In the late nineteenth century a new form of capitalism emerged in Great Britain and the United States. Before the revolutions in communication and transportation, the owners of firms managed the processes of production, distribution, transportation, and communication personally. By the end of the century, however, technological innovation and mass markets fostered the development of large-scale corporate structures, leading to a separation between owners and operators. In this new form of capitalist enterprise managers were increasingly the principal decisionmakers. This economic transformation spawned social and political tensions which compelled the public and policymakers to decide upon an appropriate response to big business.

A primary focus of public discourse was antitrust. This book explores the development of big business and the antitrust response in a comparative context. The author shows that government policies were a vital influence on the point at which managerial capitalism prevailed, first in America and then Britain, and that the search for these policies reflected the adjustment of the business order to changing economic conditions before and after managerial capitalism triumphed. Despite failures and inadequacies, antitrust often facilitated the development of flexible management organization, enabling corporations to adapt more effectively to changing economic conditions, and also increasing the opportunity of smaller firms by limiting restrictive practices.

REGULATING BIG BUSINESS

REGULATING BIG BUSINESS ANTITRUST IN GREAT BRITAIN AND AMERICA, 1880–1990

TONY FREYER

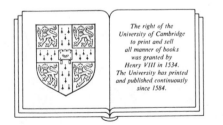

The right of the
University of Cambridge
to print and sell
all manner of books
was granted by
Henry VIII in 1534.
The University has printed
and published continuously
since 1584.

CAMBRIDGE UNIVERSITY PRESS

Cambridge
New York   Port Chester
Melbourne   Sidney

Published by the Press Syndicate of the University of Cambridge
The Pitt Building, Trumpington Street, Cambridge CB2 1RP
40 West 20th Street, New York, NY 10011–4211, USA
10 Stamford Road, Oakleigh, Melbourne 3166, Australia

© Cambridge University Press 1992

First published 1992

Printed in Great Britain at the University Press, Cambridge

A cataloguing in publication record for this book is available from the British Library

Library of Congress cataloguing in publication data

Freyer, Tony Allan,
Regulating big business: antitrust in Great Britain and America,
1880 to 1990 / Tony Freyer.
p. cm.
Includes bibliographical references (p.) and index.
ISBN 0-521-35207-X
1. Trade regulation – Great Britain – History. 2. Trade regulation –
United States – History. 3. Trusts, Industrial – Great Britain –
History. 4. Trusts, Industrial – United States – History.
5. Antitrust law – Great Britain – History. 6. Antitrust law – United
States – History. I. Title.
HD3616.O73F74 1992
338.8′0941 – dc20 91-14033 CIP

ISBN 0521 35207 X hardback

For my parents, Ida Marie Hadley and Robert A. Freyer

Contents

Preface

I thought about the theme of this book long before I considered writing about it. Alfred D. Chandler noted during a seminar I attended in 1975–1976 that the complexities of antitrust might be better understood if studied in a comparative international context. Divergent rules governing mergers and cartels, he said, influenced the point at which big business emerged in the world's leading industrial nations. The idea intrigued me because I had always thought of antitrust as a distinctive element of American law, economics, and culture. Generally, I understood, other industrial nations had no antitrust policies until the middle of the twentieth century. Yet in some form big business appeared in all those nations around the turn of the century. Thus Chandler's comment raised an interesting question: how to compare American antitrust to something which initially *did not exist* in other nations?

Other projects absorbed my attention for nearly a decade, but I did not forget the question. By the mid-1980s business historians, economists, and other scholars increasingly were exploring the international implications of antitrust. Some of this work examined the relation between cartels and mergers in a comparative context. Especially important were studies written by the British business historian Leslie Hannah and, of course, by Chandler himself. Central to the study of the wider issues was the particular experience of Great Britain. Britain was the first industrial nation, while the United States was the first nation in which managerial capitalism triumphed. The early forms of large-scale corporate enterprise appeared in both nations during the turn of the century. Britain, however, lagged behind in the development of managerially centralized corporate structures. Initially, of course, the United States possessed antitrust, while Britain did not. Yet it was possible to argue that managerial capitalism did not prevail in Britain until the British too developed antitrust institutions. This proposition heightened my interest enough that I explored its implications for six years. My findings are reported in this book.

Without the aid of many individuals and institutions the years of work would have been much less fruitful. It is a real pleasure to acknowledge the assistance of Leslie Hannah and Alfred Chandler, who supported the project from the beginning. At different points Harry N. Scheiber, Lawrence M. Friedman, and Stanley N. Katz were also most helpful. I am grateful too to Herbert Hovenkamp who provided an opportunity to publish some early thoughts in a symposium issue of the *Iowa Law Review*. I must also extend thanks to Ellen Frankel Paul and Howard Dickmen for including another early piece in their book *Liberty, Property, and Government.*

The study was enriched in more ways than I can say by the opportunity to research, teach, and travel in Great Britain. A National Endowment for the Humanities Summer Stipend and funding from the University of Alabama Research Grants Committee permitted an initial research trip during the summer of 1985. I did the bulk of the research during the summer and fall of 1986 while I was a Senior Fulbright Scholar at the London School of Economics and Political Science, under the auspices of the US/UK Fulbright Commission. I was able to return to Britain to finish the research during the summer and fall of 1989 supported by a sabbatical leave from the History Department and School of Law of the University of Alabama. For their assistance in facilitating either or both of these opportunities I wish to thank Dean Charles Gamble and his successor, Dean Nathaniel Hansford of the University of Alabama School of Law; and the University's former President Joab Thomas and his successor Roger Sayers, their executive assistant, Harry Knopke, Dean Richard Peck and his successor James Yarbrough and Acting Dean Douglas E. Jones of the College of Arts and Sciences, and Ed Mosely, Director of the Office of International Programs. I owe a special debt to Brenda Pope, the Law School's accountant, for handling the disbursement of the University's funding.

While at the London School of Economics my teaching experience added further to the work. James Potter, Dudley Baines, Paul Johnson, E. P. Hunt, Peter Earl, Geoffrey Jones, and Alan S. Milward of the Economic History Department were wonderful colleagues. The students I taught in my seminar – Mont Rogers,

Michael Kasten, Jon Burden, Sean McAvoy, Claudia MacLachlan, Till Geiger, Samyra Rashid, John Schmeidel, and Masume Hidayatullah – helped more than they knew. Still, my greatest debt is to Leslie Hannah, then Director of the LSE's Business History Unit, whose invitation facilitated the Fulbright Award.

A number of people generously put aside their own work to help mine by reading all or portions of the manuscript: W. R. Cornish, Denys Gribbin, Leslie Hannah, Herbert Hovenkamp, and Sir Alan D. Neale. Over the years I interviewed quite a few individuals who are acknowledged in the notes. I wish to give special thanks to Valentine Korah, D. G. Goyder, Hans Liesner, Sir Arthur Knight, Jonathan Green, L. C. B. Gower, Aaron Director, William F. Baxter, Sir Alan D. Neale, and Terry Calvani.

I am particularly indebted to Dr. Jeannie Ann Godfrey Dennison who gave permission to use her superb unpublished dissertation, and to Dr. Helen Mercer who put me on the track of the rich material located in the Public Record Office (Kew Gardens). I am also grateful to Denys Gribbin whose insights helped me to avoid certain errors. Along the same lines Mrs. Susan J. Cubbin and Terry Gourvish were helpful.

The staffs of the following libraries were also of invaluable assistance: the Dwight D. Eisenhower, John F. Kennedy, and Lyndon B. Johnson Presidential Libraries, the British Library of Political and Economic Science, the National Maritime Museum, Greenwich and the Public Record Office (Kew Gardens). At the University of Alabama School of Law the Library staff, especially Dr. Paul Pruitt and Mrs. Penny Gibson, Mrs. Lori Hall and the Word Processing Center, and Mr. Anderson Wynn always have given cheerful and expert aid.

I have been fortunate too in all my relations with Cambridge University Press. My first contact was with Francis Brooke. Later Patrick McCarten and Peter G. Furniss were most helpful. Concerning the production of the book it is a pleasure to have worked with John Haslam and Ms. Susie Woodhouse.

Over the years this book occupied a place in the day-to-day lives of my wife Marjorie and son Allan and they have contributed to its making in countless subtle ways. Also, I am grateful to my parents to whom it is dedicated.

Finally, while these individuals and institutions have improved the final results, as always only I am responsible for what is written.

Introduction

Late in the nineteenth century a new form of capitalism emerged in Great Britain and the United States. Before the revolutions in modern communication and transportation, the owners of firms personally managed the processes of production, distribution, transportation, and communication. Generally, these business enterprises were family run and comparatively modest or small in size. By the end of the century, however, technological innovation and mass markets fostered the development of large-scale corporate structures, engendering the separation between owners and operators. In this new form of capitalist enterprise managers were increasingly the principal decisionmakers. Accordingly, an economic order controlled by small-scale, family firms gradually gave way to one dominated by giant corporations and managerial capitalism. In both nations this economic transformation spawned social and political tensions, compelling the public and policymakers to decide upon the appropriate response to big business.

A primary focus of public discourse was antitrust. Before World War I the British considered but rejected antitrust; in America, however, it became a fundamental political and cultural value. During the 1920s, as Britain's corporate economy gradually caught up with the United States in its reliance upon managerial centralization, the demand for government intervention grew. Large and small business groups, labor, economic experts, and publicists debated the appropriate policy. Eventually, supporters of governmentally supervised cartelization and monopoly won.

During World War II, however, a new consensus emerged in Britain. Based upon the use of administrative investigation, publicity, and ultimately the selective prohibition of certain trade restraints British policymakers hoped to foster full employment and economic efficiency. As a result, throughout the post-war era, despite differences in the mode of enforcement, the theory, practice, and outcome of each nation's antitrust policy gradually if unevenly converged. Generally, British and American officials consistently condemned cartels, while maintaining a more ambiguous policy toward corporate concentration and merger. Near the end of the century, these policies encouraged each nation's corporate big business to adopt flexible management structures, facilitating adjustment to increasingly uncertain economic conditions.

In a comparative context this study explores the development of big business and the antitrust response. It attempts to show that government policies influenced the point at which managerial capitalism prevailed first in America and then Britain. The study also suggests that the search for these policies reflected the adjustment of the business order to changing economic conditions before and after managerial capitalism triumphed. Examined on one level is the relation between public policy and four distinct merger waves which over a century shaped the structure of each nation's corporate economy. At another level the study considers the relative importance of private interests and pressure groups working through the political process and the courts. On still another level the role of economic experts and economic thought is examined. Despite failures and inadequacies, antitrust often facilitated the development of flexible management organization which enabled giant corporations to more effectively adapt to changing economic conditions. After managerial capitalism prevailed, moreover, antitrust increased the opportunity of smaller firms by limiting restrictive practices.

World War I was a turning point in the development of big business. Until the late nineteenth century family firms and relatively small-scale enterprise dominated the British and American economy. During the 1880s the businessmen of both nations first developed new forms of large corporate enterprise, but it was the great turn-of-the-century merger wave which established the foundations of a new economic order. Nevertheless, in Britain the family firms accommodated large-scale corporations and, to a relatively greater extent, retained control. In America, however, small business lost that control to corporate managers. By World War I British businessmen thus adopted legal and market innovations to preserve their independence. In America, by contrast, giant corporations operated by professional managers prevailed. At the same time, loose restrictive structures increasingly were the norm in pre-war Britain, while American managers established ever tighter centralized control through corporate merger.

In both nations, the problems of meeting increased cost through more effective organization were similar. A significant difference, however, was the law. The British courts permitted restrictive agreements but generally would not enforce them, encouraging corporate owners and merchants to establish mutually advantageous cooperative arrangements through negotiation and compromise. Many American businessmen entered into similar sorts of loose restrictive contracts. Yet, by the 1890s, state and federal law made loose restrictive trade practices not only unenforceable but also subject to legal prosecution. As soon as any of the parties felt the agreement was no longer useful they could sue, charging that it was a restraint of trade. In other cases, individuals who had sold their enterprise to a competitor who then possessed a monopoly could sue to break the agreement if they decided to reenter the business. In either instance, the availability of a legal cause of action facilitated conflict rather than compromise.

Changes in government policies coincided with the start of the first merger wave. Before the turn of the century American state laws and the Supreme Court's interpretation of the Sherman Antitrust Act outlawed cartels while, ironically, encouraging various forms of mergers. Basically, there were three individual merger structures: the common law trust, the asset acquisition, and the holding company. While American courts rarely condemned the merger itself, they often struck down the restrictive covenants related to the merger. Particularly in the case of asset acquisitions, American judges almost always found the basic acquisition to be legal, but often overturned attendant covenants not to compete as violations of the common law of trade restraints. Eventually, federal authorities and the Supreme Court encouraged these ambivalent results by applying a new rule of reason. British law, by contrast, permitted most cartel practices and mergers. The courts even modestly altered the traditional restraint of trade rules affecting contracts by adopting a more flexible rule of reasonableness, ultimately enabling British firms to enforce restrictive agreements. The different legal rules governing loose and tight business structures facilitated the persistence of British family enterprise on the one hand and the triumph of American managerial capitalism on the other.

After World War I both nations' business enterprises increasingly used mergers and cartels to ameliorate the problem of enforcement. During the 1920s each country experienced a second major merger wave, with the result that the British corporate economy began more closely to approximate that of the United States. Still, significant differences remained. Not until after World War II did the depth of managerial centralization within British big corporations approach their American counterparts. Throughout the same period, the extent of peacetime cartelization was greater in Britain except during America's short-lived National Recovery Administration. During World War II each nation's government controlled the economy. Yet the return of peace paved the way for the merger wave of the 1960s, and Britain closed the gap in managerial organization. Accordingly, the multidivisional corporate structure characterized each nation's corporate economy. Convergence continued in the 1980s merger wave when conglomerates increasingly prevailed though, in each nation, these mergers were often entered into primarily to dismantle less profitable firms.

The connection between governmental policy and mergers also continued after World War I. In America the Supreme Court restricted the scope of the new Clayton and Federal Trade Commission Acts and applied the rule of reason to distinguish "good" from "bad" corporate giants. At the same time federal judges continued to outlaw overt cartel practices. By contrast, Britain's first brief experiment with antitrust under the Profiteering Acts ended in 1921. Thereafter British courts increasingly *enforced* restrictive agreements, while the government began promoting cartels and sanctioned changes in company law which fostered holding companies. The different mix of policies helped to explain the uneven development of corporate management and cartelization in each nation during the second merger wave.

After World War II Britain created permanent antitrust institutions, reversing the policy of the inter-war years. The Monopolies Act of 1948 and the Restrictive Trade Practices Act of 1956 established new enforcement policies which influenced the third and fourth merger waves. The same pattern was evident as a result of the enforcement of antitrust in post-war America. Thus, in both nations, a firm anti-cartel policy coincided with a fluctuating but generally more lenient mergers policy to encourage similar corporate structures.

The strength of business self-regulation influenced the development of managerial capitalism. From the 1880s on, business groups, publicists, and experts used the idea of self-regulation or "self-government" to describe privately negotiated and enforced cooperative agreements within comparatively loose organizational structures. The idea embraced a wide range of practices, including weak informal gentlemen's agreements, stronger trade associations, various forms of retail price maintenance, and quite sophisticated cartels. But, regardless of the form, the agreeing parties sought to restrict if not eliminate altogether competition. The use of these agreements did not end business conflict. Rather, depending upon the effectiveness of private enforcement, self-regulation maintained cooperation through ongoing negotiation or intimidation. Cooperative agreements, nonetheless, could be attractive to independent, generally smaller firms because it enabled owners to retain control. Preserving this independence, however, reduced the incentive to establish greater managerial centralization through corporate consolidation.

Creating the organizational efficiencies inherent in managerially centralized, big corporations required making what Alfred Chandler called a "three-pronged investment." First was "an investment in production facilities large enough to exploit a technology's potential economies of scale or scope." The second prong was "an investment in a national and international marketing and distributing network, so that the volume of sales might keep pace with the new volume of production." Thirdly, in order "to benefit fully from these two kinds of investment the entrepreneurs also had to invest in management." The recruitment and training of managers was essential "not only to administer the enlarged facilities and increased personnel in both production and distribution, but also to monitor and coordinate those two basic functional activities and to plan and allocate resources for future production and distribution." According to Chandler it was this "three-pronged investment in production, distribution, and management that brought the modern industrial enterprise into being."[1]

Before World War I British but not American firms generally failed in this regard. The turn-of-the-century merger wave represented the American success in making the "three-pronged investment." This success paved the way for the long-term superior performance of American big business until the middle of the twentieth century. Despite important exceptions such as Guinness, Lever, Dunlop, Pilkingtons, Courtaulds, Nobels, Brunner, Mond, and Metropolitan Carriage, however, British firms suffered "entrepreneurial failure." According to Chandler, this was the "failure to make the three-pronged investment in production, distribution and management essential to exploit economies of scale and scope." Moreover, the "time period in which that investment could have been made was short. Once first movers from other nations had entered the British market, often supplementing their marketing organizations by direct investment in production, the window of opportunity was closed."[2] During the second merger wave, British companies began catching up, said Leslie Hannah, developing "managerial hierarchies as deep... [and] as well-trained and professional, as those in America."[3] This process was still underway until after World War II.

Chandler and Hannah suggested that the persistence of cartelization contributed to Britain's entrepreneurial failure. The present study explores and provides support for their suggestion.[4] The rise and triumph of the British system of business self-regulation coincided with the failure to make the three-pronged investment which had established the basis for American industrial dominance. The system permitted and often actively encouraged smaller firms to retain their independence within looser organizational structures. It also sanctioned horizontal trade restraints between firms in the same industry and vertical restrictive agreements between producers and distributors. In either case, the ability to maintain and ultimately enforce self-regulating cartel practices discouraged the investment in "managerial hierarchies" upon which the triumph of managerial capitalism depended. Indeed, in the United States the use of antitrust to outlaw cartels channeled investment decisions toward mergers engendering greater managerial centralization. Before World War I, however, Britain's sanction of cartels contributed to making the first merger wave smaller.

A policy supporting both mergers and cartels promoted the rise of the British corporate economy during the 1920s. But not until Britain began attacking cartels did managerial capitalism prevail. Outlawing business self-regulation was part of the ongoing adjustment of antitrust policy and business to changing economic conditions. At no point after either America or Britain declared self-regulating restrictive agreements illegal did business stop resorting to them altogether. As a result, throughout the post-war era the policy of each nation's antitrust authorities converged on the need continuously to police cartel practices.

From the point that each nation instituted antitrust, the policy toward mergers and corporate concentration fluctuated. Yet, by the 1970s and 1980s, while concentration levels were higher in Britain, each nation's antitrust policy generally remained more tolerant of conglomerate and diversifying mergers than of horizontal combinations. Again, policy had converged. Unlike the case of cartels, however, officials in both countries encouraged flexible organizational structures better suited to a new post-war era of business uncertainty. Both Britain and America found it difficult to maintain competitiveness within the post-war global economy. At the same time the failure rate of mergers in both nations was high. Nevertheless, antitrust fostered a business environment in which many firms performed well, suggesting that whatever its inadequacies, antitrust often facilitated managerial effectiveness.

During the formative era of big business and antitrust the market influenced each nation's policymakers differently. The American market encompassed a vast continent in which a majority of the population did not live in major cities until 1920, fostering a clash between rural and urban market interests. In addition, the nation's federal system and constitutional tradition of judicial supremacy channeled market tensions into a wide array of political pressures suggested by the greater reliance on lawyers. In Britain, by contrast, the domestic market was not only geographically compact, but it had become predominately urban *before* large-scale corporate enterprise appeared. Also, export markets were of much greater importance to British industry than was the case in America. Moreover, Parliament was the single dominant legislative body, while the courts generally exercised self-restraint. Also, in Britain lawyers were much less important to business than accountants. As a result, compared to the United States the scope of market tensions manifested in interest-group pressures was narrower.

In both nations before World War I small and big business became distinct political interest groups. The United States differed from Britain, however, in having a majority of voters in agricultural or raw materials sectors. Small firms served these sectors. As small enterprise was threatened by the emergence of large corporations (which were usually based in a few large northeastern and western cities) they formed political coalitions with other dispossessed groups. The thoroughly urban British market, by contrast, lacked major extractive sectors so that even if big threatened small firms there was no comparable basis for such coalitions. In any case, the compact market and export trade proved to be more amenable to the repeated negotiation of restrictive agreements British law sanctioned. Once the system of business self-regulation took hold, moreover, it facilitated a degree of cooperation between large and small business which helped to protect the latter. In America, however, both the law and the market fostered conflict between the two business groups.

The different experience of small business was part of a wider social milieu facilitating consensus or conflict. British legal rules governing restrictive trade practices, corporate consolidation, and combination generally reflected a consensus favoring Free Trade and business self-regulation. In British usage Free Trade and *laissez-faire* were very much distinguishable, applying Free Trade only to a policy of no tariffs or other barriers to international trade. Accordingly, for the British, restraint of trade and Free Trade were not inconsistent. Because of greater conflicts in values and interests the primary point of agreement found in American law was, by contrast, that despite the general belief in *laissez faire* some sort of government intervention was essential.

In order to accommodate the new phenomenon of large-scale enterprise, each country's lawmakers changed legal principles. Application of those principles, however, could not transcend the ideological, social class, political, and market relations that constituted the two nations' divergent experiences with big and small business. Increasingly, many British commentators blamed the relative decline of their nation's economy at least in part on the failure to develop centralized corporate management on a scale comparable to that of Britain's American and German competitors.

Social values also influenced the course of political conflict. The British system of class distinctions created a preference for greater economic cooperation and political consensus based on freedom of contract and Free Trade. Many British business leaders belonged to the ruling class which controlled social as well as governmental institutions. Although many political issues divided Liberals and Conservatives, shared class values sustained bipartisan opposition to government intervention along the lines of American antitrust. In the United States, however, voters considered the leaders of giant corporations to be the agents of corruption. Accordingly, big business threatened not only the hope of individual opportunity represented by small business but also the republican values sustaining free government itself. Despite the general belief in *laissez-faire*, therefore, the primary point of agreement was that the rise of big business required government action. Thus, in Britain, social values facilitated cooperation between large and small business, whereas in America they fostered intractable confrontation.

In each nation, a similar pattern characterized the relation of large and small business to labor. Although the business groups of neither country liked unions, British business and labor at least agreed on opposing antitrust. In America, by contrast, big business and labor resisted antitrust, while small firms used the policy to defeat unions. This victory prevented a political coalition with the influential labor constituency. Perhaps more significant in the long run, it contributed to ambiguity in antitrust laws which worked to the advantage of corporate giants.

After World War I market tensions and social values gradually changed. During the 1920s merger wave in Britain, the faith in rationalization eroded the Free Trade consensus. With the coming of the Depression, British policymakers embraced tariff protectionism and formally promoted self-regulating restrictive agreements. The growth of the corporate economy resulting from the merger movement hurt many small firms. They nonetheless lacked the sort of political allies American small business had had in the less urbanized market before 1920. In addition, many other small enterprises remained protected within the system of self-regulation, further undercutting political pressure for American-type antitrust.

During World War II, Labour joined many Conservatives in the belief that post-war full employment and economic efficiency required the development of some sort of antitrust policy. Large and small British business groups helped to shape the consensus favoring the investigation-publicity approach of the 1948 Monopolies Act. When first Labour and then the Conservatives directly attacked restrictive practices through measures which culminated in the Restrictive Trade Practices Act of 1956, however, smaller firms fought back. But, by then, small business was too divided to overcome the new consensus favoring government intervention. Throughout the rest of the post-war era, the antitrust policies enacted by both Labour and the Conservatives remained within that consensus. The dramatic growth in the role of British lawyers in mergers and acquisitions suggested the scale of the change.

During the seventy years following World War I, the change in America was generally less pronounced. By 1920 the dissipation of the market tensions driving small business resistance coincided with the triumph of managerial capitalism. Throughout the 1920s and 1930s segments of both large and small business cooperated in a campaign against antitrust. By the start of World War II the old antagonism revived, though throughout the remainder of the century it was episodic. Gradually, Americans' greater preoccupation with economic efficiency and consumer welfare eclipsed the moralistic concerns reflected in republican values. During the economic contraction of the 1970s and 1980s the emphasis upon efficiency dominated federal antitrust policies and court decisions. Meanwhile, the increased antitrust prosecutions of state attorney generals represented a return to the older antitrust tradition. Whether the state statutes were the harbingers of a more vigorous era of antitrust response to big business was unclear. Nonetheless, that any change would fundamentally shake the commitment to economic efficiency was doubtful.

CHAPTER I

The response to big business: the formative era, 1880–1914

The stability of a ruling social class existing within a compact market created in Britain the basis for business self-regulation. In America, however, a federal system superimposed upon wider social tensions and a larger market diverted conflict into the formal channels of official policymaking.[1] The British courts and Parliament sanctioned loose combinations and restrictive practices which, despite the great merger wave, sustained the comparatively greater control of family firms and modest-scale enterprise. The illegality of these same legal forms in America weakened the influence of small business and encouraged the triumph of managerially centralized, giant corporations in the same merger movement. On the whole, then, the factors facilitating the British consensus toward nonintervention ensured that the law merely followed the interests of the established business group. The broad-based conflicts driving the American demand for government action, however, fostered the displacement of the old business order by a new one, capable of much greater domination. Yet the British failure to develop vertically integrated corporate structures reinforced the belief that underdeveloped managerial centralization contributed to the nation's relative economic decline.[2]

THE SOCIAL MILIEU AND THE MARKET

In America, but not in Britain, the rise of large corporations threatened the already existing business order. Well into the twentieth century British family firms retained more control throughout the economy. The market and legal pressures facilitating business combinations did not undercut the family enterprise because it could continue to function as a single autonomous subsidiary within a loose organizational structure. Furthermore, financial transactions among family firms influenced the development of the stock market, which in turn encouraged the merger movement. This pattern of investment enhanced family control, or at least the retention of vital influence on boards of directors of the new large-scale corporations. In other cases, family shareholder-directors continued to manage because the firms were still fairly small. Even in the often bigger publicly traded companies the owners of the formerly separate firms often retained the top executive positions. Thus the British business establishment was able to accommodate and preserve itself within the new large-scale business structures. It was a notable contrast that in the American business order the opposite was generally true. As a result, the individually owned and operated, comparatively small enterprises resisted the emergence of the big corporations. In the manufacturing sector small firms generally lost. Whereas in banking and retailing small business remained less concentrated than in Britain because the law often enforced their interests.[3]

The internal structure of each nation's business order continued, as it had since the 1880s, to diverge. Despite similarities in the level of technological and industrial development the great turn-of-the-century merger movement was smaller in Britain than America. The Americans favored tight, managerially centralized corporations while the British relied on looser, anticompetitive combinations. As business responded to changing market conditions by seeking greater organizational and scale economies through bigger firms the legal rules governing restrictive practices were instrumental.[4] Undoubtedly America's protective tariff, in contrast to Britain's tenacious attachment to Free Trade, accounted for some of the difference. "The desirability of reducing domestic competition (and the possibility of achieving high levels of monopoly profits) was," wrote Professor Leslie Hannah, "significantly enhanced by reduction in foreign competition implicit in the successive tariff increases imposed between 1883 and 1897." Yet without the ability to achieve the economies of scale upon which profitability (monopoly or otherwise) depended, protectionism would have counted for much less. It was at this very point that, according to Hannah, "Paradoxically [American], antitrust law...increased the incentive to monopolize by merger...[because it] made [loose] cartel agreements and trusts illegal methods of controlling competition, and...thus ma[de] participation in them a more risky enterprise."[5]

During the formative era of big business a "ruling class" controlled British society. As one observer noted, the period was the "last age of aristocracy, but also the one and only age of an ascendant upper-middle class."[6] The family businesses dominating the British economy constituted a powerful segment of the ruling class. Although labor and socialists resisted the "large... proportion of parliamentary representation" these business "interests" possessed, wrote the Fabian socialist Henry W. Macrosty in 1905, their traditional legal and social values nonetheless inhibited a resort to the "coarse and worn out methods of bribery" characteristic of American trusts.[7]

The perceived difference in values obscured divergent views of business self-interest in a changing market. In both nations the era of declining prices and depressed conditions gradually came to an end by the mid-1890s. In each country, too, new underwriting methods adopted on the New York and London stock exchange around 1897 increased the market for industrial stock merger issues, which encouraged the demand for speculative investment in these issues. The new investment opportunity spawned a new profession – the merger promoter, whose strategies produced not only successful big companies but also others which failed. Thus the presumed efficacy of traditional British social and legal values notwithstanding, the investors of each country embarked on risky and often questionable schemes resulting in industrial concentration.[8]

The homogeneity of British values and business interests facilitated consensus and compromise on issues involving restrictive trade practices and combination. Because British business fervently continued to support Free Trade and freedom of contract, its opposition to government intervention along the lines of antitrust surprised no one. Yet the relative stability the ruling class enjoyed also suggested why, despite protracted struggle and most employer's opposition to the trade unions, it gradually supported an eventual accommodation with organized labor permitting restrictive combinations, as well as the broader extension of social welfare measures throughout Britain. Similarly, even where clashes among business groups themselves resulted in government regulation of railroads and, to a lesser extent, the shipping industry, there was enough class cohesion to keep the government's role comparatively limited.[9]

In America, by contrast, ethnocultural antagonisms, class, and localistic differences facilitated conflict between the two business groups. On one level the struggle between big and small business involved merely two different economic interests. On another level the clash had regional implications in that the Rockefellers and

Carnegies were based in major northeastern or mid-western metropolitan areas, whereas the middlemen they displaced generally operated throughout the predominantly rural hinterlands. The nation's federal system permitted some states to protect the small proprietors while other states fostered large-scale enterprise. The constitutional division between state and federal government created further conflict.[10] Meanwhile, through the National Association of Manufacturers and other organizations, small business attacked organized labor.[11]

A more subtle but nonetheless potent source of divisiveness concerned the degree to which many small enterprisers were members of ethnic minorities seeking the American Dream. Big business threatened the welfare not only of a culturally definable business class, but also that of workers from the same group whose rise generally depended on entering the business system. No one represented this dimension of the struggle better than the Boston lawyer Louis D. Brandeis, whose clientele tended to come from ethnic groups engaged in modest-size manufactures or the wholesale and retail sector. He defended legalizing the enforcement of price fixing on the ground that it would prevent social disorder which seemed likely if big corporations destroyed the "small man's" economic opportunity. Brandeis did not consider, however, whether one reason the small enterprisers attacked organized labor was that it posed a challenge from below similar to that which big business presented from above.[12]

The British ruling elite's influence shaped public officials' response to the rise of large-scale firms. The investigation of the Royal Commission on Depression in Trade in 1886 favorably reported that Free Trade and nongovernment intervention were consistent with the view of the family business constituency. In 1898, at the height of the merger wave, the Employer's Parliamentary Council was established to represent business groups before Parliament and the government. The new organization, however, was merely an extension of business lobbying groups such as local chambers of commerce which had emerged earlier to fight the "railway interest," or which had formed in response to the rise of organized labor. Virtually all of these groups opposed antitrust. At the same time, organized labor and the socialist, their struggle with business over social welfare measures notwithstanding, also resisted antitrust, though for different reasons.[13]

In the United States factional pressures caused disagreement over the scope of government intervention, but no significant opposition arose to the principle itself. By 1890 farm, labor, and small-business groups created enough pressure that Congress passed the Sherman Antitrust Act. By 1900, divisions occurred among these groups concerning the enforcement of antitrust policy. Because the government had used the Sherman Act against the Pullman strikers, labor supported revising the law to confine its operation to business. Representatives of giant corporations wanted federal authorities to enforce price stability through business-government cooperation. Small businessmen, including retailers, wholesalers, traveling sales-men, and local manufacturers, generally favored Louis Brandeis's view that bigness was bad. They wanted the government to prevent large-scale combination and to break up the already existing giant firms. In response to the turn-of-the-century merger wave, Presidents Theodore Roosevelt, William Howard Taft, and Woodrow Wilson offered vigorous rhetoric but ambiguous policy measures. Through-out the period, however, the core of each president's political rhetoric and the government's enforcement policy accepted the distinction between "good" and "bad" big business. Ironically, even the People's Lawyer Brandeis, the adamant foe of the "curse of bigness," urged lawmakers to permit and enforce restrictive price agreements among members of trade associations composed of small dealers.[14]

The divergent British and American experiences with big business also were reflected in informed public opinion. From the 1880s to the war, neither British academic economists nor the press considered the new corporate giants to be a threat to the nation's welfare. Until the turn of the century, most observers agreed with Alfred Marshall that despite the economies gained through consolidation, big firms eventually would succumb to competitive pressures and break up. Gradually, prominent academics and leading periodicals like *The Times* and *The Economist* took the position that in certain instances bigness was natural. Commentators even went so far as to argue that the growth of large-scale enterprise represented a "rationalization" of Britain's economy which was healthy and something to be encouraged, while a few radicals advocated increased publicity to curb potential abuse. Meanwhile, British observers generally dismissed the melding of economic and moral elements reflected in the good–bad trust distinction as peculiarly American.[15]

In the United States, although many observers eventually accepted the idea that bigness was natural, opinion was much more divided. Followers of William Graham Sumner's Social Darwinist philosophy were perhaps conspicuous, but they exercised little influence on policymakers. Some academic economists, political scientists, and lawyers assumed that unregulated large-scale enterprise represented a threat to the public interest. Following the great merger wave, prevailing professional economist opinion recognized that big corporations often brought economic efficiency, which was good. Bigness, however, also raised the possibility of abuse and exploitation, which was bad. Thus the distinction between good and bad combinations prevailed, and it was the government's responsibility to foster the former and prevent the latter.[16]

Moreover, in neither nation did the doctrine of *laissez-faire* inhibit government action. Although the doctrine undoubtedly represented a general philosophical orientation popular in each country, whatever influence it had on policy was vague.[17] The incisive British observer of the United States, James Bryce, noted that though Americans conceived "themselves to be devoted to *laissez-faire* in principle...they have grown no less accustomed than the English to carry the action of government into ever-widening fields." In both nations the "dark side" of "unrestricted competition" arising from the "power of groups of men organized by incorporation as joint-stock companies, or of small knots of rich men acting in combination, has developed with unexpected strength," with the result that "the very freedom of association which men sought to secure by law when they were threatened by the violence of potentates may, under the shelter of the law, ripen into a new tyranny." Yet in America "great corporations have been more powerful than in Britain, and more inclined to abuse their power." For "crotchet-mongers as well as for intriguers there is no such paradise as the lobby of a State legislature. No responsible statesman is there to oppose them, no warning voice will be raised by a scientific economist."[18] Thus the British pattern of social conflict and politics fostered government intervention on behalf of social welfare, whereas in America the influence of corruption engendered the demand for antitrust.[19]

In addition the divergent approaches of British and American lawmakers reflected differing market relations. In America, the emergence of the large-scale business structures coincided with rapid urban growth and the relative decline of the old small-scale enterprise. During the interdepression years between the mid-1870s and mid-1890s, the nation's total population grew by about 40 percent. Rural population increased by nearly five million during the 1880s, but urban population jumped by eight million, resulting in a drop in the proportion of rural Americans from 72 percent in 1880 to less than 65 percent in 1890. This decrease was greater than in any other ten-year census period in United States history. As the older American social and economic order underwent transformation, conflict with the new business giants was inevitable. In some industries, consolidation and merger meant that the number of buyers and sellers decreased, but their aggregate size increased. Efficient transportation, a growing urban population, and centralized arrangement fostered a radically different and far more concentrated market than that of the early nineteenth century. By building their own marketing organizations, the new large-scale firms handled their buying and selling more efficiently, undercutting the significance and livelihood of the small, unincorporated enterpriser.[20]

In Britain, most major market changes *preceded* the appearance of big business. The 1851 census reported that the nation's population was divided nearly evenly between country and town dwellers.[21] By 1900, three out of four English citizens lived in towns. This predominately urban population constituted a geographically compact market in which information and transactions costs were low. Thus, the appearance of big business did not coincide with wrenching demographic and market changes and, consequently, a significant cause of conflict in the United States was not a problem in Britain. Although this compact market clearly did not preclude the emergence of large-scale enterprise, it was even more supportive of business self-government sustained through loose, anticompetitive structures.[22]

The rise of centrally managed corporations in the United States also disrupted the personal connections among producers, wholesalers, and retailers that had been characteristic of the old business order. Throughout the nineteenth century, the dominance of face-to-face contacts, tied to the economy's dependence on credit, encouraged associational factors in American business transactions that often softened the demands of the market. Thus, a wholesaler might pressure retailers to charge certain prices, but when the time for accounting came, the retailer often was able to put off the date of payment, in part because he had established a personal relationship with the wholesaler. Long-term market considerations, rather than any humanitarian sensibilities often explained such behaviour; nonetheless, it was a pervasive fact of life in the old American economic order. With the rise of the giant corporation, which placed marketing or processing roles under the control of centralized management, the personal element declined.[23]

Despite the rise of large-scale companies, personal relationships in Britain persisted. Free from legal challenge, big firms formed price-fixing agreements with distributors or suppliers. Unquestionably the large company's market power provided advantage, but the prevailing resort to negotiated relations resulted in compromise on both sides. Similarly, during the early twentieth century the same was true even for the marginal shops in depressed working-class neighborhoods like Salford.[24] Thus, prior to 1914, the durability of personal business relations in Britain diffused tensions which, in America, engendered conflict between small and big business.

The greater vulnerability of American small business also affected the struggle with labor. During the late nineteenth and early twentieth century labor strife pervaded both nations. Employers reacted to unions with their own organizations such as the British Midland Employer's Federation and the American National Association of Manufacturers (NAM). But the outcome of confrontation in each country was different. British business neither prevented Parliament from passing pro-labor legislation, nor stopped the courts from overturning antilabor decisions.[25] In addition, some British employers supported at least some cooperation with labor, in order to weaken the "opportunity for the agitator, who imbues the idea that the working class are being exploited, and that syndicalism is the appropriate remedy." Large British firms often took the lead in applying this strategy.[26] Although some American big corporations attempted to undermine labor militancy through cooperative organizations such as the National Civic Federation, confrontation prevailed.[27]

The contrasting experience of Cadbury's and the NAM helped to explain the Civic Federation's lack of success. Family management not only made Cadbury's Britain's leading chocolate producer, but also it fostered cooperative and relatively peaceful labor relations. "The test of any scheme of factory organization is the extent to which it creates and fosters the atmosphere and spirit of cooperation and good will," wrote Edward Cadbury, "without in any sense lessening the loyalty of the worker to his own class and organization." The company paid good wages, provided health care, housing, and athletic programs, and supported the Liberal Party's prolabor legislation. To sustain loyalty through respect for the worker's "class and organization," Cadbury's even encouraged the employee's membership in trade unions. One craft-union leader noted that such benevolence made it "difficult to generate interest in things that are really of benefit to the workers in groups because they come to them without quite so much trouble as others may have to put into it in other places."[28] Admittedly, Cadbury's was probably not typical. Nevertheless in America the smaller enterprises comprising the backbone of the NAM not only defeated favorable labor laws but also succeeded in limiting the unions' rights through successful court fights.[29]

The law's relative toleration of anticompetitive practices facilitated this divergent outcome. Organized labor created costs for business which larger firms often could more effectively absorb than smaller ones.[30] Yet, in Britain, large and small business gained enough organizational economies through loose combination that there existed a somewhat greater willingness to cooperate with labor. Admittedly, British labour suffered a defeat when the House of Lords weakened the right to strike in the *Taff Vale* decision of 1901. But this was a temporary set back compared to the longer-term Parliamentary and judicial sanction of unions which culminated in the overruling of *Taff Vale* in the Trade Disputes Act of 1906. One aspect of shared values, moreover, was that the trade unions really believed in *laissez-faire* which, in a sense, the Trade Disputes Act showed.[31]

The business order's reliance on lawyers and courts further suggested the relative strength of social consensus or conflict. In Britain shared values and market relations provided enough cohesion among different business interests for them to rely on commercial arbitration rather than litigation to resolve disputes. The American business order, however, was driven and sustained by law suits. Symptomatic of this difference was the fact that the parties to British anticompetitive agreements often depended on London or provincial accountants specializing in such work. One accountant often served as secretary for a dozen or more combinations, suggesting that the issues arising from the struggle against competition were relatively routine. But in America the professionals handling restrictive arrangements were lawyers. During the turn of the century a few

New York law firms became experts in adjusting each state's and the federal government's separate and distinct antitrust laws to the needs of big business. At the same time, Brandeis represented the emergence of a second, less lucrative but nonetheless important, market for legal services involving the needs of small businessmen.[32]

Thus the pervasiveness of conflict in America had a deeper cause than the difference in market relations. The reliance on self-governing, loose combinations indicated that for British voters restrictive practices and large-scale enterprise posed little or no threat to the political order. Americans, by contrast, feared that big business might corrupt republican government itself. The emphasis upon corruption encouraged Americans to distinguish between "good" and "bad" combinations, a dichotomy the British rejected. Each nation's people wanted the consumer benefits large-scale business organization made possible, but moral concerns involving the very survival of the republic complicated America's acceptance of these economic advantages.

SELF-REGULATION VS. GOVERNMENT INTERVENTION

The formulation and maintenance of restrictive agreements was a form of private self-regulation by which family capitalism preserved order without the extensive intervention of government. Self-regulation did not mean that there was little or no struggle; rather it meant that struggle was resolved through ongoing negotiated accommodation. American business dealt with conflict through legally sanctioned, tight organizational structures which displaced small enterprise. By contrast the British preserved small business within loose organizational arrangements, ameliorating conflict through a form of cooperative self-government.[33] The character and function of the law in each nation also diverged. Although the common law provided a shared tradition, the rules governing restrictive practices and combination evolved differently not only between the two nations, but also among the states and between the state and federal jurisdictions of the American federal system. Britain's popular consensus favoring Free Trade encouraged the alteration of old doctrines to create a more flexible rule of reasonableness which permitted family firms to adopt loose rather than tight anticompetitive business structures. In America, however, the interplay of federalism and the conflict between small and big business resulted in increased state and federal intervention which nonetheless facilitated the triumph of giant corporations.[34]

Big business emerged in Britain and America as the result of a similar search for stability. During the mid-1870s and mid-1890s the United States suffered severe depressions. Throughout the entire post-Civil War era prices steadily fell: the wholesale price index for all commodities in 1865 was 185, by the early nineties it declined to around 80.[35] In Britain the period from 1873 to 1896 was known as the Great Depression and, for many industries, declining prices were a problem.[36] On both sides of the Atlantic businessmen searched for ways to adjust output to the changing market and to influence prices. In order to exploit more efficiently economies of scale they tried new organizational structures resulting in bigger firms.[37]

Large-scale corporate enterprise appeared in the two nations during the 1880s but it became conspicuous during the great turn-of-the century merger wave. Between 1898 and 1900 approximately 650 British firms, valued at £42 million, disappeared in 198 separate mergers. The American movement, however, was larger and more significant: in the peak year of 1899 alone, 1,208 firms valued at over $2,064 million (c. £400 million) were consolidated. The same year in Britain 255 enterprises, valued at only £22 million, merged into bigger firms. These mergers, moreover, involved fewer industries, principally textiles and brewing.[38]

Although each nation had attained comparable technological and industrial development, various factors indicated how much smaller was the scale of Britain's turn-of-the-century merger wave. British industry as a whole employed only slightly fewer manufacturing workers than the United States, yet America's manufacturing corporations were significantly larger in terms of organizational size and employment; in terms of capital and output the American firms were still farther ahead. US Steel suggested the extent of the difference. Its physical size was greater and its managerial control of raw materials, production, and marketing was more comprehensive than that of any British steel firm. The quoted value of US Steel's issued commercial paper in 1902 was $1,322 million (over £264 million) whereas that of the largest British corporation was Imperial Tobacco, valued at only £17.5 million.[39]

British and American businessmen sought to stabilize prices by restricting competition. Competition reduced the profit margins necessary to service the heavy fixed costs arising from the maintenance of industrial and commercial enterprises. As a leading political economist of the day put it, the "waste of competition" which comes from the "inability of adopting one's plants and output to the needs of the market" could "be partly saved by combination of many manufacturing establishments in one industry under one management."[40] The search for stability also involved other anticompetitive practices. Price-fixing among firms engaged in the same business involved *horizontal* agreements; price agreements between firms in different types of business – such as between the manufacturer and the wholesaler or retailer – were *vertical.*[41]

Over the long term British more than American businessmen relied on vertical price-fixing agreements.[42] Protracted negotiations and frequent disruption characterized by constant tension shaped the course and survival of these arrangements. But after the merger wave the British had achieved relative stability without displacing the middleman.[43] In America, by contrast, many large corporate manufacturers simply took over the distribution function themselves, ultimately destroying the middleman. John D. Rockefeller explained that Standard Oil's circumvention of distributors and the selling of products "direct to the consumer...[generated enormous] criticism."[44] One of Britain's largest cement manufacturers described a relationship between himself and the merchants that was more ambivalent. He "daily impress[ed] upon our customers that the object of this company is not to injure the merchant, or to squeeze out the middleman...but in return for the hand we hold out to the distributors we ask for a 'tied trade.'" He then threatened that if the firm's products were "not actively handled and distributed by merchants, there we shall organize our own agencies, so as to secure...not a monopoly, but a fair proportion of the trade."[45]

During the 1880s and 1890s firms in each nation also formed comparatively loose horizontal business structures intended to reduce or eliminate competition through agreements regulating price, output, and marketing. One such structure was the cartel, in which the participants concurred upon trade policy and then appointed a secretary possessing full access to each member's books. After determining the proportion of total trade of each cartel member for a given period, the secretary ascertained the appropriate future percentage. From then on, for as long as the cartel lasted, the secretary monitored compliance through monthly reports. The secretary calculated each firm's total percentage of business, notifying each member whether his percentage was consistent with that which the cartel had agreed on, whereupon each firm decided whether to increase or decrease output. After 1900 British business increasingly preferred and maintained this sort of loose anti-competitive arrangement in which the constituent firms preserved independence.[46] During the same period in America, however, managerially centralized, large corporations not only displaced cartels but also the smaller enterprises.[47]

Although greater control brought increased business stability in Britain, it also enabled weaker firms to persist. British businessmen often established a fund or pool to which each member contributed, permitting the "pensioning of inefficient members." As one businessman explained, "it was a law of progress that the inefficient should go, but in practice progress was impeded because he would not go, so instead of trying to kill him… it was better to pension him off, since that costs far less." If the "inefficient man, who used to struggle to do 3 percent of the trade, likes to content himself with doing $1\frac{1}{2}$ percent, or none at all, the difference goes to the more efficient man, who, working more economically, can well afford to pay into the pool from which the inefficient man can draw compensation."[48]

This private version of a pension system suggested another significant difference between the two nations' business orders. According to one historian, the "whole principle" pervading British enterprise was "'live and let live,' because price competition was so destructive of profits; and it depended on deliberate self-restraint by the stronger firms."[49] Although Americans attempted to achieve such stability through anticompetitive self-regulation, they had little long-term success. More fundamentally, cartels and other loose anticompetitive agreements left cooperating firms relatively autonomous. Members were free to gain advantage by undercutting established prices and output quotas, thereby unleashing the very competitive pressures which they had sought to prevent. Before the great merger wave this problem plagued both British and American business. But once arrangements such as the "pension system" emerged British enterprises often maintained anticompetitive agreements, thereby preserving each firm's independence. At this, American business failed.[50]

Legal rules influenced whether loose forms of business self-regulation or tighter corporate consolidation prevailed. In each case the central issue was whether business agreements were *enforceable*. A primary reason American businessmen resorted to managerially centralized corporations was that, generally, cartels and looser arrangements were not enforceable at law.[51] Without the means of compelling compliance in court the loose agreements were, said Rockefeller, "ropes of sand."[52] In order to "stop the rot" cut-throat competition caused, British enterprisers such as the nation's leading cement manufacturers also formed loose anticompetitive arrangements. Because the "gentlemanly agreements – the passing of the 'word of honour'" were "not enforceable," however, "they were observed until the manufacturer saw his way to 'making a bit' by ignoring them."[53] Yet by about 1900 the British gradually circumvented the problem of judicial enforcement by relying on negotiated, self-regulating settlements. The "live and let live" ethos reinforced by the "pensioning" of inefficient competitors thus reduced incentives to disrupt loose, anticompetitive agreements.

Until the late nineteenth century, British and American common law allowed most price-fixing agreements. The general common-law rule was that price-fixing contracts were restraints of trade which the parties could not enforce in court. Commentators at the time and later sometimes failed to distinguish between unenforceability and illegality.[54] In 1898 Judge William Howard Taft's noted *Addyston Pipe* antitrust opinion stated correctly the general principle: contracts in "restraint of trade at common law were not unlawful in the sense of being criminal... but were simply void, and were not enforced by courts."[55] Although individuals were free to enter into most restrictive trade agreements, only self-interest bound the parties. Yet, during the 1890s, British courts facilitated the stability of loose anticompetitive agreements by not only permitting but in some cases also enforcing them. American courts increasingly sustained the opposite policy.[56] As a result, Boston attorney Louis Brandeis noted, "by denying" small business "the ability to enforce legally their [loose, cartel-like] contracts," American law encouraged large, managerially centralized corporations.[57]

Resale price maintenance, "tying contracts," and other vertical agreements between producers and distributors or wholesalers and retailers enhanced business stability. At the same time, however, their use invited abuses, including collusive or discriminatory dealing.[58] Nevertheless, from the early nineteenth century on Parliament and the British courts sanctioned all but the most blatantly criminal forms of vertical price fixing. This policy of toleration meant that British manufacturers had little incentive to take over the distribution function themselves, which would have destroyed the middleman. In the United States, however, federalism made the process more complex. Throughout the nineteenth century state and federal courts permitted resale price maintenance, but in 1911 the Supreme Court outlawed it in all but a few cases.[59] Meanwhile, beginning in the 1870s, the Court applied the commerce clause to overturn taxes on out-of-state middlemen enacted to protect local business. However, the constitutional protection of interstate trade paved the way for large corporations to establish their own marketing organizations, undercutting the independent middleman.[60]

During the 1880s and 1890s many states also established stricter antitrust rules enabling state officials to break up loose and tight combinations. Beginning with New Jersey in 1889, however, other states passed laws which expressly permitted certain forms of corporate consolidation including holding companies. In addition, Congress enacted the Sherman Antitrust Act of 1890.[61] Ironically, the Supreme Court's initial interpretation of the new law, combined with the state's ambivalent policies, facilitated, as Brandeis predicted, the turn-of-the-century merger wave.[62]

The proliferation of big business in turn heightened popular pressure for stronger antitrust enforcement. But it also strengthened the belief that there was a distinction between good and bad corporate giants. Elected officials responded to these ambiguous demands, advocating revisions of the Sherman Act and the creation of an antitrust administrative body. In 1911 the Supreme Court fostered a political consensus by adopting the rule of reason in the *Standard Oil* and *American Tobacco* decisions, making the legality of anticompetitive combinations dependent on a blend of moral and economic factors. Responding to the rule of reason the Wilson administration established a bureaucratic approach to antitrust in 1914, which nonetheless did not prevent the displacement of small business by big corporations.[63]

Meanwhile, Parliament enacted no antitrust legislation. During the 1890s, British courts preceded their American counterparts in adopting a reasonableness doctrine, which they applied to permit and sometimes even enforce anticompetitive agreements. After the turn-of-the-century merger wave Parliament also established modest administrative regulation of anticompetitive practices in the shipping industry. The absence of government efforts to impede corporate consolidation, combined with judicial sanction of loose combinations, however, reinforced the dominance of smaller-scale enterprise maintained through self-regulation.[64]

The rule of reason suggested the different factors in each nation shaping the rise of big business. During the 1880s and early 1890s the British and American legal rules governing restrictive practices and combinations increasingly diverged, paving the way for the divergent economic experience. The interplay of changing market conditions, a comparable level of industrial development, and legal rules produced a marked contrast in the scale of the two countries' turn-of-the-century merger movements. Although the common law provided a shared tradition, the courts of one nation did not accept the doctrines of the other as binding. This was true among the state courts of the federal system and, to some extent, even of federal and state tribunals. Thus, when the British and American judges began adopting old common-law doctrines to new business conditions, diversity rather than uniformity prevailed. As a result of the search for more flexible legal principles, the British courts first established a formal doctrine of reasonableness in the *Nordenfelt* decision of 1894. In America, however, the process of adopting the common law (particularly as it involved interpreting the Sherman Act), the struggle between big and small business, and the institutional constraints of federalism itself became entangled, delaying the formulation of an American rule of reason. In Britain the common law thus did not inhibit the choice between various forms of restrictive business structures, whereas in America the reverse was true.[65]

The ability to maintain vertical and horizontal price agreements might have helped to sustain family capitalism in America, as it had in Britain. Increasingly after 1900, however, state and federal courts forbade most vertical and virtually all horizontal price-fixing practices. As a result, in the 1880s there were reportedly dozens of jobbers in Boston's wholesaler sector, but by 1899 there remained only four. American small enterprises lobbied Congress for a law permitting the judiciary to enforce vertical as well as horizontal price-fixing agreements throughout the nation. But, despite the efforts of the famous Peoples' Lawyer Brandeis, they lost.[66]

THE CONTRASTING PATTERNS OF BUSINESS STRUCTURE

In each nation the interplay of market relations, social tensions, and law produced different patterns of business structure. According to Alfred Chandler, the comparatively less-developed character of Britain's corporate economy reflected not only the proximity to the world's richest and most concentrated consumer market, but also that production and distribution in these industries required less costly facilities and less complex managerial and technical skills than most other capital-intensive industries.[67] Yet, the law's toleration of anticompetitive practices also made a difference. Although generally not enforceable at law, horizontal and vertical price-fixing agreements created a sharing of risks and costs, which weakened incentives to compete by cutting prices and encouraging business self-regulation. In addition, corporate mergers and holding companies which allowed consolidating firms relative internal independence, further reduced potential sources of conflict which might have threatened the family firm's dominance of the British economy. In the United States, however, the more diverse market and social conflicts engendered the disruption of established business interests, including successful state prosecutions dissolving the trust, which in turn fostered tighter corporate consolidation through the formation of a merger or a holding company. After the great merger wave the federal government also initiated and won several important prosecutions against tight, managerially centralized corporations. Although state and federal action was certainly not the sole cause of increased managerial centralization and vertical integration, it nonetheless sanctioned certain organizational choices over others so that oligopoly rather than cartels or monopoly prevailed.[68]

The shipping industry exemplified the dynamics of self-regulation. The survival of Britain's island economy depended on trade routes stretching from London and Liverpool to the Far East. In response to the late-nineteenth-century price depression, steamship company owners, shippers, and agents developed cartels which were known as conferences. Involving numerous separate agreements controlling outward and homeward trade, the conference system sought to curtail or prevent altogether competition. The conference was a "changing, growing, almost a living organism. The coverage and membership expanded and contracted, the terms of agreement were changed and modified and changed again, to meet the wishes of members or demands of shippers, to conform to new patterns of trade and to cover additional shipping routes."[69]

Horizontal arrangements among ship owners facilitated stability. The conference subdivided earnings per ship, pooled and divided earnings among members so that each ship's registered tonnage earned equivalent gross freight, and proportionally divided cargos according to a uniform standard of value. Similarly, an important vertical agreement between the shipping companies and the shippers was the rebate, whereby the merchant received a percentage payback on freights carried in conference bottoms. During most of the pre-war era neither the horizontal nor vertical agreements were enforceable at law, and yet the ultimate benefits were mutually satisfactory enough that over the long term the conference system endured and thrived.[70]

Within the conference system itself, moreover, shipping companies combined to achieve greater economies. Following the financial panic of 1907 the Peninsular & Orient formed a holding company with a New Zealand firm.[71] The companies sought to improve their cost and investment position without jeopardizing the personal control of the family owners who had "grown up with the business." Thus the aim was to "strengthen the position of both Companies, to promote economy, eliminate possible rivalry and generally increase the efficiency of their joint work." The means was "fusion of the existing Boards of the respective Companies under such legal conditions as may be necessary for the working of the two companies separately but under a single control in which the Directors of the P&O will possess a preponderating voice." Beyond such power sharing, it was "not intended that any change" would occur in "control or management." For the shareholders the "basis of security and earning power will be broadened." But there was also the "desire to hide away the profits which have been or are being made by the…New Zealand [company] from the public in that country."[72]

In America, by contrast, the law's intolerance of loose restrictive practices encouraged even efficient cartels to adopt tighter corporate consolidation. Until the turn of the century several relatively small family producers of explosives cooperated on prices through a cartel called the Gunpowder Trade Association and a holding company known as the Eastern Dynamite Company. In 1902, three cousins replaced the policy of horizontal combination with one of managerial centralization and vertical integration, establishing a single corporate structure, E. I. DuPont de Nemours Powder Company.[73] Responding to cost considerations rather than government coercion, they voluntarily limited their control of the industry's capacity. "If we could by any measure buy out all competition and have an absolute monopoly in the field, it would not pay us. The essence of manufacture is steady and full product. The demand for the country for powder is variable. If we owned all therefore when slack times came we would have to curtail product to the extent of diminished demands," wrote one cousin to another in 1903. If, however, "we control only 60% of it all and made that 60% cheaper than others, when slack times came we could still keep *our* capital employed to *the full* and our product to this maximum by taking from the other 40% what was needed for this purpose." Thus, "you could count upon always running full if you make cheaply and control only 60%, whereas, if you own it all, when slack times came you could only run a curtailed product." The settlement of an antitrust suit in 1911 merely confirmed the market share the company's owners had themselves established eight years earlier.[74]

Other American business attempts at establishing self-regulation through loose agreements failed still more completely. Manufacturing industries such as textiles and leather met the challenge of a changing economy by resorting to price fixing and other restrictive horizontal practices. Often these sophisticated cartel arrangements were little different from the British shipping industry's conferences. Many manufacturers even published price-fixing agreement in the trade press. Contrary to the British experience, however, the American attempts at private self-regulation did not bring stability. This was so in part because throughout the period entry costs were low enough and the availability of substitute goods were sufficiently widespread to encourage competition and price cutting. In addition, however, state and federal courts consistently not only refused to enforce such practices but also usually declared them to be violations of state and federal antitrust laws. The publication of price agreements did not cease altogether until the federal government's major antitrust victories of 1911.[75] Yet the Court's decisions merely confirmed the ambivalence of American antitrust: corporate mergers were often lawful whereas looser combinations generally were not.[76]

Similarly, business self-government maintained through loose anticompetitive agreements minimized conflict throughout Britain's distribution system. Between 1875 and 1914, mass retailers increasingly challenged the itinerant drummer and the single fixed shop to dominate the nation's distribution system. Although the independent shopkeeper persisted, three types of mass retailers emerged, including chain stores (known in Britain as multiple shops), consumer cooperatives, and department stores. The British department-store pioneer was Whiteley, a leader among the multiple shops was

Lipton, and the biggest cooperative was the Co-operative Wholesale Society (CWS). The British developed substantial mail-order houses but never as big as America's Montgomery Ward or Sears. The difference was, no doubt, influenced by the fact that in Britain the market was almost entirely urban, whereas in America the majority of the population was rural. As a result the American houses sold all sorts of merchandise to small merchants and farmers in a continental market. Instead, in both product and class of customer, the British mass retailers were more specialized. Whiteley and Harrods marketed dry goods and household furnishings largely to middle and upper-middle class customers. Multiple shops sold primarily tea, sugar, meat, and dairy products or manufactured goods such as shoes and clothing to members of the working class. Up-scale customers purchased such essentials at independent shops. Two large wholesale cooperatives, however, provided retail cooperatives with everything from groceries to household furnishings for purchase by predominately working-class customers.[77]

By World War I cooperative and restrictive self-regulation pervaded the distribution system. Within and between the three types of mass retailers, as well as among the independent shops, trades worked out, according to James B. Jefferys, "systems of retail price maintenance." In addition, markets characterized by extensive specialization enabled firms to achieve economies without the creation of large organizational structures. Some mass retailers increased their size by integrating backward, purchasing manufacturing plants, yet direct personal management remained the norm. In 1915 the total retail sales of the multiple shops, cooperatives, and department stores combined averaged about 19 percent of the market. Thus there was still business, particularly in food and clothing, for independents, who often survived because they provided customers with generous credit. There were, of course, a lot of merchants, wholesalers, jobbers, and other middlemen in Britain, particularly in the late nineteenth century, and the contrast with America was a tendency, not an absolute one.[78]

Still, conflict prevailed in the American distribution system. Up to the middle nineteenth century, numerous small merchants negotiating myriad credit transactions connected foreign and eastern urban wholesalers with local shopkeepers. But improved transportation and communications opened America's growing urban and rural market to a volume of demand too great for the old distribution system to satisfy efficiently. A new group of commodity dealers and wholesale jobbers emerged, disrupting the old merchant's control. A greater challenge arose, moreover, from three new mass retailers: the department store, the mail order house, and the chain store. The mass marketers established centralized managerial structures which permitted the handling of high-volume business at such a relatively lower cost that many of the older middlemen were not competitive.[79]

Yet, the American middlemen and other small businessmen were hit hardest by the heavily capitalized, production industries. After the Civil War, seeking ways to adjust output to the changing market, to influence prices, and to exploit more efficiently economies of scale, manufacturers tried informal gentlemen's agreements, pools, and mergers. Increasingly, however, these forms ran afoul of state law. Amid the confrontation some producers developed their own distribution networks and, gradually, more manufacturers came to do their own wholesaling. Consequently, the need for the independent merchant declined. These middlemen were essential to the older agrarian order because they brought buyers and sellers together in spite of distance and poor communications. Yet efficient transportation, a growing urban population, and significantly improved communications fostered a radically different and far more concentrated market than that of the early nineteenth century. By building their own marketing and purchasing organizations, producers were able to handle their buying and selling more effectively than could the wholesalers. By the turn of the century, these changes brought about the necessary adjustments in production and distribution; they also destroyed the merchant's leading role in the production side of the economy.[80]

A conspicuous example of conflict involved the petroleum industry. During the late 1870s, many small processors responded to competitive pressures by forming a cartel under the leadership of the largest refiner, the Standard Oil Company. Standard's John D. Rockefeller established cooperation by negotiating secret rebate agreements with railroads. Rockefeller used the rate agreements to shut out new competitors and to keep members from leaving the cartel. By 1881, through exchanges of stock among some forty firms, Rockefeller and four associates held a majority of the cooperating firms' securities. The cartel controlled nearly 90 percent of the nation's refining capacity. To break Standard's hold on railroad transportation, other producers combined themselves to construct pipelines connecting the nation's major source of crude oil, Western Pennsylvania, with the east coast.[81]

Increased centralization of management under the trust device enabled Rockefeller to meet this challenge. The creation of Standard's lawyer, S. C. T. Dodd, the trust agreement authorized nine trustees to "exercise general supervision over the affairs," of the former cartel. In order to avoid the risks associated with diverse state jurisdictions, Standard also incorporated its subsidiaries throughout various states. The trust also continued vertical integration. First it ended the need for wholesalers by creating a marketing organization; then Standard began its own crude oil production. Thus by 1888 Standard had moved from horizontal cooperation in a cartel, to become a managerially centralized, vertically integrated corporate giant controlling raw materials, production, and distribution. West coast and east Texas firms followed a similar path.[82]

Yet legal conflict shaped the changing structure of the industry. Rockefeller's rebate policy generated criticism of discriminatory rates which climaxed in the outlawing of such practices in the Interstate Commerce Act of 1887.[83] Similarly, the creation of first the cartel and then the trust encouraged resistance from small, independent refiners and wholesalers. Responding to these pressures during the late 1880s and early 1890s, the Attorney General of Ohio prosecuted the Standard Oil Trust for violations of state corporation and antimonopoly laws. Defeated in Ohio state court, Standard became a New Jersey holding company in 1890, while other states initiated their own prosecutions.[84] Although the success of these other state prosecutions was mixed, the Lone Star state successfully defended the burgeoning east Texas fields from Standard Oil's takeover.[85] Meanwhile, the federal government won a major antitrust victory in 1911 against Standard Oil, ensuring the triumph of oligopoly.[86] The pattern and results were similar in other industries which had adopted the trust device, including cottonseed oil, linseed oil, sugar, and whisky.[87]

The struggle between small and big business had a similar outcome in the meatpacking industry. By the 1880s Swift and Company integrated its national network of slaughtering and packing houses into a transportation system using refrigerated railroad cars, which the company also owned. Five competitors did the same. The packers' control of production and marketing antagonized local butchers whose National Butcher's Protective

Association unsuccessfully boycotted sales in urban centers. Live-stock shippers, who also depended upon the railroad but owned no railroad cars, were a more serious threat. The railroads demanded and received rebates from each group causing costly rate discrimination. By the early 1890s, however, the efficiencies gained from vertical integration and the refrigerator technology fostered cooperation among the leading packers against the livestock shippers and the railroads, resulting in the formation of a cartel. Successfully fending off an antitrust suit in 1903, the packers attempted to establish a monopoly called the National Packing Company. This time, however, federal prosecution was more effective: the Justice Department ordered the dissolution of the monopoly, restoring the industry to the oligopolistic conditions of the 1880s.[88]

There was a similar outcome in the production industries which did not experiment with the trust device. In order to exploit most effectively the Bonsack cigarette-making machine, James Buchanan Duke built a centralized management structure to coordinate production and marketing. During the 1880s, Duke and his four chief competitors distributed their products through wholesalers, and relied upon advertising agents for publicity. In 1890, the five firms merged to form the American Tobacco Company under Duke's leadership; within five years he centralized the purchasing and sales departments. This administrative coordination enabled the firm's own salesmen to acquire primary responsibility for marketing in the United States and abroad, thus limiting the role of independent wholesalers and advertising agents. Yet the economic success of forward integration generated popular changes that the firm held a virtual monopoly. As a result, the federal government prosecuted and won a major antitrust suit in 1911 which meant that oligopoly rather than monopoly prevailed.[89]

The experience of Britain's leading chocolate producer, Cadbury's Ltd., suggested, by contrast, the effectiveness of business self-government. In the mid-nineteenth century Cadbury's was a small family business with eleven employees. It grew steadily, from a work force of 1,193 in 1889 to one of 7,100 in 1919, becoming the largest of the nation's three major chocolate producers. Increasing production through plant expansion, Cadbury's integrated forward by developing a national advertising and sales force, and backward by manufacturing its own packaging materials. But integration did not threaten wholesalers and retailers with whom the chocolateer maintained price-fixing agreements. Government investigators found that these agreements were not abused. In the wake of the 1907 panic Cadbury formed a holding company, yet the Cadbury brothers continued to manage directly the company's daily operation through a committee structure controlled by family members.[90]

Representing a second organizational approach in which many family firms cooperated within a single, industry-wide corporate structure was Imperial Tobacco. After 1900 there were as many as two hundred small British cigarette manufacturers using the new mass-processing Bonsack machine, though WD & HO Wills, the first to adapt that technology, was strongest. Competition from the American Tobacco Company of the United States in 1901 compelled thirteen leading British cigarette makers to exchange stock and merge into a holding company under Wills. The new corporate giant, Imperial Tobacco, acquired a market-share value which by 1919 made it the nation's fifth largest industrial enterprise. To control the international market the British and American companies formed the jointly owned British American Tobacco (BAT). Yet the United States government's successful prosecution of American Tobacco in 1911, enabled the British to eventually dominate BAT.[91]

Despite Imperial's corporate form, the family firms within it retained considerable independence. The internal organization structure was, according to a senior executive, "not unlike that of the Thirteen States of America, who" under the Articles of Confederation "gave the central government as little authority as possible and retained as much as they could in their own hands." Wills and the families controlling the biggest companies, now functioning as subsidiaries, formed an Executive Committee, aided by a small staff including a secretary, an engineer, a chief accountant, and a purchasing agent. Negotiations among Wills and the other Executive Committee members established prices, allocated advertising costs among the subsidiaries, and authorized annual operating budgets. Even so, the subsidiaries manufactured and sold their products separately. Primarily, the merger facilitated horizontal coordination among cigarette manufacturers, and vertical price-fixing agreements with wholesalers and retailers. Government investigations found nothing unlawful in such practices. The stable prices resulting from cooperation, moreover, permitted smaller cigarette enterprises to compete.[92]

Among light manufacturers, Lever Brothers temporarily was an exception to the triumph of self-regulation. During the turn of the century the price of raw materials needed for manufacturing soap significantly rose. To achieve greater economies, Lever Brothers led other family-run soap firms to establish a cartel. Despite attempts to keep the arrangement secret, reducing the weight of the standard-sized product while increasing the price produced a crisis during the summer of 1906. Several mass-circulation London newspapers portrayed Lever Brothers as an evil trust ruthlessly exploiting the public. Yet the results were ambivalent. The crisis broke up the cartel, setting off a period of intense competition. Lever Brothers integrated backward to control raw materials, and forward into marketing, while it slowly but steadily acquired its competitors through horizontal mergers, though the family firms retained some independence operating as subsidiaries.[93]

Contrasting market factors and legal rules contributed to a different pattern of business structure in each nation. In Britain the more compact market and the law's toleration of loose restrictive agreements reduced the incentives to form large corporate structures threatening the survival of middlemen. Highly capitalized industries and traders diffused conflict by accommodating each other's interests through an ongoing process of negotiation, perhaps best exemplified by the shipping industry's conference system. American industries as diverse as leather, gun powder, and petroleum attempted a similar course of self-regulation. But sooner or later they ran afoul of antitrust, encouraging a shift from loose to tight organizational structures and vertical integration which often destroyed the middleman. Yet state and federal law's general failure to interfere with most mergers nonetheless favored neither cartels nor monopoly but oligopoly.

THE CAUSES AND CONSEQUENCES OF MANAGERIAL
CENTRALIZATION

The rise of big corporations seemed to undermine established views regarding competition. The United States Solicitor General, arguing an antitrust suit in 1898, articulated the prevailing assumption: "Competition drives the weak to the wall, the fittest survive, but the greatest good to the greater number results... Under competition the most improved plant, the best trained labor, the most economical management, the wisest sagacity and foresight, is not only encouraged but demanded for success." In Britain business self-regulation, fostering as it did not only various successful firms but also many others which survived only because of the "live-and-let-live" ethos, suggested a picture more complex. The irony of American antitrust suggested further contradictions in that the attempt to use government intervention to preserve competition produced the triumph of big business. Ultimately, however, the interplay of contrasting social tensions, political conflicts, market relations, and business structures on the one hand, and changes in corporation law on the other, helped to explain the strengths and weaknesses of the faith in competition.[94]

Changes in corporation law facilitated the divergent structure of British and American business. The corporation not only permitted the mobilization of necessary capital, it also provided the institutional framework for establishing and maintaining ongoing organizational control. Throughout the nineteenth century, transportation companies established greater centralized control through incorporation under state laws in America, and acts of Parliament in Britain. There was, of course, no general federal incorporation law in the United States. From the 1870s on industrial and commercial firms in both nations increasingly acquired corporate charters and, by the end of the century, many of these companies had established still tighter organizational structures through merger. Unlike the self-regulating autonomous firms operating as a cartel, a merger required each company to turn over its independence to a centralized board of directors. Merger could virtually eliminate internal disruption of agreements, giving the managing board direct control over assets and earnings of subsidiaries. Organizational centralization also facilitated a wide range of inter-company contractual transactions, including the sale of assets of one subsidiary to another, the routing of profitable business to one subsidiary in preference to another, and the concealment of loss or the seeming creation of nonexistent deficits.[95]

Still, within a large corporation the degree of centralized control varied. In both nations the legal device often used to consolidate corporations was the holding company, which enabled a corporation to purchase the stock of one or more other corporations. The common law did not sanction such a purchase but, during the late nineteenth century, Parliament and several American states enacted legislation making it lawful. Yet between a thorough-going merger and a holding company the extent of operational control differed. Although both forms of corporate consolidation permitted greater direct control than a loose combination or cartel, the merger more than the holding company resulted in extensive managerial centralization. A merger usually required the consent of two-thirds of the corporation's stockholders. To form a holding company, however, only a simple majority was necessary, and the establishment of "working control" was often possible with less than a majority.[96]

In addition, American businessmen attempted to consolidate corporations under yet another legal device formally known as the trust. Technically, corporations established a trust by transferring securities to trustees who then possessed the lawful authority to run the new legal entity as one unified corporation. Standard Oil formed the first trust in 1882 and, within a decade, other industries followed suit. By the mid-1890s, however, state prosecutions ended this particular form of corporate consolidation.[97]

The smaller turn-of-the-century merger wave suggested a British aversion to managerial centralization. There were, of course, many large British firms; despite important exceptions, however, internal organization remained comparatively embryonic. In both countries the holding company was the legal device used to achieve scale and organizational economies. But in Britain the holding company was often little more than a loose federation of single-unit family firms, whereas in America it was ultimately the initial step toward establishing greater managerial centralization through merger.[98] Thus Britain's smaller turn-of-the-century merger wave, as well as the dominance of family firms within its holding companies, reflected a "general weakness of the early industry" resulting from the "persistence of control in particular hands through large blocks of shareholding [which]...contributed to excessive individualism [and]...quickly deteriorated into ignorance and insularity."[99] In America, by contrast, recurring legal battles and government intervention encouraged big business to adopt ever tighter forms of corporate merger requiring the greater development of centralized managerial structures. According to Alfred Chandler, the transition from loose restrictive agreements, to the trust, to the holding company, to even tighter mergers, meant that by 1917 only the "giant US Steel Corporation, Standard Oil (New Jersey) and a handful of smaller metals and oil firms continued to use the holding company form."[100]

There were two broad approaches to achieving organizational efficiency through managerially centralized corporations. The consolidation of firms pursuing one line of industry at the same stage of production were examples of horizontal integration. The combination of business enterprises engaged in different or successive phases of production were examples of vertical integration. Producers integrated backward to control the source of raw materials or forward to market their product. A company carrying on all phases of business, including the extraction of raw materials, production, and marketing was said to have attained complete vertical integration.[101]

The degree of managerial centralization influenced the conflict between big and small business. A Parliamentary report noted that in Britain although vertical and horizontal "types" of consolidations were "common" in several industries, "none of these have attained anything approaching a predominant position."[102] Instead of taking over the marketing function as American big business leaders such as Rockefeller had done, British producers and distributors relied on the repeated negotiation of vertical price agreements. Similarly, unlike the American business order, British small firms remained comparatively independent, even within large corporate combinations, which further defused conflict arising from centralized-managerial control. Thus Britain avoided the threat to small business, escaping the struggle which dominated turn-of-the-century America.[103]

Admittedly, the leaders of American and British big business lauded the benefits attained through managerial centralization. The steel industry's Andrew Carnegie exclaimed, "Take from me all the ore mines, railroads, manufacturing plants and leave me my organization, and in a few years I promise to duplicate the Carnegie Company."[104] Dudley Docker, a foremost British "Trade Warrior," blamed his nation's relative industrial retardation on the comparative underdevelopment of corporate management. What was "wanted principally is an outlay of *Brains*," he said.[105] In this emphasis on the merger's organizational skills and creativeness, Docker and Carnegie ironically agreed with the Fabian socialist economist, Henry W. Macrosty. Managerial centralization gave the firm, he wrote in 1907, "permanency and more complete control over production. Superfluous or badly equipped plants can be closed, mills can be specialized, concentration of establishments will enable greater economies of large-scale production to be made, and, above all, the best brains of the trade in any department are put at the disposal of all branches of the combination." In cartels or holding companies resulting in embryonic managerial organization, however, the "interests inevitably clash and dire confusion results... In the most highly organized form of amalgamation all functions are carefully defined and graded so that proper subordination is observed, and the whole edifice culminates in a small board of directors who form, so to speak, the cabinet of the industry."[106]

That so many large corporations failed after the merger wave, raised a question whether this faith in managerial centralization was justified. By 1897 British and American financiers took advantage of new underwriting methods developed on the London and New York stock exchanges for merger issues. Despite the new accounting practices, however, the corporate securities were highly speculative because of potential overcapitalization through watered stock. In both nations many of the investments proved bad. According to one observer, of 328 mergers during the period of 1888–1905 in the United States, only half were successful. Of the new firms, fifty-three failed outright; the rest earned profits that consistently were less than expected at the time the original merger occurred. The British rate of failure was not as great, but neither was it insignificant.[107]

Nevertheless, the failure rate very likely demonstrated that the underlying structure of many industries was simply not adaptable to the organizational form of large-scale corporations. In these industries, fundamental, institutional and market constraints prevented attaining the scale and organizational economies other industries achieved through managerial centralization. Accordingly, Chandler not only "established that certain patterns characterized the structure of American industry in the twentieth century," but he "went on to discover that the very same patterns obtain, with surprisingly few modifications, in other major market economies," said Thomas C. McCraw. "Only the pace and timing of appearance vary."[108] Also, each nation's experience with business failure coincided with different experiences of economic retardation and growth. Responding to the demand of the richest and most concentrated consumer market in the world, some British light manufacturers such as Cadbury's were world leaders. And yet in the development of the new high-technology industries such as chemicals and electricity Britain lagged behind Germany and the United States. This trend was part of the general relative prewar decline of

British industry in which growth continued but at an increasingly slower rate compared to its two chief competitors.[109]

Perhaps the most striking instance of Britain's loss was the iron and steel industry. Until 1870, the Bessemer processes, the industry-wide adaptation of which British entrepreneurs had pioneered, helped to make Britain the world's leader in the mass production of steel. Nevertheless, the nation's early development of this technology engendered problems by the turn of the century. American firms merged, making it cost effective to adopt new Bessemer technologies on a larger scale, thereby significantly increasing output. The numerous, relatively small family firms dominating the British industry, however, lacked the necessary economies of scale to invest in the new technology especially given rising labor costs. In addition, despite efficiencies to be gained from the sort of corporate centralization established in the US Steel merger of 1901, British producers were unwilling to give up their autonomy. Particular producers such as the manufacturers of armor plate controlled prices within a cartel, though such formal arrangements were the exception throughout the rest of the industry. Most iron and steel makers belonged to regional associations which cooperated on prices informally. Although the inability to enforce the association's agreements invited disruption by price cutters, the numerous small, often family-owned, enterprises were satisfied enough with profit-ability that they resisted merger. Consequently, when the war came Britain produced 10 percent and America 50 percent of the world's output of pig iron and steel, while Germany was the biggest exporter in the world. By then Britain imported 29 percent of the iron and steel it consumed, and half of that came from Germany.[110]

In the United States one reason why investors moved into new industries was that the adoption of managerial-centralized, heavily capitalized corporations often permitted greater long-term profit-ability than enterprises possessing looser organizational structures. It was at this very point, therefore, that American antitrust's toleration of mergers made a crucial difference.[111] An American corporate lawyer implicitly suggested the difference the law made, commenting in 1899 on the merger movement. It was "important for us in this country to observe that the English courts have not applied the doctrines of monopoly and restraint of trade to large industrial combinations, whether in the form of agreements or corpor-ations."[112]

The experience of British and American industries confirmed the degree to which, despite similar technological and industrial development, different legal rules produced opposite outcomes. During the unstable economic conditions of the 1880s and early nineties, each nation's distributors and manufacturers formed various anticompetitive business structures. In each country, too, the improved market of the mid-nineties encouraged the turn-of-the-century merger wave. Yet, in the United States, government disruption of loose anticompetitive agreements undercut the survival of small business and facilitated the emergence of large corporate enterprise. The British courts' sanction of loose restrictive trade practices encouraged self-regulation within the distribution sector itself and between distributors and producers. The long-term usefulness of these agreements also helped to limit the scale of the merger wave.[113]

The centralized organizational structure of Standard Oil and other giants, however, threatened American small businessmen. As Brandeis's unsuccessful lobbying effort suggested, middlemen and small-scale manufacturers did not oppose restrictive trade agreements per se. Rather, they resisted discriminatory price fixing by which big firms favored one individual over another, or they attacked vertical integration which destroyed the need for small enterprises altogether. During the late 1880s and early nineties, state and federal lawmakers responded to these ambiguous pressures. Many states revised their laws making prosecution of combinations easier, but often these same states exempted the anticompetitive agreements of small businessmen, farmers, and workers. At the same time New Jersey led a few states, encouraging the formation of holding companies and mergers. As a result, state laws destroyed the trust and prevented most local cartel agreements, but also allowed the proliferation of tight corporate structures. Meanwhile, after 1897, the Supreme Court outlawed most forms of price fixing under the Sherman Act, a policy continued even after it established the rule of reason in 1911. In addition, although the Court broke up two great holding companies in the *Standard Oil* and *American Tobacco* decisions of that year, its rule-of-reason theory blended economic and moral factors establishing a popular distinction between good and bad big corporations which allowed tight, managerially centralized corporations to thrive.[114]

Thus, as Chandler noted, the state and federal authorities'

preoccupation with cartel practices, while they challenged the giant firms established through merger only in exceptional cases, encouraged big business to believe that the Sherman Act permitted only the most thoroughgoing centralization of management.[115] Hannah concluded, by contrast, that the British prewar merger wave was an important economic innovation, but the "industrial partnership and the family-owned factory remained the typical unit in most branches of manufacturing." Legal forms such as the holding company, "which strengthened tendencies to large scale, had also given a new lease of life to smaller businesses. Partnerships and family firms adopted the new institutional form to their own purpose..." As a result, the "separation and professionalization of management" associated with "modern corporations still had a long way to develop."[116] Indeed, many British observers believed that their business order's underdeveloped corporate structure was less capable of achieving efficiencies associated with managerial centralization than its American counterpart.[117] In America changes in law fostered the development of managerial centralization through ever tighter corporate mergers; whereas in Britain it sanctioned the comparatively greater control of family firms.

By World War I similarities and differences characterized big business in both nations. Each country's businessmen established cartels and other loose horizontal combinations. In Britain the interplay of the market and the social order fostered internal self-regulation which aided the ultimate stability of these arrangements, but in America such practices were subject to legal attack resulting from a different set of conflicts. British and American businessmen also formed large corporations through holding companies and mergers, yet in Britain the scale on which this occurred was much more limited and the centralized organizational structure of each firm correspondingly weaker, facilitating the continued control of smaller enterprise. The high incidence of unprofitable or failed mergers indicated that in the long run many companies benefitted little from corporate consolidation. Even so, Britain's "live and let live" ethos enabled inefficient firms to survive. In America, however, market pressures, ideological tensions, federalism, and government intervention, combined to foster the triumph of managerial capitalism.

CHAPTER 2

The divergence of economic thought

The opinions of publicists and professional economists provided a frame of reference for British and American lawmakers. Yet the extent to which judges, legislators, and administrators absorbed the ideas and formal theories of the wider culture was often not readily apparent. As a new form of enterprise, big business raised new questions of economic principle engendering considerable debate and divided opinion. Although *laissez-faire* or Free Trade provided a broad ideological framework for understanding the new phenomenon, the extent to which the principle shaped public discourse was ambiguous.[1] In both nations the initial popular press and professional response during the 1880s and early 1890s questioned whether the combination movement threatened the competitive system to the point of requiring government action. Although vague concerning actual policy, American informed opinion favored intervention, whereas in the spirit of Free Trade the British declared that generally the government should not act. The second phase of the public reaction began with the turn-of-the century merger wave. By 1914 each country broadly supported a bureaucratic approach to combination, though British opinion condoned a much more modest one than its American counterpart. Ultimately, however, the most conspicuous difference was that American commentators blended moral and economic presumptions to distinguish "good" from "bad" trusts.[2]

The British view was more benign because big business did not seem to threaten government stability. Confident that a rigid social-class system sufficiently curbed the pernicious effects of competition, British media and professional opinion perceived no significant threat to either Free Trade or the government itself.[3] Americans, however, feared that "unrestrained competition" corrupted the moral foundations of representative government itself. In so far as "morals" were concerned, wrote Henry C. Adams in 1887, it was the "character of the worst... not of the best men" that gave the "color to business society." An absolute attachment to *laissez-faire* restricted "public powers within the narrowest possible limits" making "government weak and inefficient, and a weak government placed in the midst of a society controlled by the commercial spirit will quickly become a corrupt government." Corruption within a "commercial society" in turn encouraged "private corporations to adopt bold measures for gaining control of government machinery. Thus the doctrine of *laissez-faire* overreaches itself... destroy[ing] that harmony between public and private duties essential to the best results in either domain of action." At the same time this conflict obscured the organizational and scale economies, or what Adams called the "beneficent principle," resulting from many forms of combination.[4]

The divergence of economic thought reinforced British and American attitudes towards government intervention. Professional economists and popular writers were indebted to the founder of classical economics, Adam Smith. An orthodox Scottish Realist Protestant, Smith entwined concepts of value, supply, demand, desire, and scarcity to create a theory which blended moral and economic assumptions. His theory postulated that individuals had an absolute, natural right to the fruits of their own labor which the state should not disrupt. In addition, the labor required to produce something, rather than consumer demand, determined value. These ideas, in turn, supported the view that the free market produced a "natural" price, and the inalienable rights of contract and property governed this price rather than that which might be arrived solely through voluntary bargaining.[5]

During the nineteenth century, British utilitarian and marginalist theories undermined the moralist dimension of Smith's teachings. The utilitarianism of Jeremy Bentham and John Stuart Mill replaced natural-law presumptions with the positivistic norms established by the sovereign. Meanwhile, neoclassical economists such as Alfred Marshall incorporated into their writings the theory of marginal utility according to which the desire of consumers rather than the cost to producers determined value. The emphasis on positivism and consumer interest provided a basis for government policies favoring social welfare, though generally this did not extend to maintaining a competitive market. The transformation of economic theory nonetheless excised from British economic thought explicit moralistic concerns.[6]

American economists and publicists, however, remained committed to Smith's moralistic principles. A leading late-nineteenth-century textbook stated that the "principles of Political Economy are so closely analogous to those of Moral Philosophy, that almost every question in the one, may be argued on the grounds belonging to the other."[7] Thus most Americans rejected utilitarianism because it placed the goal of maximizing human desires above considerations of morals, a result many viewed as "atheistic." Although some Progressives embraced marginalism, even they often went beyond British theory in accepting implicit moral imperatives.[8] Thus Theodore Roosevelt relied on marginalist principles to formulate government policies designed to foster an efficient corporate economy, protect consumers, and punish wrongful business conduct.[9] But he justified his program in terms of a fervent appeal to moralism. Just as Roosevelt was about to become the Bull Moose candidate for President in 1912, he denounced "the corrupt alliance between crooked business and crooked politics" which had denied him the Republican nomination. "We fight in honorable fashion for the good of mankind...we stand at Armageddon," he vowed, "and we battle for the Lord."[10]

Also shaping the retention of moralistic norms in American classical and neoclassical thought were republican values. From the 1880s to World War I big business was a new phenomenon, but the rhetoric critics used to attack it was often old. The opponents appealed to a residual of republican ideals which had endured in American political discourse for at least a century. A primary influence upon the Framers of the Constitution, eighteenth-century republicanism assumed that true liberty was impossible unless the individual remained economically independent and free to participate in public affairs, which in turn fostered the good of the commonwealth and public virtue. In public discourse, the ideological linkage between virtue and commonwealth did not persist beyond the 1830s. That economic dependency resulted in the corruption of free government, however, was a distinct republican presumption influencing late-nineteenth-century agrarian and labor protest and, to some extent, even Progressive rhetoric. Small businessmen also appealed to republican values to define the challenge of big business.[11]

In addition each nation's theory of competition was unsettled. The rise of large-scale enterprise in both countries and the growing stability of loose combinations in Britain pointed toward the modern theory of oligopolistic competition in which the interplay between costs and economies gained from organizational centralization resulted in markets controlled by a few firms. Alfred Marshall's work was the first to use such concepts as elasticity of demand and marginal revenue to explain prices and output under contrasting conditions of competition and monopoly. In America, moreover, there was a large, complex literature on the problem of fixed costs and whether agreements among competitors were necessary to the survival of certain industries. And yet throughout the late nineteenth and early twentieth centuries these theories did not altogether displace the classical conception which defined competition primarily as "rivalry."[12] Thus, in 1888 the American economist Francis Walker said competition was "the operation of individual self-interest among buyers and sellers."[13]

These similarities and differences in economic thought suggested the relative meaning of *laissez-faire*. In comparison to the comprehensive state intervention characteristic of eighteenth-century mercantilism, the late nineteenth century was an era of *laissez-faire*. But considered in terms of the actual policies of government, particularly as they applied to combinations, the phrase obscured more than it explained. To be sure the prevailing Free Trade ideology insured that Britain had neither tariffs nor antitrust laws. Nevertheless the British government's role in preserving social welfare and labor combinations grew steadily. In America, by contrast, the tariff, the Sherman Act, state laws allowing certain combines but not others, and the persistent attacks on organized labor bespoke different contradictions. At the same time, both countries regulated railways and other corporate entities identified as public utilities. However useful, therefore, was the concept of *laissez-faire* as a description of ideological proclivities, its influence on actual policies, especially those involving combination, was ambiguous.[14] Similarly, although the supporters of Social Darwinism in each nation were sometimes conspicuous, their practical impact on public discourse was little more than an "exaggerated vogue." British and American economic experts and publicists freely used "biological analogies," but not to the point of embracing the full philosophical systems of either Herbert Spencer or William Graham Sumner.[15]

POPULAR OPINION BEFORE THE MERGER WAVE

During the 1880s and early nineties, big business was a new phenomenon. Publicists in both nations had encountered cartels and more informal cooperative business arrangements, particularly among railroads. But the emergence of large, highly capitalised combines within normally competitive industries such as textiles, exacerbated popular anxiety. The dominant view in Britain and America was that on the whole big business was a deviation from the "normal" or "natural" competitive system described by Adam Smith. Each country's publicists debated whether the giant enterprises would succumb to competitive pressures, thereby affirming classical economic theory, or persist, indicating the start of a new economic order. The observers also disagreed concerning the appropriateness of government intervention, though only the Americans contended that the moral foundations of republican government itself were threatened.[16]

By the late eighties and early nineties the Free Trade tradition provided the basis for understanding combination in Britain. Decades of experience with relatively unfettered competition produced among informed commentators the dominant view that Adam Smith was right. Special privilege spawned monopoly, particularly the sort of legal protection tariffs afforded manufacturers, and such protection in turn fostered combination. The monopoly held by an individual combine was often indistinguishable from a monopolistic position guaranteed certain trades through preferential customs duties, resulting in increased prices and the perpetuation of inefficient businesses. Even so, the remedy was Free Trade.[17] Admittedly, free traders also agreed with John Stuart Mill that some industries were not suited to competition. Mill had noted that urban gas light companies and perhaps railways were "enterprises [which] cannot be trusted to competition." In the "ordinary branches of industry," however, no single "rich competitor" had it within "his power to drive out all the smaller ones" and "establish himself in exclusive possession of the market." Mill affirmed, moreover, that it was the "fact" that no "important branch of industry or commerce formerly divided among many has become, or shows any tendency to become, the monopoly of a few."[18]

In these terms British journalists considered what significance the emergence of American trusts had for the classical economy. "But for [America's] protective tariff few of the trusts could exist," noted the *Contemporary Review*. Trusts were also "illegal corporations, borne of rapacity and maintained by the exercise of tyranny" with the "avowed purposes" to "destroy all competition, to diminish supplies, and to raise prices."[19] Commentators in the respectable *Times* and *Pall Mall Gazette*, furthermore, noted a parallel between anticompetitive agreements among British commodity dealers and the American trusts, which threatened the natural economic order. The commodity "rings" were like trusts which "interfered with ordinary trade" creating "an artificial increase of prices only beneficial to those immediately interested in the combination." That the rings were more like cartels than S. C. T. Dodd's Standard Oil-type trust device indicated the degree to which British commentators often lumped together forms of combination. Nevertheless, departure from "ordinary" business resulted from the "greed and rapacity of a few market riggers who are not content with the reasonable and regular profits derivable from legitimate trading." The goal of these "two, ten, twenty" persons was "to wring enormous gains from the community, in opposition to all just principles of trade."[20]

The subversion of the natural economic order potentially had serious consequences for British society. Combinations and "gigantic monopolies" wrote the pro-Liberal Party *Economist*, affected the "food or fuel" and other "necessaries of life" of the "people," "fleec[ing] the public by eliminating competition" in order to "force prices up to a point which they would not...likely...reach under the ordinary conditions of supply and demand."[21] More particularly, the *Daily Telegraph* perceived painful consequences resulting from a combination of coal dealers. "To the poor cheap coal is an article of the first necessity." To imagine that "hundreds of thousands of shareholders were making wealth out of the dearness of coal which would bring misery to a million homes is enough to turn a high and dry Tory into an impulsive Socialist."[22] On the political fringe there were advocates of nationalization and other reforms whose criticism took a more moralistic tone. "The creator designated salt and coal as necessaries of life, and the desperately wicked hearts of men have designed salt and coal syndicates," wrote the *Democrat*, "which honest men must strive to defeat and bring retribution on the heads of evil doers."[23]

The growth of combinations challenged Britain's social stratification. Newspapers representing the full political spectrum (including those sympathetic to socialism) criticized the prevailing "spirit of gambling" of which the "rings and trusts were the outcome." And yet it was a passing phenomenon, "a mere conspiracy of greed" caused by the failure of the younger generation of British businessmen to resist temptation. "Twenty years ago, ten years ago perhaps, no great merchant or banker could have been found in England willing to risk his good name by association with any kind of trade ring," wrote the *Saturday Review*. "But, apparently, the younger generation have looked upon the prodigious gains of certain American speculators – men who reckon what they jocularly call their 'plunder' by tens of millions sterling – and the spectacle has been too much for them."[24]

Nevertheless, *The Economist* argued, Britain's upper-class "society" provided a bulwark against such evils. Most of the nation's successful family firms had existed for "generations" whereas those engaged in "speculation of the grand kind for more than one lifetime" were "few" and "still more rarely English by blood. The successful speculator turns aside often because he is bitten by a sort of craze for social position, which, if he knows England, he knows he cannot win until his speculative operations are over." Similarly, American business executives "constantly" made "bargains in secret which would make an English chairman's hair stand on end at the thought of his own audacity." Such men in England, if they "ventured on the acts of despotism constantly risked in America, would be resisted by his colleagues, exposed in professional newspapers, and, perhaps, attacked in the Courts of Law, which again, are here beyond the influence of millionaires."[25]

Similarly, British journalists were confident that because loose and tight combinations would succumb to competition government action was unnecessary. Conceding that a combination might temporarily achieve significant economies the *Pall Mall Gazette* nonetheless focused on the "inevitable tendency of a huge undertaking...towards more extravagant management" so that what was "gained in one direction" was "lost in another." *The Times*, moreover, emphasized the consequences of the British preference for loose associations over the tighter forms of corporate combination prevalent in America. Thus "another manifest difficulty" was that the "stronger and more important firms who are parties to the agreement have to carry the weaker and less capable firms on their backs."[26] As a result, the initial combination movement of the late 1880s collapsed according to the natural laws of the market. "Whenever competition…exhausted the matter competed for," wrote *The Times*, "combination" was the result, "and as soon as combination has accumulated something worth competing for the reverse movement inevitably sets in. The thing goes through the ages like the ebb and flow of the tide."[27] Consequently, there was no need for government intervention because free trade and competition were "themselves sufficient levellers."[28]

Unlike their British counterparts, American journalists considered the moral, political and economic dimensions of trusts as inseparable.[29] Representative of this approach was Henry D. Lloyd, editorial writer for the *Chicago Daily Tribune* and regular contributor to such leading periodicals as the *Atlantic Monthly* and *North American Review*. In an 1881 editorial Lloyd established the parameters for attacking the creators of big business. "The methods by which the Vanderbilts, Goulds, Rockefellers…and [other]…Pashas are heaping up enormous fortunes are methods, not of creation of wealth, but of the redistribution of the wealth of the masses into the pockets of the monopolists." He denied that the "Pasha's" success resulted from a natural, evolutionary process of the "survival of the fittest," or that their fortunes were achieved because of market efficiency.[30] Admitting in 1884 that "combination" was a fundamental element of the age, he also noted the equal importance of the "demand for social control." The first was "capitalistic," the other was "social. The first, industrial; the second, moral. The first promotes wealth; the second, citizenship."[31]

Other publicists appealed even more directly to republican values. In the *North American Review* of 1887 James F. Hudson called for laws "enforcing the principle that no monopolies" were "consistent with the spirit of popular institutions." The big corporations threatened free government, constituting a new form of feudalism. "Modern Feudalism" was most evident in the rise of "great and irresponsible rulers of industry, whose power, like that of the feudal barons, burdens the people, and even overshadows the government which gave it existence. The only important distinction" was that in the "old days of force, the power of feudalism was measured by the thousands of warriors; in the days of modern plutocracy its power is measured by millions of money."[32] Shortly thereafter lawyer-publicist William W. Cook noted the dangers posed by corruption. "So long as the business of corporations is affected by government, just so long will corporations continue to bribe, brow-beat, and dominate public officials," he said. "Whatsoever" aided "plutocracy" was thus "a danger to the republic."[33]

Publications representing farmer and labor groups set forth similar views. *Appleton's Annual Cyclopedia and Register* published the resolutions of the Farmers' Congress of the United States held in Montgomery, Alabama in 1889. Those attending opposed "all combinations of capital, in trusts or otherwise, to arbitrarily control the markets of the country to the detriment of our productive industries; and we demand of the Congress of the United States such legislation as will secure to farmers and stock raisers of the country the best possible reward for their labor."[34] The split between Samuel Gomper's A.F. of L. and the Knights of Labor meant that organized labor's stance toward big corporations was divided. Although Gomper's position was not altogether clear during the late 1880s, generally he resisted government interference with the trusts.[35] But the Knight's stand was unequivocal. "When monopolies become stronger than the law, when legislatures become the servants of monopolies, when corporations can successfully bid defiance to public good and trample on individual rights," exclaimed the *National Labor Tribune* "it is time for the people to come together to erect defenses for personal rights and public safety."[36]

Bonds between small businessmen and workers persisted long enough that some united against the trusts. By the 1880s the Jeffersonian dream of independent proprietorship remained sufficiently widespread despite social-class tensions that the rallying cry for cooperation was "equality of opportunity." More significant than the division between employer and employee was the gulf separating "monopolists" and "plutocrats" from the "people."[37] By 1884 the pull of mutual self-interest was still sufficiently strong that diverse agricultural, labor, and small business groups joined together to form the Antimonopoly party. Their platform exclaimed that the nation's commerce was "now mercilessly controlled by giant monopolies, to the impoverishment of labor, the crushing out of healthful competition, and the destruction of business security." It was, therefore, the "imperative and immediate duty of Congress, to pass all needful laws for the control and regulation of those great agents of commerce."[38] Gradually the economic pressures upon

small business resulted in cooperation giving way to intractable
confrontation between the National Association of Manufacturers
and the unions. The Antimonopoly party soon died. Yet it had
succeeded to the point that prior to 1884 the platforms of neither the
Republicans nor Democrats included an antitrust plank but,
beginning with the 1888 presidential campaign, both of the major
parties incorporated one.[39]

The popular press also stressed that the large corporations' steady
takeover of the functions traditionally left to the small enterpriser
demanded government action. Groups from the Wholesale Grocers'
Association of New York to the American Hide and Leather
Company favored "extreme" legislation to stop the trusts.[40]
National newspapers and popular periodicals also reported and
commented upon the hearings of the US House of Representatives
in which Standard Oil's former competitors described their loss.[41]
C. B. Matthews, a former president of the Buffalo Lubricating Oil
Company, explained how he was "crushed out." Because, he said,
Standard controlled "more than half of the territory of the United
States, so that independents could not ship there, they have been
able to reap such large profits in those districts that they could sell
where there was competition at a point below the cost of
manufacturing for the purpose of destroying the competitor."[42]

The press also presented the views of those defending big
corporations. In 1888 the *New York Commercial Bulletin* published a
series of editorials by George Gunton, who was just beginning a
career as a noted business journalist. The "public mind" reflected a
"state of apprehension, almost amounting to alarm, regarding the
evil economic and social tendencies of these organizations," he said.
The anxiety was not "limited to professional agitators and chronic
alarmists," but was "shared in by all classes." The public outcry
stemmed from popular fear of monopoly. Gunton argued, however,
that monopoly was bad only if spawned by the "arbitrary exclusion
of competitors"; where it resulted from efficiency it was "a positive
advantage to the community." He suggested, moreover that "bad"
trusts were exceptional, whereas the efficient ones were prevented
from exploiting the public by the threat of competition. As long as
the "gates for admission of new competitive capital" remained
"always open," the "economic effect" was "substantially the same
as if the new competitor were already there; the fact that he *may come*
any day has essentially the same effect as if he *had* come, because to

keep him out requires the same kind of influence that would be necessary to drive him out."[43]

More explicit was Andrew Carnegie. In articles published during 1889 in the *North American Review*, he favored unbridled competition until combination destroyed it. The American people should "smile" at the success of "railway magnates and manufacturers" who had defeated the "economic laws by Trusts or combinations." The law of competition insured "the survival of the fittest in every department." Americans should "accept and welcome, therefore, as conditions to which we must accommodate ourselves, great inequality of environment, the concentration of business, industrial and commercial, in the hands of a few." Carnegie modified this otherwise straightforward Social Darwinist argument by urging upon the "fittest" a responsibility to use their wealth for improving the educational opportunities of the public.[44] Nevertheless, the ultimate result of this "survival-of-the-fittest" thinking was the replacement of the competitive system described by classical economists with a new economic order dominated by giant corporations.

Even so, popular views regarding combination were equivocal. Despite the scathing attack on the "Pashas", Lloyd admitted admiring "consolidation" where it resulted from men having "become so intelligent, so responsive and responsible, so cooperative that they can be intrusted in great masses with the care of vast properties owned entirely by others, and with the operation of complicated processes."[45] In 1883 the *North American Review* published an article on the Standard Oil trust, conveying a similar ambivalence. West Virginia Senator J. N. Camden, a former Standard director, emphasized the public benefits resulting from combination. The company had fostered "almost the whole development of the oil industry" during the preceding ten years, the "uniformity [of] all oil manufactures... [and the] cheapening [of] these latter to an unprecedented degree," the "introduction of American petroleum to the remotest parts of the earth," the providing of "employment to a host of men equal in number to the standing army of the United States," and brought "prosperity to every locality" in which the company operated. Against these gains Camden set the "bitterest grievances" of the "small refiners, whose real complaint was that Standard with its improved processes and immense product, had too greatly cheapened the cost of manu-

facturing and marketing refined oil."[46] He conveniently ignored
Standard's resort to practices, including discriminatory pricing,
which courts ultimately declared to be illegal.[47] Concerning the
advantages of combination, however, Camden and Lloyd ironically
shared common ground.

Like their British counterparts, Americans possessing a socialist
perspective also favored combination. Edward Bellamy's popular
fantasy, *Looking Backward* (1881), although as critical of corporate
leaders as Lloyd, nonetheless saw large-scale enterprise as the wave
of the future. Bellamy concluded that "small capitalists" were
"totally incompetent to the demands of an age of steam and
telegraphs." Despite the growing numbers of industrialization's
"victims", he lauded the "prodigious increase of efficiency" which
"national industries" achieved through the "vast economies effected
by concentration of management and unity of organization." As a
means of "producing wealth, capital had proved efficient in
proportion to its consolidation." A return to the "old system,"
Bellamy concluded, "might indeed bring back a greater equality of
conditions with more individual dignity and freedom but it would be
at the price of general poverty and the arrest of material progress."[48]

The popular anxiety concerning combination was, then, qualified.
The publicist's preoccupation with the wealthy's extravagance, or
particular forms of pernicious conduct such as predatory pricing,
suggested that the basic problem was abuse, which translated into
the general fear that private power was corrupting republican
government. Yet the growing animosity between small enterprisers
and workers, the split within the labor movement itself, and the
demise of interclass cooperation in the Monopoly party indicated
how divided were the opponents of corporate giants. This conflict
weakened their political effectiveness. The growing conflict among
the opponents of corporate abuse also facilitated a marked vagueness
concerning what remedies state and federal government might
pursue. Commentators such as Lloyd and Hudson, like the
publications representing farmers, organized labor, and small
business rarely if ever set forth specific policy recommendations.
Even the attacks on discriminatory prices and other pernicious
conduct rarely if ever prescribed anything other than court action.
Certainly there was no attempt to offer proposals commensurate
with the claim that corporate corruption threatened the very
existence of republican government.[49]

One explanation for the gap between criticism and the formulation of remedies was that the groups attacking corporate combination themselves often benefited from other forms of combination. By about 1890 the states' common law and new antitrust legislation either implicitly permitted or formally exempted the cooperative arrangements of farmers, organized labor, and small businessmen.[50] Despite notable exceptions, moreover, the US Supreme Court subsequently declared that most of these provisions violated neither the Constitution nor the Sherman Act.[51] Thus, much of the antimonopoly rhetoric implicitly distinguished certain loose combinations which were legitimate from tight consolidations which were not.

Popular publications and periodicals reflected the divergence in British and American public opinion. The initial response of British publicists to the emergence of big business was concerned but confident. Individual market "riggers" might challenge the "normal" Free Trade system but, ultimately, competition would prevail because Britain's social-class system inhibited excessive deviant behavior. Although a few commentators on the political extremes defined the problem in moral terms they were exceptional. Generally, even socialists joined the Free Traders, arguing that government action against loose or tight combinations was unnecessary. In the United States, however, moralistic concerns linking personal opportunity, individual accountability, and the corruption of republican government engendered intractable conflict. Yet the rhetoric of moral condemnation obscured a fundamental inability to establish clear distinctions between legitimate and illegitimate combinations. As a result, critics of big business demanded government action but left the remedies vague.

THE PROFESSIONAL ECONOMIST'S RESPONSE BEFORE THE MERGER WAVE

The publicists usually popularized the theories of academic economists. In Britain, the leading neo-classical economist, Alfred Marshall viewed the emergence of combination along the lines outlined by Mill and the classical school. Representatives of more radical perspectives, including the historical school and advocates of socialism supported other interpretations. Virtually all professional opinion started from the assumption, however, that most loose combinations were endemic in the competitive system or, as Marshall put it, "competition burns so furiously as to smother itself in its own smoke." They also generally agreed that the sort of tight corporate structures emerging in America were much less likely to appear in Britain where there was no protective tariff, monopolistic control of some natural resource, or geographic isolation.[52] American professional economists, by contrast, though, possessing a sophisticated understanding of fixed costs and other issues, nonetheless could not escape dealing with these issues generally in terms of moralism, natural economic laws, and corruption.[53]

Differences of opinion among British economists involved the question of whether combination was exceptional or permanent. An economist of the historical school, H. F. Foxwell, denied that competition was a "final permanent state of stable equilibrium." It was instead an "industrial war, more or less, honorably carried on" leading to the "commercial monopoly of the victorious firm." Competition was therefore, "transitional," whereas "monopoly" was "something more permanent, more fundamental than competition itself."[54] Marshall, by contrast considered such views "to be exaggerated." In Britain not tight but loose combines prevailed, and sooner or later in a competitive system they collapsed. He was confident that, "as ever, the main body of the movement depends on the deep silent stream of the tendencies of Normal Distribution and Exchange, which are 'not seen' but which control the course of those episodes which 'are seen.'" Particularly in America, Marshall declared, the "dominant force" was the "restless energy" of a "comparatively few very rich and able men." For these individuals, the degree of control permitted by Britain's incorporation device, the joint stock company, was insufficient; they preferred combinations like the Standard Oil trust which were "more mobile, more elastic, more adventurous and often more aggressive."[55]

British economists debated, too, the benefits and disadvantages of combination. Foxwell, of the historical school, noted that large-scale enterprise possessed "enormous economies in administration and division of labor, the concentration of knowledge and skill." Conversely, it avoided, the "costly litigation of rival schemes, the utterly useless expenditures on advertisement." Consumers gained also from improved quality, "uniform, easily ascertainable price," the "absence of temptations to adulteration," and the "greater variety of choice."[56] Marshall was more skeptical. The "very large firms and combinations of firms" had merely used "existing knowledge, rather than increas[ing] that knowledge." Generally, their efficiency was no better than "private businesses of a moderate size in that energy and resource, that restlessness and inventive power," which encouraged "striking out" on "new paths."[57]

Radicals and Socialists agreed with both positions, though for different reasons. J. A. Hobson, of the historical school, conceded that large enterprises were neither more nor less efficient than small firms. Nevertheless, an "industrial movement" which replaced the "regular employment of a few for the irregular employment of many" was a "progressive movement."[58] The socialists believed that combinations were an inevitable result of the inequities and conflicts inherent in competition, establishing the means for a peaceful transition to state ownership. Sidney Webb argued that joint-stock companies were prevalent enough in Britain that their "shareholders could be expropriated by the community with no more dislocation of the industries carried on than is caused by the daily purchase of shares on the stock exchange." Accordingly, H. M. Hyndman concluded, a "conscious socialist should rather endeavour to hasten on the growth [of combinations] as fast as the stage of economic and social development attained would itself admit."[59]

Meanwhile, British economists agreed that combinations were not an important enough problem to warrant significant government action. Marshall and Hobson concurred that the degree of the economic influence of big enterprise resulted not from immediate monopolistic exploitation, but from low, steady gross profits. Although regularity of modest profits was attractive to those possessing economies of scale it was not, wrote Marshall, "very tempting to anyone" lacking such economies. The fixed costs of maintaining a giant firm required plowing profits back into the production and distribution facilities, keeping profits down. Thus, at least as far as Britain was concerned, both the socialist and neoclassical economist concluded that it was unlikely that any giant firm would "ultimately obtain so great a power as to be able to shape, in a great measure, the conditions of trade and industry."[60] An economist of the historical school W. J. Ashley, who looked favorably upon the movement toward combination, accepted the need for only a limited degree of government oversight. If the "tendency to monopoly" made government "control more necessary, it also renders it more easy" requiring little more than the "simple expedient of publicity."[61] Finally, socialist economists opposed any intervention short of nationalization, which was nonetheless unattainable without a major social transformation sometime in the future.[62]

American classical economic theory reinforced the popular press's uneven approach to combination. Francis A. Walker, president of the Massachusetts Institute of Technology, asserted that "rightly viewed, perfect competition" was the "order of the economic universe, as truly as gravity" was the "order of the physical universe" and no "less harmonious and beneficent in operation."[63] Francis Wayland's belief in harmoniously operating economic laws included the conviction that labor and capital were "natural partners" which "if not interfered with, w[ould] spontaneously seek each other as birds mate in the spring for a happy fruitful union." This faith also meant that legitimate combinations contained within themselves the seeds of their own destruction. In such an order the role of government was significant though limited. Because the conduct of "all men" was not guided by "moral and religious principles" it was essential that "aggression be somehow prevented, and violations of property, in so far as possible, redressed. Hence the importance of *wholesome and equitable laws*, of an independent and firm judiciary, and an executive, which shall carry the decisions of law faithfully into effect."[64] Moreover, wrote Francis Bowen, according to a "legitimate carrying out of the *laissez-faire* principle," the government should insure that such "stumbling blocks" as immoral conduct did not interfere with the "natural order of things." In such cases "rights" were "objective realities" enforceable in "the courts."[65]

Regarding the relation between combination and competition the classicists both differed and agreed with other contemporary economists. The New School Economist (The American counterpart of the British historical school) included diverse individuals who departed from classical theory by arguing that large-scale enterprise was inevitable. New School economists also categorically rejected the Social Darwinist brand of *laissez-faire* espoused by Carnegie. Yet they disagreed among themselves and with the classicists concerning the extent to which government should intervene either to facilitate competition or to sanction combination.[66]

Although John Bates Clark was skeptical of the Sherman Act, he wrote in 1887 that to "regulate combinations is possible and, in some directions, desirable; to permanently suppress them is impossible; to temporarily repress them is either to force them into illegal forms or to restore the internecine war from which a natural evolution has delivered us."[67] Accordingly, Clark felt that vigorous prosecution under state common and statute law was sufficient. Also in 1887, Henry C. Adams said that the law should preserve the benefits of competition (including that which produced efficient large enterprise), while preventing its abuse. The proper "purpose of all laws, touching matters of business," was, he concluded, "to maintain the beneficent results of competitive action, while guarding society from the evil consequences of unrestrained competition." Adams particularly wanted the government to overcome that "unguarded competition" which tended to "lower the moral sense of a business community." There was, he concluded, "certainly a close connection between the rise of the menacing power of the corporation and the rise of municipal corruption." Adams did not dismiss altogether the usefulness of antitrust legislation. Yet, because the trusts were merely symptomatic of the larger problem of corruption, he stressed the necessity of broader government reform, including the creation of a professional civil service.[68]

During the late 1880s Richard T. Ely, the period's most influential New School economist, recognized a distinction between "natural monopolies" and artificial combinations achieved through special privilege or corrupt conduct. Although close to British classical economists in advocating government ownership of public utilities, Ely went beyond them in opposing government "interference with combinations of labor." Furthermore, he resisted antitrust legislation, such as the Sherman Act, first because it could be turned against organized labor, and secondly because private business which achieved a monopoly through legitimate or illegitimate competition was ripe for government control "in the interest of the public." Otherwise, "*competitive pursuits*" were the "*field for private activity*," and government should not intervene.[69]

By contrast, railroad economist and Yale President Arthur T. Hadley, maintained that the cost factors producing large-scale enterprise had ended the era of competition. Although "education and habit of mind" made people "believe in competition," the "present age" was one of "industrial monopoly...We have not free competition, nor can we fairly expect to have it in the future. Instead of moving toward it, we are moving away from it," he said. This was "a fact to which people are just beginning to open their eyes." Although Hadley's penetrating studies of railroads demonstrated that rate discrimination was often economically legitimate, they also revealed repeated instances of abuse, requiring government action in the public interest. He accepted, however, neither the outlawing of all combinations, nor public ownership, supporting instead government prohibition of particular abuses "such as secret favors, or arbitrary discriminations."[70]

Meanwhile, most American economists shared the view that loose, anticompetitive agreements posed little long-term threat. Just as the great merger wave was about to begin in 1897 lawyer-turned-economic publicist, Albert Stickney wrote, "The only possible loss, or damage...resulting from [loose] combinations...consists in a slight temporary raising or enhancing of prices. No loss or damage to any...individual, or to the community, can come from the mere act of combination, or agreement." In part this view was consistent with the popular acceptance of cooperative arrangements among small businessmen, workers, or farmers.[71] But it also indicated that, like the popular press, economic experts were unable to establish a clear distinction between legitimate and illegitimate combinations.

American and British professional economists disagreed. By the early 1890s the economic experts of both nations divided over whether big business was "natural," which raised the corresponding issue of whether it would succumb to or ultimately transform altogether the classical competitive system. Similarly, each country's professionals believed that loose anticompetitive practices did not in the long term seriously threaten the economic order. Controversy, therefore, focused on the legitimacy and implications of tight combinations. Despite many American economists' complex understanding of fixed costs and other issues the stronger moral or normative content of American economic thought resulted in a greater preoccupation with government intervention. British and American economists, of course, condemned behavior such as fraud or extortion which was indictable under the criminal code. But American professionals as different as Clark, Hadley, and Adams went farther, condoning government action to regulate the "unguarded competition" which "lowered" the businessman's "moral sense."[72] There was little consensus on more specific policy measures: some favored, while others opposed the Sherman Act. Yet these proponents of the "new economics" shared with the classical economists a conviction that American welfare depended on using public authority to prevent the abuse which threatened republican self-government itself.

THE IMPACT OF THE GREAT MERGER WAVE: POPULAR OPINION

The turn-of-the-century merger wave altered public perceptions of large-scale enterprise. Both British and American observers increasingly accepted the view that the new structure of business was permanent. Disagreement persisted, however, concerning whether the triumph of big business signaled the continued vigor or inevitable demise of the "natural" competitive order. Each country's informed observers considered the appropriateness of government intervention in terms which were consistent with marginalist theory favoring administrative regulation in the public interest. Yet the British extended the state's regulatory function only modestly to include the shipping industry, relying primarily on business self-government enforced through increasingly stable loose combinations. In America, by contrast, the fear that big business was corrupting republican government engendered a national debate over the revision of the Sherman Act and creation of an antitrust commission. Woodrow Wilson's victory over Theodore Roosevelt and W. H. Taft in the 1912 presidential election generally confirmed that the criteria controlling greater government action would have to accept a moral and economic distinction between "good" and "bad" corporate giants.[73]

The turn-of-the-century merger wave encouraged British publicists to modify their earlier assumptions. Generally, informed commentary progressed from the popular antipathy of the 1880s, through equivocal acceptance, to cautious approval of a few types of industrial combination. This change paralleled the recognition that shipping, an industry formerly regarded as competitive, had become a public utility like the railways, requiring limited government supervision. The transition in public thought came about partially because the relative international decline of Britain's economy heightened perceptions of vulnerability. The modest nature of the shift suggested, however, not only how entrenched was popular confidence in the competitive system, but also that family firms felt secure enough that significant government action seemed unnecessary.[74]

The publicist's response to unprecedented merger activity was not uniform. *The Times* treated both loose and tight combinations as ordinary business developments. After the merger wave in 1906 it summed up the nation's experience. A "dozen or more 'combines'" existed in "various trades – tobacco, cement, sewing cotton, spinning, chemicals and so on – very few of which have achieved any notable success even from the shareholders' point of view." More significantly, only in one or two instances had these "organizations secured a control over the home market which can be called a monopoly, and those that have done so retain that market solely during good behavior." *The Times* was confident that any attempt at monopolistic "extortion" would immediately spawn "competition both home and foreign." Moreover, if economies were attainable through "reasonable combination among makers," it was "not very wise of the public to object especially as the combinations in this country are so effectively limited in the scope of their ambitions."[75] Thus *The Times* partially accepted the view of the historical economists and the socialists that big firms were a legitimate and inevitable mode of industrial reorganization.

Still, *The Economist* probably represented a more prevalent view. Large combinations "may have legitimate objects within certain limits." Yet, they were "unequal to the task of maintaining prices against the consumer where trade slackens off and brings the influence of competition into play."[76] Nonetheless, comparatively small firms, possessing the "individual acumen, foresight and skill, which, inspired by the hope of personal gain, have done so much to develop our industries and perfect the means of production" were more efficient than a big enterprise's "board of directors whose interests" were "not so closely involved." These problems, moreover, were symptomatic of speculative schemes resulting in over-capitalization and, in most cases, eventual collapse.[77]

After 1900, however, the American invasion of Britain tested the limits of competition. Confronted by Morgan's attempt to dominate the shipping industry and American Tobacco's effort to control tobacco, British publicists condemned the spread of American "trust methods." The invasion was "without precedent in the annals of civilized trading," an "extravaganza of the wildest sort for which the consumer will eventually have to pay." More specifically, the Americans' speculative investment strategy violated the British sense of fair play. Commerce was "admittedly a free fight with legitimate knockout blows." But there was "such a thing as hitting below the belt – or to translate the metaphor – selling at an acknowledged loss with a view to raising the price later."[78] Accordingly, *The Economist* opposed the "internecine war" of a "ruinous" and "needless competition."[79]

The collapse of the invasion nonetheless brought a qualified reaffirmation of the British competitive system. Although it was essential to avert the evils of cut-throat competition, large, managerially centralized trusts were not the answer. F. W. Hirst, the editor of *The Economist*, categorically rejected the American political economist Jeremiah Jenk's arguments favoring bigness. He denied the American's "insinuation that the rule of a scattered group of factories by a Board of Experts sitting around a telephone will in the long run, in a normal Free Trade Community, prove more efficient than the older system in which every factory had its captain on the spot." Hirst and other commentators trusted in the "magic" of "personal management" which was not only more efficient than "remote and impersonal supervision," but also less susceptible to the "extravagance that inevitably results when men think in millions rather than thousands."[80] In Jenk's "American system," moreover, business leaders felt "no defined responsibility to society as a whole."[81] Accordingly, just as there existed a "unit of economic management" which was "wasteful to exceed," there was a "healthy side of competition," without which business would either "wither and decay" or become "obese."[82] In the search for the proper balance, journalists increasingly condoned cooperative self-regulatory arrangements maintained through loose associations, though they also contended that Britain was "unsuited to the rigidity of a German cartel."[83]

At the same time, there was a reconsideration of the need for government intervention.[84] Morgan's attempted takeover of the shipping industry upon which Britain's export-oriented economy depended, increased pressure for government action until Parliament responded with protective legislation. Meanwhile, some major periodicals demanded an investigation modeled after the trust inquiry carried out by the United States Industrial Commission, to determine whether broader regulation of the shipping industry was necessary. In 1906 the Liberal government appointed a Royal Commission to make such a study.[85] During the same year soap manufacturers established a cartel to better control production, setting off a public uproar debated on the front pages of several

mass-circulation London newspapers. Unlike the shipping controversy, however, there was no call for direct government action. The
public scrutiny caused the break up of the cartel, yet there was no
opposition when Lever Brothers, the largest soap producers, began
acquiring competitors through merger.[86]

The great merger wave also reoriented American popular press
opinion. Even more than during the 1880s, large corporations drove
small enterprises out of business. In 1893, 1899, and 1900 well-
publicized trust conferences met in Chicago to discuss the economic
transformation. The Presidential candidates of both major parties
stated that the trusts had become the dominant domestic issue of the
day.[87] Noted publicist Herbert Croly exaggerated only a little when
he stated that after 1896 "almost every morning paper was filled
with accounts of the...new railroad and industrial combinations."[88]
More than ever before mass-circulation magazines published stories
on the general trust problem and individual trusts. The most famous
of the latter category were the critical accounts of Standard Oil and
other corporate giants appearing in the pioneering muckraking
journals *McClure's* and *Century Magazine*.[89]

By the turn of the century a perceptible shift had occurred in the
focus of the popular press. During the 1880s Lloyd and other
commentators attacked the trusts in personal, human-interest terms,
but remained vague about remedies. Such commentary further
muddled the issue by sometimes defending combinations in principle
as the new order of the future. The merger wave seemed to confirm
the inevitability of combinations, but the continued threat they
posed to moral accountability and republican values heightened a
demand for concrete government action. The Supreme Court's
ambivalent interpretation of the Sherman Act, fostering as it had the
proliferation rather than demise of large corporations, also increased
public pressure for more effective government intervention. Increasingly after 1900, then, as a Kansas newspaper observed, the
"question is becoming more and more important daily whether
regulation and supervision of big corporations by the government
will produce better results for the entire country than fruitless efforts
at dissolution." Such comments suggested that Americans were
distinguishing between "good" and "bad" corporations. Many, to
be sure, steadfastly opposed the distinction, as did the Kansan who
observed that "As well might you refer to a 'Good' burglar. Every
combination was 'conceived in sin and born in inequity.'"[90] In

addition, a few adherents of Carnegie's brand of Social Darwinism wanted no government measures at all. But, by the presidential campaign of 1912, the latter two views were not dominant.[91]

Probably the prevailing view was that most large-scale corporations resulted from special privilege which encouraged abuse.[92] As a result, most commentators agreed that part of the remedy of the problem was publicity. "Whatever degree of public regulation or control they [the trusts] may be found to need in the future," observed an editorial in the 1901 *Review of Reviews*, "the thing first desirable is knowledge of their financial condition and business methods – in others words, publicity of a kind illustrated by the reports that banks are required to give."[93]

There was disagreement, however, over how the government should provide publicity, and whether other measures were necessary. Some defenders of big business favored federal incorporation with limited provision for a modest level of publicity. They also suggested either the repeal of the Sherman Act, or a reinterpretation by the Court according to the more flexible rule of reason.[94] Opponents of giant corporations wanted not only publicity but the strengthening of the antitrust laws. This group wanted new legislation forbidding as criminal "all combinations that restrain all competition" or that were "formed for the purpose of raising prices." Principles of "right and justice" demanded such laws to "kill the great 'octopi'" which had "reached out and gathered in all of the establishments in certain industries, not because of any economic superiority in these giant combinations but because they" were "fed" and "sustained by special privileges."[95]

The disagreement over appropriate regulation also involved conflicting views regarding whether combination or competition was "natural." The merger wave seemed to strengthen the argument that big enterprises were consistent with "natural" economic laws.[96] The defenders of this theory demanded regulation of competition in order to protect the road to efficient combinations. The American public read these views in the news reports of George W. Perkins's testimony before a Senate investigatory committee during the summer of 1911. Perkins, former partner of J. P. Morgan, a current associate of US Steel, and eventually a financier of Roosevelt's Progressive Party, told the committee that "you can only get that which approaches efficiency in business today by doing business on a large scale." He believed that Americans "perhaps sooner than we realize," must accept the "fact that in certain lines of business the efficiency of a certain company will become so great that that will be largely the controlling element in the matter of competition."[97] He meant by the last point that competition would end.

Perkins resisted the Sherman Act because it amounted to regulation by lawsuit. He favoured rationalizing the business environment by instituting administrative supervision of business combinations through increased publicity. "I think that a company that had to expose its capital stock, its methods, its treatment of labor, and its treatment of its competitors and consumers, so that all who ran might read – that you would find that that would be largely corrective," Perkins said. To implement this policy he advocated formation of a commission within the Department of Commerce and Labor, staffed by businessmen, with the power to license corporations engaged in interstate or foreign business. The company would receive the license only if it promised to abide by the rules Congress prescribed under the commission's mandate; and the entire process would operate under the light of publicity.[98]

Before the same Senate committee Boston lawyer Louis D. Brandeis opposed Perkins's views adamantly. Big combinations were "artificial, not a natural product." Accordingly, whenever they suppressed competition it was not the result of efficiency but due to either "ruthless processes" or the "improper use of inordinate wealth." Efforts to "dismember existing illegal trusts" did not, therefore, interfere "in any way with the natural law of business." On the contrary, it was an "endeavor to restore health by removing a cancer from the body industrial...not an attempt to create competition artificially, but it [was]...the removing of the obstacle to competition."[99] More important than the economic issue, however, was the threat bigness posed to republican self-government. "You cannot have true American citizenship, you cannot preserve political liberty, you cannot secure American standards of living unless some degree of industrial liberty accompanies it," Brandeis said. The corrupting influence of big business sapped both republican and industrial liberty, spawning "social unrest." The trusts had "stabbed industrial liberty in the back" causing "social unrest"; that was what was "really the matter with [big] business. Well-founded social unrest; reasoned unrest; but the manifestations of which are often unintelligent and sometimes criminal."[100]

The danger of impending disorder was so "serious," Brandeis

warned that "wise legislation" was essential. Going beyond Perkins's modest recommendations, he proposed first revising the Sherman Act to prohibit certain forms of pernicious corporate conduct including tying agreements which restricted selling prices, rebates and other discriminatory pricing practices, refusal to deal, industrial espionage, and the construction of phoney companies. Brandeis favored the Court's new rule of reason recently established in the *Standard Oil* case, but the proposed legislation should place upon the corporation the burden of proving the reasonableness of its conduct.[101] Secondly, Brandeis also supported the creation of a commission possessing "very broad powers of investigation and inquiry – publicity," but he opposed the Perkins's ideas of licensing, federal incorporation and supervision carried on by a body staffed by businessmen.[102]

Ever the successful trial lawyer, Brandeis desired in no way "to relieve the Attorney General or Department of Justice of its obligation to institute proceedings."[103] Brandeis hoped that the flexibility of administrative regulation and the rule of reason, combined with proscriptions outlawing certain forms of corporate abuse would enable the Justice Department to bring suites protecting small enterprise. He defended the reasonableness standard because the courts could apply it to uphold restrictive agreements among small business. He noted that the Supreme Court's anti-cartel decisions fostered tight combinations. If the Court reversed this policy and followed British doctrine allowing the enforcement of loose agreements, small business might enjoy scale and organizational economies while still preserving their independence.[104]

There were strengths and weaknesses in Brandeis's and Perkins's testimonies. The merger wave reinforced Perkins's contention that many industrial enterprises gained such organizational and scale economies that the classical theory of competition no longer applied. At least two-thirds of the nation's manufacturing assets were controlled by firms which possessed the sorts of economies described by John E. Searles, director of American Sugar Refining Company.[105] "Perhaps the greatest of all benefits in the centralization" was the "concentration of technical knowledge and ability of the people connected with the business."[106] Perkins's advocacy of publicity and a regulatory body, however, indirectly confirmed Brandeis's charge that, often, malfeasant conduct or special privilege rather than efficiency engendered combination. Moreover, such prominent representatives of big business as James J. Hill sustained Brandeis's charge that corporate managerial centralization and vertical integration destroyed small business. "They are the ones who have been caught between the upper and nether mill stones," Hill wrote in 1902, "they are the middlemen, and the small competitor who were unable to meet the larger concern in the open market."[107] Furthermore, if the British experience was at all indicative, Brandeis was also correct that the Court's sanction of loose combinations would partially at least limit the drive toward mergers.[108] Nevertheless, it was uncertain whether the respective regulatory approaches advocated by Perkins and Brandeis would achieve the results either of them claimed.

Each nation's press confirmed how the merger wave encouraged gradual acceptance of big business. Even those most antagonistic, such as Hirst of *The Economist* and Brandeis, conceded that the triumph of large-scale enterprise was probably irreversible. Similarly, disagreements over the ultimate implications of this transformation for the continued survival of the competitive system were inextricably linked to the issue of appropriate public response. Noting that tight corporate consolidation existed on only a comparatively small scale in Britain, publicists from Liberal to socialist generally condoned a modest extension of the government's authority to include shipping, partially as a protection from foreign invaders such as Morgan. Yet, after Morgan's retreat, observers accepted the virtues of business self-regulation through loose combinations. Because of the popular fear that big business was corrupting republican self-government American publicists presented giant corporations as a more ominous threat. But the inability to distinguish legitimate from illegitimate combinations rooted in American ambivalence toward small and big business enmeshed the debate over policy in intractable conflict. Thus, even after Wilson won the 1912 election on a platform accepting Brandeis's legislative proposals, Congress could not enact them without compromise.[109]

THE MERGER WAVE AND PROFESSIONAL ECONOMISTS

Again, the British popular press mirrored the opinion of British professional economists. Following the end of the merger wave and prior to the Panic of 1907 some economists supported business–government cooperation in the case of the shipping industry, though there was disagreement over whether this should extend to establishing a supervisory body such as the US Interstate Commerce Commission. The dominant professional view not only rejected such action, but also resisted even the modest proposal of instituting publicity through registration with the Board of Trade. D. H. MacGregor opposed both a regulatory agency and a system of "inquisitional registration." Arguing that combinations posed little threat because eventually the inefficient ones would succumb to competition, MacGregor perceived the "only...duty" left to the government was that of "insuring that the movement will owe its success or failure to the action of the openest competition with other methods," by which he meant primarily that Britain should have no protective tariffs.[110] This view was sufficiently widespread that even defenders of the merchant shippers who complained most about the shipping firms' unfair methods, had "no objection to combination in principle."[111]

Moreover, how much British economic orthodoxy was shaped by Free Trade deserved emphasis. Compared with American economists, much of the apparently cavalier attitude of British economists to combination was because Britain had a very small geographically compact market in which there was a lot of competition between firms, in the sense that was generally not true between firms in New York, San Francisco, and Chicago. Also, many British industries faced considerable competition from abroad, which American tariffs stopped. Anyone who believed in the classical theory of competition could perfectly well take the view that, given other facts of geography and tariffs, anti-trust policy was perhaps needed in the United States and not in Britain.

By 1906 very few economists broke with the prevailing professional opposition to government intervention. Even prominent socialist writers resisted government interference with combination because they believed that the trusts established the basis for eventual state ownership of the means of production. Admittedly, socialists and Labour were at this time politically powerless. Yet consideration of their views was warranted in order to suggest the degree of consensus among all British interest groups against government intervention. Socialists generally were convinced, according to Sidney and Beatrice Webb, that the combination movement represented a fundamental departure from the "industrial organization described by the classical economists."[112]

The most noteworthy exception to the socialist orthodoxy against government action short of nationalization, however, was Henry W.

Macrosty of the London School of Economics. Macrosty wrote tracts on the shipping industry advocating the creation of a government board overseeing the arbitration of all interests. He accepted legitimate combination, subject to modest government regulation. Ultimately, he extended this principle beyond shipping to include other industries, called for a state agency empowered to register combinations to "hear all complaints, and to take cognizance of all acts contrary to the public interest... [possessing] the right to conduct inquiries and to call for explanations and if the offending cartel did not amend its ways it would be struck off the register" and thereby lose the right as a lawful entity to enforce its contracts in court.[113] Thus, once the merger wave ended, Macrosty set forth an administrative approach to combinations similar to that which American economists eventually supported.[114]

Between the Panic of 1907 and the coming of war, British professional opinion gradually shifted. Except for Lever Brothers and a few other tight consolidations, corporate mergers abated. The most notable change in business structure was the increased stability of loose anticompetitive agreements. Many of these loose combinations had had shaky beginnings during the 1890s, but after the turn of the century they formed effective mechanisms of self-regulation. The courts reinforced this trend with decisions which not only allowed but increasingly also enforced vertical horizontal anticompetitive agreements. The primary cause of this greater organizational resilience, however, was business compulsion to replace cutthroat competition with the ethos of "getting along." Although the competitive system certainly did not end, it was moderated through ongoing negotiation and accommodation.[115]

Macrosty explained part of the trend. There were "two main causes of combination," he said, "the attempt to escape from consequences of excessive competition and the desire to realize the economies of large-scale production." On this point British commentators across the political spectrum agreed. But there was dispute regarding his further contention that the "limitation of competition... [was] a natural development culminating in the production of private monopoly either complete or partial."[116]

Following the classical assumption that monopoly resulted primarily from protectionism, other economists emphasized the distinction between "artificial" combinations and those achieved through "exceptional merit." Consequently, Mrs. M. E. Hirst concluded that although there were "many large amalgamations of capital in the United Kingdom, few are monopolistic in character." Similarly, her husband, the editor of the proLiberal *Economist*, declared that most large combines grew from "normal development" and "natural, traditional or economic advantages" and were "maintained only by strenuous effort." Thus the "more natural the basis of monopolistic combinations, the less serious danger their existence presents in the various spheres and relations of commerce." Other prominent economic experts accepted Macrosty's analysis, however, ascribing the Hirsts' views to classical economists who had "in their blood...the 'natural' necessity of competition," and therefore could not accept the "permanency of English monopolist associations."[117]

There was further disagreement over government intervention. One segment of opinion among publicists and professional economists argued that Britain's relative economic decline resulted from the under development of managerially centralized, large combinations. The *Economic Journal* of 1913 stressed the need for "reorganizing the management" of British industry if she was "going to hold her own in the industrial world against foreign countries." Improved management benefited consumers, producers, and "all sections of the community" by eliminating the "disastrous effects of internecine competition with the retention of its beneficial activities."[118] Thus government should not inhibit, and in appropriate ways could even assist, the formation of combinations run by efficient management structures.

Still, the more common perception favored preserving small enterprise by establishing a Ministry of Commerce. The agency would have, said the editor of *The Financial Review of Reviews*, "the duty of properly developing trade, encouraging the manufacturers and industries, directing the commercial industries of the country into sound profitable channels, and creating a never-failing link between openings abroad and manufacturers at home." Under this proposed regime the government's chief mission was information dissemination and the coordination of industrial research. In addition, a leading defender of the competitive system, D. H. MacGregor, wanted the government role to include coordination of purchasing and marketing. He even proposed, like the American Louis D. Brandeis, that government should sanction price-fixing agreements among small businessmen so that they could enjoy greater scale and organizational efficiencies but still remain independent. Railroads also pressured Parliament to expand the Board of Trade's authority to permit more flexible rates and more extensive mergers.[119]

During the late pre-war years, however, these views were implemented only to a limited degree. In 1909 the Royal Commission's report on the shipping industry recommended, and Parliament enacted, a system of government supervision similar to that proposed by Macrosty. Similarly, the prominent neoclassical economist Alfred Marshall had shifted from opposing to supporting such a system, even suggesting its adaption on a wider scale. Yet by the time the war began, the Board of Trade, the ministry responsible for maintaining oversight of the shipping industry, reported that it had acted only in a few relatively insignificant cases.[120] At about the same time pressure from middlemen prevented leaders of both the Conservative Party and the Liberal-Labour coalition from strengthening the government's ability to encourage and approve railway combinations.[121] Meanwhile although the courts sanctioned the enforcement of restrictive agreements among both large and small business, the proposal of using ministerial authority to encourage "rationalization" was not enacted.[122]

American professional economists also shared a growing consensus favoring administrative regulation, though they also disagreed concerning specific measures. American economic experts had exercised little or no direct influence on policymakers before Congress passed the Sherman Act. From the 1890s on, however, their role as commentators, opinion leaders, and, above all, political advisors changed markedly. Especially after the federal government's Industrial Commission and its successor, the Bureau of Corporations, provided investigatory testimony and statistics, public officials increasingly looked to economists for guidance on the trust issue.[123]

No one listened to such experts more than Theodore Roosevelt. During his presidency and the Progressive Party Campaign of 1912 he relied significantly on a handful of professional economic advisors, including Jeremiah Jenks. A professor of political science at Cornell University, Jenks was a leading contributor to the Industrial Commission.[124] Like most of his professional colleagues, Jenks was certain that the "waste of competition...which comes from the inability of adapting one's plants and output to the needs of the market...can be partly saved by combination of many manufacturing establishments in one industry under one management."[125] He was cautious about the political implications of trusts, stating that probably "few trusts" were "entirely evil" while none were "all good." But he was certain that antitrust statutes and court decisions had "comparatively little, practically no effect as regards the trend of our industrial development."[126] Jenks blamed the personal "character" of lawmakers rather than the corporations themselves for the existence of corruption. He also suggested that the era of the small businessman had passed.[127] Finally Jenks supported an administrative regulatory approach to big corporations similar to that advocated by Perkins.[128]

Another Roosevelt advisor, Yale's Arthur T. Hadley, broadly accepted Jenk's analysis and remedies, especially the reliance upon publicity, but disagreed regarding the larger threat.[129] Not unlike Brandeis, Hadley perceived the new corporate economy as creating "a contradiction between our political theories and the facts of industrial life. A republican government is organized on the assumption that all men are free and equal. If the political power is thus equally distributed while the industrial power is in the hands of a few, it creates danger of class struggles and class legislation which menace both our political and our industrial order."[130]

There was also disagreement among New School economists. Ely continued to rely on relatively unrestrained labor organizations and private business, while advocating state ownership of public utilities broadly defined. He accepted the need for inheritance taxes and legislative proscription of overcapitalization, and to enforce such measures he was not adverse to establishing a federal commission.[131] Rejecting public ownership as a primary policy, however, America's foremost neoclassical economist, J. B. Clark, put his faith in government intervention. By the turn of the century, Clark saw the control of the trusts as the leading economic issue of the period. In 1901 he published *The Control of Trusts*, contending that "Well in sight" was an appropriate regulatory policy. It was "one which welcomes centralization, but represses monopoly. It allows mills and shops to grow large and to combine with each other, for the sake of the economy which this growth insures; but it puts a stop on predatory uses of the power that is thus gained. It yields nothing to monopoly, but employs the statute-making power to strengthen in every way the condemnation that the common law pronounces on it." As long as the government vigorously prosecuted under the Sherman Act such "predatory" practices as discriminatory prices, Clark saw little need for a commission.[132] Although otherwise relying on Brandeisian rhetoric during the 1912 presidential campaign, Woodrow Wilson's effective use of Clark's distinction between good combination and bad monopoly helped him to win the election. The difficulty in establishing the difference, however, resulted in the enactment of ambiguous legislation in 1914.[133]

The merger wave thus facilitated a shift in the opinion of British and American economists. Whereas the two nations' professionals had disagreed over whether the emergence of large-scale enterprise required government intervention, once the merger movement occurred their views drew somewhat closer together. Increasingly they implicitly accepted, at least in principle, that some sort of official agency possessing the flexibility to deal with the more complex market and price imperatives recognized by marginalist theory was necessary. Yet the convergence on principle merely highlighted more significant differences between the British and Americans and among the Americans themselves concerning the form or powers of this administrative authority. British lawmakers instituted only the Board of Trade's quite modest oversight of the shipping industry, while they declined to enlarge the Board's powers over railway rates and mergers. In the United States the struggle involved not only the creation of an antitrust commission, but also the revision of the Sherman Act. The contrary uses Wilson and Roosevelt made of the theories of economists revealed how ambiguous was the regulatory principle.

The compromised antitrust legislation Congress enacted after Wilson's election confirmed the difficulty of distinguishing between "good" and "bad" trusts. Relatively free from concerns that big business threatened either the social or political order, British informed observers dismissed the melding of economic and moral elements reflected in the good-bad trust distinction as peculiarly American. Despite the changes the merger wave brought about, British publicists and economists advocated only a modest expansion of government intervention. As a result, self-regulating, anti-competitive business structures spread. Preoccupied with the popular linkage between big business and corruption of free government, but also desirous of the consumer benefits large enterprise made possible, it was not surprising that American publicists and economists blended moral and economic imperatives, advocating increased government action to encourage the benefits while preventing abuse and exploitation of giant corporations. The economic transformation represented by the struggle between big and small business ensured, however, that administrative would likely prove no less ambivalent than judicial policymaking.

CHAPTER 3

The political response

The interplay of politics and market relations shaped a different course of business development in Britain and America. Parliament's supremacy, changing interest-group pressures within the major parties, an effective civil service, and the judiciary's relative passivity constituted a stable political order in which the social-class system and labor's struggle paradoxically sustained the Free Trade consensus favoring noninterference with anticompetitive combinations. No significant institutional constraints impeded the family firm's preference for loose over tight business structures. Consequently, the scale of the merger wave was more modest and, the regulation of railways and shipping notwithstanding, business self-regulation took hold.[1] In America before the mid-1890s, by contrast, the insecurity of small business, the tension between republican values and private rights, federalism, and judicial supremacy encouraged divergent legal rules which influenced the ambiguous provisions of the Sherman Act. The ambivalence of state common law and legislative measures, which the Supreme Court's 1895 and 1897 decisions reinforced, facilitated the larger merger wave. This transformation exacerbated fears of corruption and the demise of small enterprise; but it also strengthened Americans' yearning for government action to prevent the abuse of bad and preserve the benefits of good large-scale corporations. As a result of the conflict between morals and economics the Court established the rule of reason and after the election of 1912 the federal government bureaucratized antitrust policymaking.[2]

THE DIVERGENCE OF LEGAL RULES BEFORE THE
MERGER WAVE

British and American law makers responded to the depressed economic conditions of the 1880s and early nineties unevenly. Revising old doctrines, the judges of both countries gradually adopted a rule of reasonableness, indicating the common need for a more flexible legal standard. The contrasting experience of each nation's courts, however, confirmed that despite similar economic and market conditions, institutional and ideological imperatives produced divergent results. The popular consensus favoring non-intervention, along with Parliamentary supremacy, meant that British judges declined to pursue the active policy-making role implicit in the reasonableness principle. American judges not only disagreed concerning the scope and limits of competition, but also the federal system fostered a pattern of interstate doctrinal uncertainty. Had American judges followed a passive course like their British counterparts, there may have been less ideological and institutional diversity. But the divergence in the incorporation laws of the states, and the Supreme Court's ambiguous interpretation of the commerce clause enmeshed the meaning of the Sherman Act in further uncertainty. As S. C. T. Dodd's formulation of the Standard Oil trust suggested, greater managerial centralization ameliorated the costs federalism imposed.[3]

Traditionally, American and British judges employed an analysis distinguishing ancillary or partial from nonancillary or general agreements to determine whether a given restrictive contract was enforceable. The courts of each nation only gradually departed from this mode of legal reasoning, developing the more flexible rule of reason. Yet, it was a particularly American perspective to treat the different types of a trade-restraint claim to which an anti-trust law might be hypothetically applied as cognate phenomena. Ultimately that frame of thought was determined primarily by the Sherman Act. But it was a fundamental aspect of British non-intervention that legal issues were treated separately. Thus a rule of reason was adopted *only* in relation to the enforceability of contracts between those party to them. Because of the federal pattern of states, moreover, there was much less uniformity in the evolution of the American common law. Some states liberalized the rules controlling the enforceability of ancillary restrictive agreements much as the

British did. Those same states, however, went beyond the British
principles regarding nonancillary restraints. Meanwhile other states
continued to follow the "old rule" in which virtually all anticompetitive agreements were void. In light of this diversity, the
failure of informed American legal opinion to perceive an underlying
cohesive standard of reasonableness during the 1880s was understandable.[4]

By the 1880s, Britain's common law did not hinder business
combinations. Forty years earlier Parliament had repealed laws
forbidding restrictive trade practices such as forestalling, regrating,
and engrossing, because those "regulations restricting the purchase
and sale of goods... were opposed to the spirit of modern [Free
Trade] legislation." Parliament thus significantly circumscribed
traditional common-law actions which had permitted easy prosecution of cooperative agreements as monopolistic conspiracies.[5]
British legal principles remained unsettled until a series of decisions
in the 1890s. The House of Lords settled the *Mogul Steamship Company*
case in 1892, declaring "that one may do anything to get rid of a
business rival provided that one does not commit a well-defined
tort." The Trades Disputes Act of 1906, though essentially involving
the lawful actions of trades unions in trade disputes, indirectly gave
legislative approval to the *Mogul* doctrine.[6]

The common-law's prescription that contracts in restraint of trade
were not enforceable was similarly circumscribed. The Lords held in
the *Nordenfelt* decision of 1894, that restrictive trade agreements were
enforceable if found "to be reasonable both between the parties and
in relation to the public interest." Although the principle of
reasonableness had lurked as an underlying principle, British judges
expressly had declined to rely upon it out of a firm regard for self-
restraint. The *Mogul* case, which addressed *tortious* liability to
outsiders injured by combination, refused even to contemplate the
murky distinctions of "reasonableness." Equally there was no real
question of reimposing criminal sanctions of the kind finally
abandoned in 1844. Since there was nothing left of treble damages,
there was no potential for legal intervention of any significant kind
in the absence of independent unlawfulness. Thus, ultimately, the
shift from "partial/total" to a "reasonable/unreasonable" test in
Nordenfelt was a relatively minor adjustment in the restraint of trade
rules affecting contracts. This was so, according to one close
observer, "largely because the judges were reluctant to assess
evidence on an economic character."[7] After 1900, some American

lawyers seeking justification for the United States Supreme Court to adopt a rule of reason argued that even before *Nordenfelt* the English common law had always followed the principle of reasonableness. Yet such a view ignored the fact that during the 1890s most British judges generally denied this very assertion.[8]

In Britain the judiciary's role in accommodating the law to a changing economy was passive. As one economist noted, by World War I the courts were "in fact, seldom called upon to enforce 'reasonable' cartel agreements, since trade associations preferred to rely upon private methods for ensuring adherence to their rules."[9] Indeed, from the 1880s on, the commercial press favored legal rules which left business affairs to business itself. In 1889, during a flurry of concern involving the invasion of Britain by American trusts, the *Chamber of Commerce Journal* nonetheless opposed any revival of laws against forestalling and regrating, as it was "obsolete and antiquated legislation framed to meet a different set of circumstances." Similarly, the press shared the favorable view of the *Mogul* decision expressed in the pro-Free Trade journal, *The Economist*: "Free trade and competition are themselves sufficient levellers, and any decision of our Courts of Law which tended to confine the limits of competition and combination...would be regarded as a public misfortune." The *Banker's Magazine* and *The Times* agreed.[10]

In the United States, by contrast, S. C. T. Dodd formulated the first trust in response to the conflicting court decisions throughout the different states. Prior to and during the 1880s state courts generally did not enforce the cartel or pooling agreements business fashioned to meet the late-nineteenth-century depression in prices. There was nonetheless considerable variation in judges' decisions involving restrictive practices.[11] "Virtually the same state of facts has in different courts led to opposite decisions," an early commentator observed.[12] Shortly after the Standard Oil trust appeared in 1882 a writer for the practitioner's periodical, *The Central Law Journal*, noted how unpredictable was the law of restrictive contracts and combinations. The "public policy" inherent in the old English rule transferred to America was, he noted, that "all contracts in restraint of trade should be declared void." By the mid-1880s, however, the "conservative feeling" of American judges adhered to the principle only as an "abstract rule." As with "most all the old rules, which were founded on common sense and experience, the exceptions have become so numerous that the old rule can be evaded almost entirely."[13]

The diversity of the judges' decisions reflected disagreement concerning the costs and benefits of competition. According to the *Central Law Journal* many judges who regarded the matter in a "superficial way" or gave it "no serious thought" still "implicitly believed to be infallible" the "time-worn maxim" that competition was the "life of trade." Thomas Cooley, Chief Justice of the Michigan Supreme Court and author of the most widely read constitutional treatises of the time, noted, however, that some forms of combination, such as railway pools, "both with reference to their legal aspect, and their effect upon the country... may not only not injure, but actually benefit trade."[14] The uneven impact of the late-nineteenth-century price decline among different states or regions undoubtedly facilitated conflicting decisions.[15]

In both nations the diversity typical of the common law also characterized corporation law. The status of the *ultra vires* doctrine, which held that a corporation was bound by the powers specifically delegated in its charter, suggested the degree of difference. According to the *Central Law Journal*, in England the rule was that "*ultra vires* contracts, and all acts done under them seem to give no rights whatever." In "many" American states, however, the rule was "directly contrary, and the corporation can enforce, or be compelled to perform such an executed contract, as if the doctrine of *ultra vires* did not exist." And yet, in the federal courts and in "a few of the states, a truer rule prevails. There, as in England, the contract itself is unenforceable." Even so one of the Supreme Court's decisions was "savagely criticized" because it allowed a corporation "to maintain a robber monopoly."[16]

Parliament supported Britain's Free Trade spirit by enacting the "most liberal company law in Europe."[17] The Joint Stock Companies Act of 1844 established basic principles governing incorporation. The law defined the difference between private partnerships which possessed no limited liability, and joint stock companies which did operate under that principle. The Act also required corporations to accept the light of publicity through registration. Amendments passed in 1855 and 1856 permitted "incorporation with limited liability to be obtained with a freedom amounting almost to license."[18]

Although such legislation spawned periodic periods of speculation and bust, modest reform efforts in 1888 met firm resistance from solicitors representing business clients. In a letter to the *Law Times*,

Freshfields and other "leading legal firms engaged in company business," exclaimed that the legislation was "evidently prepared with the laudable object of dealing with and stopping the acts of fraudulent promoters." But "if it becomes law [it will] assuredly drive from this country a very large amount of banking, commercial and other business which passes through all classes, and brings an interchange of commerce of every kind between England and all parts of the globe." The effect of any law, which would "render operations with joint-stock companies as expensive, complicated and difficult as similar operations abroad will be to reverse the process that has been going on in the past, and to send away business which would otherwise be transacted in London."[19]

Parliament thus changed incorporation law primarily to the point of encouraging business self-regulation. Following the battle over the legislation of 1888, some major British firms formed holding companies in which a central or parent corporation owned the stock rather than the actual properties of various separate companies. This legal device facilitated Britain's turn-of-the-century merger wave.[20] Yet Parliament's statutes, like the judiciary's common law, reflected a firm attachment to the Free Trade presumption that, generally, the best public policy toward private business affairs was non-intervention. As long as the law required corporations to register, thereby publicizing the operations of and relations among competitors, all was well. Indeed, as late as 1913 a leading proponent of Free Trade confidently affirmed that the "English Companies Act is a much more effective piece of anti-trust legislation than the [American] Sherman law. Judges may differ over what constitutes 'monopoly' or 'restraint of trade' but fraud and mismanagement are easier to detect."[21]

The failure of British business to seek the advantages of incorporation reflected a general satisfaction with the status quo. Beginning in the mid-1880s the limited liability corporation "accounted for, at most, between 5 and 10 percent of the total number of important business organizations, and only in shipping, iron and steel, and cotton could their influence be said to have been considerable."[22] Moreover, the motives for incorporation among even this relatively small number were mixed. Originally, Parliament enacted the limited liability principle because of lobbying pressures from "a group of middle class philanthropists, most of whom accepted the title Christian Socialists," who sought to

establish "facilities to safe investments for the savings of the middle
and working class." By 1886, however, an entrepreneur told the
Commission on the Depression in Trade and Industry that, "it has
been an advantage to my company to be a Limited Liability
Company – because I have always had as much power as a director
of this company as I had as a partner and the resources of the
company are greater than the resources of the old partnership."[23]

Still, an unshakable attachment to personal ownership and
control reinforced any British businessman's aversion to large
corporations financed through public sales of stock. The independent
owner-operators understood the loss to themselves resulting from the
view of one corporate board director: "it was an awful mistake to
put into control of the various businesses purchased by the company
the men from whom the businesses were purchased, because these
men have got into one groove and could not get out of it."[24]
Similarly, a significant problem with the holding company, was the
"opportunities [it afforded] for friction, misunderstandings,
quarrels, and even rebellion. Although the disturbers of the peace
can be removed at the next board election they may meanwhile have
wrought much mischief."[25]

The Manchester merchant and manufacturer, Samuel Ogden
articulated other reasons why limited liability seemed threatening.
"The social and personal consequences of bankruptcy, which result
from unlimited liability, impose prudence on private traders; but,
being non-existent in the case of limited companies, business
involving large risks is more easily undertaken by such companies,"
he said. "This fact considerably handicaps ordinary traders with
unlimited liability in their competition with companies with limited
liability, and has a tendency either to drive them out entirely, or to
induce them to abandon their cautious rules of conduct in trading."[26]

But Ogden may have exaggerated the extent to which the law
harmed smaller firms. In 1886 the Royal Commission on the
Depression of Trade and Industry emphasized that small-scale
industries led by innovative entrepreneurs were essential to the
nation's past economic greatness. And "if our position is to be
maintained it must be by the same energy, perserverence, self-
restraint and readiness of resource by which it was originally
created." Although the turn-of-the-century merger wave created
some important giant corporations, it did not shake the traditional
presumption. Rather, the mergers heightened business acceptance of

looser business structures which permitted self-regulation without threatening each firm's independence. In the replies to the Tariff Commission, the prevailing view was that businessmen were "not convinced that these huge trusts always worked more economically than the smaller makers at home. We prefer the individuality of the smaller makers." Furthermore, the "smaller maker puts more time into manufacture of the article and less into overlooking, and so very often secures a better article for the same money as the big trusts... By excessive management we find trusts often stifle effort." Meanwhile, many small enterprises which had formed loose, self-governing associations, found that "[c]ombines and associations of various firms in the same or similar trades to maintain one level of prices, with a heavy penalty or fine for breaking through the arrangement, leaving at the same time each firm to manage its business on its own lines" had "worked well to the profit more or less of all firms."[27]

Thus, although British law permitted both loose restrictive agreements and tighter mergers, the former predominated. Various Parliamentary statutes extended to businessmen a broad right of limited liability to raise capital through public offerings. Yet most business relied upon private incorporation or loose restrictive agreements which lacked the force of law. The outcome of Parliament's action was to allow business to decide how much or how little competition it wanted within self-imposed restraints of private accountability. And usually British business chose to reduce costs through looser associations which did not threaten the independence of small firms. Similarly, the common law sanctioned wide-ranging restrictive practices, though generally not their enforcement. The formulation of the reasonableness doctrine out of earlier precedents in 1894 hypothetically gave judges the means to more directly shape the course of business agreements. But the judiciary declined to develop the doctrine's inherent authority, thereby reinforcing Parliament's preference for nonintervention.

In America, by contrast, because each state possessed sovereign authority over corporations uncertainty prevailed. Since there was no federal incorporation statute, the benefits of limited liability were available to business only through state incorporation laws. Between 1870 and 1890 growing numbers of transportation and manu-facturing companies adopted the corporate form, facilitating the creation of large firms with million-dollar or multimillion-dollar capitalization. States encouraged this trend by enacting general incorporation laws. Before 1870 state legislatures granted corporate charters through special acts but, increasingly, states passed general laws that established broad, easily satisfied requirements regulating capitalization, payment of fees, legal rights and obligations, and other factors important to corporations.[28]

Yet the state's control created uncertainty for firms engaged in national trade. A corporation chartered in one state but doing business in other states was known as a foreign corporation. Railroads, insurance companies, and manufacturing firms were representative of the numerous foreign corporations operating in the interstate commerce of the period. Some states, such as West Virginia (incorporation cost $6.00 and annual taxes were $50.00), Delaware, and New Jersey passed general laws imposing extremely loose incorporation requirements in order to attract business. These laws bespoke a competition among states, which certainly benefited particular businesses but which also ensured that the formulation of legal uniformity was virtually impossible. At the same time, other states, such as Pennsylvania and Ohio, sought to restrict severely (and even exclude) the activity of foreign corporations by imposing strict regulations. To these states, nonresident corporations were "pirates" and "tramps" who threatened local interests. Inevitably, this divergent pattern of regulation imposed a burden on interstate corporate business.[29]

This was the legal environment in which Dodd created the Standard Oil trust. In order to undercut the competition of independent oil refiners operating in Pennsylvania, Standard needed to vertically integrate several refining plants it had purchased in that state. Because Pennsylvania's common law and general incorporation statute prohibited one corporation holding stock in other corporations, Rockefeller had hoped to rely on a special charter. Since Standard Oil was a foreign corporation chartered in Ohio, however, the legislature made the procurement of the special charter too costly by raising taxes on the company's capital stock and dividends. Thus Standard Oil apparently lacked the legal means to achieve the scale and organizational economies which would permit the elimination of competition. At this point in 1882, however, Dodd fashioned the first formal trust. Under the device the shareholders of forty companies exchanged their stock for certificates in the new Standard Oil Trust, which then turned over operating control to nine trustees. The new entity did not fit the technical legal definition of a foreign corporation, enabling the trustees to charter separate corporate subsidiaries to run the trust's property in Pennsylvania. As "local" corporations, the subsidiaries also were not bound by state laws regulating foreign corporations.[30]

The emergence of the Standard Oil Trust preceded another important alteration in the state's corporation law. In 1889 New Jersey revised its general incorporation law to permit the formation of a holding company. The holding-company statute made lawful what had limited Rockefeller in Pennsylvania: the right of a corporation to hold stock in other corporations. The purpose of the new law was to attract business to New Jersey. By forming a holding company a firm could establish a managerially centralized enterprise operating within a multi-state region. The directors of the parent firm thus acquired direct control over the assets and earnings of subsidiaries located in other states.[31]

In response to Dodd's trust device, however, most states enacted stronger antitrust legislation. The new statutes enlarged and extended the old common law's prohibition against restrictive trade agreements. More specific than the common-law rules, the acts addressed not only monopoly and contracts in restraint of trade, but other anticompetitive practices including pooling, price fixing, output limitation, territorial divisions, resale restraints, exclusive dealing, refusals to deal, local price discrimination, and predatory pricing. These provisions followed the early English common law's general rule that restrictive contracts were unenforceable and not actionable in tort.[32]

The new laws also enlarged the remedies and mode of enforcement available in government and private prosecutions. At least thirty-five states authorized fines or imprisonment, or both. The most stringent penalties allowed prison sentences of up to ten years and fines of as much as $25,000. Some statutes made each day of a violation a separate offense. Nine states allowed private parties to recover actual damages, two allowed double damages, and nine allowed treble damages. Often the statutes authorized public officials to revoke corporate charters or licenses of local and out-of-state corporations.[33]

The states' antitrust activism reflected popular fears that giant corporations threatened republican self-government and social order. As major industrial corporations adopted Standard Oil's trust device during the late eighties and early nineties, the public ignored the technical legal meaning, equating most large corporations with trusts, which were in turn perceived as just another form of monopoly. The rhetoric involving consolidation during Missouri's state-wide elections in 1888 was typical. Both Democrats and Republicans condemned trusts as monopolies, while the victorious Democratic governor warned fellow citizens that corporate centralization threatened their freedom. "Unchecked by any feeling of individual responsibility," he said, trusts "moved solely by the love of gain, unfettered by the duties of citizenship... are enabled to perpetuate themselves by the adoption of methods and the use of agents which scruple at no means to accomplish their ends." Similarly, in 1894 the Illinois Attorney General protested, "We may talk of democracy and equal rights all we please, but this country is to-day in danger from an evil... the evil of raising up a privileged class to prosper and grow rich at the unfair expense of the masses." It was thus not surprising, wrote another observer that "anarchy thrives when rich and powerful combines violate the laws and defy state authority with impunity, and when they rob and oppress the people despite restraining laws."[34]

By 1888 the trusts had become a bipartisan political issue for the two major national parties as well. Republican Party statements agreed with Democrat Grover Cleveland that the trusts threatened the virtuous citizenry upon which depended republican government. "Whatever may be their incidental economic advantages, their general effect upon personal character, prospects, and usefulness cannot be otherwise than injurious," to workers, small businessmen, and farmers, who then possessed, he said, "little hope or opportunity of rising in the scale of responsible... citizenship."[35]

Using the law to protect the individual enterpriser's independence and self-sufficiency, however, challenged the sanctity of contract and property rights. "If popular views are adopted in the construction of these statutes, and if they are held to be constitutional... they have made criminal all business of magnitude and all business conducted by means of association of persons and aggregation of capital," wrote Dodd. "I have too much faith in our constitutions and our courts to believe such a result possible."[36] Shortly before the New Jersey legislature enacted the holding company law, the state's governor expressed a somewhat more balanced view. The "right of individuals and of corporations... to combine for lawful purposes, is not to be questioned" he said. "When, however, the effect, if not the aim of such combinations is to control the market and regulate the price of articles... then their formation is against public policy, which... demands that competition shall not be restricted."[37]

Ironically these tensions also resulted in laws permitting certain forms of combination. Several states enacted statutes exempting farming associations, labor organizations, lumber, cotton or woolen mills, wholesalers and retailers, and "organizations intended legitimately to promote the interests of trade, commerce, or manufacturing [within the] state."[38] In part, these provisions were consistent with the narrow protectionism Standard Oil encountered when its resort to a special incorporation charter threatened the local oil refining interests which also had influence within the Pennsylvania legislature. More broadly, however, the exemptions recognized that laws which fostered increased local individual enterprise or group action also benefited the general welfare. Merger structures fit into three basic paradigms: the common law trust, the asset acquisition, and the holding company. State officials thus hoped to preserve the advantages of combination for local interests while denying them to foreign corporations.[39]

Politicians justified the promotion and protection of local enterprise as consistent with natural economic law. State governments often sanctioned the price-fixing practices of small businessmen through resale price maintenance and also permitted mergers so that local businessmen might pool organizational and technological expertise. Public officials could argue that these measures were necessary to enable smaller enterprise to compete fairly with foreign corporations. In order to preserve the natural law of competition and supply and demand in the one instance, government had to limit the operation of that law in the other. Intervention was essential, moreover, because trusts had subverted the natural economic order. According to a New York assembly report, the sole purpose of the trust "aggregation" was the disruption of the "natural law of supply and demand" and the destruction of "competition by... unfair methods... to secure control of both product and market." Thus legitimate business moved in accord "with the natural law" whereas the trust was "designed to and does operate against natural law."[40]

Politicians also linked the belief in republican values and the natural economy to popular fears of corruption. British observer

James Bryce noted the pervasive American belief that "great corporations" run by "one or two capitalists" working in "secret" used their great wealth to "offer bribes at which ordinary virtue grows pale."[41] The frank admissions of corporate leaders gave substance to such concerns. "It was the custom when men received nominations to come to me for contributions," noted Erie Railroad owner Jay Gould, "and I made them and considered them good paying investments for the company; in a republican district I was a strong republican, in a democratic district, I was democratic, and in doubtful districts I was doubtful; in politics, I was an Erie railroad man every time."[42]

Appealing to these popular perceptions, state authorities defeated the Standard Oil-type trust. Between 1888 and 1892 state officials prosecuted and won cases not only against Standard Oil in Ohio and Missouri, but also against the cotton oil, sugar, distilling, and utility industries which had adopted Dodd's trust device in Louisiana, Illinois, California, New York, and Nebraska. The victories resulted from state courts accepting attorney general's arguments that trusts were subject to criminal liability and civil remedies under the new antitrust legislation and old common law. When Dodd developed the trust to circumvent Pennsylvania's incorporation law its legal status was unclear. The states' successful prosecutions resolved the uncertainty by formally declaring that the trust arrangement was unlawful.[43]

These triumphs, however, only complicated the trust problem. By the mid-1890s the variation of state law prevented a uniform and consistent pattern of antitrust enforcement. Perhaps the most significant impediment to cohesive policy on the state level was New Jersey's holding company law. Individual states might prosecute combinations vigorously, but once New Jersey sanctioned contract rights which other states prohibited big corporations could escape to a secure harbor. Ironically, the victory over the Standard Oil-type trust pushed those businessmen seeking increased scale and organizational economies towards tighter forms of combination.[44]

From 1888 to 1890 the intractable though inconclusive struggle on the state level fostered federal intervention in the form of the Sherman Act. Federalism again, however, impeded effective action. Since the nation's early days federal courts had aided the development of interstate business, including state-chartered corporations.[45] Yet federal judges repeatedly affirmed the coequal power of the states over disputes concerning the restrictive trade practices of corporations engaged in interstate commerce.[46] As late as 1890 the Supreme Court upheld this doctrine in *Central Transportation Co.* v. *Pullman's Palace Car Co..* Similarly, it was well established that Congress possessed general authority over interstate and foreign commerce. The creation of the Interstate Commerce Commission in 1887 to regulate the railroads was a significant exercise of that power. At the same time, however, authorities generally agreed that corporations involved in production confined principally within a single state were not subject to federal regulation under the commerce clause. By the mid-nineteenth century the Supreme Court had decided many cases defining the scope and limits of the commerce power along these lines.[47]

Although large combinations had emerged by the 1880s in response to explicit market pressures, public opinion, politicians, and even informed commentators often ignored market considerations, ascribing the transformation instead to businessmen's corrupt and mendacious motives. Yet even many of those sharing these presumptions acknowledged that certain forms of combination resulted from legitimate individual endeavor which benefitted the community. This distinction between legitimate and illegitimate combination reflected tensions inherent in the belief in natural economic laws and the attachment to republican values and private rights. Thus the successful antitrust prosecutions represented the use of government to punish deviant behavior, but they did not acknowledge just how extensively new market conditions had resulted in a restructuring of the business order.[48]

By the mid-1890s the legal rules governing restrictive business practices were more stable in Britain than in America. Consistent with the Free Trade ideology British judges developed a rule of reasonableness and Parliament enacted incorporation statutes which facilitated business self-regulation through restrictive agreements. American federalism, by contrast, encouraged a course of government policymaking and business structure which was more ambivalent. Seeking to protect local business from foreign corporate giants, some state courts and legislatures attempted to distinguish between legitimate and illegitimate corporations. In so doing state policymakers appealed to republican values and the belief in natural economic laws. Other states, however, attracted by the jobs and opportunity big corporations supposedly provided, drew upon the constitutional guarantees of contract and property rights to sanction three basic merger structures, including large, managerially centralized corporations. In addition, the uneven standing of corporations under the Supreme Court's interpretation of the commerce clause, combined with the ambiguous character of the common law, left the meaning of the Sherman Act uncertain. Amidst such tensions big business established greater managerial centralization through the holding company and merger. Federalism thus fostered conflicting ideological and constitutional values as at the same time it encouraged state and federal legal rules which sanctioned tight more than loose business structures.

THE POLITICS OF GOVERNMENT INTERVENTION AND THE MERGER WAVE

During the years preceding the great merger wave, different political and ideological pressures influenced each country's divergence in business structure. On the stock exchanges of both nations improved market conditions contributed to unprecedented investment in merger issues by 1897. Despite similar technological and industrial development, however, American businessmen achieved a greater scale of mergers than their British counterparts, who increasingly relied on looser forms of self-regulation. Although British business, labor, and socialist groups and the dominant Liberal and Conservative political parties disagreed concerning government regulation of public utilities and support of social welfare, they shared a consensus favoring noninterference with most restrictive business structures. Of course, in Britain before World War I, the significant parties were the Liberal Party (which had minor contacts with Labour) and the Conservative Party. The Labour Party was not formed until 1900, only got a few seats in elections and never participated in a majority government before the First War. It was therefore never in this period in a position to significantly influence legislation except as a pressure group. And since most of the working-class did not vote in Britain until 1918, even as a pressure group it was fairly ineffective. The Socialists were even more politically marginal. They are referred to below primarily to suggest the extremes as well as the center of political conflict.

Thus in Britain neither legal rules nor government action hindered the choice between tight and loose combination and, despite the merger wave, British family firms more often than not chose business structures which permitted them to preserve relative independence. In America, by contrast, the interplay of the federal system, the popular belief in republican values and natural economic laws, and the struggle between big and small business ironically foreclosed the option of loose combinations. Before each nation's stock exchange recorded the upswing in merger issues, state officials began liberalizing incorporation law which encouraged holding companies and mergers, while the Supreme Court construed the Sherman Act to outlaw cartels but not tight corporate structures.[49]

The limited degree of government intervention reflected Britain's changing party politics. From the middle of the nineteenth century on, the power structure within Parliament and the executive gradually adapted itself to the exigencies of well-organized pressure groups. Before this, MPs and party officials had touted the ideal of "independence." Increasingly, however, the identification of "interested" representatives and party leaders became common. The new designation indicated that individuals or groups of MPs and politicians within the leading parties represented well-defined and effectively organized alliances based on social class or economic function. The extent of the change became apparent by the 1880s, with the mobilization of merchants and shippers in response to the success of the "railway interest."[50]

Throughout the mid-nineteenth century, Parliament and British public opinion accepted the necessity of government regulation of the railroads and other public utilities. The construction and operating costs of these enterprises required so much capital that the protection of limited liability incorporation was essential. In return for this security the charters Parliament granted the railroads imposed various regulations, including rate limits. Moreover, informed observers noted that the fixed costs of operation were sufficiently high that traditional principles of unrestrained competition did not apply. To achieve sufficient economies of scale, larger units achieved through combination were unavoidable.[51] No one understood better the oligopolistic character of railroads as "natural monopolies" than the well-known editor of *The Economist*, Walter Bagehot. "[G]iven our instincts for freedom and our Parliament," he said, the creation of several railway "competing monopolies" was inevitable.[52]

These pressures resulted in periodic Parliamentary battles and legislative compromise. From the mid-nineteenth century on Parliament's "railway interest" represented company boards of directors and those living in close proximity to a railroad's right of way, regardless of party identification. According to Herbert Spencer these individuals were "gentlemen...some of them landowners, some merchants or manufacturers; some owners of mines and shipping." Those living closest to the line gained "either by the enhanced value of their lands or by increased facilities of transit for their commodities. Those at more remote parts of the mainline, though less directly interested, are still frequently interested to some degree: for every extension opens up a new market for either produce or raw materials."[53]

During the disastrous price decline beginning in the 1870s, shippers advocated nationalization of the railways to overcome discriminatory rates resulting from cooperation. The railroads responded that rate agreements permitting local preferences were necessary to prevent the increased costs resulting from cutthroat competition. The shippers and their allies saw the measures as nothing less than monopolistic exploitation, but the railroads won. During the 1880s, however, traders were better organized in Parliament through such associations as national and local chambers of commerce. They won passage of the Railway and Canal Traffic Act of 1888 which established a Commission with authority to control rates subject to final review by the Board of Trade. A second law enacted in 1894 empowered the Commission to peg the rates at 1892 levels unless the railroads proved greater costs justified a rate increase.[54]

Business trade associations also emerged in response to the rise of labor unions. The turn-of-the-century clash between organized business and labor precipitated the formation of the independent Labour Party, which eventually reshaped the structure and policies of the leading Conservative and Liberal parties. As the dominant parties alternated with one another in control of the government, conflict generally concerned opposing views regarding the need for government intervention to preserve social welfare. In this struggle British workers gained more rights and the general public achieved greater social security than their counterparts in the United States.[55]

Where business self-regulation did not involve specific social welfare measures, however, a consensus prevailed. Thus the leading parties fervently debated whether tariffs spawned monopoly or might otherwise hurt the nation's economy. But these same parties did not oppose in *principle* the right of British businessmen to form private agreements which might facilitate monopoly control. Similarly, Conservatives resisted expanded government protection of the rights of organized labor in the Trade Disputes Act of 1906, which nullified the 1901 antiunion *Taff Vale* decision. Yet Conservatives, Liberals, and Labour agreed that only modest governmental supervision of the shipping industry's cartel practices was necessary. Furthermore, from the 1880s on bipartisan support existed for railroad regulation, permitting combination and rate fixing. Thus even as the British party system became increasingly responsive to a wide range of organized pressure groups, neither politicians nor the interests they represented demanded more than limited government action to prevent business combination and self-regulation.[56]

Conflicting pressures explained Labour's support for this consensus. Although the law sanctioned unions in principle, the *Taff Vale* decision demonstrated how easily business could turn the legal rules governing combination against workers.[57] As a result labor leaders opposed the idea of antitrust legislation not out of love for monopoly but because such laws could be used, as they were in America, to disrupt the rights of unions. Similarly, organized labor was ambivalent about the rise of giant corporations. Some unions found that competition imposed wage-cutting pressures on small business which big firms possessing scale economies could better resist. As a result, when the sale producers raised prices through combination, a pro-union newspaper approved a higher price "fairly remunerative to capital" if it resulted in paying "their workmen fair wages." Coal miners, however, doubted whether they could "meet the employers on anything like equal terms if they had to face an organization like that of the salt union."[58] Finally, virtually all labor groups opposed legislation which either specifically aided business through tariff protection or limited it through antitrust, favoring instead a broader social-welfare program governing wages and hours, unemployment and retirement, insurance, and taxation of business.[59]

Advocates of socialism also opposed government intervention in the form of antitrust. The small socialist wing of the Labour Party espoused beliefs similar to various independent British socialist parties though none of these groups exercised more than marginal influence on the issue of anticompetitive practices. Despite variation in detail, the dominant socialist position remained fairly constant from the 1880s on.[60] A motion made during a socialist conference in 1902, receiving unanimous approval, stated: "growth of gigantic capitalist trusts with their enormous power of controlling production" was "injurious to the advancement of the working classes." These combinations raised prices, reduced people's standards of living, endangered the "workman's freedom," and "menaced" the "national prosperity." The conference then declared that the "only permanent solution" was the "national ownership of these monopolies." Yet the socialists were also convinced that the British public's growing concern about the spread of the trusts "with their power of controlling not only labor but the consumer as well," would prove the "means of driving thousands into our ranks that are now outside."[61] Consequently, British socialists saw a natural evolution from competition, to the trusts, to socialism; and they opposed antitrust laws as an unwarranted interference with this inevitable evolutionary process.[62]

Meanwhile, civil servants influenced the party consensus favoring business self-regulation. Although the ruling party controlled the appointment of ministers heading the government departments, the line and staff positions of those ministries generally were career civil service personnel. The President of the Board of Trade was a political appointee but, in order to carry out the Board's mission, he relied on bureaucrats whose positions were removed from direct political pressure. As a result, the civil service possessed some independence which influenced the work of official commissions. The government appointed commissions to provide Parliament and government departments with information concerning the most difficult issues confronting the nation. Often, the demands of political expediency were such that the commissions were broadly nonpartisan in composition, including representatives not only of organized private interest groups and the political parties, but also members of the civil service who would bear responsibility for administering any measure enacted as a result of the commission's report.[63]

The ability of British business to maintain relative stability through self-regulation further diffused pressures for government action. During the 1880s and 90s many of the numerous trade associations which arose to control prices and facilitate organizational efficiencies dissolved because of competitive pressures. Yet to mitigate competition businessmen in all industries continued to prefer loose business structures over tighter ones.[64] Admittedly, a "voluntary association to regulate trade" was "necessarily an alliance of the weak and the strong, and sooner or later a time comes when a strong firm, whose products are always in good demand among the public, or which has special markets, finds a restriction of output to be burdensome," wrote socialist economist Henry W. Macrosty. He conceded furthermore that the resulting implementation of business self-regulation "always benefits weak firms who are thereby secured their share," and it was "probably...healthier if they could be forced out of existence." Nevertheless, if a "business goes into the hands of a receiver he cuts prices in order to make a good show of a large trade in order to dispose of the business on good terms, and in this way the market is more disorganized than ever." Consequently, by the turn-of-the-century merger wave self-regulation gradually took hold, even if competition prevailed.[65]

In America, by contrast, considerable public pressure compelled federal intervention in the form of the Sherman Act. Unlike Britain and other industrialized nations, the United States had very substantial agricultural and raw materials' sectors. In addition, the density of urban population was much lower than in Britain, with a majority of Americans living in rural areas until 1920. As giant corporations emerged, this sort of economic order created a sense of dependency and loss of control resulting in coalitions of small businessmen, agrarians, and advocates of inflationary credit. In Canada and Australia similar economic imperatives engendered similar interest groups demanding and winning antitrust laws. In Britain the urbanized, compact market undercut the formation of such groups.[66]

Still another difference, however, was that American pressure groups compelled many politicians to adopt the moralistic rhetoric of republican values. Beginning in January 1888, Ohio Republican John Sherman proposed that the federal government should have direct power to prosecute even those corporations engaged in production if they were chartered in two or more states. Sherman evaded the long-established constitutional principle limiting the reach of congressional authority only to those firms operating in interstate trade. The Senator merely insisted that the necessary powers had "remained dormant" in the Constitution until the "growth and progress of our country" called for their use.[67] He equated horizontally integrated, state-chartered corporate giants with bridges obstructing navigable waterways or state tax measures interfering with the free trade across state lines. Just as the commerce power extended to the latter it could reach the former. Furthermore, he said, businessmen created the trusts, to "evade the jurisdiction of the state courts." As a result, he proposed to protect the citizen's "industrial liberty" by "arming" the federal courts with the "full limits of the constitutional power" so that they could "co-operate with the State courts in checking, curbing, and controlling the most dangerous combinations that now threaten the business, property, and trade of the people of the United States."[68]

Sherman articulated a blend of market and ideological pre-suppositions similar to that espoused by state politicians. On one level he spoke as a modern economist might, emphasizing the immediate threat to competition and consumer welfare. The sole purpose of big corporations was "to make competition impossible," to "control the market, raise or lower prices, as well as... reduce prices in a particular locality, and break down competition and advance prices at will... The law of selfishness, uncontrolled by competition, compel[ed] ... [them] to disregard the interest of the consumer."[69]

At the same time, the Ohio Senator used rhetoric expressing the fear that the trusts were subverting natural economic laws and republican values. Society was "disturbed by forces never felt before," and the "popular mind" was "agitated with problems that may disturb the social order." None was "more threatening than the inequality of condition of wealth and opportunity that has grown within a single generation out of the concentration of vast combinations of capital to control production and trade and to break down competition." Congress "alone" could meet the threat. It must heed the voters "appeal or be ready for the socialist, the communist, and the nihilist." If Americans would not "endure a king as a political power" they should not "endure a king over the production, transportation, and sale of any of the necessities of life;" if they would "not submit to an emperor" they should "not submit to an autocrat of trade, with power to prevent competition and to fix the price of any commodity."[70]

Other representatives, however, disagreed. George Edmunds of Vermont denied that the commerce clause gave Congress the power to interfere with the state's police power. Republican Senator of Colorado, Henry Moore Teller, rejected the broad condemnation of all large combinations, exclaiming that "a trust may not always be an evil. A trust for certain purposes, which may mean simply a combination of capital, may be a favorable thing to the community and the country." Congressman John W. Stewart took a more balanced view. There were, he said, "two great forces working in human society in this country...contending for...mastery." One was competition, the other combination. They were "correctives of each other, and both ought to exist. Both ought to be under restraint. Either of them, if allowed to be unrestrained...[was] destructive of the material interests of this country."[71]

Finally, responsibility for drafting the antitrust bill shifted from Sherman's Finance Committee to the Edmunds Judiciary Committee. The Edmunds committee replaced Sherman's references to the power of Congress over state incorporation charters, with the general common law phases pertaining to monopoly and restraint of trade. Yet, debate during the spring of 1890 involving "monopoly" suggested uncertainty. West Virginia Senator John E. Kenna asked the framers of the measure whether it applied to "an individual" who "by his own skill and energy, by the propriety of his conduct generally, shall pursue his calling in such a way as to monopolize a trade." Senator Edmunds answered, such was "not intended" and the "bill does not do it. Anybody who knows the meaning of the word 'monopoly,' as the courts apply it, would not apply it to such a person at all." Massachusetts Senator George F. Hoar was still more precise: "monopoly" was a "technical term known to the common law," which meant the "sole engrossing to a man's self by means which prevent other men from engaging in fair competition with him." Indeed, Hoar concluded, the "great thing" about the bill was that it "extended the common-law principles, which protected fair competition in trade in old times in England, to international and interstate commerce in the United States." But these lawyers knew that throughout the states and, to a lesser extent, in Britain as well, the meaning of the common law on this and other points was in a state of flux.[72]

As a result, the measure Congress passed and President Benjamin Harrison signed in summer of 1890 incorporated considerable compromise. The stated purpose of the Sherman Antitrust Act was to "protect trade and commerce against unlawful restraints and monopolies." Put another way, Congress sought to prevent one form of business practice from interfering with other forms. Thus it declared that "Every contract, combination in the form of trust or otherwise, or conspiracy, in restraint of trade or commerce among the several states, or with foreign nations" was "illegal." Moreover, "every person" who "shall monopolize, or attempt to monopolize, or combine or conspire with any other person or persons to monopolize any part" of the nation's "trade or commerce" were guilty of violating the law. The Sherman Act empowered federal district attorneys throughout the country, under the "direction" of the US Attorney General, to initiate prosecutions in federal court. It also sanctioned "any person" whose "business or property" was injured by "any other person or corporation" engaging in action made illegal under the law, to sue for "threefold the damages by him sustained, and the costs of suit, including a reasonable attorney's fee."[73]

What Sherman had said of his initial proposal was now true of the law Congress enacted. It was "difficult," he had admitted, "to define in legal language the precise line between lawful and unlawful combinations." The distinction was left for the courts to determine in each particular case. "Lawmakers" could only "declare general principles," and then rest "assured that the courts... [would]apply them so as to carry out the meaning of the law."[74] Even so, since Congress had used common law principles over which American state courts and British judges disagreed, controversy concerning the meaning of the Sherman Act was inevitable.[75]

Similarly, the line between state and federal authority was left ambiguous. Texas Congressman David B. Culberson had said Congress "alone" could not "protect" the American "people... against the evils and oppression of trusts and monopolies." Congress had "no authority to deal generally, with the subject within the States, and the States have no authority to legislate in respect of commerce between the states... It follows therefore, that the legislative authority of Congress and that of the several States must be exerted to secure the suppression of restraints upon trade and monopolies." Once Congress passed the Sherman law, Culberson observed, "If the States will do their duty and supplement this Act, the people will be relieved of [all] the outrages inflicted upon them."[76]

Ironically, by the turn-of-the-century merger wave, the interplay between state and federal authority weakened loose but encouraged tight combinations. A few close-knit families such as the DuPonts were able through secretly negotiated contracts, to maintain cartels until after the turn of the century.[77] Generally, however, suites brought by private individuals under state and federal law successfully restricted the spread of loose anticompetitive agreements.[78] The record of state attorney general prosecutions was mixed. Between 1890 and 1902 the number of state outnumbered federal antitrust actions by 19 to 28; during roughly the same period, the total amount of fines resulting from all federal prosecutions amounted to $219,875 compared to $1·6 million won by Texas in a single case. The states, moreover, had defeated the original trust device.[79] Yet various states followed New Jersey's course of liberalizing their incorporation statutes to attract rather than punish foreign corporations. Thus, while private actions increasingly prevented cartels, and state victories ended the Standard Oil-type trusts, many legislatures increasingly allowed tighter combinations established through merger and the holding company.[80]

New York was indicative of the liberalizing trend in incorporation law. By the mid-nineties many lawmakers feared that the state was losing valuable business to New Jersey. Indeed, shortly after New York's courts struck down the Sugar Trust, the firm reformed under New Jersey's more hospitable incorporation law. The New York legislature met the challenge by revising its own corporate statutes. Because of political pressure reflected in the interplay of republican values, private rights and faith in the natural economy, the process took some years. The rationale for the change represented a subtle amalgamation of diverse values. First, the lawmakers dealt with the concerns for republican citizenship by stressing the need for reconciling individual enterprise and equal opportunity. "Political oppression" was the "refusal of equal rights," exclaimed an assembly committee report, whereas "commercial oppression" was the "denial of equal opportunities." Both were "repugnant to the people." The popular "spirit" of resistance resulting in the triumph of "equal rights" in the Constitution, would not tolerate in commercial competition the "substitution of monopoly for equal opportunity. The field should be free to all." The government must ensure, therefore, that in the "conflict of commercial rivalry, genius, labor, and capital" the public should receive the "largest liberty of expansion." At the same time, it was the government's duty to prevent "special privilege" and the "abuse of power of concentrated wealth of abnormal magnitude."[81]

The New York assembly report also justified government action by appealing to "natural" economic laws. The "right of contract," like the "right of liberty and property," were "recognized in natural law as the very foundation of human progress and development." The exercise of natural rights was, moreover, a "sacred privilege" of republican citizenship "guarded by the Constitution." Inevitably, free citizens used these rights to pursue the "natural impulse toward better conditions," including new forms of economic progress such as large combinations. Many big corporations were, therefore, the "natural evolution" and "universal concomitant of progress, marking...the progressive stages of commercial development." The government, however, must distinguish the fruits of legitimate labor from evil trusts which through "unfair and oppressive methods" constructed "an impregnable trocha around any industrial pursuit." Lawmakers should thus encourage the good "natural" achievements of individual liberty and progress and prevent the bad "unnatural" consequences of subversive behavior.[82]

By the mid-nineties, however, corporate lawyers were hard pressed to distinguish which tight forms of combinations were lawful. "More than in any other field of enterprise", wrote a later commentator, the "choice of businessmen between the holding company and some alternative form of unification" through merger, depended on the opinion of lawyers as to which legal device...[was] most likely to survive attack from a vigilant attorney general."[83] During the early nineties the few opinions of the lower federal courts construing the Sherman Act were mixed, though most favored a reading allowing combination.[84] The Supreme Court first considered the Act in the *Knight Sugar* case of 1895. US Attorney General Richard Olney argued, and the Court decided, the issue whether the Sherman Act reached holding companies such as the Knight firm engaged in production within but not marketing outside of a single state. The Court followed the constitutional distinction established in numerous precedents and recognized in the debates of Senator Sherman's proposal, holding that the Sherman Act applied only to restrictive marketing practices reaching interstate commerce. Justice John M. Harlan alone dissented, arguing that the holding company's dominance of production enabled it to control the price of marketing which brought it within the antimonopoly provisions of the antitrust law.[85]

Yet changes in the market and state and federal law intersected, clarifying the lawyer's uncertainty. The Depression of the mid-nineties had generally run its course by 1896, resulting in a period of gradually improving growth. Better market conditions encouraged states such as New York to attract business through liberalized incorporation laws which in turn encouraged mergers. Following the *Knight* decision the Court suggested that an antitrust law written to regulate business applied also to the action of Eugene V. Debs's union in the violent Pullman strike. But not until early 1897 did the Court for the first time decide the legal status of restrictive business practices which impinged directly on interstate commerce. In *US* v. *Trans-Missouri Freight Association* the Court split 5-4, holding that railroads had violated a literal reading of the Sherman Act by establishing rate-fixing agreements. Justice Rufus W. Peckham's majority opinion noted the need to protect small traders. For the dissenters, Justice Edward D. White urged a construction of the Act following the newly formulated reasonableness doctrine of the common law. By 1899 the Court decided several other important cartel cases, declaring that price-fixing across interstate lines violated the Sherman Act. Disagreement continued among the justices, however, as to whether a strict literal or the more flexible reasonableness principle should govern the Court's interpretation of the law.[86]

For corporate lawyers the convergence of the Court's decisions, liberalized state laws, and the improved market conditions was timely. In both the *Knight* and cartel decisions, the Court interpreted the Sherman Act in accord with the traditional constitutional distinction between restrictive agreements which crossed state lines and the state's control of local production. To be sure, the Court had not decided a case directly involving the non-marketing restrictive practices of a corporation operating in interstate commerce. Yet the Knight firm, although a New Jersey holding company, did 80 percent of its sugar manufacturing in Pennsylvania alone. To market its product it relied on independent middlemen. Consequently, a lawyer advising a corporate client who wanted to take advantage of the renewed economic growth of the mid-nineties looked only at what was clearly forbidden. By 1893 state courts had outlawed the Standard Oil-type trust and private suits had disrupted local cartels. Meanwhile, beginning in 1897, the Supreme Court had declared that interstate cartel arrangements also violated the Sherman Act. Thus, until the Court specifically decided a case involving a tight corporate structure engaged in interstate business, the popular view expressed by one corporate lawyer was understandable.[87] The "remedies devised against combinations in the form of agreements and trusts," wrote Edward Q. Keasebey in the *Harvard Law Review* of 1899, "seemed" to be "inapplicable" to the "actual merger of existing corporations."[88]

This interplay of market and legal developments shaped the relative scale of the turn-of-the-century merger wave. The simultaneous movement toward merger issues on the American and British stock exchanges in 1897 suggested the influence of improved economic conditions. A significant difference between the two markets, however, was the scale of merger investment. Undoubtedly, this difference resulted in part because most British businessmen preferred to achieve scale and organizational efficiencies through loose rather than tight combinations. Their American counterparts, by contrast, relied upon asset acquisition and holding companies as forms of mergers, especially after the Sherman Act destroyed the trust. Indeed it was at this point that even firms such as DuPont, which secretly had operated as a cartel, reorganized into a holding company. During the first eight months of 1899, the peak year of the merger wave, New Jersey incorporated 336 industrial corporations with a total capital amounting to more than 2000 million dollars. Of the industrial firms possessing stock and bond values exceeding 10 million dollars, moreover, New Jersey alone incorporated sixty-one, while all other states together chartered just sixty. At about the same time Standard Oil became a holding company, as did US Steel, becoming the largest corporation in the world.[89]

British business, labor, and socialist groups disagreed regarding the government's role in social welfare and the regulation of the railroads. But concerning the issue of government action to prevent anticompetitive business self-regulation, these same groups (admittedly for different reasons) shared a consensus favoring nonintervention. As a result, loose restrictive business structures dominated. In America, by contrast, ideological and constitutional conflicts coinciding with the liberalization of state incorporation law, the disruption of cartels by private suits and of the trusts by state attorney generals' prosecutions, and the Supreme Court's ambivalent interpretation of the Sherman Act between 1895 and 1899 fostered the stronger preference for greater managerial centralization achieved through more extensive mergers.

POST MERGER-WAVE BRITAIN: BUSINESS SELF-REGULATION TAKES HOLD

Although the merger wave was a significant development within the British business order, self-regulating, loose combinations spread. Internal market pressures and an external threat from American and German enterprise resulted in mergers establishing big British corporations, including Imperial Tobacco and Lever Brothers. Like American large-scale firms, these British companies integrated vertically, arousing opposition from middlemen. Ultimately, however, the British corporations enabled more distributors to survive by negotiating restrictive price and marketing agreements, whereas American big business often destroyed the middlemen by taking over their function. Admittedly British wholesalers and middlemen were taken over or driven out of business by British manufacturing corporations. Yet this loss not only apparently occurred on a smaller scale in Britain, but also in the more urbanized market, there were no other groups with which to form broader coalitions of the sort which in the United States brought about the passage of the Sherman Act.[90] As the experience of the shipping industry suggested, the toleration if not enforcement of restrictive practices increased the incentive for smaller firms to maintain relative independence within cartels. In response to the growing stability of loose business structures British lawmakers extended their regulatory function beyond the railroads to include shipping, though the results were quite modest. The British law's sanction of restrictive practices thus diffused the conflict which dominated turn-of-the-century America.

After the turn of the century British businessmen increasingly succeeded in their search for stable modes of self-governing combination. Some resorted to thoroughgoing cartels on the German model; one iron and steel producer went so far as to employ private detectives to police the compliance of cartel members. Ultimately, however, the British preference for the autonomous family firm doomed such efforts.[91] Meanwhile, other enterprises sought still tighter combinations through merger. Particularly in heavily capitalized industries such as iron and steel, Macrosty found the tendency was toward a mixed industrial structure composed of "a comparatively few large units in each branch" which then combined into "a loose organization for the regulation of their trade." In some instances, such as textiles, the trend toward merger facilitated effective enough forward integration into marketing that the survival of wholesalers was threatened. But most middlemen did not suffer this fate.[92]

Generally, British business relied on the repeated negotiation of numerous loose horizontal and vertical price and market agreements. The resort to negotiation reflected not so much an easy harmony among interests, as a willingness to compromise those interests in order to avoid the perils of competition. Hence, the "great fact" was that the "association cannot raise its prices, nor a merchant withdraw his trade without the consent of the board, and thus the two main points of business policy are placed under communal control." As a result, during the years before the war British business achieved stable cooperative associations and combinations through self-regulation rather than legal sanction.[93] Particularly after Parliament enacted the Trade Disputes Act of 1906, there were court decisions which applied the *Nordenfelt* rule to enforce restrictive agreements. Yet the courts merely reinforced an already established practice by which businessmen maintained their own agreements through private coercion, negotiation, and compromise.[94]

The rise of Imperial Tobacco suggested the degree to which self-regulation prevailed. In 1902 the American Tobacco Company purchased the successful British firm, Ogden's Limited, which was the beginning of a campaign to gain control of the trade in both Great Britain and Europe. Sixteen British firms responded by merging under the name of the Imperial Tobacco Company. In the ensuing battle Imperial won. Victory depended in part, however, on the new giant resolving tensions within its own corporate structure. Organized as a holding company, the formerly separate firms established a unitary board governing the sixteen constituent parts which retained considerable independence as subsidiaries. Through continuous negotiation and compromise the board arrived at effective production and pricing policies.[95]

Yet repulsion of the American invasion required even more extensive dealing between Imperial and the distribution trades. In addition to an advertising campaign which appealed to Britain's patriotic duty to resist the foreigner, Imperial guaranteed those retailers who sold its brands a large bonus. At the same time, the corporation purchased a retail firm more directly to control marketing. Despite considerable tension, the strategy of simultaneously encouraging cooperation and competition eventually resulted in price agreements between Imperial and alliances of middlemen.[96] Macrosty concluded that the relations between the company and retailers "have certainly not given complete satisfaction to the latter, but there is every reason to believe that they have been treated more generously than their strength could command." He noted also that the wholesalers did even better.[97]

Even without the threat of foreign competition, middlemen and their allies triumphed over a cartel of soap manufacturers. In 1906, W. H. Lever, one of Britain's leading soap producers and a Liberal member of Parliament, announced that without "closer association" within the industry, not only the reduction of jobs and profits loomed, but also "a material rise in the price of soap to the public." During the preceding years the cost of raw materials had risen steadily. As a result, Lever Brothers and other family soap enterprises established a cartel which recognized each firm's "separate existence and safeguards their individuality" under the direction of a centralized board.[98] Despite assertions that cooperation would benefit consumers, the cartel reduced the weight and size of the standard product while increasing its cost. This action unleashed a storm of criticism. Several mass-circulation London newspapers portrayed Lever Brothers as an evil trust ruthlessly exploiting the public. Motivating the press campaign at least in part was the newspapers' loss of the advertising space the soap producers no longer required because of the economies gained from combination.[99]

The strength of the cartel's opponents increased when the newspapers joined forces with grocers and other retailers. The manufacturer's price increase and weight reduction increased the retailers' purchase cost while maintaining the old retail price unchanged. But the public uproar resulting from the newspaper attack enabled the grocers to make a profit by increasing their prices beyond that established by the manufacturer, while the public blamed the trust for the rise. Also, national grocers' associations, experienced at using resale price maintenance in boycotts of cooperative stores, employed similar tactics in a nationwide campaign against the cartel. Independent distributors joined the fray, raising prices and increasing profits.[100]

Finally, the adverse publicity and disruption of traditional pricing practices broke up the cartel. In the period of intense competition which followed, Lever Brothers' motto was, wrote the company's historian, "every man for himself – and Lever take the hindmost."

Through mergers Lever Brothers began integrating backward to control raw materials and forward into marketing. The firm also sued the newspapers for libel and won. Yet, when it came to pricing policy toward middlemen, the new corporate giant did not again alter established arrangements.[101]

Still, the preference for self-regulation represented the diverse commitment to Free Trade. The interplay of cost constraints, lobbying pressures, and the political maneuvering of the Board of Trade fostered a major clash in 1909 over railroad rates.[102] The shippers and their allies defeated the government's effort to allow extensive mergers in return for tighter regulation, arguing that the "complete lack of the competitive spur" would offset any further economies achieved from the mergers. Still, wrote a railway economist in 1912, competition was "dying...And although its efforts still persist, and will persist for some years to come, they must ere long die out too. Now if our railways have not been more than adequately controlled by the joint force of state regulation and competition, the conclusion is inevitable that, in the future, competition being withdrawn, further state regulation must be introduced to take its place."[103]

The government also extended its regulatory function beyond railroads to shipping. J. P. Morgan's attempted take over of certain British shipping companies after 1900 precipitated demands for some sort of protective action. Largely for financial reasons, Morgan failed. But a Conservative government established subsidies, investment, labor, and rate requirements which insured that the control of major maritime firms would remain in British hands. Although there was a "good deal of criticism" of such a "partnership" between government and business, wrote Macrosty, it was "generally felt that a demonstration of the British determination to retain the command of the ocean trade, even at the cost of Government intervention, was both a necessary and a good thing."[104]

Between 1906 and 1909 the old and new attitudes toward government involvement with shipping received further scrutiny from the Royal Commission on Shipping Rings. The impetus for the investigation came from South African shipper interests and their counterparts in Britain, who resisted the rates and preferential rebates established by various steamship companies operating in South Africa. Although a Liberal government appointed the

Commission in 1906, the issue was not a partisan one. This view received support from the appointment of commission members which included company directors, politicians, lawyers, and civil servants regardless of party affiliation. In addition, such leading economists as Alfred Marshall applauded the creation of the Commission because it provided the first opportunity for a full-scale study of the effects of monopolistic practices in a competitive British industry.[105]

The Commission, however, pursued a limited course. It declined to explore the distinction between the conference system, as a monopolistic business structure, and the *effects* resulting from the control over rates the monopoly permitted. Thus a majority of the Commission reported in 1909 that the conferences so facilitated organizational economies and industry-wide stability that they were "necessary to the development of regular trade." These advantages, in turn, were "substantially dependent upon the system of deferred rebates...as a 'tie' upon shippers." The majority report noted, moreover, that most of the shippers giving testimony shared this view. "The proportion of general merchants appearing before us, large or small, who were in favor of the abolition of the system of deferred rebates was", the report concluded, "small." In Britain, particularly the "great majority of shippers of all classes" preferred that the "system should be retained provided that some means could be discovered of controlling the monopoly power of the Conference system and checking its liability to abuse." Even so the majority report rejected a proposal for establishing a regulatory body like that existing in the railway industry. Even the Royal Commission's lone Labour representative voted with the majority against that degree of government intervention.[106]

A minority report signed by five out of sixteen commission members both dissented and concurred. It rejected the "findings as to the advantages claimed for the shipping conferences and the deferred rebate system" which "over-rates" or "erroneously attributes" such advantages to "that system and does not give sufficient weight to the disadvantages resulting therefrom or to the danger incident to the system." The minority contended further that the "real object" of the conferences' rate practices was "to exclude competition to raise or maintain rates of freight." And yet the minority did not go much beyond the majority on the issue of government intervention. Referring adversely to the antitrust record of the United States, it doubted whether legislation "declaring illegal the deferred rebate system" was worth the cost of "probably...much litigation" and the "great interference by a government department with the details of the working of a highly complex industry..."[107]

Thus, despite disagreement over the nature of the problem, both reports essentially concurred that the remedy for potential abuse was "full publicity" achieved through the registration of conference agreements with the Board of Trade, which reported to Parliament upon request. Also, both sides supported conferring upon the Board of Trade a role in negotiating the terms and settling disputes resulting from the agreements, though there was not consensus concerning the scope of this authority.[108]

One member of the Commission, however, went further. David Barbour, an economist in the civil service, noted that the minority's diagnosis and remedy were essentially incompatible. The minority correctly emphasized, he said, that the problem involved the potential abuse resulting from monopolistic control. Yet, by accepting the majority's conclusion that government intervention was a cure worse than the disease it undercut any effective means of dealing with abuse. Shippers, either alone or united, could "never meet the Rings on anything approaching equal terms for the purpose of bargaining so long as the latter possess a practical monopoly, and retain in their hands the ultimate power of deciding the question in dispute as they think fit." Only enlarged authority of the government was sufficient to adjust the balance in favor of the weaker interest and the public. Accordingly, a "more drastic, and probably more effective and simpler, remedy would be legislation on the lines of the Sherman Act of the United States of America prohibiting combinations or associations of the nature of the shipping Rings which had for their object the establishment of a monopoly in restraint of trade."[109]

Parliament's implementation of the Commission's recommendations had minimal effect. Parliament extended to the Board of Trade the authority to publicize and arbitrate shipping agreements, though in most cases cooperation with government was not compulsory. Meanwhile, increased world-wide, pre-war trade provided growing business for merchant and steamship companies, ameliorating tensions between shippers and companies within the conferences and between the conferences and the independent lines. Consequently, little need arose for the exercise of the government's new power. The President of the Board of Trade informed Parliament that although "isolated complaints have been made to the Board of Trade as to rates charged by shipping lines, no request has been made for the services of the Board in the settlement of any dispute of a general nature between merchants and conference lines."[110]

Still, the Royal Commission's work possessed a broader significance. It was the first instance in which the government confronted an antitrust question in a competitive industry, as opposed to the struggle over railway combinations which was complicated by issues involving the popular identification of railroads as natural monopolies. Yet, although the Commission recognized that government intervention was necessary to prevent abuse resulting from restrictive practices, both the diagnosis of and the remedy for the problem were limited. Except for Barbour, neither the majority nor the minority supported granting the government more than a modest oversight function based on publicity and negotiation. By repudiating Barbour's plea for the outright prohibition of rebate practices through legislation tailored after the Sherman Antitrust Act, both sides rejected compulsion.[111]

This position reflected a failure to weigh the benefits achieved through organizational efficiencies against the costs rising from the conference's monopolistic control of competition. Only Barbour argued that the unequal bargaining power between shippers and the companies rested on monopolistic control which could eventually produce higher prices. Yet, while other economists did not raise the issue of power, they did criticize the majority report for not sufficiently recognizing the threat of increased prices inherent in the rebate system's stifling of competition. Marshall particularly advocated in-depth study of the issue to determine whether stronger government action was necessary, but nothing was done before the war.[112]

The shipping industry's experience suggested why in Britain political pressures supporting government intervention were weak. From the 1880s on, merchants and small manufacturers exercised considerable influence over Parliament and the different political parties which at different times controlled the government. At the same time, larger business groups, particularly those operating as limited liability companies such as railroads and steamship companies, exercised similar influence. On the question of railway rates and mergers, conflict was persistent enough that government periodically enacted measures establishing enlarged regulatory authority. In the so-called competitive industries such as shipping, however, these same groups did not organize on a consistent basis to achieve similar results. The move toward government action in the maritime industry was thus as exceptional as it was gradual, arising from external more than domestic factors. Moreover, Parliament's enactment of the modest supervisory authority recommended by the Royal Commission in 1909 reflected a willingness to allow no more than a minimum of government interference with Free Trade.[113]

Even so, the Commission's consensus reflected broader institutional and market relations. The law's acceptance of anticompetitive agreements and restrictive trade practices in the *Mogul* and *Nordenfelt* cases encouraged small and large business groups to meet the uncertainty of a changing market through self-regulation and combination. Although some business groups, especially during the merger wave, used incorporation statutes to build large corporations, the attachment to independence was so strong that most relied upon looser business structures. This business order in turn created a vested interest favoring limited government interference with the Free Trade system. The shippers' clash with the steamship companies showed that in exceptional cases government intervention was necessary. Ironically, the demand for such action arose from a desire to establish a balance of interests maintained through the negotiation of mutually beneficial, anticompetitive agreements. The merchants' acquiescence to the conference and rebate system in principle, while opposing what they regarded as specific abuses resulting from particular preferences, undercut Barbour's claim that unequal power relations altogether precluded the negotiation of agreements which were ultimately satisfactory to both groups.[114]

POST MERGER-WAVE AMERICA: THE BUREAUCRATIZATION
OF ANTITRUST

The merger wave engendered a growing demand for a bureaucratic approach to antitrust. The irony that state action and the Supreme Court's interpretation of the Sherman Act had strengthened big business created dissatisfaction with the reliance on judicial prosecution alone. Despite important differences in emphasis, Presidents Theodore Roosevelt, William H. Taft, and Woodrow Wilson sought to balance Americans' attachment to small business and their desire for the consumer benefits of big corporations by enlarging the federal government's regulatory authority. Meanwhile, the struggle within the Court over the rule of reason encouraged Roosevelt and, eventually, Wilson and Brandeis to support the greater interpretive flexibility that doctrine permitted. Yet, even as Wilson's election victory in 1912 resulted in the passage of the Federal Trade Commission and the Clayton Antitrust Act, the persistence of earlier ideological and political tensions enmeshed the bureaucratization of antitrust in uncertainty.[115]

The merger wave made the "trust problem" the leading issue in American politics. Democratic presidential candidate of 1900, William Jennings Bryan, exclaimed that trusts and combinations had crushed the "broader class of businessmen" engaged in small-scale enterprise.[116] The Industrial Commission established in 1898 to investigate the trusts, confirmed the degree to which the manufacturer's takeover of marketing removed the need for many independent middlemen. More than ever before small businessmen demanded government action. Frustrated by the weak enforcement of the Sherman Act under Democrat Cleveland and Republican William McKinley, they urged stronger antitrust legislation.[117] McKinley responded in a major address, asserting that perhaps the "remedy" for the current "evils" was the strengthening of "present law" in order to "more certainly...control or check these monopolies or trusts."[118]

To the defenders of the giant corporation, however, the new corporate economy was the result of natural evolution, which paradoxically required increased government intervention. Corporate consolidation "has earned the right," said corporate lawyer and former US Attorney General Richard Olney in 1906, "to be regarded as an economic evolution." Despite enormous "popular prejudice" from the general public, "bitter condemnation" from the press, "denunciation by political demagogues," and "unrelenting har[assment] by legislature and courts," the corporate giants remained "unimpaired." To Olney this was yet another "instance of the ineffectiveness of artificial restraints when opposed to the operation of natural laws." A primary casualty of "natural" combination was the "hoary axiom – 'Competition is the life of Trade.'" To reap the benefits arising from consolidation, Olney concluded, "competition regulated by law" was necessary, guided by such "meritorious objects" as "fair play, justice, and equality of opportunity and treatment."[119]

Moreover, the defenders of concentration had an ally in labor leader, Samuel Gompers. After the federal government used the Sherman Act during the Pullman strike and elsewhere to prosecute unions for actions courts found to be unlawful interference with trade, Gompers denounced those "who know little of statecraft and less of economics [who] urge[d] the adoption of laws to 'regulate' interstate commerce, [and to] 'prevent' combinations and trusts." He condemned such measures because, "when enacted [they] have been the very instruments employed to deprive labor of the benefit of organized effort...The State is not capable of preventing the legitimate development or natural concentration of industry." Consequently, Gompers advocated revising the antitrust laws to protect the interests of organized labor.[120]

Ironically, even the "People's Lawyer" Louis Brandeis, the adamant foe of bigness, wanted the law to sanction certain anticompetitive combinations. Suggesting the ideals embodied in republican values, Brandeis opposed giant corporations because they threatened participatory citizenship which depended on independent enterprise. The "proposition that mere bigness can not be an offense against society is false," he said, "because...our society which rests upon democracy, can not endure under such conditions." Implicit in this preference for small business were economic assumptions involving the need for "fair competition" protected by law. Corporate consolidation permitted control over markets and prices, and placed small dealers in a competitive position which Brandeis believed was unfair. Echoing Peckham's *Trans-Missouri Freight Association* opinion, Brandeis observed that "the displacement of the small independent businessman by the huge corporation with its myriad of employees, its absentee ownership, and its financial control, presents a grave danger to our democracy."[121]

What was to be done? Brandeis believed that the law should allow the small enterpriser to fix and enforce prices. "The moment you allow the cutting of prices you are inviting the great, powerful men to get control of the business," he said. That the big corporations were "natural" or able to lower prices because of efficiencies arising from organizational and scale economies, Brandeis flatly denied. "It is not even in accord with the natural laws of business," he said. "It is largely the result of unwise, man-made, privilege-creating law, which has stimulated existing tendencies to inequality instead of discouraging them. Shall we, under the guise of protecting competition, further foster monopoly by creating immunity for price-cutters?" Accordingly, Brandeis urged lawmakers to permit and enforce anticompetitive price agreements among members of trade associations composed of small dealers. National, state and local associations, "have gone on record, demanding that this illegitimate competition be put to an end...Big business is not more efficient than little business," he concluded. "Regulation is essential to the preservation and development of [fair] competition, just as it is necessary to the preservation and best development of liberty."[122]

State and federal enforcement of antitrust legislation reflected this growing support for government protection of "fair competition." In Missouri, Texas, and elsewhere, the courts upheld prosecutors' applications of state law which protected local enterprise from Standard Oil and other giant corporations. Public officials appealed to republican values and the imperatives of natural economic laws in attacking the big corporations, while using similar language to defend the right of local business, farm, and labor groups to combine.[123] On the federal level Roosevelt took a similar stance, exclaiming that combination resulting from natural evolution was good. The government, however, should prevent abuse. He believed that large corporations were "due...to natural causes in the business world"; he was, therefore, "in no sense hostile to corporations."[124] Yet it was "our right and our duty" to insure that they "work in harmony with [government] institutions."[125]

Following these convictions Roosevelt significantly increased the government's antitrust prosecutions. Congress passed the Expediting Act, which enlarged the Attorney General's funding and personnel in order to bring more antitrust suits. The law also required federal courts to give the Justice Department's antitrust cases priority, particularly where appeal to the Supreme Court was necessary.[126] The most conspicuous victory resulting from the new policy was the *Northern Securities* decision, in which the Court for the first time declared that a holding company violated the Sherman Act. A Court split 5-4 accepted the government's argument that a tight combination of powerful railroadmen formed solely for purposes of ending competition was illegal.[127] Corporate lawyers could no longer advise their clients with relative certainty that the Sherman Act reached loose but not tight corporate structures.[128] During the 1904 Presidential campaign the decision also supported the image of Roosevelt as a "trust buster." The Northern Securities suit, he said, was "one of the great achievements of my administration. I look back upon it with great pride, for... [it] emphasized the fact that the most powerful men in this country were held to accountability before the law."[129]

Roosevelt preferred, however, that primary responsibility for applying the antitrust laws should reside with administrators, not courts. Responding to his initiative, Congress established the Department of Commerce and Labor, which included the Bureau of Corporations. The Bureau was empowered to investigate the operation and practices of big corporations and report its findings to the President who then decided whether to publicize the information. Publicity helped legitimate business to comply with the antitrust laws; it also revealed wrongful conduct requiring government prosecution.[130] The President's effective use of the new power could also bring "fair play to the little man."[131]

Roosevelt made further recommendations known as the Hepburn Amendments, which Congress did not enact. Reaction of corporate lawyers and their clients to the *Northern Securities* decision reinforced the President's conviction that the legal and economic issues involving large combinations were too complex to be resolved through litigation alone. He proposed, therefore, revising the Sherman Act to permit the Bureau of Corporations, with executive authorization, to register and license corporate combinations operating in interstate commerce. Although registration was not compulsory, once a combination sought a license the Bureau and, ultimately, the President determined whether it was reasonable. Judicial review of the government's decision was narrowly circumscribed. In an effort to gain the political support of organized labor, Roosevelt also supported Gomper's demand to exempt unions from the antitrust laws. As years of negotiation and redrafting increasingly strengthened the registration provisions and the regulatory authority of the bureaucracy and the chief executive, however, the measures steadily lost congressional support. In 1908, when Congress considered the final versions of the Amendments, they failed to pass.[132]

Nevertheless the Bureau of Corporations did vigorously pursue another mission. Roosevelt criticized the Court's literal interpretation of the Sherman Act established in *Trans-Missouri Freight* as so inflexible that it hindered the efficient operation of otherwise lawful business. The evidence the Bureau gathered on the internal structure and operation of corporations, moreover, established a foundation for arguing that scale, productive, and organizational efficiencies often resulted from combination. In such cases, the government could facilitate economic growth and public welfare by allowing large-scale enterprise. This sort of flexibility was difficult, however, unless the Court interpreted the Sherman Act according to the rule of reason. As a result, the Bureau's lawyers began a concerted campaign of research and published reports contending that before the passage of the Sherman Act the American and British common law embodied that very principle. Furthermore, they argued, by adopting common-law phraseology the framers had intended that a rule of reason should govern the judiciary's application of the Act. Accordingly, the Court's literal reading of the law departed from both the preestablished common law and the purpose of the framers. The Bureau urged the Court to return to the "true" doctrine.[133]

The Bureau developed an incomplete reading of history in order to justify enlarged government intervention. During the 1880s British and American judges had confronted new market conditions not with a cohesive rule of reason, but through divergent and inconsistent applications of the old ancillary/nonancillary doctrines. Similarly, the debate preceding passage of the Sherman Act revealed uncertainty rather than unequivocal agreement concerning the meaning of changing American and British common law. The Court's decisions from the *Knight Sugar* case on also reflected these ambiguities. The Bureau's studies thus obscured the extent to which the initial response of state and federal authorities to big business was incremental, uneven, and experimental. By arguing merely for the restoration of a supposedly preestablished principle, Roosevelt's bureaucrats ignored the fact that they as much as their predecessors advocated a form of antitrust policymaking which was new.[134]

Even so the Bureau's defense of the rule of reason was linked to Roosevelt's goal of making enforcement of the antitrust laws dependent primarily on administrators and the President. This position was consistent with Progressivism's general desire to remove public issues from the influence of special interests, leaving them instead to scientific experts and chief executives. The Court's acceptance of a rule-of-reason construction of the Sherman Act would provide public officials the means to distinguish efficient, public-serving combinations needing support from those practicing abuses which required prosecution.[135]

During Taft's presidency the controversy linking the rule of reason

and bureaucratization of government intervention intensified.
Testifying before congressional committees, big business leaders such
as George W. Perkins repeated Roosevelt's argument that since big
corporations were inevitable, executive and administrative authority
rather than courts and litigation could best govern their lawfulness.
In addition, various corporate lawyers also advocated a judicial
doctrine of reasonableness and government action based on
administrative supervision and publicity. To protect small business
Brandeis also supported the rule of reason and (after initial
vacillation) the creation of an antitrust agency.[136] Most of the Justice
Department's suits were against small businessmen in which the
government argued that the courts should apply a literal reading of
the Sherman Act to overturn price-fixing agreements. Brandeis
hoped that the adoption of the more flexible reasonableness doctrine,
combined with scientific evidence gathered by a commission
demonstrating the need for small business cooperative arrangements,
would bring a reversal of the Department's policy.[137]

Taft, however, resisted forming a bureaucratic body, favoring
instead federal incorporation of businesses engaged in interstate
commerce.[138] He also opposed having the Courts reinterpret the
Sherman Act according to the rule of reason. Such a transformation,
Taft warned, would "thrust upon the courts a burden that they have
no precedents to enable them to carry, and...give them a power
approaching the arbitrary, the abuse of which might involve our
whole judicial system in disaster."[139]

A turning point came when the Supreme Court decided the
Standard Oil and *American Tobacco* decisions in 1911. *Harpers* weekly
observed that in recent history no other suits had "caused the
markets and the whole industrial and commercial world to pause
more perceptibly...They came to be known simply as the Trust
Cases. For months the financial markets have virtually stood still
awaiting their settlements."[140] Chief Justice White for the Court held
that predatory pricing and other monopolistic market practices of
both companies were violations of the Sherman Act. The basis of his
decision was the rule of reason. He emphasized the undesirable
consequences resulting from pernicious conduct, establishing a legal
standard permitting considerable flexibility. Accordingly, if the
Court discovered questionable corporate behavior which produced
restrictive results, it was contrary to the public interest and unlawful.
Yet White recognized, too, that many contractual agreements,
though clearly anticompetitive in their result, nonetheless were

entered into solely to achieve desirable economic efficiencies and therefore were lawful. Moral blended with economic considerations to separate reasonable from unreasonable conduct.[141]

White applied the reasonableness doctrine to break up two of the world's largest corporations. Since the *Northern Securities* decision the question had remained open whether tight corporate combinations of manufacturing firms (as opposed to railroads) chartered in one state but carrying on production and marketing functions throughout the nation were subject to the Sherman Act. White's decision demonstrated clearly that such mergers and holding companies were no longer immune to dissolution.[142] Nevertheless, Perkins observed that Standard Oil's and American Tobacco's market influence was so great that the government's victory was "a great farce."[143] Indeed, Progressives following the argument of Justice Harlan's partial dissent in each decision, introduced federal legislation aimed at overturning the rule of reason. The effort failed, however, largely because White's opinion successfully fused the moralism of republican values and traditional economic beliefs with the new market assumptions of neoclassical economic thought and marginalist theory.[144]

White's rule of reason also triumphed because Americans remained ambivalent about corporate consolidation. During the election of 1912 Roosevelt and Wilson reflected the public's divided mind. Although the "captains of industry...have on the whole done a great good to our people," Roosevelt exclaimed following theories of economic advisors such as Hadley, "yet it is also true that there are real and grave evils...and a resolute and practical effort must be made to correct these evils." As a result, "combinations and concentration should be, not prohibited, but supervised and within reasonable limits controlled [by executive administrative agencies]." Similarly, Wilson said, accepting a distinction maintained by neoclassical economist J. B. Clark, "I, for one, don't care how big any business gets by efficiency, but I am jealous of any bigness that comes by monopoly." This meant, he asserted, "I am for big business, and I am against the trusts."[145] Finally, Taft rejected the need for alterations in the Sherman Act or new antitrust legislation, though he called for a federal incorporation law and said he would abide by the principles established in the Court's 1911 decisions.[146]

Although Wilson campaigned with Brandeisian rhetoric against Roosevelt, he did not support the absolute condemnation of giant corporations. He absolutely defended small enterprise because he believed that, generally, big and small business could coexist as long as the former did not use its power unfairly against the latter. As a result, Wilson adopted Brandeis's proposals for revising the Sherman Act to prohibit certain corporate practices such as interlocking directorates and "a board or commission to aid in administering the Sherman law." Implicitly, he also accepted Brandeis's preference for applying the rule of reason in defense of small businessmen.[147]

The three-way Presidential race of 1912 reflected a growing popular consensus. Probably a majority of politically active Americans increasingly believed that they could enjoy the consumer benefits of large-scale enterprise, while avoiding its abuses. Flexible administrative intervention would achieve this goal.[148] Even so, Wilson's victory suggested that Americans rejected Taft's view of the government's role as too limited and Roosevelt's as too extreme. Wilson advocated just the right balance: legislation revising the Sherman Act to specifically outlaw wrongful practices, and a commission with enough power to protect the public interest including small business.[149] Wilson's Brandeisian rhetoric also indicated that evil occurred when the corporation used illegal tactics or devices. Consequently, the chief criterion for determining whether the corporation was good or bad became conduct, and the emphasis upon conduct led to viewing competition in moral terms. Brandeis thus viewed all competition between corporate giants and the little man as wrong per se, but Wilson and others distinguished between competition based on superior efficiency and that involving evil behavior. In either case the legitimacy of competition depended upon a standard which fused moral and market imperatives.[150]

Wilson's advocacy of "regulated competition" also reflected the continuing influence of republican values. American voters and their public leaders did not question the sanctity of property and contract rights; but when unrestrained acquisitiveness was permitted to determine the uses to which these rights were put – bringing about abuse and cut-throat competition – government regulation was essential. James C. McReynolds, Wilson's Attorney General and successful nominee for the Supreme Court, suggested the degree to which belief in legally imposed moral restraint held sway. Responding to charges that a stringent dissolution decree he had won in an antitrust case amounted to confiscation, he replied, "Confiscation? What if it is! Since when has property illegally and criminally acquired come to have any rights?"[151]

During Wilson's first term antitrust policy was bureaucratized.

State attorney generals achieved a few significant antitrust victories, particularly in Texas and Missouri, even as most states generally favored a policy which permitted big corporations as long as they accepted public-interest guidelines established in consent decrees. Private suits against local cartel practices also continued to be important.[152] Shortly before taking the office of President, Governor Wilson also won repeal of New Jersey's holding company law, though it was reenacted in 1917.[153] Even so federal rather than state action dominated antitrust prosecution. Generally, the Court upheld the Justice Department. Between 1890 and 1914 the number of suits rose steadily, though the most dramatic increase had occurred as a result of Roosevelt's Expediting Act. In about 80 percent of these cases the government won. Significantly, six out of seven of the government's prosecutions were of cartel agreements among comparatively small enterprises in the furniture, lumber, and apparel, wholesale, and retail trades. The government focused on these industries because it was easier to obtain testimony from customers and competitors proving unlawful conduct.[154]

Thus despite the occasional big case involving corporate giants like Standard Oil and American Tobacco, the Justice Department devoted most of its energies to breaking up anticompetitive, cartel practices. Although the government's record in the former was mixed, its record in the latter clearly favored the sort of competition more characteristic of small-scale enterprise. Under the reasonableness standard the Wilson Administration also supported the wider use of consent decrees, whereby the government agreed to exempt business from antitrust prosecution in return for promises that it conform its conduct to antitrust policy. In some cases these decrees enabled relatively smaller firms to survive, while in others it permitted corporate giants to achieve improved organizational efficiency. In one sense, then, at least in so far as loose anticompetitive agreements were concerned, on both the state and national level an antitrust policy favoring competition prevailed.[155]

Finally, Wilson fulfilled his pledge of new antitrust legislation. Yet the same sort of political pressures which produced a watered down version of Sherman's original antitrust law, shaped passage of the Clayton Antitrust Act and the Federal Trade Commission Act of 1914. After debate and compromise Congress passed the Clayton Act which sought to prevent discriminatory pricing between different purchasers, holding companies, exclusive dealing agreements, and interlocking boards of directors among different corporations. Mitigating the law's otherwise straightforward phraseology, however, was the equivocal command that the practices were prohibited only where the result was "to substantially lessen competition or tend to create monopoly." The Act also left unclear the legal status of the rights of labor unions. Similarly, the FTC Act outlawed "unfair trade" practices and created a five-person commission to enforce that purpose. The commission could receive complaints, hold public hearings, collect evidence, compel witnesses to appear, and issue cease and desist orders once it established sufficient proof that an unfair trade practice existed. Nevertheless the inherent ambiguity of "substantially lessen" and "unfair" trade meant that the meaning of both laws depended on judicial construction and the vigor of federal prosecution. It was, therefore, unlikely that the outcome of Wilson's new legislation would differ substantially if at all from that of the Sherman Antitrust Act.[156]

That big business disrupted the political landscape much more in America than Britain had significant consequences. Organized British business, the two dominant political parties and even the politically marginal labor groups clashed over social welfare measures, but agreed (though for different reasons) that the best general policy regarding restrictive business structures was non-intervention. This political consensus encouraged the British business order in its search for organizational and scale economies, to prefer looser forms of self-regulation over managerially centralized, big corporations. The lawmaker's unwillingness to interfere with the invisible hand of the market thus sustained family capitalism. By contrast in America the interplay of republican values and private rights, federalism, and changing market relations made antitrust a more important national priority than welfare issues. These conflicts meant, moreover, that while most interests shared a consensus favoring government action, there was little agreement on particular policies. The ambivalent response of state and federal lawmakers reflected Americans' ambiguous desire to distinguish between good and bad trusts, which nonetheless engendered the dominance of managerial capitalism. British observers contended that the failure to develop centralized management placed their nation's economy at a comparative disadvantage. Ironically, they did not perceive that a principal reason for this failure was their opposition to antitrust.

CHAPTER 4

The courts respond to big business

Consensus shaped the course of British decisions whereas American judicial opinions were molded by conflict. The consensus favoring business self-regulation, the principle of Parliamentary supremacy, and the dominance of a Free Trade ideology limited British judges to a passive role. By contrast, in America the insecurity of small business, the constitutional doctrine of judicial review, and the ideological tension between republican values and *laissez-faire* fostered judicial activism. The economic transformation big business represented required both countries' judges to alter old common-law doctrines, resulting in the more flexible standard of reasonableness. Yet, because of the legal uncertainty among the states and the vagueness of the Sherman Act, British courts established a much narrower and less significant rule of reason earlier than their American counterparts. The divergent character of legal thought and the market for lawyers' services in each country reinforced the prevalence of judicial self-restraint or activism. The pervasiveness of struggle ensured, moreover, that courts influenced the course and impact of the great merger wave much more in America than Britain.

Former President William Howard Taft explained how judicial activism and the giant corporations' corruption of republican government were linked. He declared that the purpose of the Sherman Act was to prevent restrictive practices which "had resulted in the building of giant and powerful corporations, which had, many of them, intervened in politics and through the use of corrupt machines and bosses threatened us with a plutocracy." The judiciary's constitutional independence enabled the Supreme Court to meet this challenge by employing an activistic reinterpretation of the Sherman Act in conformance with changing public opinion. "It is not that the court varies or amends the Constitution or a statute," he said, "but that, there being possible several interpretations of its language, the court adopts that which conforms to prevailing morality and predominant public opinion."[1]

British courts presented quite a different image. In the famous *Mogul* case, the trial judge Lord Coleridge perceived no threat to the political order from a cartel of shipowners who controlled the nation's tea trade. Sustaining a system of business self-government based on numerous restrictive practices, Coleridge exclaimed, "In the hand-to-hand war of commerce, as in the conflicts of public life, whether at the bar, in Parliament, in medicine, in engineering, men fight on without much thought of others, except a desire to excel or to defeat them."[2] The Court of Appeals and the House of Lords not only accepted this conclusion, but also categorically refused to transgress the accepted norms of judicial self-restraint to determine whether the shipowners had acted "reasonably" or "fairly."[3]

Perhaps the most conspicuous instance of divergence was the rule of reason. Before the 1890s both countries' judges considered the lawful standing of anticompetitive combinations in terms of the common-law distinction between ancillary and nonancillary restraints. The market and institutional transformation which spawned big business, however, created such doctrinal uncertainty by the 1890s that the need for a more flexible rule was clear. Although judges had often used "reasonable" in a nontechnical way to apply the old common-law doctrines, they had not developed a formal rule of reason.[4] The *Mogul* case paved the way for the House of Lords' first categorical statement of a reasonableness standard in the *Nordenfelt* decision of 1894. Nevertheless, as noted above, the shift from a "partial/total" to a "reasonable/unreasonable" test was a comparatively small adjustment in the trade-restraint rules affecting contracts. Some American state courts followed a similar course, though there was no uniformity.[5] Despite the protestations of Justice (later Chief Justice) Edward D. White, moreover, the Supreme Court did not interpret the Sherman Antitrust Act according to the rule of reason until 1911.[6]

Even so, British and American judges noted that the triumph of the reasonableness principle came gradually. During the lower appellate court's consideration of *Nordenfelt* in 1893, Lord Justice Nathaniel Lindley referred to a colleague who had argued that historically the "only test" by which judges had determined the validity of a restrictive contract was its "reasonableness." Yet Lindley and his court declared to the contrary that while the "modern authorities" were "gradually approximating" such a doctrine it was by no means "finally settled."[7] Similarly Taft, while still a federal circuit judge, provided a classic statement of the American rule of reason in the *Addyston Pipe* opinion of 1898. He contended what Lindley and the House of Lords denied, that a "reasonableness" principle had always permeated the common law. Taft admitted, however, that because many states had "set sail on a sea of doubt" there was no uniform rule throughout the United States.[8]

The controversy over the rule of reason reflected each nation's choice between self-regulation and governmental intervention. By the 1890s, British and American judges gradually realized that established common law doctrinal categories governing restrictive business practices were increasingly unsuitable for the emerging corporate economy. Even so, the movement toward the more flexible reasonableness standard represented not merely the articulation of a preexisting principle, as Taft and others contended, but an original doctrinal formulation rooted in a changing business order. The interaction between the courts and the wider institutional and ideological milieu shaped the point at which the formalization of the doctrine occurred. In Britain a stable social-class system evidenced by the greater control of family capitalism, and the gradual rise of organized labor as a political force paradoxically sustained a consensus favoring minimal interference with most self-regulating, restrictive business structures. Consequently, the role of courts was more passive and the constraints on doctrinal change correspondingly less significant. But in America the struggle between big and small business, as well as the constitutional limitation of labor, imposed on the judiciary a leading role. Ambivalent political and ideological pressures encouraged ambiguous state and federal legislation, particularly the Sherman Act, giving judges enormous policymaking responsibility. The intractable conflict arising from the effort to distinguish good from bad trusts drove the courts along an uneven course until an antitrust consensus emerged which the American rule of reason symbolized.[9]

THE BRITISH "RULE OF REASONABLENESS"

If American policymakers interpreted the Sherman Antitrust Act with reference to the English common law, that law was not perceived as static.[10] "In the age of Queen Elizabeth all restraints of

trade, whatever they were, general or partial," said Lord
Macnaghten in 1894, "were thought to be contrary to public policy
and therefore void...In time, however, it was found that a rule so
rigid and far-reaching must seriously interfere with transactions of
everyday occurrence."[11] Parliament also weakened the old common-
law rules, declaring in various statutes that most restrictive practices
were not actionable.[12] As a result, the "rule was relaxed," admitting
various "exceptions." Thus "restraints of trade and interference
with individual liberty of action" were allowed by the "special
circumstances of a particular case."[13] Support of the principle was
consistent enough by the 1890s that in most cases British courts
would neither forbid nor enforce contracts in restraint of trade. In
the unusual suit where the courts would actually enforce – rather
than merely not interfere – with restrictive agreements, the controlling rule was one of reasonableness. At the same time, most of the
cases tended to involve cartels on the defensive against depressed
trade. The principal result was to sustain extensive business self-
regulation maintained through loose, restrictive agreements which
ensured the comparatively greater control of family firms.[14]

One of the leading legal precedents was *Mogul Steamship Co.* v.
McGregor, Co. The case arose in 1888 between a conference of
steamship companies engaged in the lucrative China tea trade, and
the Mogul Co. which sought to enter the same market. Briefly, the
conference permitted Mogul a piece of the business. But when the
outsider demanded that it become a cartel member, the conference
balked, whereupon Mogul threatened to cut its rates low enough to
"smash" its opponent. The conference responded, however, by
reducing rates to such a point that Mogul could not survive. It was
a straightforward case of using predatory pricing to destroy a
competitor. The steamship company then sued, arguing that the
conference had conspired to prevent it from competing "fairly,"
violating common-law rules forbidding conspiracies to enter into
restrictive commercial contracts. In several lower and appellate
rulings between 1888 and 1892 British courts, including finally the
House of Lords, held that the conference's conduct was not
actionable on grounds of conspiracy and therefore not forbidden by
law. The adverse publicity caused a short-term dissolution of the
cartel, but soon thereafter it was reestablished and continued to exist
throughout the twentieth century.[15]

The judges' various opinions in the *Mogul* litigation set out the

British common-law's policy toward restrictive agreements. From the trial level to the House of Lords there were in all eleven opinions. Of these only one judge, Lord Esher, construed old precedents to support the view that the conference's actions were unfair and therefore subject to prosecution. The other ten judges – including the seven in the House of Lords who upheld the conference unanimously – provided an interpretation of the same precedents to reach the opposite result. Although all the judges agreed that acts of physical intimidation and the conspiracy to commit such were illegal, there was little if anything in the record showing that the conference had engaged in that sort of behavior. Instead Lord Justice Edward Fry observed in reasoning accepted by all but Esher, that the "scheme of the conference was by means of competition in the near future to prevent competition in the remoter future."[16]

Charles S. C. Bowen rejected the Mogul Company's and Esher's claim that "competition ceases to be the lawful exercise of trade" if "carried to a length which is not 'fair or reasonable.'" Esher's contention suggested, he said, that there was "some natural standard of 'fairness' or 'reasonableness' to be determined by the internal consciousness of judges and juries beyond which competition ought not in law to go." Fry also affirmed that it was not the "province of judges to mold and stretch the law of conspiracy in order to keep pace with the calculations of political economy." He argued that Parliamentary legislation rather than the common law was the proper way to "strike" at "peaceable and honest combinations of capital." Finally Bowen concluded that "competition, however severe and egotistical, if unattended by circumstances of dishonesty, intimidation, molestation, or such illegalities... give rise to no cause of action at common law. I myself should deem it to be a misfortune if" courts attempted to "prescribe to the business world how honest and peaceable trade was to be carried on," adopting "some standard of judicial 'reasonableness,' or of 'normal' prices or 'fair freights' to which commercial adventures, otherwise innocent, were bound to conform."[17]

The *Mogul* case also raised the issue of enforceability. The agreements among the conference members established a self-regulatory framework creating economies of scale, which enabled the conference to sustain greater losses than the Mogul Steamship Company. All of the opinions in the case addressed the central issue of whether the conference's market advantage was "unfair" or "unreasonable" competition. The courts, of course, decided that question against Mogul. On the related point of whether the cartel agreements were enforceable between the conference members themselves, however, Lord Chancellor Halsbury pointed out that they were not. Some contracts in restraint of trade were void as contrary to "public policy" Halsbury said. And "contracts so tainted the law will not lend its aid to enforce. It treats them as if they had not been made at all," even though the "parties have agreed."[18] Thus businessmen could form anticompetitive, restrictive combinations. But this very freedom also meant that they had little legal recourse against those in the combination who decided that continued cooperation was no longer in their interest. Thus the conference's victory in court did not prevent in the short-term the dissolution of the cartel itself.[19]

The *Maxim Nordenfelt Guns* case also involved the issue of enforceability, but with different results. In 1888 Swedish inventor and businessman Thorsten Nordenfelt sold for a considerable sum his arms-manufacturing business to the new British firm, the Maxim Nordenfelt Guns and Ammunition Co. In the sales contract Nordenfelt agreed not to manufacture anywhere in the world for twenty-five years various of the precision weapons he had developed, leaving that market to the new company. The contract also permitted him to remain with the firm as a senior partner. Within a short time, however, Nordenfelt resigned and reentered the armaments business in Belgium with the very weapons which the Maxim Company was selling. The firm sued in 1892, asking for an injunction to compel Nordenfelt to cease competing in accordance with his contract. He responded by arguing that the twenty-five year proscription was an unreasonable restraint of trade. Although the trial court agreed, on appeal the decision was reversed in favor of Maxim. The House of Lords in turn upheld the appellate court's ruling, despite Nordenfelt's personal appearance pleading his cause.[20]

On one level the question was simple: should the court enforce the contract with an injunction, or not enforce it because it was an agreement in restraint of trade and therefore void? But on another level the issue was complicated because, as the *Mogul* decision showed, late-nineteenth-century British courts generally interpreted freedom of contract to mean that the *enforcement* of restrictive agreements was exceptional. Moreover, British courts' regard for judicial self-restraint was such that, as Lord Watson said concerning Nordenfelt's final appeal, "In England, at least, it is beyond the jurisdiction of her tribunals to mold and stereotype national policy." And yet Watson also doubted whether "now or ever" it was the "policy of England to encourage unfettered competition in the sale of arms of precision to tribes who may become her antagonists in warfare. I also doubt whether at any period of time an English Court would have allowed a foreigner to break his contract with an English subject in order to foster such competition." This concern for public policy thus required adjusting the rules governing restraints of trade in order "to adapt to new circumstances an old and sound exception to the general rule."[21]

By the 1890s the standard which increasingly controlled the enforcement of such restrictive agreements was reasonableness. Again, however, the status of the common law was ambiguous. "In the early times all agreements in restraints of trade were discountenanced," said Lord Ashbourne, "but by degrees, as the exigencies of an advancing civilization demanded, this was found to be too rigid, and our judges considered in each case what was reasonable and necessary to afford fair protection." Thus it was necessary to consider the rule of reasonableness in light of the "vast advances" occurring since the reign of Queen Elizabeth in "science, inventions, political institutions, commerce, and the intercourse of nations. Telegraphs, postal systems, railways, steam, have brought all parts of the world in touch. Communications has become easy, rapid, and cheap." As a result the "inquiry as to the validity of all covenants in restraint of trade must, I am disposed to think, now ultimately turn upon whether they are reasonable." Nevertheless, the court of first appeal and the House of Lords broadly agreed that though this was the "doctrine to which the modern authorities have been gradually approximating" it was not "finally settled."[22]

Despite the relatively minor adjustment in restraint of trade rules affecting contracts the issue represented, the need for an authoritative statement of the reasonableness standard thus had become compelling. The "time for a new departure" to be "authoritatively decided" had risen, said Lord Morris,[23] and Lord Macnaghten provided a precise definition: "restraints of trade and interference with individual liberty of action may be justified by the special circumstances of a particular case. It is a sufficient justification, and indeed it is the only justification if the restriction is reasonable –

reasonable, that is, in reference to the interests of the parties concerned and reasonable in reference to the interests of the public."[24]

The *Maxim* decision established a principle having significance for the future. "With regard to the facts of this case, I have only to observe that they are, from a legal point of view, exceptional. Their parallel is not to be found in any of the reported cases; but they are such as may naturally be expected to occur in the altered and daily altering conditions under which trade is conducted in modern times," said Lord Watson.[25] Even so, Macnaghten's formulation of the rule of reasonableness, though extracted from a reading of earlier precedents, was subject to diverse interpretations.

From the mid-1890s on the British courts worked within the *Mogul* and *Nordenfelt* principles. In 1900 a case arose involving vertical price-fixing agreements between a manufacturer of "embrocations" for horses, cattle, and human use, and wholesalers who sold it to retailers. The manufacturer, Elliman, Sons & Co. required a wholesaler purchasing the product to sign a contract agreeing he would not sell it below a fixed price. The agreement also bound the wholesaler to procure a similar contract from any retailer buying the embrocation. Carrington & Son conveyed Elliman's goods to a retailer but failed to make the required contract, whereupon the manufacturer sued Carrington in chancery, asking the court to enforce that provision of the price-fixing agreement. The wholesaler's defense was that the agreement was void as a contract in restraint of trade and therefore not enforceable.[26]

The court held that between the manufacturer and wholesaler the agreement was valid, and enforceable. The "restraint of trade as regards Carrington & Son" was, the judge said, "really the liberty of trade as regards Elliman." The issue was merely "whether a man is entitled when he is selling his own goods to make a bargain as to the use to be made of them by the purchaser." Moreover, allowing such freedom of contract was not "against public policy." Moreover, "Elliman had the remedy in their own hands by refusing to supply their embrocation except on their own terms." Thus consistent with *Mogul*, British businessmen were at liberty to negotiate between themselves restrictive agreements. The sole argument put to the court was that the contract was invalid as being in undue restraint of trade. The court rejected the arguments; the agreement was valid. The judge refused an injunction but granted nominal damages (£1). Injunction is a remedy at the discretion of the court which will not be granted for various reasons. In this case the modest damage award nonetheless suggested that more substantial damages would be possible for future breaches of the same condition. So, in a real sense, the contract was enforceable.[27]

Even so, vertical restraints derived from a patent were within the limits of reasonableness and enforceable. The United Shoe Machinery Company owned a patented technology used by many of the world's manufacturers of boots and shoes. The American-based company used its monopoly to impose upon those leasing the technology certain tying agreements which restricted or denied altogether the use of other equipment. According to one of these vertical clauses, the British manufacturer, Somervell Brothers, contracted to use only the USMC's machinery for twenty years. After three years, Somervell found elements of the technology uneconomical for the particular demands of its business and began using other machinery. In 1906 USMC sued for breach of contract and asked the chancery court to enforce it. Somervell responded that the tying agreement was a restraint of trade and contrary to public policy. The judge admitted that he was "rather startled" at the "very considerable time" for which the contract ran. But, he said, "there it is, and we have got to make the best of it as it stands." The ground "for discontinuing the machine – namely, reasons of economy – is wholly insufficient," the judge concluded, and so there was "a breach of the contract" which must be corrected by the court requiring enforcement.[28]

An appeal from Canada revealed that the House of Lords was also willing to enforce such tying agreements. In order to complete part of its manufacturing process, Brunet, a Quebec firm, began using equipment produced locally in violation of its lease with USMC. In 1905 the company sued, arguing that Brunet had violated the "tying clause" of the lease. A special jury of local Quebec businessmen decided in favor of Brunet's claim that the vertical constraint was a restraint of trade and therefore void. Canada's highest court upheld the verdict, whereupon in 1909 USMC appealed to the Judicial Committee. Unanimously following *Mogul*, the Judicial Committee overruled the Canadian court's opinions. The controlling precedent afforded "a striking example of the lengths to which traders, in bona fide defense or promotion of their own trade interests, may lawfully push this privilege [of free trade], regardless of the injury, clearly foreseen by them, which they may thereby incidentally inflict on the trade of their rivals." Admittedly, the Lords observed, USMC possessed a monopoly. However, it was not for the courts but the provincial legislature responding to the "ingenuity and enterprise of the Canadian people" to remedy any "evil, if it exists."[29]

Yet, even where the Australian legislature had acted, the Lords found reasons to support self-regulating, anticompetitive agreements. In 1906 the new Commonwealth's parliament passed a Federal law not unlike the Sherman Antitrust Act. It declared illegal any contract or combination the intent of which was "to destroy or injure by means of unfair competition any Australian industry which is advantageous to the commonwealth... [and] the interests of producers, workers, and consumers." Provincial coal companies formed a pool designed to fix prices, distribute output among members, and provide a fund supporting weak producers. The resulting stability enabled the colliers to establish a cartel agreement with several shipping companies to further control maximum prices. The record showed that the agreements sought to ameliorate cut-throat competition, which had not only weakened the coal producers themselves but had also engendered labor strife because of low wages and unemployment. Nevertheless, in the *Adelaide Steamship* case the Australian government challenged the cartel as a violation of the nation's antitrust law. Australia's highest tribunal overruled the trial court's decision which favored the government, whereupon, in 1913, the attorney general appealed to the Judicial Committee.[30]

The Lords interpreted the statute in light of the principles established in *Mogul* and *Nordenfelt*. They rejected the argument that the Australian parliament had intended that all contracts in restraint of trade were always either void or unenforceable, since such a holding threatened the existence of "trade unions, the economic advantage of which has often been recognized in modern legislation." It also denied claims that US decisions construing the Sherman Act were relevant, rejecting the Supreme Court's use of the rule of reason in the *Standard Oil* decision of 1911. More significantly, the Judicial Committee linked the price stability the cartel agreements facilitated to the collier's ability to employ workers and pay satisfactory wages, an outcome "eminently reasonable and well calculated to prevent labor troubles." Moreover, "their Lordships" believed it was "never... of real benefit to the consumers that colliery proprietors should carry on their business at a loss, or that any profit they make should depend on the miner's wages being reduced to a minimum." There was, therefore, "a solidarity of interest between all members of the public," including consumers, workers, and the members of the cartel. Ultimately, the issue was whether these considerations established sufficient "intent" to violate the statute. The court held that the cartel agreements raised no "legitimate inference that any of the parties concerned, whether colliery proprietors or shipping companies, acted otherwise than with a single view to their own advantage, or had had any intention of raising prices or annihilating competition to the detriment of the public." Thus, the court declared that the cartel practices were permissible under the law.[31]

By early 1914 the judiciary's drift toward enforcing anti-competitive agreements was clear. Most of the salt manufacturers in Western England formed a cartel known as the North Western Salt Co. for the "purpose of regulating supply and keeping up prices, and it had the practical control of the inland salt market." The Electrolytic Alkali Co., though not a cartel member, entered into a contract with North Western limiting output and agreeing to sell to no one else for a period of four years. In return the cartel guaranteed the annual purchase of Alkali's production at a fixed price. But, despite the agreement, the company sold to a third party, whereupon North Western sued for breach of contract, asking the court to compel compliance. Alkali argued in defense that the contract was void as a restraint of trade and therefore not enforceable. Although the trial judge decided in favor of the cartel, the Court of Appeal reversed by a vote of 2 to 1. For final review the case went to the House of Lords.[32]

The Lords refused to admit the legal ground of the appeal, thereby not only permitting but also enforcing the restrictive agreements. As was true of the Australian antitrust case decided the year before, the court linked social order and business necessity. All four Lords wrote opinions, but Haldane's was representative. "Unquestionably", he conceded, the purpose of the cartel was to "regulate supply and keep up prices. But an ill-regulated supply and unremunerative prices may, in point of fact, be disadvantageous to the public. Such a state of things may, if it is not controlled, drive manufacturers out of business, or lower wages, and so cause unemployment and labor disturbance." Accordingly, it "must always be a question of circumstances whether a combination of manufacturers in a particular trade is an evil from a public point of view. The same thing is true of a supposed monopoly." Haldane concluded that the parties were the "best judges of what is reasonable as between themselves." As a result, the "detailed provisions" of the agreement at issue embodied primarily the "machinery for working out the bargain." The contract between the cartel and Alkali was therefore neither illegal nor contrary to the public interest and Alkali was bound to honor it.[33]

These cases suggested why British courts encouraged little disruption of the established business order. In every suit except these concerning the American-based corporation USMC, the litigants were generally either family firms or a lone individual such as Nordenfelt. Even the shipping companies were controlled by owners who had "grown up with the business." Moreover, the cases involved firms acting in concert through various self-regulating restrictive agreements, including cartels often on the defensive against depressed trade. Such organizational forms preserved the greater control of family enterprise so characteristic of the British economy, unlike the large managerially centralized corporations which displaced American small businessmen. The judiciary's rule of reasonableness was flexible enough to allow diverse organizational structures. Indeed, reflecting anxiety about the preservation of social stability and public welfare, the Lords enlarged the range of restrictive agreements which were enforceable at law, particularly by narrowing the construction of Australia's antitrust law. Yet as British judges worked to balance the freedoms of trade and contract they reinforced the earlier pattern of business self-regulation.

THE AMERICAN "RULE OF REASON"

Both American and British courts eventually applied a standard of reasonableness in cases involving anticompetitive agreements. But although the legal phraseology was like that which Macnaghten used in his *Nordenfelt* opinion, the American rule of reason differed in both its origin and results.[34] State courts applied principles inherited from the English common law to strike down the original trust device pioneered by Standard Oil. At about the same time big business's use of the trust declined, however, the Supreme Court decided the *Knight Sugar Trust* case, suggesting to many businessmen that the holding company and tighter mergers were lawful under the Sherman Act. Then, beginning in 1897, the Court began consistently overturning cartel practices. Taken together, these ambivalent decisions and the successful state prosecutions encouraged the turn-of-the-century merger wave.[35] Ultimately, the American rule of reason emerged in the *Standard Oil* and *American Tobacco* decisions of

1911. Yet, while the Court remained consistently opposed to cartel practices, it facilitated the decline of the holding company in favor of tighter mergers establishing even greater managerial centralization. Generally, American courts did not condemn the merger itself, but the noncompetition covenants that attended the merger. This was particularly true of asset acquisitions, where American courts almost always found the basic acquisition to be legal, but often struck down attendant covenants not to compete as violations of the common law of trade restraints.[36]

The state courts influenced the movement toward large managerially centralized corporations. During the 1880s Standard Oil and other corporate giants replaced horizontal cartel arrangements with the original trust device. A principal reason for this change was that the cooperative agreements were not enforceable at law, which facilitated cheating and undercut the attainment of organizational efficiencies.[37] Between the mid-1880s and mid-nineties, however, the attorney generals of Louisiana, Illinois, Nebraska, California, New York, Ohio and other states won from their courts decrees dissolving the trusts. The states based these actions on new legislation and court decisions which made loose corporate arrangements not only unenforceable, but also subject to civil and criminal prosecution. In altering their common law, the states thus established a more stringent policy toward restrictive practices than that sanctioned by the reasonableness standard of *Nordenfelt*.[38] The Lone Star state's courts upheld antitrust legislation which protected the east-Texas fields from Standard Oil's takeover.[39] The victories over the Standard Oil-type trusts, moreover, encouraged Senator Sherman to argue during the debates of his antitrust bill that federal authority would merely compliment the already proven power of the states.[40]

Meanwhile, in 1889 New Jersey enacted its law permitting corporations to form holding companies and soon other states followed suit. As a result, although Ohio finally dissolved the Standard Oil Trust, the company avoided destruction by reconstituting itself as a holding company in 1899. The liberalization of state incorporation statutes permitted corporations to escape state prosecution to the extent that by 1897 many big corporations sought increased managerial centralization through merger.[41]

In addition, state judges decided many private suits against anticompetitive contracts. An Alabama decision in 1900, *Tuscaloosa Ice Mfg. Co.* v. *Williams*, was typical. Williams, the plaintiff, sued the

Tuscaloosa Ice Company, arguing that the contractual agreement under which he sold his business to his former competitor, who then possessed a monopoly, was void under common-law rules prohibiting contracts in restraint of trade. The plaintiff won at trial, whereupon the Tuscaloosa Ice Company appealed. The issue was whether a contract between the two ice manufacturers, in which one party granted the other a monopoly, was unlawful under the common law. The court found that the contract was a "vicious restraint of trade, and is therefore violative of the public policy of the state and void."[42]

The Alabama court thus did not apply the *Nordenfelt* principle of reasonableness to enforce the anticompetitive agreement. There was no doubt that the contract "tends to injure the public by stifling competition and creating a monopoly," the court said, giving one company the power "to arbitrarily fix prices" thereby creating a "partial ice famine, upon which [it]...could batten and fatten at its own sweet will." Resorting to colorful language, the court observed that any defense of such practices was "exceedingly nude and bald." Yet, though the unfettered manufacture of ice in and of itself was undoubtedly important to the small town of Tuscaloosa during the hot humid summer months, when the case was decided, the court stressed further considerations it apparently regarded as equally compelling. Because of the contract to shut down one of two firms, the "public loses a wealth producing instrumentality. Labor is thrown out of employment." This in turn forced workers upon the public welfare or drove them to become criminals. Hence, profits from a contract which established a monopoly were not the "just reward" of "skill and energy and enterprise in building up a business," but "a mere bribery and seduction of...industry, and a pensioning of idleness." The "motives actuating such a transaction" were "always...sinister and baleful."[43]

Such private actions were more numerous and probably more important than the suits initiated by the states' attorney generals. From every jurisdiction for all the years up to the 1870s there were perhaps no more than 130 recorded private suits challenging restrictive trade practices. Between 1880 and 1914 however, the number rose from 70 to 200, totaling 520.[44] Hans Thorelli concluded that this private litigation "was one of the prime factors preventing the lapse of American industry into general cartelization of...the contemporary German type."[45] Thus by 1900 most states contributed to an ambiguous legal environment which destroyed the trust device and outlawed cartel practices, but ironically also fostered tighter corporate consolidation through holding companies and mergers.

Congress responded to this conflict on the state level in the Sherman Act. Few doubted Congressional power to regulate interstate and foreign commerce, including the contracts facilitating this trade. Yet authorities also generally agreed that corporations involved in production confined principally within a single state were not subject to federal regulation under the commerce clause. By the late nineteenth century the Supreme Court had decided many cases defining the scope and limits of the commerce power along these lines. Contractual agreements facilitating corporate production within one state generally were beyond the reach of the federal commerce power, whereas contracts directly touching interstate trade were subject to that power. How did this constitutional distinction between state and federal authority affect the contractual relations of holding companies and mergers whose control of production permitted a firm to compel others to accept anti-competitive or restrictive trade agreements? Where, in other words, did the state's control of production end, and the federal government's authority over commerce begin?[46] Despite the disagreement of one or two federal circuit courts, most of the lower federal tribunals answered this question by construing the Sherman Act much as had the Judicial Committee in the Australian antitrust case – quite narrowly.[47]

The Supreme Court first decided the issue in the *Knight Sugar Trust* case of 1895. The Court narrowly construed the Sherman Act's provisions prohibiting contracts and combinations in restraint of trade. The majority held that the Act applied only to restrictive practices involved directly in interstate trade, not to horizontal agreements among manufacturers involved in production within a single state. The Sugar Trust was a holding company whose production was confined principally to one state, Pennsylvania. Yet the combination of several competing Philadelphia firms, in order to attain productive economies, established a corporate entity with such economic power that it could virtually dictate the terms of interstate marketing agreements. When the federal government prosecuted the company it argued that the Sherman Act applied to contracts creating production monopolies. But, because such contracts were traditionally subject to state regulation, the Court decided, with only Justice John M. Harlan dissenting, that the Sherman Act did not reach them.[48]

Even so, the impact of the *Knight* case was equivocal. Leading contemporary lawyers counseled their corporate clients that the holding company and mergers were "valid" under the Sherman Act.[49] This widespread view of the legality of such corporate amalgamations coincided with the states' successful prosecution of the various Standard Oil-type trusts and the precipitous rise in successful private suits. Taken together these legal trends encouraged the businessman's preference for tighter forms of corporate consolidation.[50]

The Court was deeply divided over the interpretation of the Sherman Act. Shortly after deciding *E. C. Knight* during the spring of 1895, the Court upheld unanimously an injunction against *Eugene v. Debs* who had attempted to support the Pullman strikers with a secondary boycott imposed by his American Railway Union. The lower federal judges granted the injunction, holding that the labor unions were acting as a combination in restraint of trade in violation of the Sherman Act. The framers of the law, however, had not intended to bring unions under the statute. The Supreme Court, therefore, declined to accept the lower court's doubtful interpretation, basing its unanimous decision to sustain the injunction on the judiciary's general constitutional authority.[51]

Not until December 1896 did the Court hear a case involving unequivocally the legal status of business agreements which impinged directly on interstate commerce. Several months later in *US* v. *Trans-Missouri Freight Association* (1897), the Court strengthened the businessman's preference for tight over loose corporate combinations. The issue was whether a cartel agreement among competing railroads to fix rates violated the Sherman Act. The Court divided 5 to 4. For the majority, Justice Rufus W. Peckham held that the cartel's rate-fixing practices violated the antitrust law. Peckham reasoned that the Act should be read literally, without recourse to the ambiguities of the common law, including the *Mogul* and *Nordenfelt* decisions. Justice Edward D. White for the dissenters, however, argued that a more flexible rule of reasonableness similar to that established in the British cases should govern the application of the Sherman Act.[52]

The stakes in the Court's disagreement were high. The railroads contended that their anticompetitive practices were necessary to gain sufficient economies to off-set high fixed costs. Competition drove rates so low that profit was inadequate to cover these costs, forcing the railroads into bankruptcy. The lower federal court, which White and the dissenters wanted to affirm, accepted these arguments and found the cartel agreements to be reasonable. Rejecting the common law as the basis for construing the Sherman Act, Peckham refused to give priority to economic efficiency and private rights. "It is true the results of trusts, or combinations ... may be different in different kinds of corporations," said Peckham, "and yet they all have an essential similarity, and have been induced by motives of individual or corporate aggrandizement as against the public interest."[53]

But it was not considerations of economic efficiency alone which Peckham rejected. He conceded that certain large corporations such as the Knight Sugar Company, operating principally within a single state, were legal under the Sherman Act. What most concerned him were the social consequences of the changing economic order. When a "combination" controlled prices, the "country" lost the "services of a large number of small but independent dealers who were familiar with the business and who had spent their lives in it, and who supported themselves and their families from the small profits realized therein." Even lower prices gained from corporate con-solidation did not justify destroying these independent enterprisers. The "real prosperity of any country" was lost if corporate bigness forced "an independent businessman, the head of his establishment, small though it might be, into a mere servant or agent of a corporation for selling the commodities which he once manufactured or dealt in, having no voice in shaping the business policy of the company and bound to obey orders issued by others."[54]

The *Trans-Missouri Freight* opinion followed shortly after the state's successful dissolution of the formal trusts. The Court's *Knight Sugar Trust* judgment, combined with Peckham's decision of 1897, thus further encouraged the move to greater corporate consolidation and increased managerial centralization. As noted already, despite similar financial and technological factors, the scale of the mergers wave was greater in America than Britain. The convergence of state and federal decisions overturning loose horizontal agreements, combined with the apparent toleration of tighter combinations, undoubtedly stimulated the different pattern of investment in British and American merger issues beginning in 1897.[55]

Peckham, of course, did not have the last word. By 1899 (the peak of the great merger wave) the Court suggested in several decisions, including most notably the sustaining of the result in Taft's *Addyston* opinion, that common-law principles could provide guidelines for applying the Sherman Act. Yet division among the justices persisted as to whether Peckham's literal reading or White's rule of reason should govern the interpretation of the antitrust law.[56]

In the *Northern Securities* case of 1903, where two major railroads formed a holding company specifically in order to avoid competing in interstate commerce, the Court held for the first time that such a tight corporate combination was a violation of the Sherman Act. The 5-4 vote affirmed, however, the extent to which the justices remained divided. The majority supported Harlan's decision that the preservation of competition was the primary purpose of the Sherman Act. But among the four dissenters, White argued that the evidence as to the intent of the Act's framers was too ambiguous to support Harlan's interpretation. Accordingly, neither Peckham's literal reading nor Harlan's emphasis upon a single policy favoring competition permitted the flexibility provided by the rule of reason. And, given the uneven course of combined state and federal decisions since 1890, White believed, flexibility was essential. Moreover, in what became a famous dissent, Holmes categorically rejected the opinion's philosophical preference for unrestrained competition. By favoring the values of self-regulating cooperation, Holmes revealed a sympathy for the theoretical approach and substantive results of British law.[57]

The Court's consensus regarding the status of organized labor under the antitrust law contrasted markedly with its disagreement in business cases. In the *Debs* case, the Court had upheld an injunction on the grounds that the power was implied under the Constitution's judicial clause, circumventing the issue whether the Sherman Act applied. By 1908 it removed this ambiguity, declaring unanimously in an opinion to which Peckham, White, Holmes, and Harlan concurred that the Act authorized enjoining strikes and other labor actions. The decision cited *Trans-Missouri Freight* and *Northern Securities* to support the proposition that the antitrust law had "a broader application than the prohibition of restraints of trade unlawful at common law."[58]

White's dissent in *Trans-Missouri Freight Association* became a fundamental antitrust principle in cases involving Standard Oil and

American Tobacco. Both giant corporations were holding companies doing business throughout the United States and around the world. Each firm had entered into anticompetitive contracts involving discriminatory pricing and marketing practices, which they defended on grounds of efficiency. In both cases White relied upon a reading of British and American common law to decide whether these contracts were lawful. The Chief Justice acknowledged that "freedom of contract" was the "rule in English law," and under the Sherman Act "freedom to contract was the essence of freedom from the undue restraint of the right to contract." *Undue* restraint arose, he said, from pernicious conduct or acts leading to the "acquisition here and there" of "every efficient means by which competition could have been asserted," and the "system of marketing" by which the "country was divided into districts and the trade in each…was turned over to a designated corporation within the combination and others were excluded."[59] Using this "rule of reason" to interpret the Sherman Act, White held that its phrase "'restraint of trade' only embraced acts…which operated to the prejudice of the public interests by unduly restricting competition…or which, either because of their inherent nature or effect or because of the evident purpose of the acts…injuriously restrained trade."[60]

This emphasis upon undesirable consequences resulting from pernicious conduct established a legal standard permitting considerable flexibility. If the Court discovered offensive behavior which produced restrictive results, it was contrary to the public interest and unlawful. Accordingly, in the *Standard Oil* case the Court found that the corporation had engaged in wrongful predatory pricing practices and therefore ordered the firm's dissolution. The American Tobacco Company suffered a similar fate. Yet White's decisions also expressly acknowledged that the Court could find other examples of restraining conduct to be reasonable. In such cases, he said, the "words restraint of trade should be given a meaning which would not destroy the individual right to contract and render difficult if not impossible any movement of trade in the channels of interstate commerce – the free movement of which it was the purpose of the [Sherman] statute to protect."[61] Although Harlan accepted the result, he dissented from reading into the Sherman Act the rule of reason as an unwarranted exercise of "judicial legislation."[62]

White's rule of reason went beyond the British principle of

reasonableness. Essentially, White's linking of intent and behavior made those moral factors which British courts refused to consider relevant in *Mogul*, a basic interpretive standard of American antitrust law. Moreover, White's fusion of moralistic considerations and Harlan's policy of competition as the primary criteria for determining what violated the public interest significantly expanded the principles established in *Nordenfelt*. For Macnaghten and his colleagues the central issue was neither offensive behavior nor competition per se. Rather, they sought to strike a balance between merely allowing or actually enforcing anticompetitive practices. Thus the White and Macnaghten opinions agreed that many contractual agreements, though clearly anticompetitive in their result, nonetheless were entered into solely to achieve desirable economic efficiencies and therefore were lawful. The difference was that White blended moral and economic considerations to separate reasonable from unreasonable conduct.[63]

The year 1911 was the most important turning point for the Court's antitrust decisions since 1895 and 1897. Just before handing down the *Standard Oil* and *American Tobacco* opinions, the Justices reaffirmed their opposition to cartel practices by declaring that vertical price-fixing agreements between manufacturers and their wholesalers or retailers were unlawful. The case, *Dr. Miles Medical Co.* v. *Park & Sons Co.*, did not involve the Sherman Act directly, but the majority opinion noted in passing that such practices, nonetheless, were in principle contrary to the law. Only Holmes dissented, expressing a preference for the British precedents which sanctioned those very anticompetitive agreements which the Court struck down.[64]

At the same time, Brandeis lobbied unsuccessfully for federal legislation allowing price fixing among middlemen. He supported White's announcement of the rule of reason, hoping that the Court would use the flexible principle to circumvent *Dr. Miles*. Even after Brandeis joined the Court in 1916, however, neither he nor Holmes were able to achieve that result.[65] In restricted form, resale price maintenance remained legal on the state level, but it was exceptional.[66] After 1911, businessmen generally resorted to looser forms of cooperation and price fixing only in secret, whereupon such behavior became the primary focus of successful federal and private antitrust prosecutions.[67]

The rule of reason also had significant impact on the administrative enforcement of antitrust. Under the flexibility inherent in the reasonableness principle, the Woodrow Wilson Administration supported the wider use of consent decrees. The government agreed to exempt certain mergers from antitrust prosecution in return for promises that the conduct of big corporations would conform to antitrust policy. Such decrees enabled AT&T, ALCOA, DuPont, and International Harvester to achieve improved organizational efficiency resulting in either a monopolistic or oligopolistic industrial structure.[68] Ultimately, the Court also emasculated the Wilson Administration's Clayton Antitrust Act and the Federal Trade Commission. It construed the Clayton Act, despite the framer's admittedly ambiguous intent, to permit antitrust prosecutions of labor unions.[69] It also interpreted quite narrowly the FTC's powers to define unfair practices.[70]

Under Chief Justice White the American rule of reason became a basic legal principle governing business structure under the Sherman Act. Unlike the result of the reasonableness standard which British courts applied to sanction most restrictive agreements, the outcome of the American rule was ambiguous. As Chandler has noted, big business's use of the holding company precipitously declined in favor of more extensive merger between White's pronouncement of the rule of reason in 1911 and the war.[71] This was so in no small part because businessmen had reason to believe that the Sherman Act permitted only the most thorough centralization of management. The Standard Oil and American Tobacco decisions notwithstanding, the federal government reinforced this presumption through its primary emphasis on prosecuting cartel practices rather than big firms established through merger. Thus both British and American courts responded to the rise of big business by formulating a rule of reasonableness. But in America the rule encouraged the development of managerial centralization through ever-tighter corporate mergers, whereas in Britain it sanctioned business self-regulation and the greater control of family firms.

JUDICIAL ACTIVISM AND SELF-RESTRAINT

That each nations' judges applied a different reasonableness standard to sustain divergent economic results reflected a contrary approach to judicial activism and self-restraint. British and American courts acknowledged the need to respect their own precedents by exercising self-restraint. Yet no British judge could ever voice the confident assertion of Justice Harlan: "[I]f we don't like an act of Congress, we don't have much trouble to find grounds for declaring it unconstitutional."[72] Much the same was true regarding the legality of restrictive practices which did not directly involve constitutionality. In practice and theory, American more so than British judges were committed to judicial activism.

Although Parliament was supreme, British commentators conceded that within a limited sphere judicial activism was legitimate. As early as 1861 the distinguished jurist, Henry Maine, observed that a court's review of numerous precedents resulted in a "new decision" which not only "modified" but also made "more elastic" the existing law. In fact, Maine said, the legal rules were "changed. A clear addition has been made to the precedents, and the canon of law elicited by comparing the precedents is not the same as that which would have been obtained if the series of cases had been curtailed by a single example."[73] Albert Ven Dicey in 1905 was more direct: "No doubt the law-making function of the Courts has been to a certain extent curtailed by the development of parliamentary authority. Throughout the whole of the nineteenth century, however, it has remained, and indeed continues to the present day in operation... Hence whole branches not of ancient but of very modern law have been built up, developed, or created by the action of the courts."[74]

Nevertheless, where restrictive practices involved transportation facilities and the relations between business and labor, judicial self-restraint prevailed. British judges did much to shape the law themselves before broadly accepting Parliament's role in governing restrictive railroad agreements, the liability of employers for accidents, workmen's compensation, and, ultimately, the actions of unions in general.[75] Here the courts followed Dicey's view that government intervention was appropriate to "defend all citizens from dangers which certainly might be warded off, though at the cost of a great deal of trouble, by individual energy and circumspection." Such legislation rested upon the "idea (which is thoroughly congenial to collectivism) that the State is a better judge than a man himself of his own interest, or at any rate of the way to pursue it."[76]

Admittedly, the commitment of British judges to freedom of contract was such that many chaffed at what they regarded as excessive paternalism. In 1888, Lord Bramwell expressed frustration when called upon to review the reasonableness of railroad rates. "Here is a contract made by a fishmonger and a carrier of fish who know their business, and whether it is just and reasonable is to be settled by me who is neither fishmonger nor carrier, nor with any knowledge of their business..." It seemed "perfectly idle, and I cannot understand how it could have been supposed necessary, that it should be referred to a judge to say whether an agreement between carriers, of whose business he knows nothing, is reasonable or not." Nevertheless, Bramwell sustained Parliament's delegation to administrators of the power to fix rates.[77]

In doing so he exercised the same sort of restraint the Lords applied to self-regulating business agreements from the *Mogul* decision on. Indeed, in *Mogul* Bramwell agreed with Lord Morris, who was unable to "see why judges should be considered specially gifted with prescience of what may hamper or what may increase trade, or of what is to be the test of adequate remuneration."[78] Paradoxically, in these private business cases involving no explicit Parliamentary legislation it was through activism that the British courts established self-restraint. The *Nordenfelt* opinion (though a relatively minor doctrinal adjustment) nonetheless recognized the need to adapt old common-law principles to a new economic order. The result was Macnaghten's reasonableness standard which was consistent with the sort of "judicial legislation" Maine and Dicey described. Even so this limited activism produced the rule which enabled Bramwell, Watson, and others to preserve principles of freedom of contract outside the sphere of legislative intervention.[79]

The labor decisions demonstrated the consequences of the failure to balance effectively activism and restraint. In 1897, the Lords upheld a union's right to engage in restrictive action, with Lord Halsbury dissenting.[80] But, three years later, in the similar labor cases, *Quinn* v. *Leatham* and *Taff Vale*, Halsbury exercised his authority as Lord Chancellor to select a panel which questioned the earlier result. Suggesting the tenets of Maine and Dicey, he exclaimed that every precedent "must be read as applicable to the particular facts proved," and "I entirely deny that it can be quoted for a proposition that may seem to follow logically from it. Such a mode of reasoning assumes that the law is necessarily a logical code, whereas every lawyer must acknowledge that the law is not always logical at all."[81] It was, said a supporter of the decision, "idle to attack the result... on the ground that it is judge-made law, for in whatever way the House had decided, their judgment would have amounted to judicial legislation."[82] The decision, however, fostered the victory of Labour and Liberals in the next election, who then removed labor issues from the ambit of the judiciary in the Trade Disputes Act of 1906. "I feel that this Bill is most unjust," for it was not only "contrary to the spirit of English liberty," despaired Halsbury, but it also legalized "tyranny."[83]

Thus judicial self-restraint prevailed. The government's regulation of railroad rates or labor relations represented acts of Parliament binding upon the courts. Similarly, Parliament's consistent refusal to interfere with most private restrictive practices of business, symbolized by the British preference of Free Trade over tariff protectionism, reflected a tacit legislative policy which also controlled the judiciary. Within these limits judges exercised a circumscribed degree of "judicial legislation" like that found in *Nordenfelt* and the labor decisions. Yet, as Halsbury learned, such activism failed when it did not follow the broader public consensus favoring self-regulation. More fundamentally, in cases involving restrictive business agreements not governed directly by Parliament, the courts were relatively free to reshape the law as long as it sustained the continued dominance of family capitalism. Where the social and political confrontation inherent in the labor issue engendered conflict, however, the legislature determined the outcome.[84]

American judicial supremacy facilitated a broader acceptance of the judge's instrumentalist role as a lawmaker, particularly when the enforcement of moral imperatives inherent in republican values was at issue. These values supported the conviction that small business was important not only for economic reasons, but also because upon its independence and self-sufficiency free government itself depended. Grappling with these values, judges attempted to satisfy the American people's ambivalent desire to preserve small business without destroying the benefits associated with giant corporations.[85]

Ironically, the struggle to reconcile big and small business facilitated the defeat of organized labor. State courts supporting workers appealed to "natural" economic laws and moral values. "While labor and capital are both entitled to the protection of the law," declared an Oklahoma court, "it is not true that the abstract rights of capital are equal to those of labor, and that they both stand upon an equal footing before the law." Indeed, according to "good morals" labor was "natural; capital is artificial. Labor was made by God; capital is made by man. Labor is not only blood and bone, but it also has a mind and a soul, and is animated by sympathy, hope, and love; capital is inanimate, soulless matter."[86] Such notions were sufficiently widespread after the turn of the century that both Roosevelt and Wilson supported policies sympathetic to labor. The Supreme Court's unanimous resort to judicial activism in the labor injunction cases and its subsequent circumvention of the Clayton Act, however, favored the interests of small businessmen and the National Association of Manufacturers. The moralistic assumptions of self-sufficiency, independence, and individual accountability implicit in democracy's reliance upon small business, as well as the corporation's private rights, thus prevailed over the unions' right to unite and strike.[87]

And yet the state courts' attack on the formal trust device was also consistent with republican values. State prosecutions, such as California's defeat of the sugar trust, started from the principle that the state granted a corporate entity the right to operate within its borders "not for the sole benefit of the corporation or its stockholders, but in a measure for that of the public as well." Inherent in the public welfare were the benefits consumers and those seeking entry into the business system gained from competition. The "promotion of trade necessarily denotes the encouragement of rivalry in the business – competition on equal terms is conceded to be the life of trade, and to invite and to promote that competition is the established policy of our laws." Similarly, "all recorded human experience" showed that improved products were the "usual and natural result of competition – of rivalry in the business" whereas the "known tendency of monopoly is to lower the standard of excellence... to impose upon the consumer – upon the public – a deteriorated article and at an increased price." Thus, the "axiom" upon which state laws rested and the courts "habitually... proceeded" was: as "competition tends to create trade, so monopoly tends to destroy it."[88]

Meanwhile, the states' enactment of laws promoting holding companies and mergers not only encouraged passage of the Sherman Act, but also imposed upon the federal judiciary hard choices. It could exercise restraint and construe the antitrust law narrowly, leaving the states primarily responsible for regulating internal corporate affairs associated with production within a single state. Or federal courts could interpret the law broadly to include the extensive market power and practices resulting from the formation of giant, managerially centralized corporations. Initially, the federal judiciary attempted to resolve this dilemma within the framework of judicial self-restraint. In most of the early cases arising in the lower federal courts, judges followed a restricted construction of the Sherman Act which was similar to the Judicial Committee's narrow interpretation of the Australian antitrust statute. The Supreme Court established a uniform if ambivalent standard in the *Sugar Trust* and *Trans-Missouri Freight Association* decisions.[89]

The Court's self-restraint raised questions about maintaining republican values. The successful state prosecution of the trusts suggested that state officials could defend the interests of small businessmen and consumers under the *Knight* principle. Only Harlan, the lone dissenter from that rule, argued that since corporate bigness often prevented free competition within interstate commerce a broader interpretation of the Sherman Act was necessary. Peckham attempted to reconcile *Knight* and Harlan's concerns through a literal reading of the antitrust law. In order to protect the welfare of small business and consumers, Peckham stressed the language of the statute outlawing *every* combination or restrictive practice. Such a construction went beyond the common law which, of course, permitted many anticompetitive agreements. The Court's application of literalism to cartels operating in interstate trade made sense because national commerce was clearly the federal government's responsibility. In other cases, however, Peckham obscured the scope of his rule by declaring that certain anticompetitive practices, particularly those of merchants and other middlemen which only incidentally affected interstate commerce, were lawful.[90]

By 1897 state and federal decisions and a changing investment picture converged to produce the great merger wave. The resulting proliferation of large, managerially centralized corporations created pressure for a more flexible interpretation of the Sherman Act. Sustaining the result in Taft's *Addyston* opinion, Peckham attempted to meet this challenge but failed. The dissents of Harlan and White suggested other interpretations which nonetheless also required greater activism. Harlan favored reading into the antitrust law a standard requiring the preservation of competition, whereas White argued for the incorporation of a rule of reason. Although Harlan got his way in the *Northern Securities* decision, the Court's 5-4 split, combined with the ever-increasing politicization of the trust issue, made the victory transitory.[91]

Finally, after years of unswerving insistence, in 1911 White's version of reasonableness became the dominant rule governing the application of the Sherman Act. Harlan concurred in the Court's order breaking up Standard Oil and American Tobacco, but rejected the resort to the rule of reason as "the usurpation by the judicial branch of the Government of the functions of the legislative department." He dissented from that part of White's opinion which asserted that the Court possessed the "authority... to insert words in the Anti-trust Act which Congress did not put there, and which, being inserted, Congress is made to declare, as part of the public policy of the country, what it has not chosen to declare."[92]

Indeed, the rule's elasticity was soon apparent. When the Justice Department prosecuted cartel practices the Court usually upheld the government.[93] Meanwhile, using consent decrees, the Justice Department negotiated agreements sanctioning mergers and even monopolies based primarily on superior technological innovation or organizational efficiency. As a result, between 1911 and the war most large corporations replaced the holding company with mergers resulting in even greater managerial centralization.[94]

The idiosyncratic character of White's rule of reason suggested how much it was a triumph of activism. White rejected not only the explicit self-restraint inherent in the *Sugar Trust* precedent but also the literalist approach of Peckham. Like Harlan, he found in the Sherman Act an implied meaning. It was not a preference for a specific policy of competition, however, as much as a flexible standard enabling the Court to distinguish legitimate from illegitimate forms of combination. Also, although White attempted to reconcile his doctrine to the British principle of reasonableness, he significantly transformed it. Macnaghten's *Nordenfelt* opinion employed the criterion of the public interest primarily to determine when it was appropriate not only to allow but also to enforce an anticompetitive agreement. The core concern of White's rule of reason was, however, whether a blend of economic and moral considerations demonstrated an unlawful intent. The emphasis upon the factors proving intent gave judges considerable discretion to support or oppose particular social or economic interests. More particularly, the British principle of reasonableness restricted "judicial lawmaking" within a narrow compass, whereas the American rule expanded that authority to the maximum.[95]

The state of legal theory also suggested the originality of White's rule of reason. The utilitarian philosophical assumptions dominating British jurisprudence were those of Jeremy Bentham and John Austin. Consistent with the belief in Parliamentary sovereignty, their theories of positivism held that only acts directly or indirectly supported by the legislature were valid. Courts, of course, interpreted and applied whatever rules the legislature passed or sanctioned, and if its intent was evidenced solely by the common law they must adhere strictly to precedent. Positivism further restricted the judge's discretion by distinguishing sharply between law and morality, leaving the formulation of rules governing the latter solely to the legislature. In cases involving restrictive business agreements, the triumph of positivism thus reflected the judiciary's acceptance of self-restraint.[96] More particularly it justified the judges' refusal to consider the questions of fairness arising in the *Mogul* case, and explained the comparatively narrow reach of the reasonableness principle established in *Nordenfelt*.[97]

In America, despite the influence of Holmes, positivism did not diminish the exercise of judicial activism. For Holmes, it was "plain from the slightest consideration of practical affairs, or the most superficial reading of industrial history, that free competition means combination, and that the organization of the world, now going on so fast, means an ever increasing might and scope of combination." He also insisted upon the separation of law and morals, arguing that "sympathy, prudence, and all the social and moral qualities," were relatively insignificant to the "struggle for life," and this was "as true in legislation as in any form of corporate action."[98] Unlike the British, however, Americans wanted antitrust laws which left judges free to resist the inevitability of combination and sanctioned the formulation of moral prescriptions. Thus, although Holmes considered the Sherman Act a "foolish law," the positivist's regard for legislative action led him to generally support it, for "if my fellow citizens want to go to Hell I will help them. It's my job."[99] Yet, as the Court struggled to protect the "interest of the consumers and the public," he admitted finding himself "in a minority as to the larger issues."[100]

White thus rejected the narrower self-restraint Holmes followed to formulate an implied construction of the Sherman Act. Holmes himself observed how his philosophical approach differed from that of the Chief Justice, who was "always thinking about what will be the practical effect of the decision (which, of course, is the ultimate justification of condemnation of the principle adopted). I think of its relation to the theory and philosophy of law."[101]

The blending of moral and economic elements in the rule of reason was consistent with White's own business experience. From the early decisions in which he battled Peckham and Harlan in dissent to the victories of 1911 and beyond, he owned a sugar plantation in Louisiana. The technology of sugar production required organizational economies achieved through stock transactions which White apparently believed were not unlike those employed in the mergers of large industrial corporations. Yet he viewed these market relations through the lens of moral accountability. "Of course I ought to be very careful and not for any consideration in the world do anything which could seem to violate an agreement..." he wrote his lawyer in New Orleans. "Certainly, even if... [it] does not amount to any legal promise, if it implies a moral obligation, I ought to live up to the moral view wholly without reference to any narrow question of a legal contract having been made." Above all, he abhorred and carefully avoided the potential for the "fathomless depths of the lying capacity" present in such American agreements.[102]

Ultimately, White's triumph reflected the greater role American judges played in the shaping of business structure. Although *Nordenfelt* was a modest reformulation of the common law, British judges applied it primarily to adapt the established business order to changing times within the framework of positivism and self-restraint. The chief beneficiaries of this limited activism were family firms. White's rule, however, was the culmination of a struggle implicit in republican values to protect the small-business system while sustaining the private rights which made big business possible, and yet also to prevent morally objectionable behavior threatening either. From the 1880s on, achieving these seemingly contradictory goals proved to be beyond the capacity of state or federal elected officials, creating increased pressure for action by the judiciary. The Supreme Court's amalgamation of moral and economic imperatives in the rule of reason was thus the consummation of America's ambivalent desire to enjoy the benefits of both big and small enterprise.

THE COMPARATIVE ROLE OF LAWYERS WITHIN THE
BUSINESS ORDER

The judiciary's adherence to activism or restraint significantly shaped the lawyer's role in business affairs. The degree to which businessmen relied on lawyers depended on the significance of courts within the economic order, which in turn reflected a wider culture of cooperation or conflict. British lawyers, like the judiciary itself, handled relatively little litigation involving the restrictive trade practices of business. Consistent with the judge's leading role in the nation's economy, however, American lawyers were prominent in the struggle between big and small business.

The relative influence of each country's judiciary in business cases differed markedly. Despite the influence of several London solicitor firms in the revision of Britain's company law, from the mid-nineteenth century on "complacency" and "growing irrelevance" generally characterized the whole British judicial system.[103] Businessmen usually relied on commercial arbitration which, according to a Parliamentary Report, resulted in "prompt settlement" and the perpetuation of "friendly commercial relations." Whereas resort to the courts "inflicts on the suitor a long-pending, worrying law-suit, the solicitors on either side pleading in their clients' interests every technical point, and thus engendering a bitterness which destroys all future confidence, and puts an end to further mercantile dealings."[104]

Although American corporate leaders despised litigation as much as their British counterparts, they did not have the luxury of avoiding it. Thus "privately," for their "own use" business leaders often demanded of Republican presidential candidates a "prompt and careful answer," on "this question of the rights of corporations." Railroad executive Charles Elliot Perkins was more explicit but no less typical in 1894: "There are so many jackasses about nowadays who think property has no rights, that the filling of the Supreme Court vacancies is the most important function of the presidential office."[105] During the Senate hearings of 1911–1912, US Steel's Chairman of the Board, Elbert H. Gary, was just as forthright. "I think the salvation of the country really is in the courts," he said. As long as judges remained "independent of the people ... I do not think we will have any trouble from the courts. That should be the place to which everyone might look for final satisfaction." Gary turned to the courts because "one of the great disturbers and objections to the conditions and proceedings of this country is the frequent elections."[106]

The consequences of British judges' limited role were just as clear. Lord Justice Thomas Edward Scrutton observed that absolute impartiality was "rather difficult to attain in any system. I am not speaking of conscious partiality; but the habits you are trained in, the people with whom you mix, lead to your having a certain class of ideas of such a nature, that, when you have to deal with other ideas, you do not give as sound and accurate judgments as you wish. This is one of the great difficulties at present with Labour." According to Scrutton, "Labour says: 'Where are your impartial judges? They all move in the same circle as employers, and they are all educated and nursed in the same ideas as the employers. How can a labor man or a trade unionist get impartial justice?' It is very difficult sometimes to be sure that you have put yourself in a thoroughly impartial position between two disputants, one of your own class and one not of your class."[107] Even so, in every restrictive trade decision from 1892 to 1914 the Lords upheld some form of anticompetitive business practice without dissent.[108]

In the Supreme Court's business antitrust cases, however, dissents were common place. Peckham, Harlan, White, and Holmes maintained their own distinctive interpretations of the Sherman Act. In addition, private suits and state prosecutions were still another source of division.[109] Many commentators shared the view of the Oklahoma trial judges who exclaimed that "corporations and monopolies are active and tireless in their efforts to secure control of the appellate courts of this country and thereby by judicial construction defeat the will of the people as expressed in legislation." The "evil" had become "so open and notorious that many good people have almost lost hope and have largely ceased to have confidence in the fairness, impartiality, and integrity of the courts where corporations, trusts, and monopolies are concerned."[110]

Political pressures on the selection of British judges did not diminish the judiciary's favorable disposition in business cases. The Lord Chancellor made the life-tenure appointments for the trial and appellate courts below the House of Lords. The Chancellor also influenced the final appeals process because determination of which members of the House of Lords formed the panel hearing a particular case was his choice. Since the Lord Chancellor served at the behest of the Prime Minister the shifting fortunes of political parties influenced the system. It was, therefore, Lord Salisbury wrote Chancellor Halsbury during the 1890s, the "unwritten law of our party system... that party claims should always weigh very heavily in the disposal of the highest legal appointments. In dealing with them you cannot ignore the party system... It would be a breach of the tacit convention on which politicians and lawyers have worked the British Constitution together for the last 200 years."[111] Yet despite the rise and fall of Tory, Liberal, and coalition governments, the British judiciary did not challenge the Free Trade consensus favoring the self-regulating, restrictive practices of business.[112]

In America, by contrast, the influence of politics upon the courts encouraged conflict. Undoubtedly, as the Oklahoma trial judges suggested, state-elected judges were more supportive of the popular suspicion of giant corporations than were their non-elected (particularly federal) counterparts. Public pressures also shaped the state court's defeat of the formal trust device and consistent attack upon cartel practices. As business leaders from Perkins to Gary suggested, however, the federal judiciary's constitutional insulation from direct partisan interests established an independence British and most state judges lacked. Political considerations might play a major role when a federal judge was appointed. But American Presidents learned repeatedly that once a nominee for the federal bench took his seat, the bonds of political connection loosened.[113] Thus, amidst the controversy over the initial interpretation of the Sherman Act during the mid-1890s, Grover Cleveland, whose rhetoric at least was critical of big business, appointed two Justices to the Court. The first was White and the second Peckham, the proponents of the opposing literalist and rule-of-reason constructions of the antitrust law.[114] Roosevelt's appointment of Holmes was also unpredictable: in the *Northern Securities* case the Justice voted against an antitrust position the president fervently supported.[115]

In Britain the limited role of courts in business cases paralleled that of lawyers. The businessman's commitment to arbitration was part of broader self-regulating market relations in which accountants were more important than lawyers. One observer noted, the accountant was "well placed to become the person to whom the businessman first turned to discuss his day-to-day affairs... instead of mastering the intricacies of balance sheets... the average solicitor left accountants to learn the law relating to companies." The increased cost associated with the rigid division between solicitors, who dealt directly with clients, and barristers who were primarily responsible for arguing cases in court, further diminished the reliance on the legal profession. It was, *The Times* reported, "almost a mockery to see the huge framework of our legal procedure – at least two, sometimes three counsel drawing heavy fees, besides the solicitor who had charge of the case – creaking and groaning under the prodigious task of determining whether a man is entitled to £50 or £100 for the injury he has suffered from some breach of contract."[116]

The admission process governing the legal profession reinforced such restrictions. The solicitors' qualifying examination did not even cover the law of private companies.[117] The limited success of involving universities in the process of certification kept the focus of law-teaching narrow. A Royal Commission reported that the "most scientific study" of law which a "university can provide will... alone fit a man to deal with intellectual freedom, and from a wide point of view, with the questions he will have to answer... in his professional practice." Moreover, it would "produce lawyers whose advice and assistance will be a reliable guide to the legislature in framing statutes in organic connexion with the past and in harmony with the social developments of the national life." James Bryce observed, however, that the authorities controlling admission to "both branches of the profession in London," displayed a "short-sighted" and "perverse unwillingness" to recognize university legal training as relevant to the practice of law. Thus the "advocacy of the country, instead of being spread over a large body of fairly accomplished men, is concentrated in the nucleus of a few of excessive skill. The performers are few and the fees for their performance can be demanded, consequently, without limit, and under conditions one-sided and precarious."[118]

These institutional and cultural factors influenced the consensus favoring judicial restraint toward restrictive business practices. As a result, British lawyers no less than judges performed a comparatively passive role in the development of self-regulating market relations among the family firms which exercised greater control throughout the economy. Little wonder that Sir Frederick Pollock displayed some surprise when the Supreme Court rejected the British support for price-fixing agreements Holmes advocated in the *Dr. Miles* case. "Either your dissenting opinion in the *Miles*... case is right or much of our recent authority here is wrong," he wrote Holmes. Yet Pollock was sufficiently confident in the wisdom of the British decisions that he felt "the majority of your Honorable Court are being led into an archaic reaction by their anti-monopolist zeal."[119]

The American judiciary's primacy gave lawyers a greater role than their British counterparts in dealing with restrictive practices. "As between the legislative and judicial organs of a society," wrote Harvard law professor John C. Gray, "it is the judicial which has the last say as to what is and what is not law in a community."[120] And concerning the interpretation of the Sherman Act, observed a leading lawyer in 1910, the Court's "difference of opinion shows clearly that... [the law] standing by itself has no precise and easily ascertained meaning. Nearly all of the cases on the statute might have been decided the other way without furnishing clear ground for criticism. Manifestly the interpretation of the Act has been peculiarly a case of judicial legislation."[121] About the same time, James C. McReynolds, then in private practice but soon to be appointed US Attorney General and ultimately Supreme Court Justice, was more direct. "Which set of facts will prevail with the Court, in the present state of the decisions, no one can tell with certainty – much depends on the general economic views entertained by the Judges."[122]

The uncertainty business faced because of changes in the state and federal antitrust law increased the need for lawyers. In 1893, following the strengthening of state laws which facilitated successful prosecutions of the trusts, the passage of the New Jersey holding-company law and the Sherman Act, and the lower federal courts' narrow construction of the latter, S. C. T. Dodd expressed exasperation. Dodd had created the Standard Oil trust device because cartel agreements were generally not enforceable in state courts. Now the legal remedy he had fashioned to provide improved organizational efficiency was wrecked. The *Mogul* decision, "settled the law of England," he said. "In this country, nothing is settled. The law is a chaos of contradiction and confusion and recent statutes have succeeded in making confusion worse confounded."[123]

Shortly before White announced the rule of reason, Raymond described the course of change from the mid-1890s to 1910. Until the Court for the first time dissolved a tight corporate structure (a holding company) in the *Northern Securities* decision, he said, the "generally accepted belief among lawyers [was] that... a combination in the form of a corporation was valid under the [Sherman] Act. This belief rested on the well-known principle of general law that a corporation is an entity. The process of looking through the corporate form and dealing with what that form shelters is of recent growth." Moreover, except for the *Knight* case which, after all, gave a narrow construction to the Act, "every case" before 1903 dealt with a "loose combination." As a result of this preoccupation with cartel arrangements, there was "no question as to what actually occurred. Many, if not most of the great corporate combinations in the country were formed between the time of the decision in the Knight case and that in the Northern Securities case. Combination by [cartel] agreement ceased. Combination by fusion took its place." But it became readily apparent that public opinion was "equally antagonistic" to loose cartels and tight corporate combinations. On the eve of the *Standard Oil* decision Raymond concluded, "business and law have got into what it is little exaggeration to call an *impasse*."[124]

Despite the relief White's rule of reason brought the business community, corporate lawyers readily admitted that uncertainty remained. As Congress grappled with legislation which eventually passed as the Clayton Act, the leading Wall Street corporate counsel, Francis Lynde Stetson, told a congressional committee, "Nothing ever works out all right in human affairs. I think it would have worked out as well without the [Sherman] law as with it. The law never does anything concretely ... it never provides anything except a punishment." Nevertheless, in order to have a clear rule for counseling clients, Stetson acknowledged, "If I could not get anything else, I would rather take ... [the most radical, proposed] bill just as it stands. I would know then what I could advise."[125]

The interaction between changing law and business structure thus created a new market for legal services. The search for legally safe and economically efficient organizational forms spawned a few prominent Wall Street law firms such as Sullivan & Cromwell.[126] During the initial years following the founding of the firm in 1879, Algernon Sydney Sullivan and his younger partner William Nelson Cromwell, disagreed over whether states should outlaw corporations. Sullivan opposed the corporation as a "dangerous contrivance." When his partner died, however, Cromwell established corporate reorganization as the law firm's chief business. In the late 1880s, Sullivan & Cromwell adopted Dodd's trust device to create the cotton and linseed oil trusts. Faced with state prosecutions, James B. Dill, a lawyer associated with Sullivan & Cromwell, then lobbied New Jersey's legislature to enact the holding company law in order to create a way of escape for their threatened corporate investors and managers.[127]

After the Court's *Knight* and *TransMissouri Freight* decisions, Sullivan & Cromwell handled many of the major mergers during the great merger wave. Concerning the annual report of one such venture in 1899, Cromwell wrote, it "betrayed no secret of our business, nor anything that would give a competitor advantage; but we stated significant facts upon which intelligent investors desired information and with the consequence that in the first year of our existence ... the securities [were] daily growing in confidence without any fictitious methods." Meanwhile, although Cromwell advised his clients against the Northern Securities combination, they went ahead anyway and lost. The defeat did not, however, retard the law firm's long-term role in merger issues.[128]

Yet the fame and power of such Wall Street firms obscured another market for the antitrust lawyer's expertise. By the late 1880s lawyers representing smaller, unincorporated enterprise had good reason to be concerned about the rise of big business.[129] Not only did it threaten the clients upon whom they depended, but the attorney serving corporations possessed financial resources which the lawyer representing small businessmen lacked. The critics of the corporate lawyers appealed to the republican values of individual responsibility, self-denial, and moral accountability. As Philadelphia lawyer Daniel Dougherty exclaimed in 1888, the traditional regard for "industry, patience, and perseverance" was giving way to the lust for "gold and silver." He blamed the "Trusts," forming in "all lines of business," and the lawyers whose technique and skill facilitated their development. "If the bar yields to this craze for gold, individual character will be lost in corporate enterprise and the bright escutcheon give place to the flaming sign-board. Degrade the bar to a business, and at least some of its members will sink to the lowest depths."[130]

Lawyer critics of the big corporations also linked the trusts to social disorder which plagued the late nineteenth century. Since the Revolution, Americans had regarded the bar as a bastion of social order. This image diminished when the public perceived big corporations as undermining the public interest and responsible government which defended it. Indeed, it seemed as if "astute practitioners" had gained "advantage over their more scrupulous brethren ... enabling designing men to make contracts which ... [were] understood in one sense and interpreted in another."[131]

Another lawyer feared that the trusts were destroying the legal profession as a bulwark against urban and agrarian unrest. "Anarchy" was "openly avowed, even under oath in the courts of justice. Fiends ready to apply the torch and throw the bomb, who laugh at wholesale murder, who would swim in gore, who abhor religion and repudiate God..." were gathering, he said, "in the thousands in great cities cursing the law and vowing vengeance on its officers." For now, he concluded, this nightmare was "but a dark speck [which] may e'er long cover our skies and drench the land in blood." But with a "pure judiciary and bar inspired by honor, integrity, and independence, this apprehended horror...will pass, and our republic will outride every gale, and bear its countless blessings to distant generations."[132]

The lawyer who best represented the legal profession's antitrust position was Brandeis. His famous advocacy of small enterprise and denunciation of the "curse of bigness" was consistent with the interests of the clients his Boston law office represented. Most of this clientele were long-established merchants or medium-size manufacturers in the boot and shoe or paper industries, employing usually no more than seventy-five wage earners. Brandeis had no business from Massachusett's dominant industry, textiles, whose average factory employed over three hundred workers. The merchants and modest-scale manufacturers, of course, were those most threatened by the financial and structural reorganization resulting in big corporations.[133] Brandeis distrusted the investment methods Wall Street lawyers pioneered to establish the corporate giants. "I feel very sure that *unser eins* [people like us] ought not to buy and sell stock," he wrote his brother. "Prices of stock[s] are made. – They don't grow and their fluctuations are not due to natural causes."[134] Similar concerns explained Brandeis's defense of the right of small businessmen to engage in price fixing and other cartel practices. As noted already, in Britain the law's sanction of such agreements facilitated the survival of family firms and reduced the incentive to establish managerially centralized, corporate enterprise.[135]

Ironically, the state and federal prosecution of cartel practices Brandeis opposed often aided the interests of small business. The steady rise in successful private antitrust suits from 1890 on fostered competition by facilitating the entry of new firms into the business order. Moreover, in these suits although many of the litigants were modest-size enterprises as in the *Dr. Miles* case, in other cases one of the parties was a corporation which lost. This litigation, including the opportunity to win treble damages, thus constituted an important market for the lawyer's antitrust expertise.[136] The federal government often triumphed as a result of the judiciary's general hostility toward cartel arrangements. From *Sugar Trust* to the War the Court never accepted the Brandeisian view that corporate bigness was per se unlawful. Instead, the focus was always on explicit price-fixing behavior, rebates, or other actions which were relatively easy to prove by the complaints of aggrieved parties. Federal lawyers' primary preoccupation with cartel prosecutions – which resulted in victories about 80 percent of the time – was not, therefore, surprising.[137]

The comparative significance of lawyers in each nation's business order suggested the judiciary's differing function. The reliance of British enterprise on accountants was consistent with both the limited use of adversarial methods for resolving commercial controversies and the courts' acceptance of self-restraint. More broadly, the narrow demand for legal expertise and the courts' relative passivity, suggested that family firms felt secure enough amid economic change to depend upon cooperation and self-regulating restrictive, loose combinations. The British reasonableness standard represented, then, the law accommodating market relations rather than market relations accommodating the law. In America, however, the greater independence of the judiciary gave judges and the legal profession a primary role in the struggle between small business and large corporate enterprise. Dodd and Brandeis stood for the divergent market for legal services which emerged from the new economic order. Sullivan & Cromwell's practice, moreover, revealed how the shift from the trust to managerially centralized corporations *followed* new state and federal statutes and court decisions. At the same time, the activities of Brandeis and others encouraged the economic opportunity of small business. Thus British courts and lawyers influenced business structure primarily through passivity, whereas the American legal establishment significantly shaped the nation's acceptance of the moral distinction between good and bad trusts.

CHAPTER 5

The impact of World War I, 1914–1921

The war changed attitudes and policies toward combinations and restrictive practices. During the period of hostilities, each nation's governmental authorities approved cooperative and restraining agreements within the business order, a policy which for different reasons the two labor movements also supported. Even so, during the post-war reconstruction era of 1919–1921 neither British law nor the short-lived Profiteering Acts represented more than a limited public or official concern for the welfare of small business, despite the unprecedented growth of monopoly. After the Armistice, by contrast, various American interests debated whether the continuation of cooperation and the antitrust laws were reconcilable. Meanwhile, neoclassical economic thought and a popular if qualified faith in rationalization eroded the British Free Trade consensus, sustaining a modest expansion of the state's supervisory role. And yet the ambiguous experience of the Standing Committee on Trusts suggested a need for a stronger policy. In America the agreement of Louis D. Brandeis and Herbert Hoover on the usefulness of trade associations indicated that the ascendancy of neoclassical economic thought had not altogether supplanted republican values. As a result, the federal government's and the Supreme Court's application of the rule of reason permitted considerable ambivalence in the enforcement of antitrust.

WAR-TIME COOPERATION, PRESSURE GROUPS, AND GOVERNMENTAL POLICY

Although America entered the war nearly three years after Britain, each nation's war effort was similar. Mobilization required an unprecedented level of government–business collaboration, stimulating, often for the first time, trade organizations for the allocation of raw materials, cooperative research projects, and control of prices and output. Military experiences compelled the national authorities to administer directly such public utilities as railroads and shipping. Public officials also directly or indirectly operated coal and other traditionally competitive industries on a "national" basis. By 1921 the British expression "back to 1914" and the American call for a return to "normalcy" epitomized the popular yearning sustaining the end of government control. The cumulative organizational experience of the war, however, had a lasting impact on each country's interest groups and policymakers.[1]

Even so British and American policy toward combination partially converged. By 1917, *The Economist* wrote, the Board of Trade had responded to war-time necessities and interest-group pressures to the point that the promotion of trade combinations constituted a "considered policy." Yet after the Armistice popular anxiety over rising prices compelled the government's first consideration of Trade and Monopolies legislation, and the enactment of the first significant industry-wide effort to police restrictive practices in the Profiteering Acts of 1919-1920. Generally, however, the British government merely modified its Free Trade policy of nonintervention, enlarging its supervisory role in order to publicize abuses.[2] Prior to the United States joining the Allied side American pressure groups urged increased forms of cooperation and combination, and correspondingly the relaxation of antitrust enforcement. During the brief period of hostilities they won. But in the period of post-war reconstruction the traditional pattern of antitrust conflict revived, though it was modified by controversy over trade associations.[3]

The comparative role of lawyers and the courts suggested the contrasting nature of change. By the end of the war the British Report of the Committee on Trusts noted that those overseeing the day-to-day operation of restrictive business practices were accountants. In the same report a lawyer judged that it "would be inept" to rely upon the bar, bench, and "still less a jury" to resolve the "complicated economic problems" often raised by combinations. In the United States, however, whether they liked it or not both the supporters and opponents of big business relied primarily upon lawyers. Wall Street firms provided counsel for large corporations, while Louis D. Brandeis represented another side of the American bar defending the interests of small business. Ironically, during the post-war reconstruction members of both groups of lawyers assisted in developing the trade association. It was "not without importance," stated the attorney in a leading case, that the trade association had "become an established feature of American industrial organization, on the strength and advice of counsel that the practice is legal."[4]

In Britain the course of business combination during the war and reconstruction was uneven. Trade associations proliferated, particularly in the distribution sector and older heavy industries such as iron and steel. By 1919 there were over 500 local or national associations operating throughout British industry, directly or indirectly controlling output and prices.[5] In many cases, moreover, a single dominant firm represented Britain in an international cartel. Thus, increasingly, one or two large firms occupied near or virtual monopoly within a respective market, while smaller enterprises maintained themselves through horizontal and vertical price agreements.[6]

Because of the war governmental supervision of business restrictive practices and combinations modestly increased. The pre-war banking sector underwent extensive amalgamation, facilitating the centralizing role of the Bank of England. In cooperation with City bankers, moreover, the government provided financial backing for a merger between "two great consolidations" controlling the British dye industry, creating British Dyes Limited. But such cases of direct government action were exceptional.[7] Meanwhile, in 1920, the government established an interdepartmental Advisory Committee on Bank Amalgamations to report to the Treasury and the Board of Trade on any proposed consolidation scheme, including any arrangement for control by purchase of shares or otherwise. The committee had no statutory powers, but British banks routinely submitted their intended mergers. It permitted only a very few mergers in 1918–1919, but essentially froze the British Banking Sector into the "big five" for the next fifty years.[8]

Another official agency emerging from the reconstruction period oversaw the relationship between imports and employment. A section of the Safeguarding of Industries Act of 1921 empowered the Board of Trade to refer to a committee of enquiry for any complaint regarding the price of imported goods (other than food or drink) which might unfavorably affect employment. The committee was to determine whether the imports were sold at a price below the cost of production, or at prices which, because of currency depreciation,

were below the price British firms could profitably manufacture
similar products. The committee's enquiries enabled the Board of
Trade to periodically report whether British manufacturers were
competing "with reasonable efficiency and economy." The committee consisted of five persons selected by the Board of Trade's
President from a permanent panel he also appointed primarily
composed of individuals with "commercial and industrial experience." Throughout the interwar years the Board published a few
reports but on the whole the process proved ineffective.[9]

Coinciding with the enlarged governmental supervision of
combinations and restrictive practices were improved methods of
business lobbying. During the war wealthy owners of big firms
dubbed "monopoly capitalists" purchased London newspapers to
influence policymakers.[10] "A newspaper in London is a source of
political power," wrote a coal company owner in 1914, "and... I
prefer that sort of hobby to the ownership of a yacht... my object
being to influence the opinions not so much of the man-in-the-street
but those of Parliament and Clubland."[11] A still more focused body
was the Federation of British Industries (FBI) formed in 1916.
Through letter-writing campaigns, organized delegations visiting
top officials, newspaper stories, and more informal personal contacts
the FBI, often in conjunction with the efforts of individual firms or
industries, pressured public officials.[12] Without "industrial organization" exclaimed a proponent of unified effort in 1914, "we cannot
successfully compete with American and German industries, which
owing to their superior [organizational] method, work en masse. We
are far too individualistic as a rule. We have to combine to hold our
own."[13]

Nevertheless, between big and small business there were tensions.
During the war large "monopoly capitalists" espoused replacing the
"traditional British individualism" of family capitalism with
"collectivism and regimentation" which they believed had given
Germany and America a competitive advantage. "[I]ndividualism
stands for opportunism and national aimlessness," said one proponent of rationalization in 1918. "Just as Germany is the home of
collectivism, so Great Britain is the home of individualism and that
is why in the past Germany has a [cooperative or centralizing
organizational] policy and we have had none."[14]

The "rationalization" rhetoric used by large firms aroused
ambivalent anxieties regarding the status of small enterprise.

"Combination holds great possibilities of economical and efficient production and of improved distribution at lower cost," stated the government's Report of the Committee on Trusts in 1919, "but it does not invariably or necessarily ensure their attainment." Where the "passing of independent firms under unified... control... grows beyond the compass of one man's personal detailed direction[,] 'system' must replace that direction, and system can easily degenerate into bureaucracy and red tape." In addition, "behind the shelter of monopoly a comfortable somnolence may descend upon the whole concern; the fear of change is a well-known characteristic of large administrations, and the large unit may become stagnant or even reactionary." The Report also noted, however, that "Free competition... [permitted the survival of] the ill-endowed and... ill-placed small man, cling[ing] tenaciously to life... on the brink of ruin year after year, a source of weakness and danger to the whole industry and of expense and waste to the community at large." For many industries it was "quicker and cheaper to pension him off than to starve him out." Even so the "get-along" ethos which influenced the pre-war triumph of business self-regulation fostered adamant opposition to American-style antitrust.[15]

During the war era the greater institutionalization of organized labor further influenced the combination and rationalization movements. The pre-war Labour Party was a vocal but comparatively minor pressure group; a majority of workers were not even enfranchised until the war. Between 1914 and 1920, however, despite periodic worker unrest and election defeats, Labour won not only major social welfare gains but also passage of legislation requiring the Ministry of Labour to inquire into and arbitrate worker disputes.[16] During the pre-war years, supporters of organized labor had resisted the American approach to antitrust in part because the government (as was the case in the United States) could turn such authority against unions.[17] At the very time Labour confronted the Industrial Control Act of 1919 its representatives influenced the Report of the Committee on Trusts, the recommendations of which Parliament followed the same year in passing the first Profiteering Act. Pro-Labour representatives also helped to guide the investigations of the Standing Committee on Trusts, the investigatory body within the Board of Trade created under the new law.[18]

Labour's support of the Profiteering Acts coincided with the views of radical and neoclassical economists. Each favored nationalization under exceptional circumstances and the establishment of a commission possessing wide governmental control over prices. Labour nonetheless also agreed with Marshall and the popular press that, generally, publicity was the best guarantee against business abuse. Thus in their commitment to a modest governmental role and emphasis upon the regulation of abuse, both Labour and the defenders of business opposed American-type antitrust.[19]

American business leaders began discussing similar issues not long after hostilities in Europe erupted. Engineer-entrepreneur Herbert Hoover, Wall Street speculator Barnard Baruch, Hudson Motor Company executive Howard Coffin, and machine-tool manufacturer Edward Hurley were active in preparedness efforts before America entered the war. They emphasized how the economic exigencies of war and the eventual peace required greater cooperation within the business order and between business and government.[20] "Nowhere is the cooperation among businessmen, and between them and government, more essential than in the development of our foreign trade," Hurley said in a speech before the American Iron and Steel Institute in 1916. "The success of our European competitors is evidence enough of this."[21] These leaders also linked the economic benefits of cooperation to a broader concern for general organizational structures and legal forms, suggesting, despite antitrust laws, that the government tolerate or in some cases even promote loose and tight combinations.[22]

Similarly, before America formally entered the war, various pressure groups advocated the adoption of cartel-like practices. Small business and older industries such as textiles, whose fundamental structure inhibited achieving scale economies through managerial centralization, advocated looser arrangements particularly "open pricing" agreements. Coinciding with efforts to eliminate price competition was a move toward trade associations which permitted greater efficiency without threatening survival of individual firms. Although supporters of trade associations did not agree on the scope and limits of price agreements, there was general accord that government might provide a useful function.[23] Louis Brandeis urged the FTC to direct more of its limited resources toward developing cost-accounting systems for small business. Enhanced control of price and marketing factors would reduce the risk of small business failure. Hurley, one of the first commissioners Woodrow Wilson appointed to the new FTC in 1915, favored Brandeis's idea, in part because improved accounting methods facilitated the sort of cooperation he considered essential to America's possible involvement in hostilities.[24]

During the initial proceedings of the Federal Trade Commission the chief lobbyist for the small and older industries was Brandeis. He contended that the "real way to mend ... terrible competition" was "to play the game with the cards right up on the table." By which he meant that the Commission would become a "central fact-gathering bureau" for modest-sized firms and thereby "erect a great bulwark against the trusts" by providing "the small businessman what is procurable only by the great industrial concerns through their research laboratories and bureaus of information." Ever the attorney, Brandeis denied that the FTC should provide actual legal advice regarding what practices might violate antitrust laws: that was the "business of the lawyers and the Department of Justice."[25] Linking the attack on big corporations to the efficiencies derived from indirect government assistance of small business nonetheless reinforced the movement toward cooperation.

Another group advocating cooperation were exporters. Beginning in 1916 the National Foreign Trade Council and the American Manufacturers Export Association lobbied Congress for legislation exempting from the antitrust laws the cooperative agreements of associations whose purpose was to encourage the nation's export trade.[26] Congressional opponents contended that it was "utterly impossible to authorize combinations and agreements and monopolies of all kinds and sorts with reference to our foreign trade and at the same time preserve intact our protection of the Sherman Law with regard to domestic trade." The measure's supporters emphasized, however, that a safeguard against abuse was the empowering of the FTC to investigate practices "in restraint of trade ... and destructive to competition." If necessary the FTC could "dictate the terms" by which to make the practice "unobjectionable" and where there was "failure" to "observe these rules," the "offending association" would be "turned over to the Attorney General."[27] Such assurances were convincing enough that the Webb-Pomerene Export Trade Act became law in 1918. The following year the Edge Act, which permitted financial combinations to further overseas investments, also was enacted.[28]

Farmers and labor won antitrust exemptions, though with mixed results. Since the 1890s states had permitted farmers to form loose cooperative organizations, establishing lawful exceptions to state antitrust laws. Kansas Republican Arthur Capper got Congress to provide a similar federal antitrust exemption in the Capper-Volstead Act of 1922. Labor's experience was more disappointing.[29] Legislative compromise had resulted in the Clayton Act's ambiguous provision that the antitrust laws were not to be construed to prohibit labor unions or the lawful conduct thereof. Labor and its congressional supporters hoped that the provision would prevent antitrust prosecutions of workers. Lower federal tribunals and the Supreme Court, however, narrowly construed the Act against unions.[30]

The position of large-scale corporations was ambiguous. Following the Court's coincident formulation of the rule of reason and dissolution of Standard Oil and American Tobacco in 1911, the nation's corporate giants underwent further managerial centralization. The replacement of the holding company with more centralized internal operational control was well advanced by the nation's entry into the war. Yet the emphasis upon pernicious conduct which determined the categorization of either a "good" or "bad" trust under the rule of reason resulted in a diverse organizational pattern.[31] In a very few cases such as ALCOA and AT&T, federal officials condoned monopoly based on technological and market economies achieved through internal growth and organizational efficiency.[32] As Chandler noted, however, generally antitrust prevented outright monopoly and facilitated oligopoly. Although "federal action under the Sherman Act never transformed an oligopolistic industry back into a traditionally competitive one [of smaller firms]," he wrote, in various important cases it "helped to transform monopolistic industries into oligopolistic ones... [while it] increased the number of competitors in already oligopolistic industries."[33]

By 1917, then, advocates of big corporations looked upon antitrust with mixed emotions. Various state and federal investigations provided a forum for the expression of the Brandeisian attack on the "curse of bigness." Faced with such criticism representatives of corporate giants lobbied against increased regulatory authority.[34] They opposed the imposition of uniform financial accounting methods which public officials could have used to identify patterns of corporate concentration and thereby strengthen antitrust enforcement. Amid the reelection campaign of 1916 and increased involvement in the war, however, the Wilson Administration surrendered to pressures from business groups, farmers, and public accountants allowing the regulatory proposals to die.[35] Meanwhile, the flexibility inherent in the Court's rule of reason and the bureaucratic administration of the FTC provided the means for increased cooperation. Wilson himself inspired this perception as America drifted toward war. By 1914 he had so distanced himself from the Brandeisian rhetoric of the 1912 campaign, said Mr. Dooley, that "you can play the President's messages on a harp."[36] According to Walter Lippmann, Wilson had shifted from describing "big businessmen" as lacking any concern for the public welfare to lauding their "spirit of accommodation."[37]

Even so big business displayed a greater willingness to cooperate with labor than did small business. Opposition to stringent antitrust enforcement created common ground between the managers of large firms and unions within the National Civic Federation. Business leader Charles Flint agreed with the AFL's Samuel Gompers that the "trust or centralized control over production was a natural development of industry and that [antitrust] legislation ... was really a limitation on the industrial and commercial development of the United States."[38] As Brandeis's espousal of FTC-sanctioned, loose associational structures suggested, moreover, small no less than big business perceived the benefits of cooperation. Regarding the enforcement of antitrust, however, small firms confronted a dilemma. Modest-sized enterprises wanted vigorous antitrust prosecution of labor and corporate giants; but they also urged a relaxation of the law's opposition to cartel-practices which was the primary focus of the Justice Department's antitrust enforcement.[39]

Despite such tensions, business–government cooperation was well established by the time America went to war. As part of the nation's mobilization, big and small business, labor, farmers, and other groups accepted the government's centralized administrative control. Still, bureaucratically imposed norms of standardization, coordination, and efficiency altered rather than ended lobbying pressure. Private interests joined public officials within separate government departments pushing for short-term demands. Meanwhile, business leaders involved in the pre-war preparedness effort were given opportunities to develop broader, long-term institutional cooperation between industry and government. AT&T's Gifford became Director of the Council of National Defense, Hoover chaired the Food Administration, Hudson Motor-executive Coffin headed the Aircraft Production Board, Hurley left the FTC to become President of the United States Shipping Board, and banker Meyer took over the War Finance Board. Baruch chaired the War Industries Board. Retired-millionaire Brookings and business publisher Shaw worked under Baruch as chairmen of the WIB's Price-fixing Committee and Conservation Division respectively.[40]

A public stance of restraint and caution permitted these business leaders much room for private maneuver aimed at weakening the enforcement of antitrust. Throughout the war, Baruch and his assistants at the WIB encouraged firms in each leading industry to form private price, production, and distribution agreements. Through their efforts the nation's war economy was cartelized. Baruch acknowledged that these practices clearly violated the antitrust laws, but he justified their use on the ground of wartime necessity. Faced with opposition from the Justice Department he urged the Wilson Administration to approve a policy "that such act or actions, when done for the benefit and in the interest of the Government, are not violations of...[the Sherman Act], and do not...[subject] individuals...to penalty." During the summer of 1917, according to the Attorney General, Wilson decided "that if we attempted at that moment to vindicate the [antitrust] law, we would disorganize industry. We both agreed that we should let up on these people so that they would have no excuse for not contributing to their full capacities in the prosecution of the war."[41]

Nonetheless, during the war neither publicly nor privately did Baruch firmly support a campaign in Congress to abrogate the antitrust laws.[42] Perhaps the most important test of Baruch's stance on antitrust occurred, however, after the Armistice. Encouraged by the passage of the Webb-Pomerene Act of 1918 and the Edge Act of 1919, Secretary of Commerce William C. Redfield and others advocated wholesale relaxation of the antitrust laws. In the name of postwar reconstruction large and small business groups urged continuation of the cooperative institutional relations and policies established during hostilities. Secretary of Treasury Carter Glass hoped Wilson would approve creation of a committee or board which would "endeavor in voluntary co-operation with business interests to arrive at a level of prices upon which business activities would be more actively resumed." As a member of the US delegation in Versailles, Baruch equivocated. He told Wilson "that although this may be called a stabilization of prices, it is a fixing of minimum prices" and as such could violate the Sherman Act. And yet a worsening economic situation increased the political problems of the Wilson Administration. Finally, Baruch condoned and Wilson approved the creation of the Industrial Board.[43]

State governments concerned about rising unemployment, small business, older, less efficient industries, and certain corporate giants supported the Board. But the attempt to ameliorate the painful readjustment to a peace-time economy through governmentally approved price-fixing agreements failed. Increasingly during 1919–1921 the public blamed business profiteering for the troubled economy. Meanwhile, to encourage acceptance of price agreements the Board assured US Steel and other firms that the Justice Department would continue its war-time relaxation of antitrust enforcement. Responding to popular discontent, however, the Justice Department in fact resumed vigorous prosecution. Whatever credibility the Board may have had thus disintegrated, ensuring its demise and confirming the wisdom of Baruch's initial concerns.[44]

The government's revived antitrust enforcement also influenced Hoover and the trade association movement. War-time exigencies had justified extensive cooperation through hundreds of trade associations, particularly the circulation of market and price information. With the coming of peace both the FTC and New York authorities began well-publicized investigations of the associations, revealing that information distribution facilitated price fixing. As Wilson's Administration ended and that of Republican Warren Harding began, these reports prompted the action of the Justice Department. The campaign against the "open price" associations put Hoover in an ambiguous position. During the war and reconstruction period, Hoover maintained a middle course between those advocating the abrogation of antitrust laws and others defending their vigorous enforcement.[45] He favored a voluntary dissemination of market information in order to prevent waste, "to stabilize commerce and industry as it works strongly to prevent over-expansion and over-speculation, over-stocking of foreign goods, etc." On these points Hoover agreed with Brandeis. As a result, Hoover not only declined to join the antitrust revisionists, but also assured Harding upon appointment as Commerce Secretary that the voluntary cooperation of trade associations and the fair enforcement of antitrust laws were compatible.[46]

In both nations war-time exigencies pushed combination and concentration issues to the forefront. Despite the lag in America joining the Allied cause, from 1914 to 1921 British and American public officials and private interests considered the costs and benefits associated with greater cooperation, the enlarged scale of enterprise, and a proliferation of restrictive practices. During the war itself the government of each nation permitted and even encouraged various forms of combination. After the Armistice, however, the traditional patterns of British nonintervention and American antitrust-centered conflict reemerged, though not without alteration. The British modestly expanded governmental supervision of business and the Americans instituted a few antitrust exemptions. Even so in Britain self-regulating loose restraints and monopoly grew, while in America oligopoly prevailed in big business and competition among smaller firms persisted.

PRESSURE GROUPS AND CHANGING ECONOMIC THOUGHT

During the war-time era, each nation's popular commentators and professional economists revised economic thought. Since the nineteenth century the traditional British economic principle was, of course, Free Trade. In America a blend of moralistic and economic presumptions identifiable as republican values circumscribed the vague public regard for *laissez-faire*. In both countries the war's need for wide-spread cooperation and the corresponding implication of this for the strength of monopoly and restrictive practices brought about a reassessment of traditional economic assumptions. British newspapers, government reports, and professional economists supported enlarging the supervisory function of the state in order to publicize abuse. Once government investigations suggested that this modestly expanded role was enough to protect small business and consumers from increased or discriminatory prices most observers confidently opposed further intervention. In America there were unsuccessful demands for the continuance of the war-time suspension of antitrust enforcement. Perhaps more significantly, while Brandeis never repudiated the "curse-of-bigness" idea, he joined Hoover and professional economists contending that cooperation in the form of trade associations was compatible with the American antitrust tradition.[47]

The British public press supported rationalization as long as both small and big business benefited. The "primary object" of the "movement to secure cooperation," stated *The Times* in 1918, was to permit "production...on a large and economical scale." Manufacturing under war conditions had demonstrated that "substantial economies" resulted from "large-scale working" and it was "felt that production will be carried on still more economically and with greater efficiency if joint use can be made of technical knowledge and financial and marketing resources were pooled."[48] A favorable view of the principle of rationalization did not extend, however, to ignoring small business. *The Economist* criticized the government's sanction of combination where it threatened modest-sized family firms. This "considered policy" of the Board of Trade was "socialistic...[it was] carried on in the face of protests from chambers of commerce and from merchants, who naturally object to money paid by them in taxes being used for the ruin of their own business."[49]

The issue was evident during the debate over the first Profiteering Act of 1919. Amid reports of "butchers going to Ascot and haberdashers buying houses in the country" the press nonetheless condemned the attempt to make the "small man" the "scapegoat" for business abuses. If small firms disappeared due to inefficiency popular opinion was little concerned. But *The Times*, *The Economist*, and the press generally stated that the elimination of waste and attainment of economies of scale identified with the rationalization movement were a good thing only as long as all segments of British business benefitted.[50]

On the issue of maintaining government supervision after the war the press reflected the views of economists. In the United States, Germany, and elsewhere "many industries have sprung up like mushrooms," wrote Alfred Marshall, which were "mainly controlled in Britain by firms whose traditions go back several generations and which are therefore disinclined to sudden changes and violent courses of strategy." The strength of such traditions suggested that the "duty of the state" was "not to hinder the action of great forces of economic evolution; even when they involve the destruction of old businesses, which have no other fault than that of being unable to turn those forces to good account." Yet those same traditions also meant that government action was necessary to prevent unfair competition, particularly exploitation of monopoly marketing position through discriminatory prices. The government's "protective intervention" was thus "not called for on behalf of incompetent competitors with the trust, but it is called for when the trust sets itself to destroy a rival, who is prepared to sell things of good quality at lower prices than the trust is charging for them elsewhere."[51]

As to the mode of this "intervention" there was some disagreement. Marshall advocated primarily the establishment of an official body possessing discretionary authority to publicize incidents of abuse. Several of Marshall's neoclassical followers, and radical economic experts affiliated with Labour and the socialists, favored giving a tribunal greater control over prices and restrictive practices. Under certain circumstances they also supported nationalization. But even these individuals agreed with Marshall and the popular press that generally the best way to protect the public from abuse was publicity.[52] During the war and reconstruction a primary reason the radicals were willing to put off state ownership was that they were out of power. Thus a socialist pamphlet in 1919 stated, we "do not desire to see state-owned trusts controlled and managed by such an incompetent and extravagant government as is in power at the present time." Even so virtually all observers from the representatives of large and small business within the FBI, to the press, to neoclassical and radical economists agreed that American-style antitrust was unnecessary. As the socialist pamphlet observed in another context, "there would be innumerable loopholes through which the trust could escape this method of control."[53]

The first major British inquiry involving trusts was the Committee on Commercial and Industrial Policy in 1916. The Ministry on Reconstruction formed the Committee; its membership included primarily representatives of commercial and manufacturing interests. Contending that the preponderance of small-scale family firms retarded British industry's competitiveness with Germany and the United States, the Committee urged that various trades should "where possible, either by amalgamation or by means of working agreements...enlarge the units of production and thereby avoid the duplication of effort which is incidental to highly diversified production on a small scale."[54]

The committee's report suggested that the government might in some cases actively encourage business combination and, in other instances, publicize abuse. Generally, however, it favored nonintervention, adamantly rejecting American-style antitrust laws. The government might establish a department to investigate and request evidence from combinations, and the Board of Trade could at its discretion publish the information. Yet, above all, the report stated, "government interference in or control of the operation of combinations should be carefully restricted to cases in which these operations can be clearly shown to be inimical to national interests."[55]

Expecting that the combination movement would not abate at the war's end, the government appointed the Committee on Trusts in 1918. The government's primary concern was to mollify the popular belief that rising prices were the result of monopolistic practices. Unlike the Industrial Committee which was composed primarily of businessmen, the membership of the Committee on Trusts included not only commercial interests but also Labour leader Ernest Bevin, socialists Sydney Webb and J. A. Hobson, and W. H. Watkins of the cooperative movement. Economist John Hilton served as secretary while the Liberal M.P. and former war-time minister Charles A. McCurdy was chairman.[56]

Even so the report of the Committee on Trusts went beyond that of its predecessor. Published early in 1919 the report was relatively unconcerned that "Trade Associations and Combines" were "rapidly increasing" in Britain and "may within no distant period exercise a paramount control over all important branches of British trade." Indeed, it declared bluntly that the age of classical competition was over. The report was concerned, however, about *potential abuse* of private power once the government removed wartime controls. Accordingly, the issues were, wrote Hilton, "Firstly, how far are the theoretical gains of combination realized in practice? And, secondly, how far can a compactly organized industry exact in practice monopoly prices and profits from the consumers?"[57]

The Committee adopted Hilton's conclusions. To forestall potential abuse the "light" of publicity was the "sovereign antiseptic and the best of all policemen." The institution of governmental mechanisms, including a permanent tribunal reporting to the Board of Trade, would ensure that "extortion should be publicly pillared" and thereby prevented. Accepting the traditional assumption that even pre-war socialists shared regarding the basic integrity of British businessmen, Hilton noted, "In quite respectable business conduct, as in other human affairs, many things are done which would not be done if there were a greater probability of their being made public."[58]

American-style antitrust legislation was "far worse than futile." Influencing Hilton's rejection was the ironic impact antitrust had in America on small business. By "making combinations of independent manufacturers criminal conspiracies," the Sherman Act had encouraged the "fusion of [small] firms into great combinations." Hilton observed that the spread of British trade associations reflected the "importance rightly attached in this country to the preservation of the 'small' man." If these loose business structures became illegal as they were in America the small enterpriser "must inevitably go down before the 'big' concern." In "one or other of its forms" combination was "inevitable, and the choice before the country" was "not between free competition and competition restrained by associations, but between associations and consolidations; and the association, if welcomed and encouraged, would have all the advantages of consolidation without its dangers."[59]

Representatives of Labour, the socialists, and the cooperative movement signed an Addendum to the Report advocating further action. Bevin, Hobson, Watkins, and Webb found "nothing to disagree with" in the report's recommendations, particularly pertaining to the establishment of mechanisms for public investigation and supervision of business. Moreover, there was no need for "any action... to prevent or obstruct combination or association in capitalist enterprise." Not only did the experience of America and other nations suggest that such interference was futile, but "association and combination in production and distribution" were "steps in the greater efficiency, the increased economy, and the better organization of industry... [which was] both inevitable and desirable." It was nonetheless also clear that the "change from competitive rivalry to combinations" required the institution of safeguards "against the evils of monopoly" and the means of procuring for workers and consumers a "large share of the economic benefits of the better organization of industry." The creation of a "Trust and Combinations Department within the Board of Trade" whose principal duty would be publicizing abuses thus was a vital first step. Excess profits taxes and government operation or outright ownership of some industrial units, as well as encouragement of the cooperative movement would check profiteering and exploitative price increases. Price controls were also essential.[60]

By comparison, American popular and expert economic thought was more diverse. Throughout the pre-war years the debate over the cost and benefits of combination and concentration was complicated by republican values. As the Brandeisian belief in the "curse of bigness" suggested, republican values mixed moral and economic imperatives, emphasizing the implications big business had for American self-government and democracy. Although Brandeis himself never doubted that bigness was inherently evil, after 1914, he, Wilson, and probably most Americans focused increasingly on the need for more cooperation between government and business and within the business order itself. Some interest groups advocated doing away altogether with antitrust, though big and small business and small business and labor were divided on how best to attain such a major change in policy.[61]

During the war and reconstruction no one articulated more clearly the faith in a more moderate course of action than Hoover. Like Brandeis, Hoover's public discourse retained moralistic elements consistent with republican values, particularly appeals to self-reliance and "rugged individualism." But, like Brandeis, too, Hoover argued that these values were, if properly applied, consistent with such cooperative structures as the trade association. Hoover did not accept the Brandeisian "curse-of-bigness" idea, but neither did he support an end to antitrust. The People's Lawyer and the "engineer-organizer" shared a profound distrust of a government dominated by the few, whether big business, organized labor and farmers, or bureaucrats. They agreed, too, on the benefits gained from voluntary cooperation through trade associations and the need for some sort of assistance from the FTC. Admittedly, Hoover would have preferred the FTC and the Justice Department to advise business in advance as to whether a particular practice violated antitrust laws. Brandeis, by contrast, contended that business should rely on the lawyer's advice to provide proper understanding of the government's and the court's decisions. Still, both before and after his appointment to the Supreme Court in 1916, Brandeis worked for an interpretation of the rule of reason which supported the trade-association policies Hoover advocated as Secretary of Commerce.[62]

The favorable view of trade associations Brandeis and Hoover shared converged publicly in 1921. In that year the Supreme Court decided that the price-sharing practices of the Hardwood Association violated the antitrust laws. Hoover argued for a more liberal interpretation. Permitting the "co-operative competition" of trade associations enabled small business to operate more efficiently, he said. He also urged the government to vigorously enforce antitrust against giant "capital combinations" whose power threatened democracy, self-reliance, and individual opportunity. It was just such a distinction that Brandeis supported, dissenting from the Court's Hardwood Association decision.[63]

Advocates of big business represented yet another perspective. In 1917 journalist Walter Lippmann reissued his book first published three years earlier entitled *Drift and Mastery*. He noted a "revolution in business motives." "Younger businessmen" accepted the ideas expressed by such diverse figures as Brandeis, Federick Taylor, and Wilson's Commerce Secretary Redfield that "if they are to conduct business they must do it efficiently." By applying "administrative science," they could replace the "old commercial morality of the exploiter and profiteer" with the values of "stewardship" and "cooperation." Big and small business, consumers, and labor would benefit. The strengthening of "federal organization" suggested "a possible compromise [between old and new attitudes] in which the administrative need for centralization is combined with the social demand for industrial policy."[64]

Big business did "brutal and stupid things," Lippmann conceded. But the "real news about business" was nonetheless that American large-scale industry was "administered by men who are not profiteers. The managers are on salary, divorced from owner-ship... They represent the revolution in business incentives at its very heart. For... they stand... outside the shrewdness and strategy of competition. The motive of profit is not their personal motive, that is an astounding change." The day-to-day administration of "great industries" did not permit each manager to "halt before each transaction and ask... What is my duty as an Economic Man looking for immediate gain? They... live on their salaries, and hope for promotion, but their day's work is not measured in profit."[65]

Notwithstanding certain reservations, professional economists also embraced the values of organizational efficiency and cooperation. By the election of 1912 most American economists preferred an approach to antitrust enforcement which relied on an administrative agency rather than litigation, a view the war reinforced. Economists condoned antitrust in part because they found useful the statistical data the FTC and other agencies generated. They also supported antitrust, no doubt because government agencies and Congress solicited the opinion of and often employed economic experts. In

May 1918 Columbia University's Wesley C. Mitchell stated, the "war has demonstrated" that the "need for scientific planning of social change has never been greater, the chance of making those changes in an intelligent fashion...has never been so good." It was "probable that for a long time to come, perhaps always, we shall increasingly use intelligence for guiding the social economic forces." Most economists thus approved "a policy of conscious social control through government agencies," observed Mitchell, and that "practical bias" was "another indication that the preconceptions of economic theory are changing."[66]

Yet the emerging American economic theory reflected tensions involving the purpose of antitrust. Most of the nation's economists, such as the leading neoclassicist John Bates Clark, accepted government intervention in principle. But beyond that there was disagreement. Some put their faith primarily in publicity, whereas Clark saw that merely as a first step toward more comprehensive antitrust regulation.[67] The war encouraged another movement eventually known as institutionalism. For such proponents as Thorstein Veblen, Wesley Clair Mitchell, and John R. Commons, neither classical nor neoclassical economics possessed sufficient theoretical or methodological tools for explaining and dealing with the organizational issues and problems the war engendered. Institutionalism therefore incorporated into economic analysis a greater emphasis on history, statistics, and newer corporate forms, particularly labor unions, large-scale corporations, and trade associations. The legal rules governing the marketplace rather than the market itself were, moreover, most important.[68]

Because of the war British and American economic thought partially converged. The growing belief in rationalization eroded British Free Trade assumptions. The qualified acceptance of rationalization and the quite modest degree of government intervention supported by the press, official reports, and professional economists suggested nonetheless that gradual decline rather than death best characterized the influence of the old faith. The proliferation of monopoly and restrictive practices concerned British popular, professional, and government commentators primarily because of rising prices. Once this threat ended in 1921 the government's reliance on loose supervision in only a few areas of the economy such as banking and exports indicated the return of a relatively low level of public anxiety regarding the issue. The status of small business received some attention, though the new consensus favoring limited official supervision applied there as well. The American interest in cooperation parallelled the British acceptance of rationalization. It was strong enough among a few groups to produce the call for virtually doing away with antitrust. Generally, however, the nation's popular and expert observers narrowly circumscribed the Brandeisian curse-of-bigness idea inherent in republican values, emphasizing that moralism, self-reliance, individual opportunity, and increased forms of cooperation were compatible with antitrust enforcement. The agreement of Hoover and Brandeis on trade associations suggested the strength of this popular belief.

LAW, PRESSURE GROUPS, AND THE STANDING COMMITTEE ON TRUSTS

During and after the war there were noteworthy if limited changes in Britain's official policy toward monopoly and combinations. The courts sanctioned new company-law provisions, fostering concentration and the growth of large corporations. Yet the British judiciary's commitment to self-restraint and a corresponding unwillingness to consider the implications of economic theory also encouraged the proliferation of self-regulating cartel practices. Thus more than ever before monopoly and restrictive practices characterized the British economy. As a result, the government's consideration of a Trade and Monopolies Bill, the passage of the Profiteering Acts, and the history of the investigative tribunal they established suggested a new if temporary level of public concern.[69]

Changes in Britain's company law encouraged tighter corporate concentration through merger. Reinforced by court decisions, self-regulating, loose business structures had acquired increased stability throughout the pre-war years. Yet, while the law permitted registration of loose restrictive agreements under the Companies and Partnership Acts it denied their enforcement in court. Consequently, these agreements required continued renegotiation. In 1912, however, Parliament sanctioned the formation and registration of "a properly constituted limited liability company for the investment of all moneys received from the members," whereby if three-fourths of the members so voted the company could sell a portion of the shares to other members at a nominal price. In 1916 the courts held that the agreements of such a company were enforceable. The effect of the change was much like that of American state-holding company and merger laws: it encouraged corporate consolidation.[70]

At the same time the law also continued to permit but not enforce most cartel-like restrictive practices. In 1915 *Morris* v. *Saxelby*, an engineering firm required a highly skilled employee to agree that if he left the company he would not pursue his trade within the United Kingdom for a period of seven years. When the worker moved to another employer the old firm sued for breach of contract but lost both at trial and in the appellate court, (though the vote on the appeal was 2 to 1).[71] Finally, in 1916, the case reached the House of Lords. There were, said Lord Shaw, "two freedoms to be considered – one the freedom of trade and the other the freedom of contract" and it was "a mistake to think that public interest is only concerned with one; it is concerned with both." Admittedly, "jurisprudence has reflected the evolution of economic thought by accentuating at one period freedom of trade, and at another freedom of contract; but the stage of balance and reconciliation which has now been definitely reached is...a restatement of the perennial problem." Accordingly, the Lords affirmed the lower courts' opinions, refusing to enforce the contract.[72] In subsequent decisions before 1921 the lower courts and the Lords sanctioned cartel-like restraints including price fixing, but did not compel compliance.[73]

The *Saxelby* case suggested the consequences of the judiciary's self-restraint toward restrictive trade practices. In the Report of the Committee on Trusts published in 1919 John MacDowell traced the evolution of the law pertaining to combinations. By the turn of the nineteenth century the courts affirmed that the "interests of the parties to contracts and those of the public may not always coincide, and that combination may be accompanied or followed by serious disadvantages." Nonetheless MacDowell noted that any attempt to base the law on the "existing economic order" required a more flexible definition of "public policy." He wished that the courts would consider the "economic effect of contracts and combinations...as...would...trained economists." MacDowell favored such a policy so that courts might better distinguish between "good" and "bad" restrictive practices, as was permitted by the US Supreme Court's rule of reason. But, as the leading cases of *Mogul* and *Nordenfelt* showed, British courts declined to take into account the wider economic consequences of business conduct. And, given the "usual experience obtained at the Bar or on the Bench," MacDowell doubted that British judges generally were equipped to

follow such a course. He recommended, therefore, the creation of a
regulatory tribunal or commission empowered to distinguish good
from bad agreements according to a broadened definition of public
policy.[74]

The 1919 Report of the Committee on Trusts which influenced
passage of the Profiteering Acts, recommended just such a tribunal.
The legislation empowered the Board of Trade to investigate
complaints of business prices, costs, and profits. If inquiries
established that profit was unreasonable the Board could declare the
reasonable price and order the seller to refund any amount in excess.
The Board was also to obtain from all sources information as to the
nature, extent, and development of trusts and similar combinations.
The Board delegated this duty primarily to a Standing Committee
on Trusts (SCT). The SCT appointed numerous sub-committees
which conducted investigations into the extent and development of
trusts and combinations throughout British industry. The second
Profiteering Act experimented with empowering the Board to
negotiate price agreements with trade associations and other
industry representatives. The intent was to achieve desirable scale
and organizational efficiencies among British firms with only a
minimum of government intervention.[75]

The Acts lapsed after less than two years. Public pressure had
declined sufficiently by 1921 that the President of the Board of Trade
could justify their short duration on the ground that investigation
had uncovered few instances of monopolistic abuse. Although the
SCT's findings were not altogether consistent with the President's
claim, it did reflect the government's limited view. The government
drafted a Trade and Monopolies Bill but it was not submitted to
Parliament. During the Parliamentary debates of the Profiteering
legislation, moreover, Labour and Liberal representatives as well as
some civil servants and ministers of war-time departments advocated
legislation establishing wider controls of the sort urged by the
Addendum to the Trust Committee's Report of 1919. The pressure
brought about a strengthening of the Act's authority so that,
according to *The Times*, the government would not make the "small
tradesman ... a scapegoat," but instead would protect society against
"the big man at the top." The government defeated, however, a
Labour-sponsored Amendment which would have enabled the
Board's investigatory tribunal to order the end of monopolistic
practices and to impose penalties. Even so the Amendment, like the

Profiteering Acts themselves, embodied little more than a modest institutional response to a specific and narrow problem of high prices.[76]

The SCT, too, reflected this limited purpose.[77] Although the Board of Trade expanded the Committee's membership from 10 to 18, in most cases neither the appointed members nor those serving on the subcommittees received pay. John Hilton, economist and former secretary of the Trust Committee, was on loan from another government department. Other committeemen represented different political and social interests. One claimed to speak for the Chamber of Commerce, another said "I represent a part of the capitalist class, but I hold a fair view of every subject I tackle." Still another identified with the "poor retailer," and another was a member of the cooperative movement "representing the consumer."[78] The SCT's first chairman, a Liberal MP and former minister of a war-time department, had served on the 1918 Trust committee. His successor was also a Liberal MP. Several other members were supporters of Labour, including the socialist Sidney Webb. Of the first appointments to the SCT, about half were veterans of the 1918 Trust Committee.

The Board of Trade circumscribed the SCT's reach. The Committee's first chairman, Charles A. McCurdy, said at the first meeting in October 1919 that according to the Board's charge they were to investigate complaints of profiteering and high prices and profits, and in the process obtain information on the development of trusts and combines. He emphasized that the SCT's duties were general and statistical, providing information to assist the government in preparing the Trust and Combines legislation which would in turn establish a "general bureau of information." He emphasized that the committee was *not* asked to inquire into specific grievances or "scandals." Accordingly, the SCT could only request that firms give evidence, and it was left to the Board to decide whether the results of investigations were to be published.[79]

Yet, despite such constraints, the SCT steadily expanded the narrow role McCurdy outlined. Suggesting the perspective of the rationalization movement, one member said that the SCT's inquiries could encourage the "formation" of "a good trust with the proper safeguards ... [of] the public." McCurdy urged the committee not to "deliver judgment as to whether a man was getting a reasonable or unreasonable profit, but to confine themselves to the facts." Webb nonetheless pressed for investigatory conclusions which revealed the "actual costs of an article" separate from the mere presentation of factual data. Thus the committee asked accountants for a definition of costs. Noting that "Interest on Capital" was "an item of cost...subject to much debate," the experts replied that "Income Tax [and] Excess Profits dut[ies] do not enter into costs but are an appropriation of profits." What was, therefore, "really needed was an opinion on Replacement value," including "total outlay in production of a commodity."[80]

The SCT investigated Britain's largest and most successful firms, including Lever Brothers, the soap manufacturers, Cadbury's and Fry's chocolate, Imperial Tobacco, and J. & P. Coats of the textile industry. The SCT soon discovered the nature and extensiveness of horizontal and vertical price-fixing practices. The findings of the "Chocolate subcommittee" were typical. The majority report stated that despite extensive price fixing, the self-regulating character of restraining agreements generally did not result in abuse. The minority report conceded this point, but emphasized that "there could be no alteration of the prices without notification to the other parties to the agreements, and...if one of the parties increased their minimum prices the others would automatically follow," so the "agreements did provide machinery for raising prices without regard to costs, and did consequently act as a restraint on trade." But both reports implicitly agreed that the system of self-regulation nonetheless protected the smallest retail firms run by "widows, single women, and disabled soldiers." If, without the system "profits to retailers" were reduced "too much...[it] would have the effect of driving them from the trade and of throwing the whole business on the grocers." Yet another member noted that fixed rates were "preferable...to maintain the small retailer in existence."[81]

McCurdy stated a sanguine consensus. The "actual operation of the [restrictive] agreements depended very much on the spirit in which they were carried out." They "obviously could be made to operate in a very restrictive way...which might obviously have an effect on prices. On the other hand, such an agreement might be used for no restrictive purpose, but for the purpose of economical and harmonious working between firms." By the end of 1919 McCurdy summarized the SCT's findings in terms which were equally optimistic. "I think many of us had the idea...that we were going to find cases of concrete scandals, upon which specific action could be taken. We have not come across such things." At the same time, however, "the fact that the allegations are widely believed and the fact that we have taken up a half dozen cases, and have found that there is much to be said on both sides, and that nothing in the nature of a very dreadful scandal has come to light" had made "some contribution towards relieving the present tension in the country...and if we can enlighten the public in this way we are doing something good."[82]

McCurdy's optimism, however, was premature. Early in 1920, as the SCT's subcommittees investigated Coats, Lever Brothers, and other big firms, it became evident that the Board of Trade was succumbing to external pressures. The President eventually ordered no further investigation of Cadbury's and other prominent firms. At about the same time the Board also published a favorable report on high prices. According to one committee member, the Board was treating the SCT with the "utmost disrespect." Noting the uneasiness the "great ogres" undoubtedly felt because of the "considerable amount of information on the subject of fixing retail prices" the SCT uncovered, another member observed that the Board's action was "not delay" but "mangling."[83]

As the year progressed, the Board of Trade reemphasized that the SCT was not "to enter into controversies in the Press with regard to Reports." Meanwhile, Coats and the FBI carried on an extensive newspaper campaign. They refuted the SCT's conclusions regarding the definition of costs and profits, contending among other things that the income tax "should be deducted in arriving at the profit." A SCT member said it was "obvious that there was efficient machinery for discrediting the reports."[84]

During the spring and summer of 1920 tensions came to a head. The Electric Lamp Manufacturers' Association responded to the publication of the SCT's report on the industry with an effective lobbying effort. To the Prime Minister and the President of the Board of Trade the Association wrote letters rejecting the Report's findings, while the FBI's supportive statements received sympathetic notices in the newspapers and Parliament. The industry attacked the Report's charge that price-fixing agreements between the manufacturer and middlemen unfairly kept prices high, contending that as long as the agreements were not exclusive competition was not extinguished. Also, the agreements facilitating the industry's dominant market position were based either on court-approved patent monopolies or justified by the exigencies of foreign competition. The Board of Trade's rejection of the SCT's appeals suggested, Hilton observed, that increasingly it was considered an "outside body."[85]

Ultimately, McCurdy resigned and was replaced by Liberal MP John Murray. Ironically, the controversy coincided with the Board's extension of the SCT's investigatory responsibilities. Business, press, and Labour Party pressures on the Cabinet (including the President of the Board of Trade) and Parliament resulted in passage of the second Profiteering Act. A key clause permitted a firm or industry to "contract out" of the law's proscriptions, with the approval of the Board. In effect, the new provision enabled business and government to establish mutually advantageous pricing practices consistent with the views propounded by the rationalization movement. At the same time government supervision theoretically maintained the public welfare. Amidst the Electric Lamp controversy, the SCT sent a deputation to the Board's President, Sir Robert Horne, expressing concern for the Committee's future. In response, Horne authorized the SCT to "assist the Board by undertaking the whole of the preliminary work in connection with such [price] schemes, including the examination of proposals put forward and the necessary negotiations with the representatives of the trades and industries concerned." Final approval of the "schemes" was, of course, left to the Board. The SCT's members believed that the President had vindicated their earlier actions.[86]

Again, however, optimism proved unwarranted. Within the SCT itself tensions arose when the representative of the cooperative movement demanded that not only the names but the interest-group affiliation of the subcommittee members should appear on the reports. Although a majority of the committee reluctantly accepted this demand, Chairman Murray emphasized the risks. "A report that goes out stating the specific interests represented at once suggests that the public should not look at the joint findings but look where the men come from and argue as to their views from that stand point. That seems to me to be rather disruptive."[87]

Meanwhile, individual industries and the FBI reoriented their lobbying efforts, urging the Board to appoint a permanent committee made up of civil servants and businessmen possessing authority to negotiate the price schemes. In addition, the Board approved modifying some of the SCT's findings prior to publication after discussions with industry representatives. Committee members noted concerning one such incident that the firm's representatives were "very bad advocates, we had them whacked." Yet, as a result of the Board's actions, "a lot of combines will be going behind our backs."[88]

The SCT suffered further setbacks involving the Board of Trade's preparation of the Trade and Monopolies Bill. As McCurdy had noted in the Fall of 1919, the Board had responded to pressures from Parliament and within the Cabinet by drafting the legislation. It would have empowered the Board of Trade to make enquiries into the nature, extent, and effect of monopolies and the methods by which monopoly was maintained. The Board could require the production of documents and other information, though it was to treat this material confidentially. Either the Board, based upon its own investigation, or an individual could register a complaint with the Railway and Canal Commission charging "unreasonable" prices or other restrictions. The Commission could issue a restraining order which dealt with an abuse or regulation of prices. Emphasizing its record of effective inquiries, the SCT urged Horne to make it permanent under the proposed legislation. But, instead, the President reported to the House of Commons that "based on the Reports" of the SCT, he "did not see the necessity for legislation dealing with Trusts and Combinations."[89]

The Board's use of the SCT's own reports to abort further consideration of the Trade and Monopolies Bill was enmeshed in wider tensions. Committee members argued that their reports "showed the need for just such legislation." They conceded nonetheless that the Board was "closer to the legislative process and pressures" than was the SCT. Gradually it became apparent that the Board found it easier to await the natural end of the Profiteering Acts early in 1921 than to perpetuate the conflicts with business the SCT's reports had engendered. Firms became increasingly unwilling to cooperate with the SCT's investigations, even in connection with the pricing schemes. Meanwhile, the investigations turned up further controversial information, whereupon the British chemical industry claimed that the publication of a report would benefit its German competitors. More sensitive still was the discovery that the wartime ministry headed by former chairman McCurdy had engaged in questionable price-raising practices.[90]

By early 1921 events moved toward a climax. Because of the

SCT's reports, Labour favored Parliamentary consideration of the Trade and Monopolies Bill but Liberal MP and corporate executive Sir Alfred Mond successfully opposed the idea. Once it became clear that the Board of Trade had already decided against proposing it, Webb resigned. Not long afterward the representative from the Chamber of Commerce demanded that the SCT disband, whereupon he too resigned, exclaiming how "glad" he was that the "Committee was treated with the contempt it deserved." As the funding and mandate established under the Profiteering Acts neared an end, the SCT urged the Board of Trade's President to push for the monopoly legislation. The nation needed, said one member, "some sort of policeman between organized industry…and the consumer…to watch" the trusts.[91]

Finally, the SCT requested a meeting with Sir Robert Horne, President of the Board of Trade, to discuss a recommendation. The proposal reflected the experience gained from approximately eighteen months and 70 meetings, resulting in the publication of thirty reports. Judging the "success" of the SCT's work on trade combinations "by the number of convictions obtained in the Courts or by the value of specific price reductions which followed intervention by the Committee would be a mistake," stated the proposal. "Prevention is better than cure. So far as concerns improper action by trusts, prevention rests on publicity. In certain outstanding cases, however, the investigations and reports have had a definite influence on the action of trusts…cit[ing] reductions in the price of soap, sewing cotton, glassware, electric lamps, etc." Moreover, the SCT's findings had "discredited…extravagant views…regarding supposed depredations of trusts…[demonstrating] that the standards of honesty in the [British] business world" had not "become debased." They also demonstrated the "elements of efficiency, economy, and co-operation which" were "to be found in most trade combinations. These results of the work conduce to social harmony."[92]

Nevertheless, the SCT's investigations taught "one uniform lesson." The movement toward combinations, "good or bad, obvious or obscure" was "more likely to grow than to abate," reaching out in "many directions." Unless the government established "permanent machinery of inquiry and redress…to deal with trusts neither will the consuming public think its interests safe nor will those interests be in fact safe." The SCT urged, therefore, the

Board to submit legislation supporting the continuance of the Committee after the Profiteering Acts lapsed. To disband the "trained staff" and "scrap the machinery" which had "run, at small cost, to the great gain of the public" was "neither wise nor economical." For the "results" were obtained by cooperation rather than coercion. "Remonstrance…generally overc[ame] resistance."[93]

The President of the Board of Trade, however, accepted neither a deputation from the SCT nor its recommendation. As the Profiteering Acts ended so did the SCT. At the final meeting on May 21, 1921 one member observed, "the Government intended to put a stop to the work of the Committee, which had discovered too many truths for their liking."[94]

The short but evocative history of the SCT suggested the nature and limits of concern for monopoly and restrictive practices. The SCT's published reports, like its proposal submitted to the Board of Trade's President in early 1921, were consistent with the recommendations of Committee on Trusts in 1919. Despite noteworthy exceptions, traditional British business values and interests prevented serious abuse during the war. But in the future that could have changed, so formal methods of maintaining publicity were urged. The life of the SCT indicated the strengths and weaknesses of this assessment. As McCurdy summarized early in the Committee's investigations, the "get along" ethos sustaining the system of self-regulation preserved the interests of big and small business without major instances of abuse or exploitation. Nevertheless, persistent lobbying pressure from the FBI and individual industries, as well as the Board of Trade's sympathetic response, suggested that in the future problems were likely without permanent supervision such as that recommended by the SCT.

Even so, the Board's restriction of the SCT's investigations suggested that publicity alone was unsatisfactory. It was apparent that members of the SCT perceived little risk from cartel practices or monopoly per se. The chief concern was preserving small business and maintaining prices which seemed reasonable to consumers. In light of the increasing dominance of monopoly, however, the Board's final refusal to submit the Trade and Monopolies Bill and the subordination and eventual demise of the SCT itself indicated that such a goal was probably too narrow. In addition the Electric Lamp Association's tenacious defense of restrictive practices to ward off foreign competitors, combined with the FBI's attempt to achieve direct government sponsorship of such restraints, suggested that business was more concerned with self-preservation than the efficiencies promised by the rationalization movement. Thus the brief experience of the SCT notwithstanding, by 1921 neither the law nor government action reflected more than a temporary concern for the growth of monopoly and restraints in British industry.

THE VICISSITUDES OF AMERICAN ANTITRUST ENFORCEMENT

From 1914 to 1921 American national authorities and the courts reshaped antitrust law. Although several states, especially Texas, won important victories against corporate giants, after 1918 state antitrust activity was no longer significant.[95] The Court's formulation of the rule of reason in 1911 established a flexible standard for the US Justice Department's prosecution of both loose and tight business structures. The passage of the FTC and Clayton acts in 1914 potentially further strengthened federal authority, though the ambiguous phraseology of the laws meant that ultimately their reach depended on judicial construction.[96] The Justice Department under both Wilson and Harding applied the rule of reason in support of a wider use of consent decrees. The government agreed to exempt from prosecution certain mergers in return for promises that the conduct of big corporations would conform to antitrust policy. In the AT&T and ALCOA cases such decrees sanctioned monopoly. In most other cases involving corporate giants, however, the decrees resulted in an oligopolistic industrial structure. Meanwhile, despite the efforts of Brandeis, federal antitrust prosecution focused primarily on cartel practices among relatively modest-sized enterprises. The Court also circumscribed the FTC's powers to define unfair practices and interpreted the Clayton Act to permit antitrust prosecutions of labor unions.[97]

Against managerially centralized big corporations the government's record of success was mixed. Encouraged by victories over Standard Oil and American Tobacco, the Justice Department moved against US Steel, International Harvester, American Can, and other tight corporate structures. The blend of moral and economic values implicit in the rule of reason, however, provided considerable flexibility in determining the outcome. In 1916 lower federal courts upheld the Justice Department's linking of market factors and pernicious conduct, deciding against the Corn Products Company and American Can. Although the enforcement decrees the judges ordered were weak, the interplay of antitrust prosecution and market pressures meant that oligopoly prevailed.[98]

After America entered the war the Wilson Administration suspended prosecution of International Harvester and US Steel. By the time the cases were settled the war-time experience had weakened the tensions between efficiency and moralism inherent in republican values. Although popular anger over profiteering heightened concern for the latter, the yearning for reasonably priced consumer goods paradoxically created enthusiasm for the former. As a result, in the fall of 1918 International Harvester and the federal government agreed on a consent decree which required modest divestiture and an end to a system whereby it had confined marketing to single agents in various small towns. According to Chandler, the result prevented monopoly and fostered oligopoly.[99]

US Steel prevailed over the government but the economic outcome was the same. In *US* v. *US Steel* (1920), over the government's opposition the Court applied the rule of reason to sanction one of the largest corporations in the world. After examining thoroughly the conduct of the corporation's management, the Court found no evidence of pernicious practices. Of course, the firm's organizational structure, huge capitalization, and control of productive resources as a holding company created efficiencies which impeded the entry of new competitors. But with steel producers already in the business, US Steel competed "fairly." Thus, in the record of the case, Youngston Sheet & Tube Company asserted that US Steel had engaged in "nothing but the fairest competition in every respect for the last seven or eight years."[100] To the Court this competitive behavior was more reasonable than the government's contention that US Steel's market power prevented new firms from entering the industry. The Court held therefore that as long as there was "no adventitious interference ... to either fix or maintain prices" bigness was not in and of itself bad. Nevertheless, US Steel's brush with prosecution probably encouraged its strategy of avoiding merger to increase market share, which strengthened the steel industry's independent firms and, therefore, oligopoly.[101]

The meat-packing industry's encounter with antitrust had a similar outcome. Fearing legal challenge in 1912, the meat packers dissolved the National Packing Company, a corporate structure they used to maintain a monopoly. Anxious that suits pending in other industries might result in prosecution of their own industry, the meat packers asked the Justice Department to review the dissolution plan.

The government approved the plan and instituted an injunction, ending the likelihood of further legal action. Shortly thereafter, however, Armour and Swift, the two largest packers, began expanding into distribution and retail operations. From 1917 to 1919 the FTC made a thorough study of the meat-packing industry, documenting various vertical distribution arrangements which resulted in extensive control of prices. The FTC's report recommended a divestiture of the distribution organization. The Justice Department prepared a suit, but in order to avoid prosecution the packers began negotiations which culminated in a consent decree limiting their business to meat packing and wholesaling. Yet, as soon as an agreement was reached, the packers began lengthy litigation which stalled enforcement of the decree for fifteen years. Nonetheless, during the interim the government's sanction of the original plan remained in effect, maintaining an oligopolistic industry.[102]

In other cases involving tight corporate structures the record was mixed. In several suits the government challenged the monopoly position of the United Shoe Machinery Company. Through the control of certain patented technology, the company was able to prevent competition by maintaining vertical lease agreements with users of the USMC's machines. The unique monopolistic character of patents raised complicated issues regarding the applicability of antitrust. The initial grounds upon which the government attacked United Shoe were not, therefore, on the basis of the patents themselves, but that of the production and distribution monopoly resulting from the leases. Even so, in 1917 a majority of the Court decided in favor of the company. Just as the government lost the 1917 case, however, it began a new criminal suit alleging violation of Section 3 of the Clayton Act, which Congress had drafted primarily in order to outlaw the sorts of restraints United Shoe maintained. On appeal, with only one dissent, the Court sustained the government though, in the long run, United Shoe retained its controlling position because of market not legal reasons.[103] Meanwhile, in cases involving railroad mergers the Court upheld the government, supporting oligopoly in the transportation industry. Thus *United Shoe* was one of the few cases involving big corporations in which monopoly triumphed, whereas the railroad decisions represented the more common result in which oligopoly prevailed.[104]

The prosecution of the restrictive practices of small business had somewhat clearer results. The Justice Department's antitrust suits rose steadily until 1915, leveling off during the war years. In about 80 percent of these cases the federal government won. Significantly, six out of seven of these suits were against cartel agreements among comparatively small enterprises in the furniture, lumber, and apparel, wholesale and retail trades. The government focused on these industries because it was often not difficult to obtain testimony from customers and competitors proving unlawful conduct under the rule of reason. Thus, despite the occasional big case involving corporate giants like Standard Oil and US Steel, the Justice Department devoted most of its energies to breaking up restrictive cartel practices. Although the government's record of success in the cases involving the giants was mixed, its record of victory in the other classes of cases clearly favored the sort of classical competition more characteristic of small-scale enterprise.[105]

Thus Brandeis's advocacy of cooperative restrictive practices among small enterprises made only modest headway. Before joining the Court he had supported the rule of reason partially because it provided the doctrinal flexibility to circumvent the proscription against vertical price fixing established in *Dr. Miles*.[106] On the Court, Justice Brandeis consistently supported the same position. In *Chicago Board of Trade* v. *US* (1918) the government challenged a practice on the grain exchange known as the Call. By regulating the hours of daily trade the Call effectively fixed prices. As Brandeis said succinctly: "Before the adoption of the rule members fixed their bids throughout the day at such prices as they respectively saw fit; after the adoption of the rule, the bids had to be fixed at the day's closing bid."[107]

For a unanimous Court, Brandeis applied the rule of reason to sanction self-regulating cooperative restraints. The lawfulness of "an agreement or regulation cannot be determined by so simple a test as whether it restrains competition," he said. The "true test of legality" was whether the restraint merely regulates and perhaps thereby promotes competition or whether it is such as may suppress or even destroy competition." Implicit here was the distinction between regulated competition and regulated monopoly he had incorporated into Wilson's New Freedom platform during the 1912 campaign. For Brandeis, "regulated competition" meant sustaining restraints among small business so that it might attain the organizational efficiencies enjoyed by big business, while the distinction also permitted the prosecution of large corporations. The Court must therefore "ordinarily" consider the "facts peculiar to the business to which the restraint...applied," including the "history of the restraint, the evil believed to exist, the reason for adopting the particular remedy, the purpose or end sought to be attained." The Court considered such factors "not because a good intention will save an otherwise objectionable regulation or the reverse; but because knowledge of intent may help the court to interpret facts and to predict consequences."[108]

Brandeis's emphasis on various factors defining "intent," subtly broadened the criteria for applying the rule of reason. The Court might distinguish between "good" and "bad" price-fixing agreements, thereby strengthening the ability of small firms to form restrictive combinations. During the war-time era Brandeis won a modest limitation of the *Dr. Miles* proscription of vertical price restraints. But in the field of trade associations, initially at least, he lost. One group favored trade associations primarily as a subterfuge for outright cartelization, while another group opposed all but the most circumscribed cooperation as contrary to the antitrust laws. Brandeis, like Hoover, sought a middle course. As long as trade associations published and distributed price and market information without restriction, and participation was voluntary, he considered such practices lawful under the *Chicago Board of Trade* reading of the rule of reason.[109]

In *American Column & Lumber Co.* v. *US* (1921), however, the Court rejected the Brandeisian construction, holding that a voluntary Open Price Plan among relatively small firms was a combination and conspiracy violating the Sherman Act. In separate opinions Holmes and Brandeis dissented, though Holmes agreed with the economic test of intent Brandeis used to defend the association.[110] Brandeis concluded with questions which epitomized his view that without the right to form loose business structures, modest firms would die, engulfed by corporate concentration. "May not these hardwood lumber concerns, frustrated in their efforts to rationalize competition, be led," he asked, "to enter the inviting field of consolidation?" If that happened "may not another huge trust with highly centralized control over vast resources, natural, manufacturing, and financial become so powerful as to dominate competitors, wholesalers, retailers, consumers, employees and, in large measure, the community?"[111]

Similarly circumscribed was the FTC. Once the Commission

began operations in 1915 it briefly fulfilled the Brandeisian idea of providing small business with accounting information so that they could more effectively plan and eliminate waste. The FTC also conducted investigations. Not only did it probe such corporate giants as the meat packers, but it also studied trade associations which often were composed of smaller enterprises. Early in the Harding Administration an FTC inquiry into "Open Price Associations" encouraged the Justice Department's campaign to limit trade association activities. During the same period business groups failed to convince the commission that it should give advice as to whether a possible restrictive practice potentially violated the antitrust laws.[112]

The Supreme Court's construction of the FTC's powers curbed its effectiveness. In the *FTC* v. *Gratz* (1920) a majority of the Court overturned the FTC's order that abrogated as "unfair competition" a tying agreement binding the purchasers of steel ties. Suggesting the moralism implicit in the rule of reason, Justice James C. McReynold's opinion found no unfair competition in "practices never heretofore regarded as opposed to good morals because characterized by deception, bad faith, fraud or oppression, or against public policy because of their dangerous tendency unduly to hinder competition or create monopoly." Since the record showed neither pernicious conduct nor monopoly power, the FTC lost.[113] Brandeis, however, dissented. Probably because the Gratz firm was an agent of Carnegie Steel Company, Brandeis viewed the FTC's order as a regulation of big business monopoly in favor of smaller merchant competitors. Recounting the history leading to the Commission's establishment, he argued that its "purpose in respect to restraints of trade was prevention of diseased business conditions not cure." The "great trusts had acquired their power in the main, through destroying or over-reaching their weaker rivals by resort to unfair practices." Through "supervisory action," therefore, the Commission's duty was "to protect competitive business from *further* inroads by monopoly. It was to be ever vigilant... Its action was to be prophylactic."[114]

Ironically, when the Court upheld the FTC's dissolution of resale price-fixing agreements among small firms, Brandeis again dissented. The Court in a 5-4 decision sustained the Commission's order based on findings that the Beech-Nut Packing Company had maintained exclusive dealing practices with distribution agents and customers, thereby unfairly preventing the competition of other middlemen. The issue involving vertical price fixing was similar to that raised in *Dr. Miles.* As he had in that case, Holmes wrote a dissenting opinion favoring the British courts' general toleration of vertical and horizontal restrictive trade practices. Brandeis, who had supported the FTC in part because he hoped it would provide a flexible administrative means by which to circumvent *Dr. Miles,* joined Holmes's dissent.[115]

Regarding the enforcement of antitrust against organized labor Brandeis also lost. During the war, despite sporadic disorder, the government's preservation of cooperation between business and labor suspended small enterpriser's use of labor injunctions against organized labor. Thus, not until hostilities ended were there significant tests of the Clayton Act's purported labor exemption. In 1921 the Court decided two cases narrowly construing the Act's ambiguous language against unions. In one, Brandeis, Holmes and John H. Clarke dissented; in the other Brandeis partially concurred because the Court at least sustained the general lawfulness of the Act.[116] In a third case that same year the Court held that an Arizona law prohibiting the state's courts from issuing labor injunctions violated the Fourteenth Amendment. The law was, said the Court, an unwarranted "legalized experiment in sociology." Again, Brandeis, Holmes, and Clarke dissented.[117]

Brandeis's post-war dissents suggested the continuing dilemma of American antitrust. From the beginning the enforcement of antitrust reflected Americans' ambivalent attachment to both the opportunity small business represented and the consumer benefits big enterprise made possible. The Court's rule of reason and the creation of the FTC seemingly provided the flexibility to satisfactorily resolve this tension. The simultaneous impetus the war gave to cooperation and exploitation, however, emphasized anew how difficult it was – except in cases involving organized labor – to establish a clear-cut policy. The Justice Department and the FTC vigorously prosecuted certain big and small, tight and loose business structures. Yet, on the whole, the blend of moral and economic values implicit in both the Court's and the government's application of the rule of reason resulted in ambiguity. Notwithstanding ingenious constructions of the rule of reason, Brandeis no more than his opponents resolved the dilemma.

As an era of peace began there was a short-term convergence of each nation's business practice and official policy. Although Britain experimented with more intrusive government intervention in the Profiteering Acts and the Standing Committee on Trusts, the erosion of the Free Trade consensus was insufficient to sustain more than a modest and selective extension of official supervision. American public authorities and private interests also sought, by relaxing the enforcement of antitrust, to expand the degree of cooperation between business and government and within the business order itself. As the Court's treatment of the trade association suggested, however, neoclassical economic thought had not displaced republican values to the point that it solely influenced the application of the rule of reason.

The different interests of pressure groups shaped this contrasting experience. As the investigations of the Standing Committee on Trusts confirmed, the growth of large-scale corporations did not diminish British manufacturers' extensive reliance on vertical price-fixing agreements, which preserved the interests of middlemen. Equally there were many areas where there was no effective monopoly and where self-regulating restraints were ineffective, as many rationalizers complained. The main reason for this beginning in the 1920s was surely that there were few tariff barriers in Britain, so for goods which could be imported there was no possibility of an effective domestic cartel. As a result, once the government responded to the public's demand that small as well as big business should have equal opportunity to benefit from rationalization, there was little support for greater government intervention. Despite its interest in the Trade and Monopolies Bill, Labour, too, shared this consensus. In the United States, by contrast, the Court's ambivalent treatment of trade associations and big corporations indicated that after the Armistice the division of interests was too great to avoid the revival of conflict. Thus, in Britain, monopoly and self-regulating restraints increasingly dominated. In America, by contrast, oligopoly prevailed in big business and classical competition characterized smaller enterprise.

CHAPTER 6

Tentative convergence, 1921–1948

By 1948, the two nations' responses to big business had undergone partial convergence. During the 1920s a merger wave occurred in which British business began to follow a path toward the greater managerial centralization American firms had pioneered at the turn of the century. Still, a lag in managerial organization persisted in which business self-regulation and trade restraints prevailed to a greater extent than was true of the United States. Cartelization increased in both nations during the Great Depression, and in Britain it was facilitated by the adoption of tariff protectionism. In America, however, the triumph of cartelization was brief. By the immediate post-war years British policymakers fashioned a coherent policy established in the Monopolies Act of 1948 which, nonetheless, like the temporary measures enacted after World War I, relied primarily upon publicity. In the United States, by contrast, public officials and the courts continued to follow an ambivalent course toward loose business arrangements and managerially centralized large firms. Thus, the differing impact of pressure groups and economic thought, which all along had encouraged different results, meant that a convergence in policy was tentative.

THE NEW PARAMETERS OF COMPARATIVE BUSINESS STRUCTURE

During the 1920s, the Great Depression, and World War II each nation's business structure partially converged. The merger wave in Britain established the basis of a corporate economy which more closely approximated that of the United States. To overcome the massive economic collapse of the 1930s both countries' public officials promoted cartelization, and World War II required even more extensive business–government collaboration. Nevertheless there were noteworthy differences. The merger movement in Britain created a corporate order characterized by monopoly and trade restraints, whereas in America oligopoly prevailed among giant corporations and outright cartelization was illegal. More fundamentally, the managerial organization of British corporations was generally less developed than that of their American counterparts, with US firms more widely adopting a divisionalized structure. During the Depression the extent of cartelization and monopoly was significant in both nations engendering new antimonopoly policies during and shortly after World War II.[1]

During the 1920s each nation's merger wave differed. During the era of World War I certain restrictive practices became enforceable under the law which encouraged British businessmen to adopt the holding company. At about the same time in the US, by contrast, the Court's application of the rule of reason encouraged big business to develop a more unitary operational structure.[2] This structural difference suggested the correctness of Hannah's observation that while the merger wave of the 1920s established the foundation of the British corporate economy, "of the largest 100 US manufacturing corporations … over half of their major mergers occurred before the First World War. Thus, the picture of British firms 'catching up' in the rationalization movement of the 1920s with a structure of industry which had been created earlier in the United States is confirmed."[3] Yet, as Carl Eis has shown, the relatively weak enforcement of antitrust, along with market changes and rising stock prices nonetheless encouraged the American merger wave. In Britain, however, the government's influence on the merger movement was even less direct and the extent of trade restraints was therefore correspondingly greater.[4] In America the merger movement of the 1920s "involved a smaller number of multi-firm consolidations and produced relatively fewer transactions yielding a single dominant enterprise." Its "distinguishing characteristic was the creation of oligopolistic market structures through mergers that formed strong 'number two' firms in industries formally controlled by a single company and reinforced some existing, comparatively weak oligopolies."[5]

Different legal rules shaped each country's merger experience. The Supreme Court retreated from the trust-busting construction of rule of reason affirmed in 1911 to the big-not-necessarily-bad policy proclaimed in the *US Steel* decision of 1920. The change in the Court's interpretation shaped lawyers' advice to corporate executives as they restructured the business order during the merger wave.

Although managerial and market factors were clearly important, the Court's changing application of the rule of reason also influenced the contrasting results of the first and second American merger movements. According to Hannah, "The union of many firms into a consolidation with a very high market share, which had been the hallmark of the first merger movement, was relatively rare in the 1920s..." Apparently the "somewhat lackadaisical enforcement of antitrust law could successfully discourage market leaders from merger for monopoly, although mergers among lower-ranking firms continued, thus tending to create an oligopolistic industry structure."[6]

Britain's law thus helped to bring about a corporate economy characterized by greater cartelization. The change in company law solved the problem of enforceability by strengthening the financial and organizational incentives to form a holding company, facilitating the merger wave. At the same time, however, the courts not only allowed cartel practices, but also increasingly permitted the enforcement of looser trade restraints. Thus legal rules stimulated both corporate concentration and cartelization until, more than ever before, monopoly and restrictive practices prevailed. The law promoted the foundations of a corporate economy; but, co-incidentally, it gave formal sanction to the forms of self-regulation and the "get-along" ethos which were less efficient.[7]

The comparative status of the holding company in each nation suggested the impact of the law. In such firms as Cadbury's and Fry's or Imperial Tobacco, the holding company enabled the owners of separate, smaller firms to retain relative autonomy.[8] In addition, such consolidations were often formed in order to take advantage of tax exemptions rather than to attain organizational efficiency per se.[9] Meanwhile a loophole in the Clayton Act prohibited the purchase of stock by holding companies as a means of limiting competition, but indirectly encouraged more unitary structures by permitting one corporation to acquire another corporation's assets.[10]

A significant consequence of Britain's "catching up" was thus the comparative underdevelopment of managerial organization. The shift from loose cartelistic structures, to the holding company, to the consolidated operating company preceded the emergence of a still more flexible "decentralized and divisionalized" corporate structure. As Chandler noted, "centralization and consolidation followed by rationalization must precede decentralization and divisionalization."[11] During the 1920s Alfred Sloan pioneered the divisionalized organizational structure which followed two basic principles. First, each "organization headed by its chief executive shall be complete in every necessary function and enabled to exercise its full initiative and logical development." Second, "Certain central organization functions are absolutely essential to the logical development and proper control of the corporation's activities."[12]

Sloan's system permitted greater diversification, particularly regarding the marketing function. Although American business continued to rely primarily on the unitary structure throughout the 1920s, the Sloan strategy became increasingly common. "Diversification" had become "a settled policy with many companies... [thereby] insuring... continuity in earnings," wrote one commentator in 1929. "More than one shrewd observer of current happenings in industry has suggested that one of the impressive changes now going on in business is the tendency to spread out, not to form a monopoly of a single product, but to bring into the management of a single group of men a group of kindred industries," noted another observer in 1928. "Business seems to grow by accretion, either through this kind of merger of kindred companies or by adding complementary lines." Meanwhile, it had become more apparent, wrote an executive in 1927, that the "business executive of this period of commercial history must look at his business from the standpoint of its ultimate aim – the sale of the product." Of course, production and purchasing were vital. "But these and every other movement of business seem... dependent on the several basic functions of sales." Thus, especially because of the orientation toward marketing, the second merger wave in America "consisted of more mergers in which vertical integration, geographic and product line extension, and... diversification were strong features."[13]

In Britain the adoption of the divisional structure was limited. Imperial Chemical Industries was one of the few large British firms which achieved a decentralized and divisionalized corporate structure. Resulting from the merger of Brunner, Mond, Nobel Industries, British Dyestuffs, and United Alkali in 1926, after the British government expressed concern over the initial emergence of Germany's I. G. Farben, ICI was among the world's most effective giant corporations. It joined DuPont and I. G. Farben in an international cartel dominating the world-wide chemical industry.

British business success in such dynamic industries was, however, exceptional. And yet, in other cases, British business avoided adopting a more unitary operational structure, often preferring to preserve the relative autonomy and greater personal management of individual firms within a holding company.[14] In any case the aggregate evidence was that the British economy did very much better than the American economy in the 1930s, despite not having as many multi-divisional corporations.[15]

Influencing this divergent level of managerial centralization were different attitudes toward profitability. In American firms, Chandler observed, the "basic goals appear to have been long-term profit and growth. Growth ensured increased assets for large investors, including founding families. Growth also ensured long-term income and long-term tenure for managers and, in many cases, for workers. In Britain the goal for family firms appears to have been to provide a steady flow of cash to owners who were also managers." Significantly, for the few British companies such as ICI, UniLever, and British Petroleum which adopted the more effective managerial organization, the "goal became, as it was for such American companies, long-term growth of assets financed through retained earnings."[16] William Benton, Vice President of the University of Chicago and a successful businessman reached a similar conclusion. During a visit to Britain in 1943, he observed that a "major difference of outlook between our two countries" was that the "British believe in *capital*, we believe in *capitalism*. You think capital is more indestructible than we do. With us, individual initiative comes first. Capital, which underwrites and rewards enterprise, comes second. You put capital and security [of] income first."[17]

The difference in business structure also was reflected in the differing market for the lawyer's services. The merger wave of the 1920s, as well as the government's promotion of cartelization, created a new demand for the consultation skills of a few major British solicitor firms such as Freshfields. Contributing further business was the Imports Duties Advisory Committee which effectively administered a kind of anti-trust policy as a result of tariffs. In banking, the Bank of England was also involved in both promoting mergers, and exercising some supervision over the formation of cartels by banks on interest rates. Eventually even smaller firms whose clients included exporters often were called upon to draft cartel agreements. While accountants remained of primary importance, even they increasingly relied upon solicitors' advice in matters involving mergers and cartels. A leading treatise on the holding company, which went through several editions from 1923 to World War II, was kept in print by T. B. Robson of Price, Waterhouse & Co. Throughout the work Robson noted at what point a lawyer's advice might be useful, writing that "each case must obviously be considered on its own merits, and if necessary the holding company's legal advisors should be brought into consultation before any action is taken." Still, although problems posed by minority shareholders sometimes required going to court, litigation was exceptional. Since tax advantages and other considerations permitting the relative autonomy of individual firms often were the motive behind a merger, the process was routine enough that accountants rather than lawyers remained in the leading role.[18]

In the United States the reverse was true. Between World Wars I and II a fundamental issue for American big business was the relation of the holding company to other forms of corporate "fusion." According to a leading study of the American holding company published by James C. Bonbright and Gardiner C. Means in 1932 these were "questions within the purview of a lawyer rather than of an economist." This was so in part because of federalism: the rules governing corporate consolidation in the separate states often differed. Lawyers were indispensable during and after the merger wave, moreover, because the "pure" holding company increasingly became the first step toward forming a more centralized managerial structure. In "recent years," wrote Bonbright and Means, "stock control has first been centralized in a pure holding company...later to be displaced by a complete fusion of the constituent companies." As in Britain, minority stockholders might "place fatal difficulties in the way of complete integration." Yet, unlike Britain, the mix of state and federal law regulating takeovers encouraged dealing with the minority shareholders as a preliminary to more complete managerial control. In addition, there remained the corresponding market for private suits against large firms and cartel practices.[19]

Each nation's merger wave ended in the Great Depression. By 1929 the foundations of a new corporate order existed in Britain, though the degree of organizational efficiency was less and the scale of monopoly control greater than in the United States.[20] The economic collapse beginning in 1929 was such, however, that both nations resorted to extensive cartelization.[21] In Britain, Acts of Parliament, private restrictive agreements, and trade associations generally sanctioned the "most extensive, though not always co-ordinated control instituted by the producers, distributors, and consumers," wrote one commentator in 1937. "As a feature of industrial and commercial organization, free competition has nearly disappeared from the British scene."[22]

Briefly, the same was true of the American economic order under the National Recovery Administration. During the Depression the unitary structure which dominated the nation's big business by the 1920s proved little more effective than Britain's holding companies. Like their British counterparts, therefore, American business leaders urged the government to sanction cartels in order to prevent price competition. The Roosevelt Administration instituted this policy through the NRA, which suspended enforcement of the antitrust laws and attempted to stabilize commodity values through fixed prices. The policy failed, however, not only because within eighteen months the Supreme Court declared the NRA unconstitutional, but also because price fixing did not increase production. No longer sympathetic to the business point of view, Roosevelt supported Thurman Arnold's zealous antitrust campaign. Revitalizing and significantly expanding the Antitrust Division's traditional anticartel policy, Arnold "broke up" the cartels and other trade restraints. The government also won cases which imposed greater oligopolistic competition upon managerially centralized firms.[23]

Meanwhile, the Depression revealed the effectiveness of Sloan's organizational strategy. Whether British or American big business relied upon the holding company or unitary organizational structure, they turned to cartels primarily in order to reduce production and raise prices. Even so, stabilized prices encouraged caution regarding increasing production because of the concern that prices would again fall. Thus, cartelization meant that prices increased, but not production. The flexibility of the divisionalized and decentralized managerial structure, however, enabled firms to compete more through research, development, and advertizing than price. Prices were secondary to a marketing and sales strategy which required product differentiation.[24] In America, according to Neil Fligstein, the "proof of the success of the sales and marketing conception came during the Depression. Firms...dominated by the...[unitary] conception of control did poorly." But firms such as

Swift & Co., DuPont, US Rubber, General Electric, RCA, General Motors, "whose managers and entrepreneurs concentrated on finding markets for goods, any market for any goods, were successful."[25] In Britain the high regard for ICI as a model of managerial efficiency suggested implicitly that British observers recognized this too since it was one of the nation's comparatively few firms possessing the divisional structure.[26] Significantly, the divisional structure was adopted by many of the American firms which had reorganized in response to the "lackadaisical" enforcement of antitrust after the US Steel decision.[27]

World War II was a turning point in government policies influencing business strategy and structure. First in Britain, then in the United States, war-time production required industries to operate at full capacity. As was the case during World War I, in order to mobilize and allocate resources officials sanctioned cartelization. The British government worked through trade associations. In the United States there was also extensive cooperation between government and business, including the general suspension of Arnold's antitrust campaign, at least in so far as it involved domestic enterprise. Nevertheless, many business leaders, economists, and government authorities in both nations concluded that a post-war international economic order capable of sustaining full employment and healthy consumerism depended upon more efficient business organization and free markets. As a result, after 1943 American policymakers increasingly advocated aggressive prosecution of international cartels and big corporations. Similarly, unlike World War I, British policymakers succeeded in developing enduring machinery for regulating monopoly and trade restraints. Although this machinery was not enacted until 1948, the new policy consensus it represented was an important preliminary step toward overcoming the organizational lag in British business.[28]

Between the 1920s and 1940s the convergence of both nations' business order was uneven. Differing attitudes toward profit, reflected in contrasting financial and market contingencies and a more limited demand for legal services, were undoubtedly important factors. Yet each country's legal rules were also significant. The ambivalent application of the American rule of reason generally forbade overt price fixing while it often encouraged more efficient forms of corporate concentration. British law promoted mergers and thereby the rise of a corporate economy; its simultaneous sanction of cartelization and loose organizational forms, however, discouraged the widespread adaptation of more efficient managerial structures.

PRESSURE GROUPS AND CHANGING ECONOMIC THOUGHT

As each nation's business structure tentatively converged, pressure groups applied new economic theories. The dominant economic analysis assumed that "imperfect" rather than classical competition best characterized the operation of market relations among firms.[29] Economic experts, business and labor interests, and policymakers applied this principle in Britain to undermine the Free Trade consensus and in America to significantly redefine republican values. Nearly all interest groups in each nation supported government intervention; disagreements involved means rather than ends. Different outcomes reflected different social and political institutions; but by the end of World War II there was more agreement than ever before among the two nations' public officials that monopoly and restrictive practices were problems requiring government action.

In both nations the organizational transformation wrought by war, merger wave, and Depression encouraged economists to revise their theories of competition. Economists increasingly agreed that imperfect competition characterized by oligopoly or monopoly had displaced the classical competition identified as rivalry between small units. In 1933 this trend culminated in the publication of books by Britain's Joan Robinson and America's E. H. Chamberlin. They rejected the classical assumption that monopoly and competition were exclusive, showing that both factors influenced the pricing practices of most firms.[30]

Yet economists of both nations had mixed views regarding the implications of imperfect competition. Concerned primarily with the relation between government action and employment, J. M. Keynes did not address the monopoly issue directly. Nevertheless, Keynes's theories were potentially useful to advocates of competition who argued that without corrective government intervention monopoly and restrictive practices impeded attainment of full employment. America's A. A. Berle, G. C. Means, and Arthur Burns pushed the Robinson–Chamberlin theory to the point of contending, however, that competition was dead. In order to end extensive unemployment and prevent corporate "autocracy," they said, massive government planning along the lines of NRA, rather than mere antitrust prosecution was required.[31]

To other economists the restriction of competition was less ominous. J. A. Schumpeter believed bigness permitted firms to limit inefficient competition based on price in favor of "competition from the new commodity, the new technology, the new source of supply, the new type of organization (the largest-scale unit control for instance)."[32] Finally, a young lecturer at the London School of Economics, R. H. Coase, sought to "bridge... a gap in economic theory between the assumption... that resources are allocated by means of the price mechanism and the assumption... that this allocation is dependent on the entrepreneur-coordinator." Coase focused on the degree of vertical integration within a corporate structure. The extent of vertical integration determined the firm's ability to limit external market transactions. The more the firm eliminated these transactions, he reasoned, the greater its efficiency.[33]

Initially this transformation in economic theory benefited the advocates of cartelization. Business groups in both nations contended that World War I had created a new economic order in which cooperation had superseded competition. In Britain this view was most directly identified with the rationalization movement; by the mid-1920s its assumptions dominated public discussion of the economy.[34] According to one observer, the merger wave of the 1920s was so extensive because the war had "driven home to our organizers of capital and our masters of finance that... we were behind the times." The traditions of "automatic regulation and unconscious specialization – independence and aloofness – were antiquated." In order to "maintain our place as an industrial and manufacturing nation we would have to co-ordinate and amalgamate our big concerns into single units all closely inter-related."[35] Although some representatives of small enterprise dissented, throughout the period the rhetoric of both large and small British business groups generally favored government promotion of cartelization, particularly through trade associations.[36]

The rhetoric and alignment of business pressure groups was similar in the United States. In 1928 a Justice Department investigator declared that a trade association's cooperative agreement embodied the "business man's idea of the proper and reasonable solution of the universal problem of over production. It represents probably in most cases a very slight extortion of the consumer, but it is by no means proved that the benefits, first of all to the producer, both employer and worker, and later even to the consumer from the stabilization of industry, do not outweigh this."[37] In America, of course, those advocating such cooperative trade restraints had to contend with antitrust legislation. Accordingly, their support for "business self-government" in the form of trade associations coincided with a campaign to weaken or suspend altogether the antitrust laws. Just as big and small business generally supported rationalization in Britain, so the proponents of antitrust revision included both groups. Noted Robert F. Himmelberg, the "major line of division within the business community was between the more and the less profitable industries... Industries from the less profitable sector tended to support revision, quite irrespective of the average size of member firms."[38]

During the 1930s the triumph of the theory of "self-government" through cartelization was uneven. In the United States during Roosevelt's first administration the antitrust revisionists won passage of the NRA. When it collapsed, however, Roosevelt revitalized antitrust enforcement by making Thurman Arnold head of the Antitrust Division.[39] Throughout the period in Britain, by contrast, the advocates of rationalization remained influential. In 1943 a British MP and Government Minister who, during the 1930s, had been associated with the "iron and steel international cartel," told an economist in the Board of Trade that the cartel was "good for the iron and steel industry in their export markets, and that there was no occasion, therefore, for the Government to cavil at it." Moreover, "in a product like steel it was necessary to fix the price not with relation to costs of production, since these vary so greatly, but with relation to what the market would stand." Given such benefits, the economist observed, it was not surprising that the Minister expected "quite clearly" that the cartel "would be brought to life again after the war."[40]

In both nations the economic thought of organized labor was less uniform. Since the nineteenth century British and American labor groups had considered the issue of monopoly and restrictive practices primarily as an extension of larger social-welfare concerns, particularly unemployment, prices, and nationalization.[41] Yet from 1921 to 1945 the stance of each nation's labor movement steadily diverged. At crucial points certain American labor and business interests joined forces favoring antitrust revision and the NRA. But when Congress, the government, and the courts finally established that unions were exempt from the antitrust laws, organized labor's interest in the issue declined.[42] In Britain, however, the Labour Party persisted in its uneven course until World War II when it came to share the dominant view that some form of administrative machinery was necessary because monopoly and restrictive practices threatened full employment. British Labour also differed from its American counterpart in believing that the regulation of monopoly and trade restraints was consistent with nationalized industries.[43] Professor Harold Laski, a member of the Labour Party's executive committee said in 1943 that should Labour replace Churchill's Coalition Government the "first thing that I should want to do would be to nationalize the banking system; to nationalize the land; to nationalize mines and power and transport."[44]

Similarly, throughout the period the British proponents of competition disagreed. Various British economists endorsed the views of Marshall and A. C. Pigou, who since World War I had called for the institution of a tribunal with power to investigate trade restraints and monopoly and to recommend action where unfair competition or prices was proven. Within this group conservatives relied principally upon publicity while others favored supplementing it where appropriate with nationalization. In either case, the underlying assumption was that imperfect competition among large managerially centralized corporations was more efficient than cartelization.[45]

Throughout the 1920s and 30s the British proponents of competition had little influence. During World War II, however, their significance increased. In 1943 British economist W. Arthur Lewis examined the relevance of American antitrust.[46] Adamantly opposing cartelization, Lewis concluded that "nothing [was] to be said in favor of [loose] trade combinations." As for managerially centralized big firms, those which achieved size through organizational efficiency were of little threat. But the "fact" was that "many inefficient firms [were] able to grow by taking advantage of defects in our social organization." Lewis was not adverse to the government ensuring that small firms received adequate financial assistance, so that the "big firm would not so easily gobble them up." In any case, it was often defects in the law of patents, restrictive practices, and other areas which aided the "would-be monopolists." But lawmakers as well as "plain men" had accepted the "fallacies"

that because of cut-throat competition business resorted to monopoly
and restraints in order to establish stability and aid employment. Yet
the contrary was true, Lewis said, for monopoly kept "prices stable"
but "high," which "makes some richer and others poorer."[47]

The American antitrust experience provided guidance for
remedying these defects. In Britain loose "rings and combinations"
were a "much more common" "type of monopoly" than the
"industrial giant," Lewis observed. If effective antitrust machinery
existed in Britain it could suppress cartel practices with "little
practical difficulty," as the American record of successful prosecution
of cartel agreements demonstrated "overwhelmingly." The contention common in both the United States and Britain that antitrust
had "failed" arose not from prosecutions against cartels, but those
involving managerially centralized corporations. American corporate lawyers, it was true, had evaded the Clayton Act's
proscription of the acquisition of shares by purchasing physical assets
to bring about merger. Similarly, American courts, and their British
counterparts, had interpreted laws governing patents and other
restraints too narrowly. Lewis conceded that this "experience does
indeed prove that it is useless to try to prevent rival firms from
merging into big corporations." The triumph of size, however, did
not mean that competition was impossible. Where the government
provided adequate resources, as was the case with Arnold's Antitrust
Division, there was "no doubt that antitrust legislation can be a
most effective deterrent of monopolists, and save the public millions
of dollars."[48]

Based on this record, Lewis drew two broad conclusions. First,
"without question" government intervention could prevent
cartelization, and thereby preserve competition throughout broad
sectors of Britain's economy. Although such action could do little to
prevent big corporations, effective prosecution of monopolistic
abuses would at least facilitate imperfect competition. Second, to
achieve this competition the creation of new administrative
machinery was essential. The government's "major reliance" should
be not the courts, but "enforcement by a government department
with adequate funds." The "traditional repository for powers of this
kind" was the Board of Trade, and Lewis recommended establishing
within it a "special 'Department of Monopoly Control.'" The
department would possess "police powers, including men capable of
nosing out restraints from conflicting evidence of witnesses and files

of complicated papers...economists trained to analyze the pattern of an industry and the effect of its peculiar restraints...[and] lawyers, able to present a good case." In order to preserve "private enterprise," he emphasized, "it must be made to compete." This meant making private enterprise "not the master but the servant of the public." Britain was "almost the only important country without legislation to...control the activities of monopolists," Lewis concluded. "If private groups are not to submerge the public interest, Parliament must take bold action to control monopoly."[49]

Unlike their British counterparts, the American proponents of competition worked within an existing antitrust tradition. During the 1920s J. M. Clark and Frank Albert Fetter argued for antitrust policies which recognized the economic consequences of imperfect competition. "The economists have not lost faith in the virtues of free competition in industry where it actually exists or is possible...But they see clearly that in actual life these conditions have become more and more rare," wrote Fetter in 1924. The remedy was a vigorous enforcement of antitrust legislation "fully emancipated from the bonds of a mere price conception."[50] In 1925 Clark emphasized that all law was "a means to a social end." Conceding that the "inertia of precedent persists and the value of stability is highly emphasized," he wrote that "nonetheless economic facts are more and more finding their way into legal briefs, and the evolution of law in response to changing economic circumstances is coming to be recognized as one of the accepted conditions of present-day life."[51]

A leading proponent of this sort of economic analysis during the 1920s was Herbert Hoover.[52] During the 1930s and 1940s the argument for linking antitrust enforcement to economic conse-quences became still more influential. Economists at the University of Chicago, including F. H. Knight, George Stigler, and Henry Simons fashioned theories for attacking big business, emphasizing economic analysis rather than moralism.[53] Assistant Attorney General Arnold agreed that effective antitrust enforcement de-manded this change of focus. Confusion arose because in the past antitrust prosecutors and businessmen alike "considered...intent as more important than...results." Enforcement had been a "problem of corporate morality" with "courts and prosecutors...busy pursuing that will o' the wisp, corporate intent, while economic results were ignored." But the "trust problem" was "not a problem of private morals... not a question of the good or bad intention of the monopolist." What mattered, said Arnold, were the "economic results growing out of their operation of the price and marketing machinery."[54]

Yet American more so than British defenders of competition were ambiguous concerning the value of small enterprise. Economists such as Lewis believed that firms which became large through efficiency rather than trade restraints benefited the public, while in other cases the small firm was no less efficient than the big firm. They did not particularly worry about the fate of the "little man," as long as the government ensured everyone an adequate supply of credit. In the United States, however, the heritage of republican values associated with Louis Brandeis made such a dismissal of small business difficult. Neither the Republican Hoover nor the Democrat Arnold could succeed politically unless they recognized the special status of small enterprises.[55] Thus, on the one hand, Arnold said it was "as meaningless to say that small units are better than big units as to say that small buildings are better than big ones." He denied, moreover, that any "governmental group" sought to break up efficient mass production" based on large units. The government would intervene primarily where industry had "gone so far on the path of monopoly control that competition can never be restored." On the other hand, prosecution was necessary in order to eradicate the "thousands of price-fixing agreements and instances of coercion of small business which... [were] changing this country into an industrial autocracy." Such a practical approach benefited from the "great advantage of applying the Rule of Reason... [which permitted consideration of] one problem at a time in the light of its particular facts."[56]

American policymakers nonetheless adopted the theory of imperfect competition to attack big business. Despite the contention that antitrust issues were not "a matter of moral judgment in any sense whatsoever," the social values underlying antitrust enforcement nonetheless favored free government, full employment, vigorous consumerism, and healthy small enterprise. In order for "democracy... to survive it must be vigilant, strong, forceful, and constantly able to defend itself against concentrated economic power," wrote economist T. J. Kreps. "It must prevent exploitation of the people by such corporate bureaucrats intoxicated with their economic power. It cannot let matters take their course." Where the "rules of industrial empires control the state, the inevitable result is fascism and the destruction of liberty."[57]

During World War II the supporters of cartelization in both nations encountered mounting resistance. America's campaign against international cartels and other foreign-policy concerns coincided with the growing influence of the British advocates of competition pushing for the development of antimonopoly machinery.[58] The transatlantic pressures favoring government intervention aroused the anxiety of such cartel defenders as ICI's Lord McGowen. "I see no hope of collaboration between British and American business unless the United States repeals its Sherman Anti-Trust Act," he told William Benton in 1943. "Can we in England look forward to that?"[59] In the same year economists in the Board of Trade noted that discussions with British business representatives "lead rapidly to questions of Government policy on international cartels and monopoly of the home market."[60]

The differing attitudes toward government intervention reflected different values and institutions. Paradoxically, wrote constitutional scholar Robert E. Cushman in 1941, British social and political relations favored the extremes of business self-regulation and government-run industries. Americans, by contrast, supported "maximum governmental regulations but [shied] away from collectivism." In part this was so, Cushman said, because British business was generally "sound and conservative." The "glaring abuses" and "callous disregard by private capital of its public responsibilities" which in America fostered extensive regulation, never were in Britain "serious or prolonged enough to dominate government policy" to require such action. Another "factor pulling for conservatism in British regulation of business" was that "vested economic interests in England enjoyed virtually unchallenged political supremacy much longer than in the United States." Thus, in the case of collectivized industries, "title and control [passed] from the prior owners to a government dominated by the owners' own economic group." In addition, unlike American regulatory bodies which often lacked public respect, the British held their Civil Service in high regard. Finally, in Britain Parliament had supreme authority to define the meaning of the public interest, whereas in America the "vital difference" was that the court made that "determination."[61]

The uneven convergence of the response to big business was

reflected in British pressure groups' use of changing economic thought. Economists in both nations recognized that imperfect competition had replaced the classical notion of competition. By the late-1920s Britain's faith in Free Trade had given way to a new consensus favoring government promotion of larger business structures. Yet there was disagreement over the extent to which economic efficiency among these larger units was best served by government action stimulating cooperation or competition. Big and small business groups and both major political parties espoused rationalization, especially through the formation of trade associations while some economists and supporters of Labour supported competition. During World War II the proponents of competition gained greater influence, but they expressed little more concern for truly autonomous small enterprise than did their rationalizer opponents.

In the United States pressure groups put the theory of imperfect competition to somewhat different uses. Representatives of both large and small business and organized labor not only favored trade associations, but advocated relaxation of antitrust to encourage cooperative arrangements. These interests achieved, however, only limited success. Applying the rule of reason, policymakers from Hoover to Arnold used the new economic theory to emphasize "economic results" rather than the moralism which had been central to republican values. Yet these same policymakers could not escape the traditional ambivalence shaping antitrust enforcement. Americans wanted the consumer benefits derived from big business while maintaining a steadfast commitment to individual opportunity represented by small enterprise. These antitrust enforcers appealed to economic theory to renew the attack upon "inefficient" giant corporations in order to preserve the free institutions which permitted "efficient" small and big business to thrive. As a result, republican values did not disappear, they were transformed. During World War II the Antitrust Division kept these values alive by winning support for action against international cartels.

LAW AND THE DIFFERING IMPACT OF PRESSURE GROUPS

In both nations, despite similarities in rhetoric and alignment, the impact of pressure groups differed. The passing of Free Trade engendered a new consensus. Most large and small business interests, organized labor, and other political and professional groups agreed that market productivity and full employment required government action on the issue of monopoly and trade restraints. Disagreement over whether the ultimate outcome should be a cooperative or competitive business order nonetheless did not disrupt business self-regulation and the "get along" ethos which insulated small as well as large firms from the most vigorous competitive pressure. The courts and Parliament sanctioned this result. In America, by contrast, interest-group cooperation in the campaign against antitrust was, except briefly under the NRA, ineffectual. While policymakers from Hoover to Arnold favored economic analysis over moralism, their actions and central presumptions continued to reflect the basic tensions inherent in republican values, including the respect for small business. The Court's and the government's application of the rule of reason sanctioned this struggle, encouraging oligopolistic competition among giant corporations and the survival of small enterprise.

After 1921 the willingness of British officials to consider limited government intervention along the lines of the Profiteering Acts and the Standing Committee on Trusts faded. In 1924, under a Labour government, the Board of Trade prepared various proposals growing out of the Trade Monopolies Bill drafted in 1920. These proposals relied principally on publicity. When a claim concerning restrictive practices arose, either the Board or the Railway and Canal Commission was empowered to make inquiries and, if necessary, to publish reports. Another version of this Bill suggested giving the Board or Commission powers to forbid particular practices. In 1925 a few members of the Labour Party introduced one variant of these proposals as a private member's "Trusts and Combines Bill." None of these measures received significant support. There were no further noteworthy proposals until after World War II began, though in 1923 and 1925 the Board of Trade established internal supervisory boards responsible for overseeing consumer prices in the building and food trades. These measures relied solely upon publicity and business good faith.[62]

By the mid-1920s a consensus emerged favoring governmental promotion of trade restraints under the guise of rationalization. Since the turn of the century official toleration of trade restraints had permitted smaller firms to remain relatively independent within self-regulating trade associations and other large organizational structures. The triumph of rationalization meant that increasingly such self-regulation received direct government endorsement. Also, it enabled smaller enterprise to persist in Britain despite the merger wave of the 1920s. In 1926 both Conservative and Labour Parties generally approved marketing coal through cooperative agreements. Little concerned about monopolistic abuses amid falling prices and prolonged industrial depression, successive governments fostered or encouraged rationalization of various industries and services on the basis of large units especially trade associations.[63] The Final Report of the Balfour Committee on Industry and Trade published in January 1929 concluded that: "On the whole and on balance we feel that, in the circumstances of the present industrial situation, the case for immediate legislation for restraint of such abuses as may result from combinations cannot be said to be an urgent one."[64]

Throughout the 1930s the government's policy of rationalization favored the perpetuation of trade restraints among smaller firms. The Final Report of the Greene Committee on Restraint of Trade published in 1930–31 concluded that although resale price maintenance was sometimes inconsistent with the public interest, the problem was not significant enough to justify any major change in the law. The Report nonetheless declared that if at some future time the government considered public policy concerning trusts, monopolies, and restrictive practices, the "possibility of support being given by the price maintenance system and boycotts ought not to be overlooked."[65] The conclusions of the Macmillan Committee Report on Finance and Industry of 1931 took a similar stance. The Tory chairman of the Committee, Harold Macmillan, enlarged upon the view that "planned production" was unlikely "while industries are organized on competitive lines." It was thus "a matter of primary importance to produce an orderly structure in each of our national industries amendable to the authority of a representative directorate conducting the industries as self-governing units in accordance with the circumstances of the modern world."[66]

Parliament enacted legislation promoting cartelization. Beginning with the Coal Mines Act of 1930, Parliament sanctioned business "self-government" under official supervision. The Finance Act of 1935 granted cartelized industries tax advantages. Once Britain imposed a protective tariff through the Import Duties Act of 1932, the Import Duties Advisory Committee used its authority to approve cartel agreements in various industries, including iron and steel. The British government even explored a possible cartel arrangement with the German iron and steel industry as late as 1938. Labour supported these measures in principle.[67] The attempt to establish some safeguards for consumers in the Consumer's Council Bill, prepared and introduced into Parliament by the short-lived Labour Government in 1930, got nowhere. Meanwhile, Labour supported the Conservative's initial steps toward nationalization through the formation of various "Public Corporations" in the transportation, communications, and electricity industries.[68]

From the 1920s to the 1940s the British judiciary reinforced the triumph of cartelization which preserved the independence of small firms. During the interwar years the courts generally did not prevent restrictive horizontal agreements between large or small firms in the same industry, or vertical ones between producers and distributors, including resale price maintenance.[69] Following the *Mogul* doctrine which required proof of actual malice in order to challenge restraints, the courts sanctioned the "monopolist" who used "measures designed to hamper the business of competitors." In order to "protect themselves and their members" trade associations "could offer preferential terms in exchange for exclusive dealing, black list and boycott dealers who broke resale price and other conditions...without any fear that the Courts would hold such agreements unreasonable as between the parties or against the public interest." This narrow construction of what constituted "unreasonable" and the "public interest" denied a right of action to those harmed by trade restraints, and the "monopolist and association could be as ruthless as they chose in pursuit of their own interest so long as they were not actuated by malice!"[70]

Cartelization prevailed in court cases involving struggles between relatively small, owner-operated firms. A 1925 case pitted "a trade union of newspaper retailers" against "a committee of newspaper proprietors." The retailers sought to prevent the proprietors from forming exclusive contracts with new retailers. Both groups pressured wholesalers: the retailers threatened to switch a restrictive agreement to another wholesaler, while the producers threatened not to supply the wholesaler if he continued dealing with the retailers. The retailers sued, seeking an injunction to block the producer's withholding of goods.[71] The court refused to intervene, taking an "attitude of neutrality towards economic groups struggling for enforcement of their economic aims," which indicated "how far social reality was already removed from the state of affairs idealized by the *Mogul* case, where every individual had full economic freedom and, so Bentham thought, all would come out well for the community.”[72]

The courts also sanctioned the use of business coercion to *enforce* restrictive practices. According to a contemporary observer, from the 1920s to the 1940s “comparatively loose contractual” arrangements gave way to “tighter structural organization, mostly in the form of trade…associations. The principal object of these associations is the maintenance of minimum prices by a rigid control of wholesalers and retailers.” During the merger wave competition between producers was “decisively curtailed or excluded.” These horizontal combinations facilitated the formation of trade associations “whose main object” was “usually the fixing of wholesalers’ and retailers’ prices.” The associations concluded agreements with “different sections of the trade by which both wholesalers and retailers undertake not to supply or buy from price cutters. The principal means of enforcement is the black list system.”[73]

In *Thorne* v. *Motor Trade Association* (1937) the House of Lords declared that certain forms of the black list were legal. As long as the system was part of “a reasonable pursuit of legitimate business interests…it [was] neither criminal blackmail nor civil conspiracy.” The decision was a “further important step” toward legitimating “collective action for the protection of economic group interests.” The Lords “authorized corporate action which eliminated freedom of trade for the individual, and it refused to interfere, except in very rare cases. The attitude was still neutrality with abandonment of the liberal economic ideals of previous generations.”[74]

The British courts also supported restraints imposed through cooperation between business and labor against another business. On Scotland’s Outer Hebrides the original Harris Tweed industry relied in part on local crofters who spun yarn and wove cloth by hand in their cottages. On Harris island a group of mill owners, who also qualified under the Harris Tweed trademark, had their yarn spun on the mainland using cheaper techniques, but then had the cloth woven by the Harris cottage crofters. Nevertheless, a larger group organized as the Lewis Mill Owners’ Association controlled the industry. Through a cooperative arrangement with this group the dock-workers’ union refused to import yarn from the mainland. The Millowners’ Association wanted to secure a minimum selling price, while the workers sought to protect a collective bargaining agreement with the Association. The mills relying upon the imported yarn challenged the two groups, alleging conspiracy. The Lords, however, rejected the claim.[75]

Wrote one critic of the *Harris Tweed* decision, the "employers' association and the worker's union co-operated against [and defeated] a number of outsiders who were owner-producers."[76] Perhaps ultimately this preference was more important because it fostered greater protection for unions from criminal tort litigation. The decision was also significant, however, because the court pushed traditional self-restraint to new limits, sustaining broad substantive results benefitting the established business order. It thus reflected a course of decision in which British judges "often... have taken sides in economic issues, though often unconsciously and mostly in the form of improvised and unscientific theories." Even so this limited degree of activism reinforced the inefficiencies inherent in the "get-along" ethos.[77]

By World War II the triumph of rationalization did not prevent the increased influence of those promoting competition. Britain's faith in Free Trade was gradually displaced by a new consensus favoring official promotion of business cooperation within large, self-regulating units. Labour supported the new consensus, believing that price stability helped to maintain employment. Small business supported the consensus because it sanctioned the preservation of relative independence through horizontal and vertical restrictive agreements. The managers of large firms such as ICI supported the consensus because it legitimated the corporate economy emerging from the merger wave, without arousing concern about monopolistic abuse. During World War II, however, some pro-competition economists, Labour leaders, and Tories became convinced that cartelization inhibited the attainment of full employment and a free market economy once victory was won. Prominent London newspapers endorsed this argument, and the United States pushed the same view in bi-lateral negotiations of major international agreements. By the end of the war a policy compromise emerged which reflected the tension between those favoring government intervention to police but otherwise allow monopolistic practices and those demanding official action to prevent such restraints. Established in the Monopolies and Restrictive Practices (Inquiry and Control) Act of 1948, the compromise reflected the presumption that investigation and publicity were sufficient to prevent abuse.[78]

Cartelization followed a different course in America. Between

1921 and 1933 three approaches involving the relation of the antitrust laws to loose cooperative and tight corporate structures emerged. The first position, following a traditional view of antitrust, contended that government should preserve competition. The second and opposite view was that of the antitrust revisionists. Not particularly concerned about the creation of managerially centralized big firms, the revisionist favored establishing "cooperative self-government" through trade associations.[79] The middle position was that of Hoover's "cooperative competition." He defended the "cooperative action" of "trade association activities" to attain a "progressive economic system" without destroying competition by "creating dominations of groups that would stifle equality of opportunity." Seeking to avoid the "twin evils" of big business "monopoly" and big government "socialism," Hoover believed in "the interest of maintaining the small business unit." Nonetheless, he opposed overt price fixing. He accepted managerially centralized big firms as long as they attained their market share through efficiency; and, under certain limited circumstances, he even advocated granting antitrust exemptions. Such qualifications aside, however, Hoover's cooperative competition was consistent with the ideas of Louis Brandeis.[80]

Throughout the 1920s Hoover's middle course prevailed. Initially, Attorney General Harry Daugherty and the Supreme Court inhibited Hoover's program of using trade associations to circulate and publish statistical information in order to improve business efficiency. After Harlan F. Stone replaced Daugherty in 1924, however, Stone's new assistant attorney general William J. Donovan won the *Maple Flooring* case, a Supreme Court decision consistent with Hoover's policy. Two years later, in a decision Hoover also supported, the Court accepted Donovan's argument in *Trenton Potteries* that trade associations engaged in overt price fixing violated the Sherman Act. Also in 1927, however, the Court rejected Donovan's attempt to increase competition among more managerially centralized big firms in the *International Harvester* case. Even so, Hoover was sympathetic to Donovan's unsuccessful argument. Meanwhile, Hoover condoned Donovan's new policy of advising business on the legality of proposed cooperative practices. He favored, too, the Federal Trade Commission's new administrative machinery established to negotiate and approve trade practice agreements.[81]

Hoover resisted identifying himself with the campaign of the antitrust revisionists. The revisionists used Hoover's rhetoric to promote forms of cartelization they called "self-regulation." Hoover, however, rejected their proposed overthrow of the per se ban against price fixing established in *Trenton Potteries*. Instead of antitrust revision, he urged more "economic analysis" in the government's antitrust cases and the Court's decisions, curbs on the effects of the 1920s' merger wave, and more aggressive punishment of abuse so as not to undermine the legality of trade associations. After Hoover became President in 1929 his new Attorney General William D. Mitchell dismantled the advisory-opinion procedure Donovan had created. Moreover, Mitchell replaced Donovan with John Lord O'Brien, who took a more aggressive stance toward antitrust prosecutions. In 1932, following O'Brien's argument which incorporated the sort of economic analysis Hoover suggested, the Court ordered leading meatpackers to comply with a consent decree they had resisted for fifteen years. "Mere size ... is not an offense ... ," the Court held, "but size carries with it an opportunity for abuse that is not to be ignored when the opportunity is proved to have been utilized in the past." Also, Hoover's new appointments to the FTC gradually returned to a more adversarial approach toward trade agreements. The Depression, to be sure, compelled Hoover in the name of his "associational" policies to condone certain antitrust exemptions in the petroleum, rubber, motion picture, and electrical industries. Ultimately, however, oligopolistic competition rather than cartelization prevailed in these industries.[82]

Thus antitrust revisionism triumphed not under Hoover's "cooperative competition" but Roosevelt's NRA. By 1931 the less profitable big and small industries supported recovery proposals generally identified with Gerard Swope of General Electric and Henry I. Harriman of the Chamber of Commerce. The Swope Plan required suspension of antitrust laws so that the government could plan recovery through legally enforceable cartel agreements implemented by trade associations.[83] Hoover condemned the Swope Plan for requiring the "organization of gigantic trusts" to carry out "price fixing" through "the repeal of the entire Sherman and Clayton Acts and all other restrictions on combination and monopoly."[84] A compromised version of this planning-cartel program became the Roosevelt Administration's NRA.[85] Meanwhile, the Court upheld cartel agreements within the coal industry in *Appalachian Coals Inc.* v. *US* (1933); two years later, however, it struck down the NRA which had imposed similar agreements.[86]

The Roosevelt Administration's subsequent reaction against the NRA appealed to the interests of some small business. In a bid to gain the support of small enterprise Congress enacted the Robinson-Patman Act of 1936 and the Miller-Tydings Act of 1937. The former attempted to protect small retailers from chain stores; the latter permitted states to pass fair trade laws which allowed small firms to engage in certain trade restraints. To a limited extent these laws loosened the restrictions against resale price maintenance and other restrictive practices along lines Louis Brandeis had urged following the Court's *Dr. Miles* decision of 1911. The legislation also afforded American middlemen some of the opportunities their British counterparts enjoyed.[87] Roosevelt also approved the appointment of The National Economic Committee, which created an active group of lawyers, economists, and academics who used the new economic theories to renew the attack on big business in the name of small enterprise and free government.[88]

Still, the most conspicuous indication of the policy reversal was the appointment of Thurman Arnold. Arnold transformed the Antitrust Division, winning from Congress record appropriations to support a significantly enlarged professional staff which included economists as well as lawyers. He also instituted new prosecutorial techniques and a zealous public-relations campaign intended not only to gain public support but also to educate business on how best to comply with the antitrust laws. Ironically, Arnold's revival of antitrust was to a certain extent consistent with Hoover's principles. Most of the prosecutions Arnold's Antitrust Division instituted and won were against price-fixing schemes in such industries as steel, oil, electrical goods, milk, and cement. Hoover, of course, had favored the Court's rejection of overt price fixing in *Trenton Potteries* and the use of economic analysis to force compliance with antitrust principles in the meatpackers' case.[89]

Most importantly, the theory underlying Arnold's prosecutions favored an analysis which considered the structural and economic consequences of business organization and practice. Like Hoover, Arnold urged the courts to apply a rule of reason avoiding moralism in favor of economic analysis. "Competition" was, Arnold, said, "a kind of game which requires a referee. Without a referee... the men who form gangs will win. Often antitrust offenses involve no moral turpitude. Sometimes they are protective measures taken in order to survive against the aggressive tactics of... [the] buccaneer." It was "important to recognize that antitrust enforcement is not a moral problem. It is the problem of continuous direction of economic traffic." The purpose of effective government intervention was "to penalize" the "reckless" or those "in too much hurry."[90]

Policymakers' attachment to small business, nonetheless, required a redefinition of republican values. Both Hoover and Arnold used the theory of "economic results" to attack "inefficient" big firms. They used the same economic assumptions in the prosecution of price fixing among small firms. Emphasis upon "efficiency" thus replaced the Brandeisian appeal to the moralism inherent in republican values. On the whole, however, the effect of the new approach was to establish the economic assumption that small business was often as efficient as big corporations. Theoretically, small enterprise did not threaten free government, open markets, and individual opportunity as did big business. Accordingly, the attack on giant corporations in the defense of freedom indirectly fostered the presumption that encouraging small enterprise benefited both economic efficiency and democracy. The linkage between liberty and efficiency displaced moralism as the standard governing the application of the rule of reason. But that same linkage merely reshaped republican values and, in the process, reaffirmed the unique status of small business in American life. Unsurprisingly, dispersed small business interests were Arnold's primary supporters.[91]

The ALCOA case of 1945 marked the emergence of this new antitrust doctrine. In 1912 the Justice Department had granted ALCOA a consent decree on the ground that although it had attained a monopoly there was no moral culpability. Yet from the 1920s on the Justice Department and FTC, as well as private suits, challenged ALCOA's monopoly. Until World War II the federal courts sustained the company's contention that under the rule of reason there was no evidence that its monopoly resulted from pernicious intent or conduct. Arnold, however, instituted a new suit emphasizing the economic consequences of the monopoly.[92]

Finally, in 1945, Judge Learned Hand declared a pioneering application of the new antitrust thinking. "We need charge it [ALCOA] with no moral derelictions after 1912; we may assume all it claims for itself is true," he said. It was only important "whether

[ALCOA] falls within the exception established in favor of those who do not seek, but cannot avoid, the control of a market." Hand concluded it did not. Although ALCOA had relied on organizational efficiency alone, he could "think of no more effective exclusion than progressively to embrace every opportunity as it opened, and to face every newcomer with new capacity already geared into a great organization, having the advantage of experience, trade connections and the elite of personnel." Ultimately, he concluded, it was better "to prefer a system of small producers, each dependent for his success upon his own skill and character, to one in which the great mass of those engaged must accept the direction of the few."[93] The result of the decision was a modest consent decree which nonetheless fostered for the first time within the aluminum industry oligopolistic competition.[94]

Between the 1920s and 1940s the impact of each country's pressure groups differed. In both nations a coalition of small and big business advocated increased cartelization. The emergence of a corporate economy in Britain, however, did not disrupt vertical and horizontal trade restraints which permitted large and small firms to coexist. Pushing the tradition of self-restraint to the limit, the British courts sanctioned these cartel arrangements. The faith in Free Trade had given way to a consensus favoring government intervention, though there was disagreement over whether policymakers should promote cartelization or competition. By World War II business interests claimed that achieving full employment and increased production in the post-war era required market stability maintained through cartelization. Many within the Labour Party, some Tories, and a group of economists, however, took the position that the attainment of these post-war policies was unlikely unless the government fostered competition. Even so, encouraging both corporate consolidation and looser forms of business cooperation, the law diffused conflict between large and small enterprise, but at the cost of perpetuating the inefficiencies associated with business self-regulation and the old "get-along" ethos.

In America, by contrast, the business-group coalition prevailed only briefly and then became fragmented. From World War I on, less efficient big and small firms advocated increased cartelization by pushing for a relaxation of the antitrust laws. Their efforts triumphed temporarily between 1933 and 1935 with the passage of the NRA. But the Court's declaration that the measure was unconstitutional, followed by Arnold's revitalization of antitrust, demonstrated that the victory was transitory. Throughout the period the Court adhered to the activism inherent in the American rule of reason, remaining ambivalent toward managerially centralized big firms, but consistently opposed to overt cartelization. Even so from Hoover to Arnold, American policymakers attempted to preserve both the consumer benefits of large-scale enterprise and the opportunity associated with small business. The moderate support of trade associations and "cooperative competition" reflected the balance Hoover struck, whereas after 1935 the Robinson-Patman and Fair Trade Acts, as well as Arnold's antitrust campaign, suggested the balance established by the Roosevelt Administration. Despite the cooperation between large and small enterprise during the antitrust-revision campaign, then, conflict ultimately prevailed. As the ALCOA decision suggested, the enforcement of transformed republican values encouraged the more efficient divisional structure and oligopolistic competition, while also preserving the benefits of small enterprise. During World War II the Antitrust Division appealed to the same values in its campaign against international cartels.

AMERICAN INFLUENCE, INTERNATIONAL CARTELS, AND THE REVIVAL OF ANTITRUST 1942–1948

The international cartel issue arose out of American domestic concerns. Arnold's efforts to maintain the antitrust campaign during World War II stimulated widespread public interest in the cartel "threat," which in turn fostered intensive government action. By the time Johnson and Benton visited Britain in the Fall of 1943, the issue had become the object of foreign-policy negotiations between the two nations. These negotiations coincided with Britain's initial development of policies toward trade restraints and monopoly eventually culminating in the Monopolies Act of 1948. Yet the same social and institutional factors which, since World War I, made the convergence of business structure, ideas, and policies tentative circumscribed the American influence on British policymaking.[95]

The war curtailed antitrust enforcement in domestic business. After Pearl Harbor Arnold's Antitrust Division adjusted to the extensive business-government cooperation the war-time mobilization required. As it had in World War I, the US government generally suspended the antitrust laws to meet the emergency. Nevertheless, Arnold improved upon World War I's record by establishing a role for the Antitrust Division. The Division's budget of $2,325,000 and staff of 583 reached a peak in 1942, declining relatively little during the rest of the war. As the government's administrative control expanded throughout the whole economy, the Antitrust Division exercised an oversight and advocacy function, particularly to ensure that small business received an appropriate share of government contracts. At the same time, however, the Antitrust Division postponed most of its major prosecutions, including those in the transportation, building, and food industries.[96]

A major reason for the Division's continued level of funding was its campaign against international cartels. Following the Division's investigations for the TNEC during the late 1930s, Arnold had sought prosecutions against collusive patent agreements. Previous court decisions had sanctioned extensive patent restraints. In order to overcome this obstacle he testified before congressional committees arguing for the reform of patent law. Still, there was little public interest in the patent problem until after the war began. The Division's investigations revealed that many patented goods which were indispensable to the war effort were directly or indirectly subject to international cartel agreements, many of which originated in Germany. Such powerful German giants as I. G. Farbenindustrie and America's Standard Oil had maintained extensive restrictive patent agreements.[97]

In testimony before congressional committees Arnold presented vivid accounts of "conspiracies" among leading corporate giants in the United States, Great Britain, Germany, and other nations. As a result the international cartel issue became "notorious." Americans believed "that cartel agreements between American and German firms had gravely weakened the national defense. The charges were spread over the front pages of newspapers, and the man in the street was soon talking about the 'cartel menace' and the sinister activities of I. G. Farbenindustrie." The investigations and prosecutions of international cartels increased throughout the war.[98]

By the time Arnold left the Antitrust Division to become a federal judge in 1943 the State Department, other agencies, and a special interdepartmental committee were studying the issue. House and Senate Military Affairs Committees also established special subcommittees to study the economic and political aspects of the problem. Edwards authored extensive studies which became the basis of a major congressional report on "Cartels and National Security," published in November, 1944.[99] At about the same time the State Department's Cartel Committee prepared a private memorandum entitled "Advance Clearance of Business Agreements in International Trade."[100] These and other published and privately circulated reports influenced important discussions between US and British representatives concerning the post-war economic order.[101]

Within the United States many business groups and the press generally opposed international cartels. Those concerned about commodity exports after the war agreed with Vice-President Henry A. Wallace's statement in March 1944 that "cartels [were] the greatest menace to the American business principles of free enterprise and equal opportunity."[102] Eric Johnson, president of the US Chamber of Commerce, and his friend William Benton of the University of Chicago, expressed similar views during their visit to Britain in the Fall of 1943.[103] The National Foreign Trade Council, by contrast, appealed to the government to provide advance clearance of international business agreements; it also sought an end to the Justice Department's prosecution of Webb-Pomerene co-operative arrangements.[104] The Council agreed with Sir Edgar Jones, Director of the World Trade Alliance, who said, "If Great Britain and the United States will take the lead and get the producers of each main product to prepare schemes for world export regulations, then general employment can be insured."[105] Yet from late 1942 on, as the Antitrust Division's revelations about the influence of German cartels made front-page news, most of the press sided with the views of Johnson, Benton, and Wallace.[106]

American professional economists and popularizers of expert opinion also generally attacked international cartels. Government economists on leave from such economics departments or business schools as Stanford, Oberlin, Northwestern, Reed College, and Buffalo, rejected the ideas of Joseph A. Schumpeter, who argued that by preventing "cut-throat" competition cartels enabled firms to invest in costly research and technological innovation.[107] Typical of this critical opinion was Northwestern University economics professor Corwin Edwards. From the late 1930s on he was affiliated with the Antitrust Division. In 1945 he edited and contributed to a collection of essays written by fellow economists serving in the government entitled *A Cartel Policy for the United Nations*. In this book, and articles published in the *New Republic*, Edwards popularized the anticartel position he had argued in government reports. Various popular books cited this evidence at length, including Guenter Reiman, *Patents for Hitler* (1942), Joseph Bortein and Charles A. Welsh, *Germany's Master Plan* (1943), Assistant Attorney General Wendell Berge's, *Cartels: Challenge to a Free World* (1944), and David Lasser, *Private Monopoly, the Enemy at Home* (1945).[108]

The pressure from interest groups, public opinion, and government authorities shaped official anti-cartel pronouncements. In September, 1944 Roosevelt stated that international action against cartels was vital to the nation's post-war economic policy. "More than the elimination of the political activities of German cartels will be required," he wrote. "Cartel practices which restrict the free flow of goods in foreign commerce will have to be curbed. With international trade involved this end can be achieved only through collaborative action by the United Nations."[109] Shortly thereafter the State Department published a statement noting that it had been considering such a policy since the fall of 1943.[110] The month following Roosevelt's statement the Senate's Kilgore Committee published its report entitled "Cartels and National Security" which received widespread public notice and commentary. This growing attention coincided with the Allies' policy discussions during and after the Bretton Woods and Dumbarton Oaks conferences of the summer of 1944.[111]

The Kilgore Committee's Report reflected the interplay between domestic and international pressures. The attainment of full employment after the war required expanding industrial output one and a half times over that of the pre-war period. Achieving such an increase was impossible unless markets and production were free from "cartel restrictions." Germany instituted these restrictions before the US entered the war, and was deploying its economic resources through the same means to prepare for a "third war." The pre-Arnold Antitrust Division's "failure" had encouraged American firms to join these "German cartelists" in order to replace "cut-throat competition" with "stability." US business participation had given Germany access to vital American technology in return for minimum benefits; it also had paved the way for shortages and scarcities in strategic industrial sectors at the time of Pearl Harbor.[112]

The Report made several recommendations. It urged the dismantling of German armament industries and expropriation of

German property throughout the world under the auspices of the United Nations. More importantly it advocated vigorous action against restrictive practices to avoid jeopardizing post-war full employment. To achieve this goal multilateral rather than unilateral reciprocal agreements and the elimination of all trade barriers were essential. The establishment of joint economic organizations among governments was necessary also, in order to determine the most efficient exchange of products, including increased American exports. The Report urged the creation of an international economic body to prevent restrictive practices, particularly in the patent field, and to facilitate the effective exchange of scientific knowledge and technological innovation. The Report also advised adopting the International Economic and Social Council proposed at Dumbarton Oaks and the "international monetary and credit proposals initiated at the Bretton Woods Conference."[113]

Publication of the Kilgore Report coincided with the State Department's rejection of a scheme to relax the enforcement of antitrust laws. The National Foreign Trade Council put forth the "old" proposition that advance clearance of proposed business plans in foreign trade was necessary because the antitrust laws were uncertain. The problem was especially acute in foreign trade, the Council contended, because the "divergences of law regarding monopoly in different parts of the world require a diversity of business practices on the part of exporters to which a statute designed primarily for domestic trade [was] ill-suited, and that considerations of foreign policy impinge and should be taken into account." The Council proposed legislation applying the standards of reasonableness to business agreements in international trade on a different basis from the "standards applied to such agreements in domestic trade." The proposal also sought "advance but revocable clearance of foreign-trade agreements by a designated agency, preferably the State Department."[114]

In an internally circulated memorandum the State Department's Cartel Committee stated the reasons for rejection. In certain exceptional cases such as the oil industry Congress permitted the various cabinet-level departments to exempt international agreements from antitrust prosecution for specified periods. The Council's proposal required, however, formal administration of such authority on a continuous basis. Despite "many years" of "intermittent agitation" for advance clearance by the Justice Department of domestic-trade agreements the issue was "dead." The "basic reason" for this denial was the "impossibility in borderline cases of an advanced administrative determination of the reasonableness of a plan when the test of reasonableness depend[ed] ultimately on the effects of the plan in the special circumstances surrounding a particular industry." The committee asked, therefore, whether it was likely that the "situation" would be "sufficiently different in post-war foreign trade to justify a procedure consistently rejected for domestic trade?" Complicating the question further was the Justice Department's and Federal Trade Commission's vigorous prosecution of Webb-Pomerene "activities." An extension of the Antitrust Division's attack on international cartels, these prosecutions made the law governing foreign-trade agreements more rather than less stringent. Thus it was "doubtful" that Congress would enact the Council's proposal until it was "more clear than it now [was] that the successful pursuit of our foreign policy require[d] legalizing arrangements of questionable present legality."[115]

The US Government's acquiescence to the Antitrust Division's anticartel policy influenced foreign-policy negotiations with Britain. The Atlantic Charter stated broad political objectives for the post-war world including a United Nations. Yet the main provision pertaining to the international economic order was Article VII of the Master Lend-Lease Agreement. Agreed to by both nations on February 3, 1942, Article VII provided that the "benefits" the United States received in return for aid to Britain would "not... burden commerce between the two countries, but... [would] promote mutually advantageous economic relations... and the betterment of world-wide economic relations." Through "agreed action" both nations and "all other countries of like mind" committed themselves by "appropriate international and domestic measures" to the "expansion... of production, employment, and the exchange and consumption of goods which are the material foundations of the liberty and welfare of all people; to the elimination of all forms of discriminatory treatment in international commerce, and to the reduction of tariffs and other trade barriers."[116]

Article VII's proscription of discrimination applied primarily to government-imposed tariffs or quota systems. According to Edwards, however, the provision was elastic enough to include cartels.[117] Until President Harry Truman abruptly terminated the Lend-Lease Agreement during the summer of 1945, American and

British representatives periodically meant to discuss the implementation of Article VII. The Antitrust Division's revelations that Germany's international cartels jeopardized the American War effort were front-page news by the beginning of 1943. During the Fall of that year American and British negotiators extended the "Article VII talks" to include the international cartel issue.[118]

From early 1944 to the end of the war the importance of the issue increased in both nations. Edwards carried on formal and informal exchanges with counterparts in the Board of Trade. In May, 1944 he noted, a "formal statement incorporated in the White Paper on Employment Policy" called for "appropriate action to check practices" which may have brought "advantages to sectional producing interests but work[ed] to the detriment of the country as a whole."[119] During the summer of 1944 each nation's stance toward the regulation of international cartels was addressed at the Dumbarton Oaks and Bretton Woods conferences. Edwards observed further that the Minister of Reconstruction suggested that the problem warranted new legislation, perhaps including the creation of "some sort" of court to investigate restrictive practices.[120] By 1945 he noted the extent to which the press and the British government itself were gradually becoming more critical of cartels and monopolies. *The Economist* and a "great London newspaper" were engaged in a "campaign against cartel abuses."[121] Corwin did not suggest, however, that American action had significantly influenced the new British pronouncements.

After the war, the significance of the international cartel issue soon declined. The bilateral negotiations involving creation of the International Trade Organization continued until 1948 when the US Senate declined to ratify the Havana Charter. Failure to pass the Charter further reduced the anti-international cartel issue to insignificance. Although Labour's President of the Board of Trade, Harold Wilson, mentioned the Charter when he introduced the Monopolies Bill early in 1948, domestic concerns were clearly the primary rationale. Later the same year the Bill was enacted as the Monopolies and Restrictive Practices (Inquiry and Control) Act. The jurisdiction of the Commission the law established extended to international cartels, but this provision resulted more from domestic pressures associated with the export sector than American influence.[122]

In any case, between 1945 and Truman's election victory of 1948, domestic concerns once more dominated antitrust enforcement in America. Throughout the period probably the primary concern of most Americans and their elected representatives was inflation. In an attempt to curb the cost of living, Attorney General Tom Clark and the Antitrust Division devoted most of their resources to the prosecution of price fixing. Confronted with uneven appropriations from the Republican-controlled Congress, the Antitrust Division understandably emphasized the sorts of cases which traditionally were easiest to win. Also, price-fixing suits did not clash with the antipathy against big government prevalent in public opinion polls, newspaper editorials, and among large and small business. The courts encouraged this same policy by continuing the course established during the 1920s of condemning overt price-fixing practices as per se violations of antitrust.[123]

In addition, however, there was mounting pressure for governmental action against corporate concentration resulting from mergers. Despite the common distrust of big government, tension existed between large and small business concerning mergers. In correspondence with the Truman Administration and the FTC the President of the National Federation of Small Businesses suggested this conflict when in 1948 he pointed out that small enterprise would benefit from antimerger legislation. In response to such pressure Attorney General Clark had established an antimerger section within the Antitrust Division. During the war, Thurman Arnold and Wendell Berge had attempted, with only limited success, to ensure that a fair share of defense contracts went to small firms. Yet Clark's new section probably grew primarily out of post-war concerns for the welfare of small enterprise. The National Federation's President noted that the asset loophole of the Clayton Act invited mergers between large and small firms. But if the loophole was closed, the Small Business Federation predicted, small firms might have more incentive to resist acquisition.[124] The ALCOA case of 1945 provided a legal theory emphasizing economic effects which conceivably reinforced the demand for legislation. By the year of Truman's presidential campaign, Clark and the Antitrust Division had filed suit against nearly half of the nation's 100 largest firms. The Division's head exclaimed, "We will out trustbust Teddy Roosevelt."[125]

Another champion of antimerger legislation was the FTC. In 1941, relying on evidence gathered by the FTC, the TNEC recommended closing the asset-acquisition loop hole of the Clayton Act. After the war the FTC drew upon this earlier research to point out the need for a full-scale study into the rising incidence of mergers. Truman took special interest in such an investigation, seeing to it that in November 1946 the FTC received additional funding for what was otherwise a modest annual congressional appropriation. A preliminary report entitled "The Merger Movement" included a graph which showed a dramatic increase in mergers, though in point of fact it was insignificant compared to the major waves of the turn of the century and the 1920s. Nevertheless, the graph supported the FTC's appeal to amend the Clayton Act with an antimerger provision. The Commission issued the final report, entitled "The Present Trend of Corporate Mergers and Acquisitions," in March, 1947, which argued forcefully for the antimerger amendment. The findings of the FTC supported Truman's call for the closing of the loophole in his economic address of 1947.[126] The FTC's investigation and Truman's interest in the issue coincided with the Justice Department's first-ever attempt to use an antitrust suit to *prevent* a merger in the *Columbia Steel Co.* case, which was filed and tried during 1947.[127]

These measures received sympathetic support from certain members of Congress. Long-time antitrust advocate, Wyoming Senator Joseph O'Mahoney, and congressmen Emmanuel Celler and Estes Kefauver (soon to be elected Senator representing Tennessee) adhered to the Brandeisian "curse of bigness" tradition. Throughout the 1940s they pushed what were the most significant of twenty-one Bills introduced to amend the Clayton Act with an antimerger clause. In their efforts the three men agreed with the FTC report. Unless the "growth of concentration" was halted, the "giant corporations" would "ultimately take over the country, or the government will be impelled to impose some form of direct regulation in the public interest." America was either "going down the road to collectivism or it must stand and fight for competition as the protector of all that is embodied in free enterprise."[128]

This philosophical predilection underlay antimerger provisions which Congress considered in 1947. Each one included revisions of the Clayton Act which not only closed the asset loophole, but also allowed the courts to order divestiture of assets resulting from illegally merged firms. The Supreme Court had held that since the Clayton Act applied to stock not asset purchases, courts could order only divestiture of the former. The proposal revisions thus would have in both cases allowed as a remedy divestiture. The opponents of the final Bill incorporating these proposals argued, however, that it was both too extreme and contrary to leading Supreme Court decisions. The latter point received support when the federal district court rejected the government's attempt to prevent the merger in the *Columbia Steel Co.* case. After parliamentary maneuvering in both the House and Senate the Bill was defeated. The Supreme Court, during the summer of 1948, also decided against the government in the appeal of *Columbia Steel*.[129]

But neither Truman nor Celler and Kefauver gave up. The President made the antimerger amendment an issue in his election campaign of 1948. Celler kept the issue alive in the House and Kefauver did the same after moving to the Senate. Moreover, the dissent of William O. Douglas in *Columbia Steel*, joined by three other justices, encouraged further litigation. Even so, by 1948 the potential for new legislative and judicial initiatives in American antitrust remained very much alive.[130]

The tentative convergence of each nation's response to big business reached a turning point during World War II. British proponents of competition for the first time attained significant influence which coincided with the American campaign against international cartels. The injection of the issue into vital foreign-policy discussions might have strengthened the hand of those advocating competition. Ultimately, however, narrow domestic factors primarily shaped each nation's position, diminishing the American influence on Britain's formative period of antimonopoly policymaking.

CHAPTER 7

A British antimonopoly policy emerges, 1940–1948

The exigencies of war compelled Britain to develop administrative machinery for regulating monopoly and trade restraints. During World War I cooperation between business and government had sufficiently eroded the Free Trade consensus that the authorities established the Profiteering Acts and the Standing Committee on Trusts to police monopolistic and restrictive practices through the use of publicity. After 1921 this mode of government intervention was replaced by a policy promoting large corporations and looser cartel arrangements, especially trade associations. Permitting the enforcement of trade restraints, the courts reinforced this promotional policy. From 1941 to 1945 debate within the Government centered on whether to continue the inter-war policy or to develop a stronger interventionist approach. Undoubtedly the single most significant decision facilitating greater intervention was the Coalition Government's commitment to the attainment of full employment as a primary goal of planning for postwar economic reconstruction. Debate persisted, however, over what degree of official intervention was sufficient to ensure full employment. The Gaitskell-Allen memorandum urged a policy which directly fostered competition. Indirectly, diplomatic pressure from the United States during 1943–1948 supported a similar principle. Ultimately, however, the interplay of domestic pressure groups, politics, and ideology resulted in a new consensus which favored institutionalizing the earlier reliance on publicity through the enactment of the Monopolies and Restrictive Practices Act of 1948.[1]

DEFENDERS OF CARTELIZATION VS. PROMOTERS OF COMPETITION, 1940–1942

Monopoly and restrictive practices issues emerged initially as British officials began planning for postwar reconstruction. During the first part of the war a Minister without Portfolio, Arthur Greenwood, had general responsibility for postwar reconstruction planning. Under Greenwood the Internal Economic Problems Committee had jurisdiction over economic issues. By late 1940 it was apparent that the transition from a war to a peacetime economy involved more than merely the termination of military-oriented production. Throughout the economy public officials controlled prices, rationed supplies and, in many cases, had imposed compulsory concentration of smaller firms to create fewer industries (often organized as trade associations) with greater capacity. As part of postwar reconstruction the controls and compulsory concentration raised complex issues. The Internal Economic Problems Committee left much of the study of these issues to the President of the Board of Trade, Hugh Dalton. Within the Board two organizations examined problems relating to industrial structure, including monopoly and restrictive practices. The first was the Board's Reconstruction Unit, headed by Henry Clay; the Unit's secretary was Cambridge-trained economist Ruth L. Cohen. The second organization was the Central Committee for Export Groups, composed of Business Members who advised President Dalton, and various permanent or temporary civil servants, including Clay and economist professor, G. C. Allen.[2]

Within the Reconstruction Unit monopoly and restrictive practices issues arose in connection with trade associations. According to one study, business sought to use government sanctions to make membership in trade associations compulsory. The "compulsion of all firms in a trade to act for purposes delegated by the Government will make it easier to overcome the reluctance of recalcitrant firms to co-operate in schemes for regulating output and prices." The report observed, however, that conceding "to any and every...group in the community legal power to coerce a minority of the group by a majority vote" was "a false view of democracy."[3] Accordingly, it was unlikely that associations would use "such powers...exclusively in the general interest of the public." By December 1941, a Board official noted that since the "attitude of the Government" toward the associations was "being raised...so frequently ... at some stage it will probably be necessary to formulate a board of trade view."[4]

A temporary civil servant affiliated with the Reconstruction Unit, Sir Charles Innes, prepared a preliminary examination. The pro-restrictionist memorandum envisaged two possible policies toward trade associations. The "pre-war policy of modified encouragement to Associations with special legislation where necessary" was one. A "more forward policy giving powers to Trade Associations to regulate their industry under some general Act subject to adequate control" was the other. The memorandum recommended the second. Innes advocated the formation of an Industrial Council or Commission in which business would make official policy, subject to government supervision. He based this preference on an analysis of the functions the associations would be expected to perform after the war. Strong associations could better negotiate with the government to implement the reconversion of industries to peace-time operation, particularly, coordinated plans for export, the regulation of prices and output, and, where necessary, the preparation of redundancy schemes.[5] Generally, the Innes memorandum supported views industrialists put forth during the Greenwood Ministry's initial discussion of reconstruction. Yet Innes and the industrialists drew upon economic theories of rationalization public officials had used since World War I to justify expanded cooperation within industry and between business and government.[6]

Cohen, however, rejected both the recommendations and the underlying theory of the Innes memorandum. Favoring a policy of competition, she stated a third policy option was "that of discouraging Trade Associations which regulate prices and output – a policy" which was "usually known as 'preventing restraints of trade.'" Cohen thought the "State...not...the future consumer" should bear the cost of reconversion. The pro-restrictionist preference for governmental promotion of trade associations followed the "protective policy" of the 1930s which had seemed necessary because of the Depression. But, assuming that the free world would adopt an "expansionist" post-war economic policy, Cohen perceived little need for "compulsory Trade Associations." More importantly, she felt the restrictionist approach "rated too low their dangers," particularly the creation of "undue rigidity in the industrial structure," first because the Association might hold up prices in industries where consumer demand had declined, and second because it could restrict the entry of new firms. These factors in turn hampered reducing costs through improved organizational efficiency.[7]

Cohen also emphasized the link between inefficient business structure and politics. A further "objection to allowing industries to regulate and fix prices and output" was that their "energies" became "devoted more and more to political wrangling and less and less to the actual improvement of efficiency." She admitted that severely cutting back on trade associations during the war was "now politically impracticable." As a result, regardless of the different views within the Board of Trade concerning trade associations, Cohen thought that as of December 1941 it was "politically most undesirable" for the Board to announce "a general statement." It was, after all, "a subject of the greatest importance on which the political parties differ considerably. With a three-party coalition no statement which could have any real meaning would be acceptable to all parties in the Government."[8]

Falling between the two views was Clay, the Head of the Reconstruction Unit. He emphasized that the "need for giving powers to Trade Associations to regulate their industries varies greatly from industry to industry... [as did] the degree of the dangers to which Miss Cohen has referred." It was particularly important to distinguish managerially centralized firms such as ICI from the looser trader associations. The "big merger organization" conferred "considerable benefits on industry through planned production, a strong bargaining position with foreign competitors, and benefits in the way of the organization of methods of increased efficiency." Although these "amalgamations" were not without "dangers," they were generally "sensitive to public opinion," and "greatly superior" to a "number of firms working in isolation or a Trade Association... purporting to work for the industry as a whole." And yet, "under a system of private enterprise" effective trade associations were necessary in order to achieve prosperity in the post-war era. Accordingly, "these industries and the Government [should] get to planning for... regulation... [despite] the political considerations."[9]

The Central Committee for Export Groups added further to the discussions within the Board. Since 1940 governmental officials and industry had formed about three hundred Export Groups to manage foreign trade, factory space, allocation of raw materials, the utilization of labor, and the control of prices. These groups included the Federation of British Industries, the National Union of Manufacturers, the Association of British Chambers of Commerce, and certain other trade associations; they were represented by the Business Members on the Central Committee advising President Dalton. Early in 1942 the Business Members sought to influence postwar reconstruction planning through preparation of a policy paper. "The conception that the economic system works by itself is today," the paper stated "completely discredited…left to itself the economic system results in recurrent crisis of production and distribution…" To remedy the problem the Business Members proposed an "elaborate industrial structure resting on government compulsion. The structure included an Industrial Council representing each industry organized around compulsory trade-association membership. Additional layers of private and public bureaucracy balanced the interests of business and labor. To this proposal there was considerable opposition. Central Committee members Clay and Allen, as well as Cohen and others, resisted an attempt to persuade Dalton to publish the Business Members' position in the form of a White Paper. Cohen wrote "that a factual study of the existing associations, their strength and functions was necessary before any further progress could be made in developing a policy toward them."[10]

The contentiousness resulted in an examination of the law of restrictive trade practices. The Solicitor General made clear, however, that the critical view represented "a dangerous interpretation" and he denied any "responsibility for it."[11] Yet, generally, the advocates of competition argued, courts applied the rule of reasonableness to enforce "a contract in restraint of trade…if it is reasonable as between the parties and not injurious to the public interest." The courts were "disposed to hold that the interests of the public are not necessarily served by cut throat competition and unremunerative prices in a particular trade." Thus "trade agreements have in fact seldom, if ever, been invalidated on the ground of injury to the public interest." As a result, parties to such agreements "had expert opinion to the effect that agreements on these lines would be enforceable at law."[12]

Another staff member noted the economic problems the law fostered. "The present state of the law may be intelligible to lawyers, as it is certainly a source of income to them; but it is an obstacle to stable and effective agreements for regulating prices and output without preventing monopolistic agreements." Essentially, contemporary British law did not effectively distinguish between efficient and inefficient business structures. Supporters of "compulsory" trade-association membership ignored the fact that associations represented the "majority of an industry rather than the active and efficient minority, and, by keeping up prices, very often prevent the efficient from driving the inefficient out of business." Similarly, the law failed to recognize that where "technical conditions favor it, the large-scale concern, like ICI," was "likely to be much more enterprising and efficient than a Trade Association." In other cases, "technical conditions favor[ed] a large number of moderate sized concerns" in which "enterprise and originality" were "usually due to the initiative of individual firms... rather than to Associations."[13]

By the summer of 1942 business exerted steady pressure. According to one Committee member the goal of the study was to "put the case for encouragement of Trade Associations and discouragement impartially," suggesting the "problems... raised by both policies" and recommending one the Government might adopt. Yet, at the same time, the Export Groups and the Business Members lobbied within the government and Parliament and in news releases for broad official sanction throughout industry of trade-association membership as a means of controlling prices and output. They advocated loose governmental supervision under the auspices of some such body as the Import Duties Advisory Committee.[14] Throughout the spring and summer of 1942 there circulated among the various units within the Board newspaper clippings from *The Times*, *Finance & Commerce* and other papers. The stories expressed divergent views concerning the interests of "Big Business and Little," consumers and the government. Even so the papers articulated only mild concern about possible threats to small business, emphasizing primarily the interest of consumers and the need for some sort of government regulation to protect it.[15]

The private and public conflict sharpened internal disagreement over the evolving study. "The proposals of the Export Groups and the Business Members" one staff member argued forcefully, seemed "to have taken over the main features of the Fascist co-operative state against which we were fighting." Governmentally sanctioned control of prices through trade associations merely reinforced the various industrial groups' "interest in getting all they can out of the consumer." The Board of Trade's recommendation to the Internal Economic Problems Committee should, therefore, "aim to limit and to direct the activities of trade associations immediately after the war into the channels where they can work usefully without the possibility of doing later harm to the community." These activities included co-operative research, export marketing, the collection of information and statistics, and providing a general medium of communication between industry and government. Above all, however, "something much more effective than the Import Duties Advisory Committee" was "necessary as a price-controlling machine in the long run and ... much more direct control ... would be needed than that afforded by mere investigation and publicity."[16]

Nevertheless, another member favored giving qualified support to the position of the Export Groups. The Export Groups were not, he admitted, "entitled to speak for their industries in regard to these larger home trade problems." The "fundamental question" was whether post-war officials should foster Trade Associations for "limited purposes ... without the Government laying itself open to the charge that it is encouraging Associations for other more controversial activities." Above all, the Exporter Groups should not expect that government would "in any way" maintain "in all cases" the "principle" of compulsory membership.[17]

In August 1942 the staff completed a policy draft. It stated objectively all sides of the trade-association issue as it had evolved since the war began. Although the paper conceded that trade associations had a legitimate function, it rejected the business lobby's preference for officially sanctioned, compulsory membership. For consumers and society at large there were, it stated, "grave dangers in this type of self-government of industry." Giving to the "interested parties" the power to enforce and manage prices and output engendered higher prices, the maldistribution of resources, the perpetuation of inefficient firms and "uneconomical" scales of production, and discouraged if not prevented "new entrants." The "pace of an association" was therefore, "only the pace of its slowest firm." In addition, "joint action ... to regulate output and prices ... often obstructed the unification and rationalization of an industry" through merger. It was "important to guard against small-scale concerns associating themselves in a rearguard action against the creation of large-scale concerns on the grounds of technical and commercial efficiency." The paper conceded that big managerially centralized firms would also "possess monopolistic powers, which will equally need control." But, perhaps because big business tended to be more responsive to public opinion, small firms organized in loose business structures represented a greater threat.[18]

Finally the paper suggested the appropriate scope and limits of government action. The law regarding trade associations was "equivocal and obscure" and the courts "abstain[ed] from any systemic attempt to prevent socially objectionable practices." Thus the task of revising the law was too large to justify immediate attention. With the coming of peace policymakers might consider the "American practice which frankly and deliberately – though not wholly successfully – outlaw[ed] arrangements that may lead to monopolistic practices." The "chief conclusions" were that the creation of "representative trade organizations" was necessary if they were "voluntary and...confined to 'representational' functions." At the same time it was essential that "Government organs for investigation and control should be strengthened." Since the "war controls of prices and output" would continue in peacetime, however, there was "ample time to create such organs and to review the law governing monopolistic practices and agreements in restraint of trade."[19]

By the end of 1942 the contentiousness convinced Dalton that no White Paper was possible, ending efforts to rely upon trade associations as the primary means of reconstruction planning. Nevertheless, the confrontation within the Board indicated the future course of policymaking. It rejected taking a position for or against the Business Members' view that post-war reconstruction required maintaining some form of cartelization. The studies indicated that the administrative rather than the judicial elements of American-style antitrust might be worth considering; yet they also remained neutral as to whether government should explicitly enforce competition. Similarly, there was agreement that the primary goal of any policy should be market efficiency; but whether that was best achieved through competition among managerially centralized big firms, or cooperation within cartels remained an open question. Except in so far as trade associations were involved, the Board's studies expressed little direct interest in the status of small enterprise. Finally, there was general agreement on the need for strengthening the government's "organs for investigation and control." But what that meant exactly was left unclear.

PLANNING FOR POSTWAR EMPLOYMENT AND THE
GAITSKELL-ALLEN MEMORANDUM, 1942–1943

The earlier competition policy considerations acquired greater importance because of increased public concern for post-war full employment. By the fall of 1942 American, British, and Soviet military victories in the Pacific, North Africa, and on the eastern front heightened interest in post-war national and international "expansionist" commercial policies. Particularly important in Britain was the publication at the end of 1942 of the Beveridge Report. Although the Beveridge Report focused on social insurance and welfare services, it also suggested a general need to develop a post-war policy of full employment. Labour and various young Conservatives had become convinced that full employment was unlikely unless public officials resolved the "monopoly problem." In a broadcast speech of March 22, 1943 Prime Minister Churchill said there was "a broadening field for State ownership and enterprise, especially in relation to monopolies of all kinds."[20] Out of this new emphasis on the relation between full employment and restrictionist practices, a pathbreaking report by Hugh Gaitskell and G. C. Allen emerged.

Responding to the Beveridge Report, the Government reoriented reconstruction planning toward an emphasis upon full employment. After much internal discussion, the Coalition Government publicly committed itself during February, 1943 to the Report's recommendations. Just before formal commitment was given the Economic Section of the Ministerial committee prepared a policy paper which included as one of eight topics requiring study restrictive practices in trade and industry. According to the Economic Section's paper, a primary "connection postulated between employment and expenditure" was the "absence of monopolistic price raising and the prevalence of reasonable stability in the general wage level." Contention within the Cabinet over the Section's policy statement resulted in the establishment of a Steering Committee to prepare studies of how to implement the Beveridge Report's recommendations. The Steering Committee charged the Board of Trade to study the trade-restraint problem. At the beginning of 1943 the Board already had established the Internal Reconstruction Department, headed by Alex Kilroy, with G. C. Allen as Deputy. Cohen also received enlarged duties.[21] Throughout this same period, as we shall see, there was increased pressure from the United States involving international cartels, though it was of secondary importance.[22]

By the middle of 1943 the restrictive practices issue was prominent in Government news releases, Parliament, the press, and public statements of business groups and the political party organizations. Influencing the debate were well-publicized US Senate investigations and antitrust prosecutions of various international cartels, which included ICI.[23] The Board of Trade responded in a "secret" memorandum on "Restrictive Practices in Industry." The "postwar policies for maintenance of employment, the expansion of output and the control of monopoly should be closely related to one another," it stated. Because "[p]ublic attention" focused on this question "confusion and misunderstanding will prevail unless and until...[the Board developed] some authoritative statement of Government policy." The memorandum also gave serious consideration to the need for promoting industrial re-equipment and technological innovation through government aid.[24]

Yet, during the spring of 1943, exchanges between economists Alex Kilroy and G. C. Allen revealed the tension between defenders of cartelization and proponents of competition within the Board's Internal Reconstruction Department. "The Prime Minister's broadcast gave us something of a jumping-off ground on the control of monopolies," said Kilroy. She was "sure" the Board would "have more pressure from business" than they realized "on the question of national monopoly and international cartels." Several Chambers of Commerce and the World Trade Alliance had convinced many business leaders and some leading governmental officials that restrictive agreements, "whether negotiated between industries or between Governments...[established] 'order' in international affairs, and the absence of such agreements...[ensured] 'chaos.'"[25]

The Business Groups wanted a continuation of the state's pre-war encouragement of cartel practices once peace came, Kilroy said. Sympathetic to this position, she asked, "Could we not work towards the principle that we are not against monopolies *per se* – but against the abuse of monopoly, and that where any group of manufacturers obtains a monopolistic position they come automatically under control on behalf of the consumer by the state?" "Assuming such a general principle were approved, what would be the powers and administrative machinery necessary to carry it out?" Kilroy believed manufacturers were "entitled to guard themselves, or be guarded against...*uneconomic* competition." She wanted to avoid returning to the post-World War I "attitude...[that] cheapness was all and cut-throat competition...was thought to be the most likely road to the millenium."[26]

Favoring competition, Allen rejected this argument. Manufacturers preferred "monopoly to competition" when it enabled "them, by restriction on output and price control, to rid themselves of risk and to maintain or to increase their own profits." This was not "in the community's interest merely because manufacturers desire it. The business man's job [was] to carry risk and not to rid himself of it at the consumer's expense." The central issue was what sort of economic system they were "preparing for after the war." Adoption of the "expansionist" international trade proposals the American and British leaders were discussing would create, Allen said, "an entirely different situation from that which existed between the wars."[27]

State policies during the inter-war period favored the "development of cartels because international trade policy was not expansionist, and so cartels with their restrictive policies were following along the same lines as Government policy. It was because policy was restrictionist that cut-throat competition developed. That kind of competition does not appear in the expansionist regime," Allen said. An "expansionist cartel" was an "illusion." Monopolies of "all kinds (except those run by the State)" were "certain to follow policies contrary to the policies of expansion, full employment and freer international trade which" Britain and America were "trying to get accepted." Finally, Allen doubted whether mere "supervisory machinery" alone was sufficient to deal with the problem. The "only policy" that was "consistent with the other [expansionist] economic policies" was "for the State to be hostile to private monopoly."[28]

The disagreement between defenders of cartelization and supporters of competition influenced the Board of Trade's decision that a full-scale study was necessary. Beginning in April, 1943 C. K. Hobson explored further the American antitrust "experience," including a description of major legislation and court decisions, an assessment of their effectiveness and weakness, and the evaluation of such American commentators as Arthur R. Burns and the Temporary National Economic Committee. Another study traced in detail the gradual evolution of British governmental policymaking from 1918 to 1939. Additional research examined the state of the English law of restrictive trade practices. Other studies analyzed the economic consequences of the historical and institutional record. This research supported the principle of increased government intervention in the form of a commission to encourage competition.[29] According to a Board memorandum it indicated the need for a policy of "stimulating competition and enterprise and discouraging monopoly and unenterprise ... [which] points more directly towards full employment." Yet these inquiries also demonstrated that while such a policy would be "welcomed by many sections of public opinion ... [it also] would undoubtedly create much opposition, and even strong resentment, in some business circles."[30]

Kilroy was skeptical. Again responding to Allen, she thought the emerging pro-competition policy overemphasized the "disadvantages and dangers of monopoly and cartel arrangements." Although "a large number of firms and organizations had, through these arrangements, the opportunity to 'fleece' the consumer ... [there was] little concrete evidence that they did so." Kilroy conceded there were "cases of *known* harmful monopolistic practices"; they were, however, "relatively few." Arguably, given the relatively small British home market, the nation could ill afford "small units of production and the answer to the large US market" was "more amalgamation in British industry." For these national and international reasons, then, the "official attitude to a certain measure of cartelization and organized marketing and price fixing was on the whole favorable in the inter-war years." After World War II, she thought, "these reasons will continue to have weight, particularly ... [because of] the desirability of avoiding *unnecessary* change and *sudden* disturbance to employment." Kilroy thus resisted the attempt "to prevent the development of monopolies or to discredit monopoly and cartelization as such." Yet, recognizing that such restrictive practices possessed "great power for harm to the consumer if abused ... [she believed there was also] a strong case for some form of Government control or supervision of any such arrangement."[31]

In July 1943 the Board's enquiry resulted in a major report in which Allen's views prevailed. Allen joined Labour activist and Oxford-trained economist Hugh Gaitskell to write "The Control of Monopoly."[32] A turning point in the British government's approach to the monopoly problem, the study synthesized the research of Hobson and others. It included five sections: the problem of monopoly, a review of the pre-war position, changes introduced by the war, proposed policy, and the mechanism of control. Employing a loose definition of monopoly, it identified "types of monopolistic organization ranging from close combines or giant firms that dominate a trade, to loose terminable associations...employed for limiting competition." Noting that this "organization" increased costs for consumers, the study emphasized the "disadvantages of monopoly to the community" particularly those of reducing the "demand for labor, retard[ing] the transference of output to the more efficient producers and so increas[ing] the difficulty of achieving full employment and of raising the standard of life."[33]

The Gaitskell and Allen memorandum located its proposals within a context of policy which had evolved since World War I. The judiciary had largely departed from the old general proposition that restrictive agreements were not enforceable. The judiciary's relative passivity toward restrictive practices had increased the lawyer's role in formulating such agreements. "The economist would still applaud...[the old] judgment," the memorandum observed, "but the lawyers have been unfaithful to th[ose] legal principles...and monopoly ha[d] thus found the legal position increasingly favorable to its extension." The law, however, was only one factor. The two economists recalled the short-lived experiment with the Profiteering Acts and the Standing Committee on Trusts which was followed by the policy of governmental supervision and promotion of restrictive agreements during the inter-war years.[34]

The Government's sanction of trade associations to mobilize the wartime economy extended the promotional policy. This mode of governmental intervention gave the civil service "invaluable experience," with the result that "on balance" it was "better equipped than before the war to discharge the responsibility of industrial control." And, given the sophistication of business "self-government," such experience was essential. For, "producers or traders" were "not as a rule docile, obedient creatures waiting for a judgment which they will accept cheerfully and without question." They were "far more frequently, active, anxious and sometimes angry principals in a series of negotiations, who wish to get the best terms and are prepared to exercise whatever pressure they can to achieve this end." Consequently, the government's involvement with trade associations to fix prices had "become more like collective bargaining – in which the various trade associations represent the producers and the Government does its best to protect the consumer."[35] The wartime "strengthening of trade associations" helped to "promote monopoly" whereas price controls and other action represented "measures of control by which the State... defended the public interest against organized producers."[36]

For Gaitskell and Allen the "keystone" of the memorandum was a "proposed policy," incorporating three broad goals. First, governmental action should prevent the emergence of "private monopoly, except in industries where the economies of large-scale organization" were such as "to require the concentration of the greater part of the output in a single firm." Secondly, it should control monopolistic practices which appeared despite preventive action. Third, it should control the "activities of any great firm or close combine which" was "responsible for the greater part of the output of any class of product." The forms of "preventive action" were two-fold, each tied to the attainment of full employment and greater productive efficiency. One was "negative," intended to remove "any provisions of the law," such as those involving patents, libel, or restraint of trade, which favored the "appearance of monopoly." The second was "positive," to prohibit, except under license, practices toward which the law was "neutral" including the "limitation of production or for the division of markets... [or] agreements to destroy capacity." Moreover, the governmental authority would grant the licenses "Only when considerable excess of capacity... appeared in any line of production, and when a scheme of contraction... [had] been worked out to remove that excess."[37]

This policy opposed cartelization but favored managerially centralized big firms. The intent of the prohibitions, Allen and Gaitskell emphasized, was to "destroy or weaken the terminable association or cartel." The prohibitions "clearly" did not, however, "touch the close combine or giant firm which pursue[d] a monopolistic policy." Toward the large managerially centralized corporate "concerns" the intended policy was "not that of breaking them up" which might "sacrifice... the economies of large scale," but rather one of "preventing them from taking anti-social action." Noting the uneven consequences resulting from the enforcement of the Sherman and Clayton antitrust legislation, the two economists suggested government control of certain "objectionable practices," including "any device to exclude newcomers or to tie customers to certain firms, for example, boycotts, tying clauses, deferred rebates, resale price maintenance agreements." They also noted that under certain circumstances, where a thorough enquiry determined it was necessary, the government should have the power to set maximum prices. Finally, they recommended mechanisms for publicizing the corporate giant's conduct. Yet, they observed, "in the last resort, Government ownership may well be the only means of dealing with [certain] giant firms."[38]

The memorandum then outlined the "mechanism of control." The implementation of the "proposed policy" required a division of authority between the various government departments "responsible for the various industries on the one hand and a permanent Commission or Tribunal appointed by, and reporting to, the minister responsible for general economic policy, on the other hand." The Commission's "main functions" included investigation of restrictive practices and recommendations to check them, enquiry into the prices charged by monopolists or semi-monopolistic concerns, and the licensing of restrictive agreements and practices, especially those involving exporting firms or associations. The Minister responsible for general economic policy to which the Commission reported was the President of the Board of Trade. The Commission was empowered to recommend action involving its "main functions," including the publication of reports. The various government departments would have responsibility for carrying out the Commission's recommendations.[39]

Within the government departments the response to the Gaitskell and Allen memorandum was not enthusiastic. The study began circulating within the Board of Trade and other departments on 17 July, 1943. Shortly thereafter, echoing the concerns Kilroy expressed earlier, the Business Members objected to the "undertone of complaint against monopolies," particularly those formed during the inter-war period. Some representatives of the business lobby did, however, advocate establishing some sort of tribunal "responsible to the appropriate Minister, with the power to survey and check prices, and to obtain the relevant data for the purpose."[40]

G. L. Watkinson was more receptive. Gaitskell and Allen had effectively combined an understanding of the "inside knowledge" of government departments with a willingness to face "out-side...political difficulties." Their report clearly revealed that "during the war the movement towards monopoly ha[d] been strengthened, and after the war the country should have some sort of insurance against the possibility that private enterprise may, through monopolies, be in a position to serve private interests at the expense of national interests." Above all, he noted, achieving the policy of full employment required insuring against prices that were "too high" and industrial efficiency which was "too low." Watkinson discussed the usefulness of broadening the policymaking role of the proposed commission. He suggested it might "undertake the task of *encouraging* the formation of large-scale business units in... [a] very wide field." He pointed out, too, the need for the commission or some other official agency to "promote the development of new processes and inventions." He also raised an issue virtually ignored by Gaitskell and Allen: the "finance for small- and medium-sized businesses... [through] some central organization."[41]

James E. Meade recommended enlarging still more the commission's role. He favored the negative "apparatus of anti-monopoly safeguards" the memorandum proposed. To encourage industry's acceptance of the policy, however, he further suggested pursuing a "positive... State–industry relationship." Such a promotional policy might include direct official encouragement of "industrial efficiency" through merger, reform of the patent system, subsidization of industrial research, and product standardization among "backward firms." In order to carry out these policies, Meade proposed giving broad investigatory powers to the Board of Trade and an "independent panel" of experts made up of cost accountants, engineers, and managers (but not lawyers). The panel thus "would have a very important positive role to play in the improvement of British industry."[42]

The Steering Committee asked Dalton for the Board's report on restrictive practices just about the time Gaitskell and Allen completed their "Control of Monopoly." The two authors urged Dalton to submit a shortened version of the memorandum to the Steering Committee. Opposition was too great, however, and Dalton accepted Sir Arnold Overton's extensive revisions. Overton limited the proposals to industry alone. In addition, responsibility for the registration of agreements was lodged in the Board, which was empowered to refer those it considered contrary to the public interest to a Commission. If an investigation revealed a violation of the public interest the Board could suspend or ban the practice. Big as well as small firms were subject to the Commission's investigations, and the Commission was authorized to recommend as a remedy price controls. Dalton sent this compromised version of the memorandum to the Steering Committee, which could choose between either the prohibition of certain cartel practices or Overton's more moderate inquiry approach. Although vigorous resistance to the Board's statement arose from Lionel Robbins of the Economic Section, the Committee on Reconstruction eventually accepted Overton's approach as the basis of paragraph 54 on restrictive practices in the White Paper on employment policy published in May 1944.[43]

Thus, in the short term, the Gaitskell and Allen memorandum did not result in action. In August, 1943 a Board of Trade survey of the British press on post-war commercial policy during the preceding month revealed that domestic and international views were unsettled. Of particular importance was the increased concern American policymakers expressed toward international cartels, coinciding with the growing activism of such cartel defenders as the World Trade Alliance. Amid these tensions the Board moved cautiously. Near the end of November, 1943 the Ministry of Supply requested advice from the Board on whether it should raise with industry the "question of restrictive practices in order to discourage attempts by trade associations to develop such practices." Cohen's reply was that "until decisions are taken on the general policy to be followed in this sphere, we should prefer that you do not raise this point yourselves."[44]

Still, the memorandum indicated how far policy discussions had moved since the preceding summer. Gaitskell and Allen rejected the neutral stance of the earlier papers, arguing that preventing cartels and fostering competition should be the central policy in order to achieve full employment. It was on this point that the affinity with American antitrust was clearest, though Gaitskell and Allen, like the earlier studies, supported an administrative rather than a judicial approach to government intervention. The memorandum favored managerially centralized large firms, while it also recognized the need for policing abuse and suggested that in certain instances nationalization might be desirable. Also, the memorandum stated in what cases law reform was necessary. These recommendations, coupled with the authority to prohibit trade restraints, grant licenses, and regulate prices required a much more extensive role for the proposed tribunal than had been suggested earlier.

INDIGENOUS PRESSURES PRIMARY, 1943–1945

From late 1943 to early 1944 the Government hesitated to announce an official policy toward monopoly and trade restraints. But early in 1944 the Board decided that a "statement... would clear the air for industry and the public, and would make it easier for the Department to answer complaints and to deal with requests for the Board's views on proposed agreements, price arrangements, etc."[45] During the rest of the war the interaction between foreign and domestic pressures shaped legislative proposals intended to reconcile the attainment of full employment with greater official intervention against restrictionist practices. For the Government, however, domestic considerations remained of foremost importance, and they shaped a Bill which was not only weaker than that recommended by Gaitskell and Allen, but also than that urged by the United States.

Churchill's "election statements" during the spring, 1943 advocated official action against trade restraints in order to achieve full employment. This statement of official policy and the ongoing newspaper campaign against monopoly and restrictive practices encouraged the Board to conclude that there was "obviously some degree of embarrassment in any long postponement of legislation on this subject." Moreover, the inability to answer business enquiries and complaints regarding "particular practices... in the absence of a defined Government policy... presents officials with a difficult and embarrassing situation." Delay became still more difficult after the Government published the White Paper on Full Employment and the Beveridge Committee published another report in May and November of 1944 respectively, proclaiming that a national policy of full employment required action against monopoly and restrictive practices. Meanwhile, the issue became enmeshed in the American–British discussions of postwar commercial policy. In "international talks" scheduled for the summer of 1944, a Board memorandum observed, the "whole question of restrictive practices, including monopolies and cartels (especially international cartels) arises in connection with the US commercial policy proposals." Thus the "Board of Trade view" was to "proceed... fairly soon" with legislation "on the lines of that considered by the Coalition Government."[46]

Throughout 1944 the Board reviewed successive drafts of legislation prepared by the Solicitor General. In January Alex

Kilroy and others discussed two basic questions which were to remain central to the emerging legislation.[47] In the fall of 1944, the FBI published a report stating that a government tribunal possessing the "right sort" of authority to publicize business practices would benefit the trade-association movement.[48] Reflecting the consensus shared by the business lobby, press, and government authorities, the legislative proposal included a Restrictive Practices Commission (RPC). Yet there was little agreement on the referral process. Although the Board was responsible for administering the Commission, the "main question" was the "functions of the Board of Trade and of other Departments in relation to the RPC." A difficult jurisdictional and political problem thus arose involving "a proposal to refer an industry" which was responsible to a Department other than the Board of Trade. The Solicitor General recommended a "joint reference." Board representatives admitted that it was "clearly undesirable that a number of Departments should refer cases to the Commission in an uncoordinated way." But where did "coordination" begin and end? If a Department preferred not to "refer an industry for enquiry at a particular time because of the state of its own negotiations with the industry, it would fall to them, not to the Board of Trade, to resist pressure for an enquiry." The Board did not want to be "left holding the baby and being apparently unwilling to work machinery for which it [was] responsible."[49]

The second basic question involved the authority of the RPC itself. According to one memorandum the issue was whether a "Commission of Inquiry" and the "mere publication of findings" were sufficient, or was "some element of sanctions" also necessary?[50] A related matter was whether the RPC's jurisdiction should extend not only to major private industries but also to services, such as "hairdressing," and the professions. Regarding private industry, moreover, Gaitskell suggested using its "powers to reduce pre-war profits."[51] Another memorandum noted the usefulness of including references to the "effect of... [restrictive] practices on the expansion of international trade and on the operation of commercial treaties which, if included, will be extremely good talking points with the Americans." As for the standard guiding the exercise of this power, a consensus within the Board favored using the "public interest." The central question was, however, whether it was better to leave what that meant "entirely undefined."[52]

The question of authority also involved whether the RPC would follow a legalistic or a more informal administrative procedure. Regardless of how the issue of referral was resolved, noted another memorandum, it was clear that the Commission should "avoid legalistic procedure." Accordingly, it was advisable not to call the RPC "a Tribunal" since it suggested the "judgment seat. Unless industry" accepted "an informal method of procedure" it would be "extremely difficult to resist representation by Counsel, examination and cross-examination and all the legal procedure which, when money is no object (as it is apt to be in commercial cases), can be drawn out not only over months but over years."[53]

Secondly, the non-legalistic procedure required a definition of the role of the staff. The Commission's chief duty was to discover the facts and then to recommend action to the Board based on the "public interest." The Commission thus required sufficient staff "to make a careful study of most aspects of the industry... [including the authority] to call for and inspect papers... books of account relating to costs, prices and output and in many cases... information about similar industries in other countries." Such work required the "right staff" having access to "persons of administrative experience, accountants, and economists with a knowledge of business, in numbers adequate to undertake several investigations simultaneously." In addition the "Commission... need[ed] persons with legal knowledge to deal with the obtaining of information and to advise on company law and general legal matters." This institutional arrangement of commissioners and experts would enable the RPC and the representatives of industry to reach "substantial agreement... on matters of fact, and to a limited extent on the interpretation of the facts. The Commission would thus be able to cross-question the industrialists as to the correct interpretation of those matters which call for further enquiry in an expeditious manner."[54]

By late 1944 the Board and Reconstruction Committee neared agreement on a draft legislative proposal. Although the relation of the Board to other Departments in the referral process remained unresolved, a consensus gradually emerged regarding the authority of the RPC. During the fall John Jewkes of the Office of the Minister of Reconstruction provided a thorough critique of an advanced proposal "purely from the point of the economist." Essentially Jewkes wanted the Commission to apply a "public interest" standard which possessed substantive economic content. In part this meant prohibiting industry's attempt to restrict entry and "methods of unfair competition." It also included other considerations involving whether the agreement or combine "unduly" interfered with prices, profits, technological innovation, and, above all, the achievement of the Government's policy of full employment not only in a single industry but throughout the "economic system as a whole." Furthermore he cautioned against suggesting that the proposed RPC was somehow similar to the IDAC, "since the very mention" of that "body...throws Mr. Bevin and one or two other Labour Ministers into paroxysms of rage."[55]

The Board's response to Jewkes was unfavorable. A memorandum of December 7 exclaimed, "Jewkes' letter takes us into questions of economic policy and will waste time." The emerging consensus favored the RPC applying a flexible yet vaguely defined standard, while the definition of monopoly was left imprecise. Primarily, however, the Commission was to determine whether "any particular practice or agreement [was] *contrary* to the public interest." Still, no effort was made to "pre-judge any question," and it was of "cardinal importance" that the proposed measure "should show no bias either in favor of or against restrictive practices or monopolies as such." Thus the Commission was "asked to consider the effect of the practice on the export trade and not to hold that a big export trade [was] a good thing." It was "not to hold that high prices [were] bad or that low prices [were] good." Board officials had "decided that unless we adopted that plan we should be passing into law a particular set of economic theories."[56]

Yet the Board retained from the Gaitskell–Allen proposal the basic enforcement policy. The December, 1944 memorandum stated that the government should invalidate all restrictive practices except those licensed by the Board of Trade. The intent was to shift the burden of proof from the government to the parties, which required them to provide conclusive evidence that their agreements were consistent with the "public interest" and as such supportive of competition and the goal of full employment. It was also agreed to exclude services and state-chartered public utilities from the Commission's jurisdiction. In addition, the "parties concerned" were "free to have legal assistance." Earlier the Board and Reconstruction Committee had agreed that in appropriate cases the RPC should have the power to fix prices. Finally to what extent the

Board published the Commission's findings was left to the President's discretion, though the memorandum conceded that the "Americans might eventually demand a stronger policy."[57]

During early 1945 internal rather than international concerns primarily shaped the final stages of legislative drafting. In the Solicitor General's Office D. N. Fyfe incorporated the changes worked out between the Reconstruction Committee and other Departments, including the Board of Trade.[58] Within the Board G. L. Watkinson, Alex Kilroy, G. H. Andrew and others followed developments closely.[59] In February Kilroy's minute sheet noted little objection to Fyfe's draft heads. As for the American influence, she observed, "some progress was made in the discussions" with the US representative in the talks on International Commercial policy. "He did not argue strongly for the drastic Washington proposal to prohibit all the main classes of cartel practice as bad in themselves," she wrote. "Instead he pressed that we would recognize that cartel agreements were capable in particular cases of frustrating the intentions of Governments and asked that, where it was agreed that they were frustrating the International Commercial Convention, we would...take...measures...to remedy the position."[60]

At about the same time agreement was reached on the departmental referral issue. After protracted inter-departmental exchanges the Reconstruction Committee concluded that "on balance it would be preferable not to deal with this matter by statutory provision or to mention Departments other than the Board of Trade in the Bill."[61] Andrew noted the strengths and weaknesses of having the Board alone make referrals to the RPC. There was a "constitutional point" that Parliament "should not oblige one Minister to consult another." In addition, relying solely on the Board permitted the "work placed on the Commission...[to] be properly regulated, and [the]...public responsibility...clearly defined."[62]

However, Andrew noted, the arrangement was not without risks. It instituted "a Parliament responsibility which may on occasion be embarrassing," requiring the President "to answer questions, not only about cases which have been referred (this would be comparatively easy since the facts would be available) but also about cases which ha[d] *not* been referred...[and therefore] to answer on inadequate information about the facts." Similarly, since the Board was "legally" responsible for publishing the Commission's report, occasions could easily arise in which it had "very superficial knowledge of the trade and the cartel in question." Andrew conceded that the "fundamental case against cartels" was that they "reduce[d] employment and general prosperity, but complaints usually arise because consumers of particular products... [were] injured."[63]

Watkinson indicated the probable considerations influencing the Reconstruction Committee's decision. The Board "of course, as a matter of normal practice consult... [other Departments] when they were likely to have information useful to us, but there [was] no need to mention that in the legislation." A decision to "refer cases to the Commission will turn largely on the technical policy of handling these restrictive issues, and most, if not all, the knowledge of this will be in the Board of Trade." Thus, he concluded, it was "unlikely" that "other Departments" might "help us."[64]

By the end of 1944 the Cabinet requested the Solicitor General to transmit the Reconstruction Committee's final legislative proposal to the Parliamentary Counsel. Reflecting the consensus hammered out during the preceding year, the proposal constituted the substantive basis for the Bill which the Counsel prepared for Parliament's vote, early in 1945. The Counsel's "draft heads" provided for a Restrictive Practices Commission which, upon the recommendation of the Board of Trade, was empowered to investigate monopolies and trade restraints between two or more firms. The Commission was to judge whether or not the monopolies and restrictive practices violated the public interest, though the criteria for this traced a thin line between the general and the specific. The Commission could, however, only recommend to the Board appropriate action. The Board of Trade was required to report the Commission's findings to Parliament, but publication of the complete report was unnecessary unless publication would definitely benefit the public interest.[65]

Thus the only remedy was publicity and this was fairly circumscribed. The draft Bill incorporated the Overton modifications rather than the prohibition and licensing provisions which were central to the enforcement policy of the Gaitskell and Allen memorandum.

Parliament, however, did not pass the Bill. As early as March, 1945 Watkinson wrote "Doc" Allen, who had returned to teaching, that "for your private information a good deal of thought is being given to [antimonopoly] legislation (not of the 'outlawing' kind but on the more moderate basis you mention): whether there will be time for it in this Session is, however, rather doubtful."[66] Indeed, early in May, the Lord Chancellor informed the Reconstruction Committee that because of the mass of legislation already introduced, the "Restrictive Practices Bill...cannot now be passed this [1944–45] Session."[67] In August 1945 Watkinson indicated the impact of this on the Board. The President considered certain "restrictive practices" as "desirable and even necessary adjuncts to the present industrial regime," and therefore did not wish to launch any general attack on them or go too fast or too far in seeking power to deal with them. As far as the Americans were concerned, he concluded, "it should be possible to avoid difficulties by explaining that the flood of domestic legislation had made it necessary to postpone restrictive practices legislation."[68]

Watkinson was correct: the crowded Parliamentary legislative agenda did indeed lead to the postponement of consideration of the RPC Bill. The popular consensus was strong enough that passage in a later session seemed certain.[69] However, the proposal which the Parliamentary Counsel submitted for legislative approval was weaker than that put forth in the Gaitskell–Allen memorandum. The rejection of the prohibition/licensing policy in favor of mere publicity circumscribed the enforcement capability of the RPC. This choice of policy, moreover, was consistent with the FBI's recommendation of October, 1944 that a tribunal possessing limited powers of publicity would benefit the trade-association movement. Attainment of postwar full employment, at least in so far as it depended on official action against restrictive practices, thus was linked to a modest extension of governmental intervention. Even so the weaker policy prevailed not only over the British defenders of competition, but also despite diplomatic pressure from the United States.

AMERICAN INFLUENCE AND THE LIMITS OF CONVERGENCE, 1943–1948

British–American foreign-policy discussions concerning international cartels and the formulation of the RPC Bill coincided with the British Government's commitment to full employment as a primary postwar goal. From the fall of 1943 to the war's end in August, 1945 the cartel issue was part of bi-lateral negotiations growing out of the Lend-Lease Act of 1941 and provisions of the Bretton Woods and Dumbarton Oaks agreements. The Americans urged the British to develop machinery for the registration and prosecution of restrictive agreements, similar to that proposed in the Gaitskell–Allen memorandum. Despite the protestations of Allen and other proponents of competition, however, the British rejected the American position. Thus policymakers and business groups accepted the proposition that in so far as full employment required amelioration of restrictionist practices, publicity was enough.

Before the fall of 1943 British negotiators did not realize how important the international cartel issue was to the Americans. Once the United States entered the war, it placed the Lend-Lease aid on a new basis in the Agreement of Principles Applying Mutual Aid, signed February, 1942. Article VII of the Agreement stated that all "agreed action" aimed at the "expansion of production, employment and the exchange of and consumption of goods" required the "elimination of all forms of discriminatory treatment in international trade, and to the reduction of tariffs and other trade barriers." Beginning in 1942, British negotiators led by Lord Keynes and including Lionel Robbins and J. E. Meade (who figured in the Board's discussion of the Gaitskell–Allen recommendations) periodically visited Washington to work out arrangements under Article VII. By the time these talks commenced in earnest, Thurman Arnold's revelations before Congress had stirred American public opinion against international cartels. As a result, by the fall of 1943 the Americans insisted upon including that issue in the Article VII negotiations. Because the British were "ill prepared" to discuss the problem, they were noncommittal on American proposals which would have led to Parliament enacting legislation requiring registration and potential prohibition of international cartels. Eventually these discussions led to consideration of the International Trade Organization. The British, however, never accepted the American anti-cartel provision.[70]

During the spring of 1944 the restrictive practices issue influenced British–American foreign-policy negotiations. Despite pressure from the United States, sentiment within several Government committees responsible for reconstruction planning favored a weaker restrictive practices proposal than that put forth in the Gaitskell–Allen memorandum. The "decision...on restrictive practices," wrote Ruth Cohen on May 1, was "bound to make discussions with the Americans on international cartels, and therefore on commercial

and commodity policy, more difficult than they would have been if
the [stronger] proposals...had been accepted." Allen agreed. The
"recent decision seems...to have destroyed the possibility of any
agreement with the Americans," he said. "How can there be any
basis for an international agreement if we cannot lay down...the
circumstances" in which the government would "intervene together
with the principles which would guide it in judging whether
practices are 'good' or 'bad' or the kind of action which it would
take in the event of a judgment that a particular practice was
'bad?'"[71]

This weaker policy approach thus ran counter to American policy
recommendations involving international cartels. Since the British–
American "discussions" beginning in the fall of 1943, one of the US
proposals regarding the post-war commercial order was that
individual nations should enact anti-cartel legislation. American
negotiators called for the "registration of all international agreements" which established "enduring relationships between business
enterprises," including those which involved the "acquisition of
ownership interests by one enterprise in another; and measures to
make the registered information available to participating Governments and to any appropriate international body or bodies." In
order to reduce the "dangers resulting from international cartelization" they also urged "national legislation concerning corporation,
patent and trade mark law, and other relevant commercial matters"
as well as review by periodic "international conventions."[72]

Cohen explained the conflict between her Government's emerging
restrictive-practices proposal and the American anti-cartel recommendations. No "definite policy" along the lines the Americans
urged was likely until "HMG, the Parliament and the public"
learned "more about the operations of trusts and cartels," she wrote
on May 1, 1944. Even so, in their exchanges, the Board and the
Reconstruction Committee increasingly agreed "to begin by
investigating complaints and where these [were] substantiated [to]
bring in proposals for remedy before Parliament...by legislation."
The Committee preferred "this policy to registration" because
government authorities could "build up...procedure gradually"
with "far less danger of 'whitewashing' agreements registered but
not disallowed." After all, a "quick" investigation was unlikely, and
"if any agreement were registered and subsequently found undesirable, the participants would have their come-back that the

Government had known for some time about their activities and that they had planned production programs, their investment, etc., assuming that the agreement would not, after a considerable lapse of time, be disallowed." Cohen admitted that "this argument" was not "water-tight." She hoped therefore to "discuss with the Americans" the extent to which the enquiries of the Board or "a tribunal" would receive "publicity" and the "grounds on which the Board... would... recommend action to Parliament."[73]

This conflict over policy had a significant impact on relations between American and British business. During the spring of 1944 the British Embassy in Washington prepared a critique of US public criticism of British business, particularly cartel practices. In mid-May the Embassy sent the critique to London accompanied by a letter noting new tensions. Since March there had been "a definite change for the worse in the attitude of the Department of Justice" toward "cooperation between American and British [exporting] industries... previously considered legitimate under the Webb-Pomerene Act." The Department's "attack," according to "influential American business men," made it "almost impossible for any leader of industry, or trade association to enter into discussions or attempt to collaborate with a British or foreign group." Thus even though "official US post-war trade policy call[ed] for collaboration with the British Empire, the Department of Justice seem[ed] determined to prevent any inter-industry understandings [except those directly sponsored by the US government itself]." American businessmen believed that the "question merit[ed] attention in the highest quarters." Since Americans raised this "matter... in many contexts," the Embassy requested guidance from London concerning British commercial policy so that its staff could "make some positive contribution, quite informally of course," when the question arose.[74]

The Embassy's critique argued forcefully that the American position was extreme. There was greater US interest in cartels and monopolies than "more serious subjects of trade policy." The concern, however, was "more emotional than rational. Clear thinking ha[d] been obscured by clouds of nationalist propaganda and invective." As a result, to "not merely... the ordinary public," but a "considerable number of public leaders the term 'cartels'" was associated with "a philosophy and with practices" which were considered "nefarious and un-American." The term itself was used "very loosely" so that the "disapproval conjured up" by it was "poured nonchalantly" on "every kind of agreement, whether quite private or semi-private, which deals with restrictions on the production or distribution of industrial goods or raw materials, tending to monopoly." The chief protagonist was the Justice Department's Antitrust Division, which had initiated cases against international cartels and delivered testimony before congressional committees. These committees, in turn, followed the Division's critical line. During a fact-finding visit to Britain during the fall of 1943 the President of US Chamber of Commerce, Eric Johnson, and his "traveling companion" University of Chicago Vice-President, William Benton, concurred in the government's position. A new office within the US State Department supported certain forms of international cooperative agreements, but its views were obscured by those of the "extremists."[75]

Throughout the rest of 1944 the Board of Trade monitored American sentiment toward cartels. When the Senate's Kilgore Committee published its report entitled "Cartels and National Security" in November 1944, Board officials prepared thorough summaries. The Board of Trade and Reconstruction Committee developed the restrictive practices proposal at the same time as they received this information. The British respected the individual studies by experts such as Corwin Edwards which provided most of the evidence the United States Government and the press used to attack international cartels. As the Embassy critique indicated, however, the conclusions drawn from such evidence were primarily emotional or xenophobic, which reinforced the grudging recognition by such advocates of competition as Cohen and Allen that internal domestic tensions primarily shaped British policymaking on the "monopoly problem."[76]

Major American and British policy statements of 1944 indicated the tension between national and international concerns. During July the historic Bretton Woods Conference resulted in major agreements shaping the post-war economic order, some of which required negotiations involving international cartels. In May, the British Government had published the White Paper on Employment Policy and one of its provisions specifically called for action on restrictive practices and monopolies. The pioneering Beveridge Report on full employment published in November had a similar provision. These national and international policy statements reflected the domestic and foreign pressures influencing the contemporaneous drafting of the restrictive-practices proposal which the Solicitor General formally submitted to the Parliamentary Counsel in early 1945.[77]

Nevertheless, American and British negotiations on international cartels suggested the continuing primacy of domestic factors. In January, 1945 American and British officials met at the Board of Trade to discuss "cartel policy." The American representative repeated the proposals set forth in the fall of 1943 calling for the registration of all private international business agreements and the prohibition of all "normal types" of cartel practices. According to the British, despite the continued adherence to "very drastic proposals," the Americans "showed signs of a much more moderate attitude." They said it would be "a big step forward" if the British concurred "in condemning bad though unspecified cartel practices and would undertake to take all practicable means to prevent the continuance of private agreements which" the two "agreed were frustrating the intentions of the proposed international Commercial Convention," including the creation of an International Trade Organization. Underlying the American instance was the considerable domestic political pressure the international cartel issue had engendered.[78]

The British emphasized, however, the domestic pressures influencing their policymaking in the field of restrictive practices. They noted the official antimonopoly stance taken in the White Paper on Employment Policy, characterizing it as a "definite step forward." Yet Parliament would have to "hammer out" any legislation and the legislative program was "already crowded" so that the prospect of passage was dim "unless the war went on longer than [they] all hoped." The British admitted that cartel agreements posed an "international problem...over and above and apart from the [nation's] domestic problem." They urged the usefulness of considering the international problem, however, from the "domestic angle."[79]

Even so, the British said, the White Paper's provision reflected "a considerable change of opinion." During the inter-war period the "British Government had encouraged the formation of larger industrial units (mainly in the hope of achieving greater industrial efficiency) and this in turn had assisted the creation of monopolies." During the war there emerged "a clear realization" of the "dangers" of that policy. Nevertheless the British were "not convinced that these...'treaties of alliance' were always wrong, although...they held dangers for the consumer." Nor, they said, was "entirely free competition...either obtainable or always right: one held dangers for the consumer, the other for the producer." In light of this uncertainty, it was "not possible on the international side to go further than [was]...possible domestically."[80]

The basic question, then, was that of establishing a "method" for distinguishing "virtuous" from "vicious" cases. British experience and social values prevented following the "American practice" which was "to lay down by law certain, general prohibitions" which were then interpreted by the courts. British traditions and institutions thus "blocked" any attempt to enact a "Sherman law...[because of] endless arguments that it would prohibit certain things which ought not to be prohibited." Within and without the British government the "conception" which would "likely" receive "more favor...in the international as in the internal sphere, would be to examine particular cases in the light of general principles. In this way a body of precedents could be built up which would have persuasive weight in arguing future cases."[81]

In both the domestic and international sphere, therefore, the British envisioned relying on "publicity for a sanction, but not excluding the possibility in appropriate cases of ad hoc legislative action." Generally, publicity was sufficient because British industries seemed "more amenable to Government persuasion than perhaps" was the case in America. British "cartel member firms" were usually "anxious not to come into conflict with the Government." Finally, the British representatives agreed to discuss anti-cartel measures administered by an International Trade Organization, as long as they were consistent with domestic policies and institutions.[82]

Despite the final Allied victory during the summer of 1945, the cartel issue engendered heightened tensions between British and American negotiators. The state of opinion after six months of "informal talks" was apparent in the meeting of June 27. The discussion focused on the relationship of cartel practices to the attainment of general commercial, employment, and commodity policies in the post-war world economy. A comparison of each nation's position on restrictive practices revealed "considerable difference." The British favored the "gradual building up of a...'code of practice,' while the Americans adopted the 'statutory approach.'"[83]

After the meeting Andrew wrote that there seemed "no likelihood of agreement on this subject taken on its merits as the Americans [were] exactly where they were two years ago," except for no longer demanding the registration of certain corporate and patent arrangements. "In the last resort," he noted, the British government would "presumably have to decide how far it will accept American ideology on these matters in order to get other political or economic advantages."[84] Yet the Americans made "general financial discussions" contingent upon the British changing their cartel position. It seemed "hardly conceivable that a complete break should be allowed to happen between ourselves and the Americans on the cartels question," said another Board official, "though obviously it [was] very difficult to see where an accommodation could be found between their present and our present point of view."[85]

Domestic concerns dominated the Board's consideration of the monopoly-restrictive practices issue up to 1948. Pressures arising from British–American negotiations involving the International Trade Organization influenced the drafting process.[86] The debate over whether government intervention should rely upon publicity alone or publicity coupled with sanctions to aid the attainment of full employment and improved economic efficiency, however, indicated that domestic factors shaped policymaking primarily. The Board's staff conceded that because of antitrust legislation America was "less cartelist than the UK." Yet no significant interest within or without the government favored the "break-up of monopolies into competing groups" especially the large-scale managerially centralized firms such as ICI, Unilever, and J. P. Coats. Many economists nonetheless recognized that the limitation of competition through cartels reduced business efficiency, kept prices up, and threatened full employment. Accordingly, some sort of official machinery was "possible (within limits) to break down obstacles to competition and to stimulate the free play of private enterprise."[87]

The Board's staff submitted legislative recommendations to the President of the Board of Trade, Harold Wilson. The Labour Party's "election manifesto" required an end to "anti-social restrictive practices." The problem was to agree upon the institutional mechanism which permitted "determining which practices [were] anti-social" and whether "sanctions" were "necessary...and if so what they should be." In certain instances price controls and the reform of such fields as patent law might be insufficient. Because resale price maintenance touched so many economic and political interests, action in that field should await the findings of a special investigatory committee.[88] In addition, the broad political factors associated with the triumph of the Labour Party itself influenced the decision not to consider nationalized industries as part of the monopoly-restrictive practices issue. A staff member conceded that "Everybody's attitude to this problem depends of course on their own political and economic outlook." He suggested, however, that if the Government's policy was obtaining "maximum efficiency and output in the non-socialized sector of our economy – i.e. to make capitalism function where it is allowed to function, it will at least be necessary to have machinery for enquiry into cartels..."[89]

The staff favored a commission empowered to make "careful investigation." Given the precedents from World War I and II, the options were either that the Government might propose the creation of a "Commission of Inquiry" only, or it could in addition prescribe "some element of sanctions." The Reconstruction Committee of World War I had urged unsuccessfully the need for sanctions, and during World War II the Government did not accept the similar recommendation of the Gaitskell–Allen memorandum. Accordingly, by the fall of 1946 the Board's staff were of the view that publicity "should exercise a restraint over abuse," while it declined to accept the general utility of "sanctions."[90]

Meanwhile the ITO issue and the Justice Department's renewed antitrust campaign converged. The staff noted with concern the Justice Department's court victory in the ALCOA case of 1945. Wendell Berge, Thurman Arnold's successor, had initiated "22 antitrust cases, some...involving prominent British firms," the Board staff observed. He would "almost certainly seek more publicity... about 'cartels' assisted no doubt by some carefully synchronized 'exposures' by the sympathetic Kilgore...Committee."[91] Since 1943 the Americans consistently had insisted upon an anti-international cartel policy linking registration and prohibition. Although the evidence which the Justice Department's Corwin Edwards had gathered revealing the "use of cartels as weapons of aggression" impressed the British Government, it considered the American position to be "doctrinaire." A policy requiring such "fundamental change" was "highly contentious" and given that the Government's "legislative programme [was] full" there was "no present possibility of getting through an Act of Prohibition." Of course the Labour Government was "returned on a 'planned economy' not a *laissez-faire*' program." Privately negotiated cartels were "not part of a planned economy ... but the purely prohibitive step proposed by the Americans [was] not the only alternative."[92]

The Government considered the American position on international cartels, but domestic concerns remained primary. Prior to the summer of 1946 bilateral negotiations were scheduled, though where exactly Britain stood in relation to the United States in the "international discussions on the subject of restrictive practices, cartels, and monopolies" was unclear. Accordingly it was likely that legislation growing out of such discussions "might have to wait for a long time." Given the Labour Party's "election statement" there was "obviously some degree of embarrassment in any very long postponement of legislation on this subject." In addition, the question of legislation spawned repeated inquiries from industry. Finally, it *was* apparent from the preliminary international commercial talks that at "the least" Britain would be expected to enact "legislative powers of inquiry." The "balance of the argument" therefore favored a "decision to proceed with legislation as soon as time can be found."[93]

Between the fall of 1946 and spring of 1947 the Board drafted legislative proposals. The advocates of competition urged the stronger emphasis on sanctions embodied in the Gaitskell–Allen memorandum. They revived the idea of registering restrictive agreements, though the corollary proposition of "licensing or prohibiting them" was dismissed "without any question." The defenders of competition saw registration as the minimal sanction consistent with the inquiry–publicity approach.[94] In order to comply with the ITO idea, Lord McGowan of ICI publicly had supported registration of *international* agreements. But registration of "internal agreements" was "not ... proposed by any industry." The "main problems of registration" were, its opponents stated, the "definition of the agreements to be registered and of the persons obliged to register them." It was "important to the success of our policy on this subject that business men should not feel they are being subjected to quite unnecessary impositions." This view recognized the need to comply with whatever might be agreed in the negotiations for the ITO, but deferred specific recommendations until "our obligations ... have become more certain."[95] Ultimately, the ITO issue became virtually irrelevant, however, because the US Senate declined to ratify the Treaty of Havana which would have established the organization.[96]

Wilson introduced the legislation in the 1947–48 parliamentary session. The draft Bill included a commission with the "non-controversial power to enquiry (though not sanctions)."[97] The Labour Government believed that the use of cartels to "restrict production or employment" as a "means of protecting those engaged in industry" was incompatible with postwar goals of full employment and productive efficiency. Nevertheless, the Government rejected a "general trust busting policy" of "sweeping hostility to all monopolies and restrictive agreements...[which] would include in its condemnation genuine efforts to secure production economies by planned rationalization and industrial integration."[98] It was "better to judge each particular case on its merits, holding an independent enquiry to establish the facts and basing its conclusions on the results of the enquiry." Such a policy was approved in the "Election programme of both the Conservative and Labour Parties." Delay in proposing the Bill already had been "commented on in *The Times* and other newspapers fairly recently." Still, Kilroy observed bluntly, "Our commitment to the Americans may make it necessary for us to have a Bill but it is clearly better that we should not appear to be legislating primarily to please the Americans."[99]

The composition of the commission, and the need for related investigations received close attention from the staff. The Board recommended and the Government approved the appointment of special committees to investigate certain controversial restrictive practices. For example, resale price maintenance (RPM) was bound to arouse such controversy among producers and distributors, including numerous small businessmen, that the Government left the issue to an independent committee.[100] Similarly, the Board approached cautiously the section of the Bill involving selection of the Monopoly Commission's first chairman, who would serve full time and have chief responsibility for the staff. Above all, the chairman "should be a person of standing, not unacceptable to industry, the Unions or the Labour Movement, not closely associated in the past with any of the big cartels and with plenty of drive without being headstrong."[101]

The Marshall Plan complicated the preparation of the Government's Bill. The Marshall Plan, announced June 5, 1947, potentially raised new issues involving the convergence of international and domestic policies. Proposals for "dovetailing plans for production and consumption of particular commodities" suggested that "European producing countries [might]...agree to an allocation of

European markets among themselves...and not from outside." The British Government's and both political parties' "domestic attitude towards cartels" was that they were "not bad in themselves, but [were] capable of causing injury" and therefore should be subject to "public enquiry and exposure." Given the ITO discussions, there was "nothing necessarily inconsistent with these internal and external policies in the growth of inter-European agreements whether between Governments or private parties." Certain American "opposition newspapers" might present, however, "Europe's response to the Marshall offer in the light of one vast cartel designed to keep American competition out of Europe permanently."[102]

After months of uncertainty, Parliament began considering the Bill in early 1948. Since the preceding September, amid growing concern over consumer shortages, the press and other authorities stated that "we can only save ourselves and our country by a greater production." Restrictive practices of "any kind" were "anti-social...[and] a grave danger to the country. Anything which restricted our capacity to produce must be got rid of with all speed." Wilson responded to questions in Parliament, promising that the legislation would be forthcoming "as soon as the demands on Parliament time permit." Finally, in April, 1948 Parliament had before it the Monopoly (Inquiry Control) Bill.[103]

The measure finally enacted was somewhat broader than the Bill which was initially introduced. Both the Labour and Conservative Parties agreed in principle that trade restraints threatened the post-war British economy sufficiently to justify Parliamentary action. There was general agreement too that the commission–enquiry approach was most appropriate. "We all agree about what we want," said one MP during debate, "and we all agree we do not want to follow the lines of the American system." Both Parties also concurred on excluding labor practices and nationalized industries from the commission's jurisdiction. Yet there was considerable discussion as to whether the Bill as proposed would be effective. Wilson said that the primary reason for introducing the measure was to deal with the domestic problems of monopoly and restrictive practices. A secondary reason involved the diplomatic obligations associated with the negotiation of the ITO and anti-international cartel agreements. Conservatives challenged Wilson concerning the appropriate size of the Commission, the scope of its investigative authority, the meaning of "public interest" as a standard of business accountability, the sort of business conduct to which the standard applied, the reliance on Parliament as the final judge as to remedy, and even the distinction between monopoly and restrictive practice.[104]

Out of this debate the final legislation emerged. Reflecting the attempt to make the scope of the law more specific, its final title was the Monopolies and Restrictive Practices (Inquiry and Control) Act of 1948. It established a Commission, prescribed the conduct or situations included within its jurisdiction, defined the scope of investigative power, required the publication of reports, and suggested the sort of remedial action which might result from the reports. As a result of the debate, the "public interest" standard was somewhat more explicitly defined in relation to particular forms of monopoly or trade restraints. Beyond making control of one-third of the supply of a commodity the basis for inquiry, however, the Commission was left considerable discretion to establish such a standard based on case-by-case investigation.[105]

The Act empowered the Commission to investigate individual industries or large firms. In addition, under Section 15 the Commission could make special, more general inquiries into issues within its jurisdiction. The power to refer complaints or problems to the Commission was lodged in the Board of Trade. After the Commission prepared its report, the Board placed it before Parliament which decided appropriate action. There was no provision for criminal prosecution. Only a civil remedy, such as an injunction, was allowed. To a greater or lesser extent both the Labour and Conservative Parties were confident that in most cases where abuse was discovered improvement would occur as a result of publicity alone. This was the limit of government intervention. As one Liberal MP noted, the measure was a "puny infant," rather than a "lusty and noisy fellow."[106] More broadly the Act of 1948 represented an experiment circumscribed first by a reasonably informed understanding of the problem as it had evolved in Britain since World War I, and secondly by the presumption that the system of business self-regulation warranted less public control than that recommended by either the Americans or the Gaitskell–Allen memorandum.

CHAPTER 8

Uneven convergence since World War II

Throughout the post-war era the British and American policy response to big business gradually converged. Both nations experienced two significant merger waves, each of which peaked during the late sixties and eighties. By the 1980s the managerial organization of the British corporate economy approximated that of the United States. Not only had managerial capitalism finally displaced family capitalism in Britain, but the dominant corporate structure in each country was the large diversified corporation. The Monopolies Act of 1948 was merely the first step in a series of British and eventually European anti-cartel and merger measures which replaced business self-regulation with public control, facilitating the triumph of a corporate economy. In the United States a revival of antitrust enforcement from the late 1940s to the late 1960s, which nonetheless underwent transformation by 1990, also shaped corporate development. In Britain contrasting interest-group pressures and theories of economic efficiency sustained a new consensus favoring government intervention, while in America these same factors fostered the eventual demise of republican values.

THE PARAMETERS OF CONVERGENCE IN BUSINESS STRUCTURE

In both post-war nations similar patterns of business organization, government intervention, economic theory, and pressure group activity emerged. As had occurred in the turn-of-the-century United States, the British government's adoption of a reasonably clear anti-cartel policy combined with a greater toleration of mergers coincided with the triumph of managerial capitalism over family enterprise. The system of self-regulation did not disappear but it was circumscribed by a new system of public control. While post-war levels of corporate concentration were higher in Britain, in each country conglomerate and diversifying mergers were the norm by the 1980s.[1] The fluctuating political clout of small business, the reception of efficiency theories, and the changing role of the legal profession in each nation reinforced this gradual convergence.[2]

Despite minor mini-booms, merger activity in both nations was relatively flat until the 1950s, after which it steadily rose to a peak in 1968. There was a comparative lull beginning around 1973, which lasted until the mid-1980s, when another significant merger wave began. By 1990 this wave too had abated. In the United States the level of corporate concentration rose from 21 percent at the turn-of-the-century to 33 percent by 1969, though throughout the entire post-war era it remained fairly constant. In Britain the concentration level in the manufacturing sector rose from 26 percent in 1953 to 40 percent in 1970, and despite fluctuations it too remained relatively stable overall during the next twenty years.[3]

In each country merger activity followed a similar pattern. The American merger movement of the 1960s had little effect on competition because compared to earlier waves, the proportion of horizontal mergers was small and shrinking. Horizontal mergers were "clearly dominant" during the turn of the century, and probably still amounted to two-thirds in the 1920s. By the 1960s, however, conglomerate had superseded horizontal mergers to such an extent that the horizontal mergers accounted for only one-eighth of the total mergers. During the 1980s conglomerates again prevailed, but dealmakers initiated takeovers (leveraged buyouts or LBOs) primarily to break up subsidiaries which often were then sold to purchasers in the same line of business.[4]

By the late 1960s horizontal mergers were dominant in Britain. But by the early 1970s a "striking change" occurred, as the proportion of horizontal mergers declined and that of diversifying or conglomerate mergers increased. In terms of asset value diversification accounted for approximately 7 percent of mergers by 1969; during the early 1970s this rose to 29 percent, and, in the early eighties it had reached 40 percent, peaking in 1985 at 54 percent. "The corresponding proportion of horizontal mergers fell from 89 percent in the late 1960s to about 66 percent throughout the 1970s, to 57 percent in the 1980s and 42 percent in 1985," wrote one commentator. The impact on concentration and competition was similar to that in the United States. "The significance of this change is that whereas horizontal mergers increase concentration within an industry, diversifying mergers typically do not." Finally, as in the United States, a rising proportion of the diversifying or conglomerate mergers were "not in fact the joining of two hitherto independent companies, but the sale of a subsidiary by one company to another."[5]

Thus, during the post-war years, British managerial structure came more closely to approximate that of the United States. The increase in the level of corporate concentration paralleled the continuing decline of small firms. From 1958 to 1963 alone the share in net output of manufacturing corporations employing fewer than 200 workers fell from 20 percent of the total to only 16 percent. Over half of this decline in small firms reportedly was due to buyouts by bigger competitors. Even so, the scale of takeovers reflected the decline in the proportion of family-controlled firms. Although the demise of family capitalism dated from at least the 1920s merger movement, the post-war era witnessed the triumph of managerial capitalism. As managerial centralization prevailed in the 1960s, corporations increasingly adopted the multidivisional organization, which in turn facilitated diversification, including the conglomerate mergers of the 1970s and 1980s.[6] Hannah suggested that the "distinct postwar trend to conglomerate bigness" in the United States and Britain probably was "linked with the general development of the science of management and the nature of the modern 'visible hand' of the corporation." During the early development of the corporate economy in each country "management skills were industry – or product specific, but as functionally specialized techniques ... developed and top management – particularly financial management ... [became] increasingly professionalized, skills have become more easily transferable."[7]

Still, in neither Britain nor America was managerial centralization or multidivisional organization a guarantee against failure. In the post-war merger waves of both nations the failure rate was high. A White Paper published by the Department of Trade and Industry in 1988, surveying numerous studies of merger activity in each country, concluded: "Evidence on post-merger performance that has emerged since ... [1978] supports the earlier findings of disappointing or inconclusive performance." Yet this record merely confirmed the importance of effective management in the creation of large corporate enterprises which did succeed. "In the long run," Hannah said of the British corporate economy "as Alfred Chandler has pointed out in the context of the United States, it is principally those corporations which succeed in improving administrative coordination which will survive."[8]

As was the case in the United States, the demise of cartel practices encouraged corporate concentration. In 1955 a Monopolies Commission report showed that the pervasiveness of restrictive trade practices retarded full employment and efficient operation of the economy. Responding to concerned public opinion, the Conservative Government enacted the Restrictive Trade Practices Act of 1956. The legislation reflected a bipartisan party consensus against cartelization; during the next thirty years Labour and Conservative governments periodically passed or recommended still more stringent provisions. British business leaders and the writers of expert studies agreed that although the interconnection between mergers and cartels required further study, most research showed that in "many industries" mergers occurring after termination of cartels were "probably the major cause of increased concentration."[9]

The Monopolies Act of 1948 established an administrative process based on investigation and publicity. After passage of the 1956 Restrictive Trade Practices Act, the Commission's authority was limited until 1965 when the Labour Government extended its jurisdiction specifically to include mergers. Between 1966 and 1971 the effectiveness of this change was offset by the Industrial Reorganization Corporation (IRC) which promoted primarily horizontal mergers. In 1973 the Fair Trading Act set up the Office of Fair Trading and the Department of Trade and Industry replaced the Board of Trade, potentially strengthening the enforcement of competition. The RTP court handled cases of cartels, whereas the investigation of monopolies and, by 1965, mergers, remained the business of the Commission. And yet, throughout the post-war era the number of references the Minister made to the Commission was not large. During the merger wave of the late sixties and early seventies the government's Mergers Panel reviewed 833 mergers. The number actually referred to the Commission for investigation, however, was just 20.[10]

Nevertheless, action on the cases which were referred consistently attacked concentration resulting from horizontal mergers in the name of competition. Coinciding as it did with a firm anti-cartel policy, the prosecution of horizontal mergers encouraged investors to shift toward conglomerates. From the early 1970s onward the percentage by asset value of conglomerate or diversifying mergers rose steadily. Periodically, the government did prosecute conglomerates, especially in order to prevent the takeover of certain long-established British firms by foreigners. Overall, however, a competition policy which centered on concentration facilitated conglomerates since, unlike horizontal mergers, conglomerates usually did not increase concentration levels.[11]

Government intervention also encouraged conglomerate mergers in the United States. The Celler–Kefauver Act of 1950 closed the Clayton Act's asset loophole. Until the late 1960s antitrust officials used the Act primarily to attack horizontal mergers. Accordingly, investors sought organizational and scale economies through conglomerates which dominated the late-sixties boom. The boom ended by 1973 after President Richard Nixon's antitrust authorities began prosecuting the conglomerates. Nixon soon reversed the position, however, and thenceforth Republican as well as Democratic antitrust enforcement again declined to interfere with conglomerate mergers. Influencing this policy shift were major divestiture suits in which the courts decided against the government. By the mid-1980s, under the Reagan Administration, the combination of judicial decisions and lax enforcement encouraged a second conglomerate merger wave, though this time the goal of acquisition was generally to sell off subsidiaries.[12] By 1987, however, the attorney generals of all fifty states, both Democrats and Republicans announced uniform anti-merger guidelines intended to "give business the message that the states are united in their determination to stem a 'rash of mega-mergers.'" Also, certain states passed and the Supreme Court upheld more stringent anti-takeover legislation. The scale of takeovers aroused enough public concern that the Republican Administration of George Bush advocated strengthened antitrust enforcement.[13]

In both nations other factors influenced the uneven course of merger movements. The British 1948 Companies Act, and the American Hart-Scott-Rodino Act of 1975, required firms to disclose more complete profit and asset information, encouraging takeover bids. The new information enabled predators to circumvent corporate directors and appeal to shareholders through direct bidding. Despite technical differences in the two laws, by the 1970s uncontested and contested takeover bidding thus contributed to the prevalence of conglomerate mergers. Meanwhile, expert analysis confirmed that the timing of merger activity was more closely related to stock prices than other variables. The precise nature of the relation between stock prices and merger activity remained nonetheless "an enigma." In any case, the underlying motives shaping mergers involved the search for scale and organizational economies which in various instances probably were inseparable from the urge to monopolize.[14]

In each nation the business opinion of those supporting diversification and conglomerate mergers eventually converged. Harold Geneen, the leader of ITT's diversification during the early 1960s, summarized the experience of American finance-oriented managers who pioneered the takeover strategy. He understood that the "most important aspect" of antitrust policy was that the "concentration of markets within – I repeat – within industries" was of primary concern to government authorities and the courts, until "horizontal and vertical mergers" had "virtually ceased." It was "for this reason that only the so-called diversified or conglomerate mergers remain to business as a method of seeking more effective forms of management efficiency and growth, which could be translated into stockholder values without concentration of markets within an industry."[15]

Nearly twenty years later Sir Gordon White made a related but different point. "Entrenched management and trade union attitudes, resistant to inevitable change have been a major cause of Britain's post-war industrial decline," he said. Therefore public criticism of "complacent and generally poor management of these sunset industries on the one hand and the lack of political will on the other," was "much deserved." Ironically, he suggested that government had not acted early enough in applying the "nebulous concept of the public interest" to encourage the type of takeover "merger activity... [which had] been a failure of post-war Britain and the US." Mergers and takeovers, "particularly contested takeovers" were vital to the "essential process of modernization in the US and UK," and "[w]hatever role the government authorities choose to play in this, it should not be part of government policy to protect inept and inefficient managements from being replaced." White did not contend that all takeovers were beneficial. He was nonetheless certain that the "vital restructuring of much of the core of British industry... should have taken place long ago."[16]

Nevertheless, by the 1980s there was a growing concern that Britain's traditional social-class values were weakening. Early in 1987 a financial scandal involving Guinness raised criticism that the traditional values had eroded as a result of "Casino Capitalism" in which the "clubbish old order" in the City's financial district had given way to a "meritocracy, with East Enders competing on equal footing against Eton graduates." Conservative as well as Labour MPs agreed with a Conservative's statement that increasingly the City had come under the influence of individuals "long on cunning but short on morals." Edward Heath, the former Conservative Prime Minister, condemned this as still "another aspect of the unacceptable face of capitalism."[17] Shortly thereafter the Liesner Committee published reports recommending improved merger and restrictive practices policies. These reports in turn coincided with the preparation of the European Community's new merger regulation of 1990, which nonetheless built upon Britain's accession in 1973 under the articles of the Treaty of Rome.[18]

The public expressed similar concerns in America. The insider scandals of 1987 prompted the view that "without a sense of responsibility," the nation's business was "in trouble." A *Los Angeles Times* editorial commented that the "whole takeover craze" reflected the reality "that in present-day America you can make a mountain of money a lot faster by...legal financial manipulation, than by helping a company make and market a good product." Yet the decline in morality was an even greater issue than legality. There was "something corrupt" about "brainy young business people," who were paid hundreds of thousands of dollars annually, "scheming for their companies to dip into pension funds on which rank-and-file employees are depending for their retirement." This moral decline indicated the loss of "enlightened self-interest" and "some sense of responsibility" to society as a whole. America, to be sure was a capitalist country but the nation's "democratic society" did not perpetuate the capitalist system "as a favor to the rich and well-born; on the contrary...a free-enterprise system produces a better life for everybody." When the "people on top...failed to understand this simple truth" Americans used the "power of government to teach them a lesson." The antitrust laws and other government regulations were "reactions to excesses by businessmen who failed to understand the need for self-restraint."[19]

In this conflict the impact of interest groups was nonetheless difficult to measure. In America the turn-of-the-century and 1920s merger waves diffused the political clout of small business. Accordingly, during the postwar era small enterprise won only sporadic triumphs, generally supporting the status quo. Labor, consumer, and environmental groups also remained within the traditional American consensus which feared the abuse but embraced the consumer benefits of big business. Meanwhile, big business itself increasingly pursued a more accommodating if vacillating approach toward government intervention, unwilling to challenge the levels of corporate concentration antitrust enforcement imposed.[20]

In Britain small business was a relatively quiescent pressure group until the post-war era. Despite the rise of the corporate economy during the 1920s, small enterprise and family firms remained comparatively protected by national tariff barriers and privately enforced business self-regulation. Except in support of retail price maintenance (RPM), small companies did not mount significant political resistance until the Commission's investigation of trade restraints resulted in the pathbreaking Restrictive Trade Practices Act of 1956 and the abolition of resale price maintenance in 1964. By then, however, business interests were sufficiently divided on particular issues that they supported the bipartisan consensus favoring government intervention to ensure at least a modest degree of competition. Similarly, the media and public officials often espoused the interest of consumers. At least with reference to monopoly and restrictive practices, however, policymakers found that generally consumers lacked the organizational cohesion to be an effective pressure group. Labour, of course, did possess considerable political clout, but its support of mergers or competition depended upon whether in any given case either one might foster employment and social welfare.[21]

Interest groups and official policymakers appealed to changing economic theories. In both nations post-war economic experts built upon the work of Joan Robinson, E. H. Chamberlin, and R. H. Coase, developing the theoretical implications of oligopolistic competition. After studying in the United States during 1952–53, British civil servant A. D. Neale published in 1960 an incisive analysis of American antitrust which remained in print throughout the rest of the century. Traditionally, Neale said the "rationale of antitrust [was] essentially a desire to provide legal checks to restrain economic power" rather than a "pursuit of economic efficiency as such."[22] Increasingly from the 1970s on, however, efficiency theories identified with Coase influenced American antitrust. An Englishman and former instructor at the London School of Economics, Coase elaborated upon and extended his theories of firm organization while teaching at various American universities including, finally, the University of Chicago. Critics contended particularly that the famous "Coase theorem" amounted to essentially "a normative bias against state interference in the market, disguised as a 'theorem'." And yet some defenders of the organizational approach, especially as it applied to antitrust, turned the theorem "into a *defense* of certain kinds of wealth redistribution."[23]

Neale suggested how much of American antitrust was applicable to Britain. He favored "leaving oligopoly alone except so far as it becomes formalized in outright collusion," usually identified with horizontal combinations. If a "problem of 'big business' power" arose, and there "may be such a problem just as there may be problems of bureaucratic power or trade union power – it will tend to be seen as a political and social problem outside the special field of economists or 'trust-busters.'" As far as cartel practices were concerned, however, the American antitrust record was impressive, indicating that British policy should maintain a "strong presumption... in favor of simple prohibition – *per se* rules – enforced by criminal proceedings and thereafter by the legal advisers of business."[24]

In post-war America the theoretical definition of efficiency and its relation to competition changed. Since at least Herbert Hoover and Thurman Arnold economists, antitrust authorities, and lawyers have talked about efficiency. But they nonetheless remained under the influence of the republican values associated with Louis Brandeis. In the ALCOA decision of 1945 the Court linked economically oriented efficiency concerns emphasizing levels of corporate concentration to the social benefits resulting from attacking bigness. By the late 1940s economists, government and private lawyers, and the courts incorporated these values into a new theory of competition. According to Eugene Rostow the "old preoccupation of the judges [was] with evidence of business tactics they regarded as ruthless, predatory, and immoral" whereas the new theory "assimilat[ed] the legal to the economic conception of monopoly... regarding as illegal the kind of economic power which the economist regards as monopolistic." Chicago economist Henry Simons summarized one dimension of these theoretical presumptions in 1948, writing that "the compelling reason for stamping out private monopoly" was that it facilitated "an accumulation of government regulation which yields, in many industries, all the afflictions of socialization and none of its possible benefits; an enterprise economy paralyzed by political control; the moral disintegration of representative government in the endless contest of innumerable pressure groups for special favors; and dictatorship."[25]

By the 1960s, however, this analysis of competition came under vigorous attack. Although the assault came from various quarters, generally it was identified with the University of Chicago, particularly the law school's Law and Economics program headed by Aaron Director.[26] Among the many opinion leaders and policymakers Director's teaching influenced was Robert Bork. From the 1960s on, Bork's writings as a Yale law professor and judge helped to reshape antitrust theories. In *Fortune* articles written during the 1960s he said "Too few people understand that it is the essential mechanism of competition and its prime virtue that more efficient firms take business away from the less efficient." Bork did not question economic theory when it taught that where "certain business behavior is likely to result in monopoly profits and misallocation of resources... [it] should be illegal." But he was certain that such behavior was exceptional. "All other behavior should be lawful so far as antitrust is concerned, since, in relation to consumer welfare, it is either neutral or motivated by considerations of efficiency. The market will penalize those that do not in fact create efficiency."[27]

At the same time, a somewhat different perception of efficiency was popularized by Donald Turner. A law professor at Harvard and head of the Antitrust Division from 1965 to 1968, Turner rejected the explicit social and political values identified with the ALCOA decision's analysis. He was more concerned than Bork, however, about the impact of concentration levels on prices.[28] One of Turner's lieutenants in the Antitrust Division, Edwin Zimmerman told a group of antitrust lawyers that "our tradition of self-regulation and of reliance upon the marketplace becomes endangered when the marketplace no longer serves effectively to make... decisions... in an efficient manner. If by reason of concentration... public confidence in the marketplace erodes... the demand for... government regulation is greatly enhanced."[29]

During the 1970s and 1980s British and American economic theories remained distinct. In the United States, from the early 1970s on the tension between the approaches represented by Bork and Turner shaped court decisions and government antitrust enforcement, limiting horizontal but facilitating conglomerate mergers. For the first time in nearly a century, however, the republican values defended by Brandeis were of minimal importance.[30] In Britain, the emphasis was also upon efficiency but competition theory was influenced little if at all by the Chicago School's law and economics movement. Reassessing ideas stated during the 1950s and 1960s, Neale and others regarded the economics of monopolistic or imperfect competition which was the basis of much Chicago doctrine as not very realistic as a model of modern trade and industry; an analysis of competition in terms of various forms of rent-seeking, some benign, some less so, seemed more useful.[31] But, as was the case in the United States, British policy focused more on horizontal than conglomerate mergers, though British concentration levels remained higher.[32]

Each nation's legal profession influenced the comparative impact of pressure groups and economic theory. As Neale noted in another context, many problems of antitrust enforcement could be overcome by the "lawyers advising businessmen."[33] In post-war America small enterprises usually were litigants in suits involving cartel agreements. In these cases, except where "fair trade" and other exemptions existed, the government and the courts consistently enforced a policy of competition. When concentration levels and mergers were at issue, however, the status of small business waxed and waned.[34] Until the early 1970s private litigators, the government, and the courts remained responsive to Brandeisian values linking republican self-government, free enterprise, and small business. But from the mid-1970s on judges, government prosecutors, and the private antitrust bar adopted efficiency theories associated with the Chicago School, according to which the primary goal governing decisionmaking was consumer welfare.[35]

Antitrust principles increased the role of the British legal profession. Before World War II, Freshfields and a very few other London solicitors' firms helped to draft cartel and merger agreements. Since the courts increasingly upheld the enforcement of restrictive agreements, disputes involving the reasonableness doctrine periodically also demanded the services of barristers. Yet generally this market for legal services was limited, leaving the bulk of the work to accountants. After 1948, however, the passage of anti-monopoly and anti-cartel legislation enlarged the legal profession's role. By the 1960s the solicitors' and barristers' professional organizations instituted merger and restrictive practices committees whose expertise influenced public debate and policymaking. British corporations often had no legal departments, and there was no British equivalent of the large Washington law firms having close contacts with government antitrust agencies. Both as advisors and litigators, however, the legal profession increasingly helped large and small firms to maneuver within the parameters of official policy.[36]

Britain's anti-cartel legislation in various specific ways increased the legal profession's business. The Restrictive Trade Practices Act created a court which established the demand for client representation. Business counsel developed ways around the Act's prohibition and registration provisions, facilitating Parliament's enactment of an even stricter law abolishing RPM in 1964.[37] From the creation of the Office of Fair Trading in 1973 to the Liesner Committee proposals of 1988, the government attempted to contain the legal profession's creative search for new restraints. The Liesner Committee also recommended legislation which would have increased the opportunity for private actions. The recommendations did not support treble damages and contingent fees which facilitated private suits in America. Nevertheless, legislation establishing a private action in tort was considered an important change which "could provide a useful supplement to the efforts of the [governmental] authority and liability for damages should be added deterrent to the making of anti-competitive agreements." Finally, entry into the Common Market brought Britain within the anti-cartel provisions of European Community law, creating still more business for lawyers.[38]

Further strengthening the role of the British legal profession was merger and monopoly law. The investigation–publicity approach, based on the government's reference of cases to the Commission established in 1948, generally avoided an adversarial process requiring representation of counsel. Rarely did a case go to court. Thus lawyers might appear on behalf of a business client in an advisory role when the OFT was deciding whether to make a reference. The same was true once a reference investigation was underway in the Commission. Generally, however, both solicitors and barristers advised clients prior to their appearance before the government's Merger Panel or the Commission itself. In addition, from the 1960s on teams including solicitors, barristers, and accountants advised firms concerning major merger and acquisitions in either Britain or the European Community. Barristers did have a greater role as litigators in cases involving the EC's law. Gray's Inn, especially, developed an expertise in representing British clients before the Court in Luxemberg and the Commission in Brussels and this business was likely to increase as a result of the EC's 1990 merger regulation.[39]

In the United States, of course, the lawyer's role in antitrust was always central. In the late nineteenth century Sullivan & Cromwell and other Wall Street firms had emerged primarily to serve corporate giants. Paralleling the rise of the corporate bar, was the other market for antitrust legal services symbolized by Louis Brandeis. Like their corporate counterparts, these lawyers were counselors, litigators and lobbyists. The availability of treble damages and contingent fees meant that throughout the twentieth century approximately 90 percent of the antitrust cases filed were private suits. After World War II the private antitrust community, including both sides of the bar, was strengthened through the formation of the Antitrust Section of the American Bar Association. From the late 1940s on this Section maintained close and generally cordial ties with the FTC and the Antitrust Division. Numerous periodicals, such as the Section's *Antitrust Bulletin*, also provided a steady flow of expert opinion and analysis.[40]

A leading antitrust lawyer marked how business expectations had changed the sort of advice sought from counsel. In 1971 former ABA president Bernard G. Segal wrote that traditionally many business-men relied primarily upon the lawyer's political lobbying function. This role, of course, remained important. Segal found, however, that "enormous progress has been made and that the businessman's respect for the antitrust laws and his desire for and adherence to the advice of his antitrust counsel have reached new and favorable heights." Once business tended to "call on his counsel for advice after the ship has already entered perilous waters," Segal observed. "Today, when a company is contemplating a merger, acquisition, joint venture, or other action having antitrust overtones...the antitrust lawyer...[is] called upon promptly. Often, the negotiations are shaped by his advice."[41]

Indeed, lawyers' advice shaped the post-war merger waves. As government prosecutors and the courts successfully attacked horizontal mergers during the 1950s and 60s, corporate lawyers recommended shifting to diversification and conglomerate mergers. "In the post-war years, there have been some special pressures and temptations to diversify. The trend of antitrust enforcement has made it difficult for many corporations to expand in their own industries," reported *Fortune* magazine. Similarly, a commentary on mergers in *Business Week* noted, "whatever happens, it won't be because all recent mergers were entered into blindly. There's plenty of evidence that they have been made only on careful advice of counsel. Most of the current deals do not look as though monopoly has been their goal. Rather, they seem aimed at some legitimate aims such as diversification." After Harvard Law professor Donald Turner took over as head of the Antitrust Division in 1965, moreover, *Business Week* reported that he was trying only "to channel the merger movement away from 'horizontals'... and, to a lesser extent, vertical mergers... into the conglomerate stream. Private lawyers are well aware of this attitude and advise corporate clients, 'If you're thinking about conglomerate mergers, do it now'... the [legal] climate... will never be better."[42]

As far as litigation was concerned, American lawyers played their most significant role in private suits. Between 1960 and 1978 the number of private suits filed jumped dramatically from 228 to 1,611. Until 1986 the number did not fall below 1,052, before dropping to 654 two years later. Segal attributed the rise to three significant developments in post-war antitrust law. First, the Celler-Kefauver Act led Turner and others to formulate new theoretical concepts which extended the grounds for bringing private cases involving mergers. Secondly, the massive electrical equipment litigation created new remedies and sanctions for antitrust violations, including the imprisonment of corporate executives. These factors generated "private treble damage actions, with their immense verdicts and huge settlements, which would have been incredible not long before," and which had "large and chilling effect on the potential antitrust violator." The third development was the "flowering of a plaintiff's antitrust Bar." Accordingly, antitrust corporate defendants confronted a new class of private plaintiffs, including the "country's largest investor-owned electric utilities, state and local and even foreign governments, and important industrial companies." Beginning in 1977 courts applied new economic theories to reduce the number of private suits but, a decade later, the number was still nearly three times greater than that of 1960.[43]

American lawyers put economic theory to greater use than did their British counterparts. Until the early 1970s the Americans followed the brand of competition theory which recognized that excessive concentration threatened social values as well as economic efficiency. And yet, once the courts began adopting the efficiency theories associated with the Chicago School, private lawyers changed course.[44] In Britain, however, judges looked upon the testimony of economists espousing different theories as presenting something like a choice between "two witch doctors." Among British economists, moreover, Chicago-type theories made few inroads. In addition, the Commission and the Court of the European Community adopted the economic theories followed by American antitrust during the 1950s and 60s. British solicitors and barristers used this economic theory in their advice involving references, and in their represent-ations of business clients before the UK and EC regulatory commissions and the courts. But, as London University's Valentine Korah said, neither Britain's government authorities nor business interests accepted the Chicago School premise that business leaders were "market maximizers."[45]

Ultimately, the contrasting role of lawyers and status of economic theory reflected different judicial philosophies. In Britain, the enactment of antitrust legislation from 1948 on resulted in periodic court cases in which judges occasionally displayed activistic tendencies. In early cases testing the scope of the Restrictive Trade Practices Act some decisions expressed greater concern than others for possible unemployment resulting from the termination of restrictive practices. Also, lawyers' ingenuity in developing cartel or monopoly practices often stayed ahead of administrative or legislative remedy.[46] British judges, however, hesitated to address such problems through broadened construction of already existing statutes, leaving the decision of whether a new law was necessary to the executive. Thus Lord Chief Justice Parker said that "in modern Britain, where no agreement exists on the ends of Society and the means of achieving those ends, it would be disastrous if courts did not eschew the temptation to pass judgment on an issue of policy. Judicial self-preservation may alone dictate restraint..." Lord Devlin put the argument favoring self-restraint more pointedly. Most judges, he said "do not seriously question the status quo," usually adopting a vision of the public interest shared by "any body of elderly men who have lived on the whole unadventurous lives."[47]

The American judge's acceptance of changing economic theory eventually also resulted in greater restraint. Despite the ALCOA decision of 1945, the post-war Supreme Court vacillated in its acceptance of a theory incorporating both social and consumer values. The Court did not fully embrace such a theory until the 1950s and 60s. At the same time, however, American judges increasingly came under the influence of contrasting strands of efficiency theory, one associated with the work of Turner, the other identified with the Chicago School. By the early 1970s, the Supreme Court led a dramatic shift away from the ALCOA-type analysis to the new theories, which dominated antitrust at least until 1990. Thus, in merger as well as many cartel cases, American courts increasingly exercised a degree of restraint.[48]

Yet judges used economic concepts selectively. Generally they relied upon the "technical...analysis of language...rather than economic modeling." Judges proceeded "inductively by examining the language of judges in order to extract principles from particular decisions, rather than deductively by carrying prefabricated hypotheses to the data."[49] Undoubtedly, wrote another commentator in 1989, "Chicago models" were "widely" accepted as the conceptual basis for antitrust law but the models did "not dictate...a policy choice." Generally, judges "relied on the models to guide the inquiry in...doctrinal contexts as a way of structuring and resolving critical empirical issues through the process of proof in litigation." In private suits or government cases, these theories limited the "jury's discretion in areas in which it manifestly lack[ed] experience, yet does not foreclose plaintiffs from producing evidence that refutes the efficient explanation for the practice." The Supreme Court in particular "resisted the Chicago policy program's wholesale reformulation of antitrust because it require[d] estimates that go beyond the traditional judicial role."[50]

Notwithstanding important differences, each nation's post-war business structure and official policies gradually converged. Completing a process begun during the 1920s in Britain, the managerial capitalism of corporate giants finally replaced family capitalism identified with smaller firms. As official sanction of self-regulation ended, Britain completed the course pioneered by the United States. As was the case in America at the turn of the century, the triumph of British big business during the 1960s coincided with the government's formal opposition to cartels combined with a looser policy towards mergers. Similarly, in each nation the government's emphasis upon horizontal mergers facilitated the prevalence of conglomerate and diversifying mergers during the 1970s and 1980s.

The interplay of economic theories, pressure groups, values, and law insured that in each nation important differences would remain. But the interconnection between business structure and antitrust policy suggested that the slow yet steady convergence would continue.

BRITISH POLICY IMPLEMENTED, 1948–1968

The post-war implementation of Britain's first significant monopoly and restrictive practices legislation occurred in two principal stages. After the passage of the 1948 Monopolies Act, Harold Wilson began several important initiatives which led to Labour's 1951 White Paper attacking resale price maintenance. The Conservative Government's revision of the Monopolies Act in 1953 and a Monopolies Commission report on trade restraints in 1955 were preliminaries to the second stage, the passage of the Restrictive Trade Practices Act of 1956. The Act instituted the sort of sanctions and enforcement provisions recommended in the Gaitskell–Allen memorandum. The Conservatives further incorporated the spirit of the memorandum in the Resale Price Act of 1964. Ironically, a Conservative Government enacted measures which during the war had been too controversial for either party to enact into law. Similarly, the Monopolies and Mergers Act of 1965 was the Labour Government's legislation, but it grew out of proposals included in the Conservative Government's 1964 White Paper. The consensus reflected in this and other legislation influenced the first post-war merger wave which peaked in the late 1960s.

After Labour enacted the Monopolies Act of 1948, other competition issues arose. Neither Labour nor Conservatives favored interfering significantly with the growth or development of large corporate structures. The potential point of contentiousness involved, therefore, cartel practices, resale price maintenance (RPM), and trade restraints in technical fields such as patents. The Gaitskell–Allen memorandum and, to a lesser extent, US policies against international cartels, suggested a basis for registration and ultimate prohibition of most restrictive practices. The Monopolies Act demonstrated, however, that both major parties could agree only to adopt a policy which relied upon publicity as distinct from some sort of direct sanctions. Whatever influence the ITO and international cartel issue might have had on changing this policy consensus dissipated once Congress declined to ratify the Havana

Charter in 1949. Similarly, except for passage of the Patents Act of 1949 which largely formalized monopolistic rights under patents, the President of the Board of Trade, Harold Wilson, was unable to make progress on stronger measures against RPM or other forms of trade restraints before Labour went out in 1951.[51]

Nevertheless, political pressure mounted for further action against restrictive practices. Early in June, 1949 the Lloyd Jacob Committee charged with investigating RPM published its report. First, the Report recommended that no official action should be taken which would "deprive an individual producer of the power to prescribe and enforce resale prices for goods bearing his brand." The Committee questioned, however, the justification for *collectively* enforced RPM. The Report attacked any collective attempt "to obstruct the development of particular methods of trading, to impede distribution by another manufacturer of competitive goods, or to deprive the public of improvements in distribution." Secondly, it recommended that formal "steps should be taken to render illegal the application of sanctions which extend beyond the remedies open to an individual producer for any breach of... [RPM] conditions."[52]

The effort to distinguish officially tolerated *individually* enforced RPM from various forms of collective enforcement which might be outlawed created ambiguity. Business objected that the distinction was artificial and unrealistic. Other factors contributed to uncertainty. The official platforms of the leading political parties stated that trade restraints inhibited the attainment of productive efficiency and full employment. These Party programs and the press were particularly anti-restrictionist when it came to the distribution sector. Yet the Labour Government believed that expanded price controls and nationalized industries were essential to the public interest.[53] Meanwhile, the day before publication of the Lloyd Jacob Committee Report, Dame Alex Kilroy, Secretary of the Monopolies Commission, declared that the Commission would address the RPM issue only as it arose in particular references. The Commission intended, she said, "to obtain detailed evidence, covering RPM and other matters as well, about the industries referred to them, and their conclusions on the RPM aspects of these cases will be reached in the light of this evidence as a whole."[54]

Wilson's action reflected the pressure for further measures. On the same day as the Lloyd Jacob Report appeared he stated in Parliament that through consultations with trade associations and the Ministers responsible for price controls the Government would "consider the most satisfactory means of ensuring that price maintenance by individual producers shall not injure the interests of the consumer." It was appropriate to consider abolition of *collective* RPM given the revelation of "a widespread system of trade association controls, whose scope, complexity and cumulative restrictive effects" pervaded the distributive trades.[55]

Wilson defined the threat to the "consumer's interest" in both general and particular terms. Condemning the intricate network of private self-regulation and enforcement which prevailed within the distribution sector, the President of the Board of Trade expressed the hope that business would cooperate with the Government to resolve the problem. Nevertheless the "Government are fully determined to ensure that the general public shall not suffer from the private restrictions of price competition." Yet Wilson also viewed Co-operative Societies and self-service shops as particularly vital to the consumer's interest. In the discussions with business he would "make clear that discriminatory restrictions against consumer dividend or discount systems employed by Cooperative Societies…must be abolished." In addition, the "public must be allowed to reap the benefit of low-cost methods of distribution (in particular self-service shops) by way of reduced retail prices."[56]

Throughout the rest of the Labour Government's existence Wilson's efforts achieved little tangible results. Until shortly before Labour went out of power in the fall of 1951, Wilson encountered steady opposition from business groups. In July 1949 newspaper headlines stated: "A rebuff for Harold Wilson. His suggestion to stop collective price fixing has been turned down by the Proprietary Articles Trade Association."[57] In February, 1950 a pro-restrictionist lobbying group called the Fair Price Defence Committee refused, noted a Board of Trade observer, even to discuss seriously the voluntary suspension of "self-imposed restrictions and controls… obviously sitting tight…until they see the character of the next Government."[58] At Wilson's urging the Board solicited business views through a circular letter and questionnaires but, by early 1950, the staff concluded that the "exercise" had been "a frost."[59]

The FBI and the National Union of Manufacturers (NUM) were also uncooperative. The two organizations "completely rejected" the Lloyd Jacob Committee's conclusions as a "false interpretation of the evidence." They emphasized that the trade associations practicing RPM were registered under trade-union legislation and were therefore lawful. If the Government wanted to abolish RPM it should change the law. In addition, the Monopolies Commission was a "further instrument for investigating and controlling restrictive practices." The FBI and NUM leaders also argued that the actual forms RPM took throughout the distribution sector were too varied to permit a uniform policy which distinguished individual from collective private enforcement. Many trade associations, moreover, did not discriminate against Cooperative Societies. They also denied that self-service stores were cheaper than the "small shopkeeper" operating under RPM agreements.[60]

Given this resistance, departments within the Board of Trade and other Ministries discussed policy considerations. A paper prepared by a young civil servant, A. D. Neale, during summer, 1949 indicated the course of discussion throughout the period. The paper outlined the position of business groups and the likelihood of their minimal cooperation. Although political exigencies made it incumbent upon the Government to pursue consultation, eventually the "only real alternatives" might be either legislation prohibiting collective enforcement of RPM or doing nothing. Neale conceded that, in order to preserve unanimity, the Lloyd Jacob Committee stopped short of recommending outright prohibition. The business groups' adamant stance against voluntary action indicated, however, that legislative prohibition was very possibly the only effective means to bring about "more competition among distributors." The consultations with business groups and preparations for legislation required close cooperation with the Ministries of Food, Supply, and Fuel and Power, as well as other departments. Neale noted, too, that these cooperative efforts must not appear to preempt the concurrent but independent investigations of the Monopolies Commission.[61]

As the resistance to Wilson dragged on a legislative proposal became increasingly unlikely. By the spring of 1950, Wilson prepared to submit a memorandum to the cabinet reporting that the Conservative opposition, while in principle not resisting measures to control collective RPM, nonetheless felt any action should await the Monopoly Commission's report. Wilson conceded the "difficulties of finding a legal formula" covering "all cases" of collective RPM. Perhaps some form of tribunal was necessary." He also requested the Board to prepare a "note...setting out the case for and against the *registration of all price fixing and cartel arrangements* and of trade associations who consider this to be one of their functions." Still, Wilson "recognized the difficulty of finding a formula which would cover all the unwritten arrangements between producers to achieve this end." Finally, he "expressed concern at the long period taken by the Monopolies Commission to issue their first reports."[62]

Before leaving office in November 1951 the Labour Government issued a White Paper on RPM. Drafted by A. D. Neale, the White Paper broadly indicated the intention to legislate to prohibit collective enforcement, with some provision for exceptions. In April, 1951, Wilson had resigned from the Government over the Budget and his place at the Board of Trade was taken by Sir Hartley Shawcross. The White Paper was approved by the Government and issued by Shawcross before the November election. At the time the Trade Union Congress took the White Paper as its official position.[63]

Initially the Conservative Government's response to the problem of RPM was equivocal. Early in 1952 the issue arose as the Board of Trade prepared its third annual report on the operation of the Monopolies Commission. A draft of the Report suggested that the Board might, under Section 15 of the 1948 Monopolies Act, refer to the Commission the problem of exclusive dealing. Kilroy, however, questioned the idea because not all forms of the practice were necessarily bad.[64] Yet Kilroy's comment touched larger policy considerations. Referring to the Labour Government's White Paper recommending legislation dealing with RPM, Board officials feared embarrassment if, in the "near future", it referred "exclusive dealing to the Commission under Section 15." The Board might "be offering a great hostage to fortune... almost daring the Opposition to criticize Ministers for not rushing into legislation" to prohibit RPM.[65]

Yet public pressure for stronger action against restrictive practices mounted from 1952 on. The Board knew that thorough investigation of the various discriminatory methods associated with business self-regulation would provide a basis for official action. Accordingly, in December, 1952 the Board made its first and only general reference under Section 15 of the Monopolies Act. The Board referred to the Commission certain "collective discrimination" agreements, including exclusive dealing, aggregated rebates, collective boycotts, and the implementation of RPM. According to the terms of the reference, the Commission investigated not the merits of the practices *per se*, but rather their effects throughout industry.[66]

Under the 1948 Monopolies Act the Commission could not compel groups or individuals to give evidence. Even so, the fact that the evidence gathered was given voluntarily probably enhanced the credibility of the Commission's findings. About 160 trade associations offered evidence revealing the full range of discriminatory practices associated with the system of self-regulation. The trade associations, of course, generally defended the practices as necessary to avoid the rigor of competition. Approximately ninety other individual or group statements, however, complained about the effects of the discriminatory practices. In addition the Commission solicited the opinion of Britain's largest manufacturers and distributors who did not resort to such practices. It also received information from such representative organizations as the Federation of British Industries, the Trades Union Congress, and the Co-operative Union. A majority of the Commission concluded, however, that consumers lacked forms of adequate group representation, and so evidence from consumers was conspicuously absent.[67]

In 1953 the Government also proposed legislation intended to remedy the Commission's delay in making reports. Despite pressure from the Conservative Party's own constituents to do so, the Government did not examine the nationalization issue. The points considered for revising the Act of 1948 were, therefore: the technical status of the chairman, enlargement of the Commission's membership and staff, and a more precise definition of the standard of public interest, particularly as it related to general references under Section 15. Throughout the first half of the year the Conservatives' efforts to make the bill "non-contentious" resulted in legislation which was even narrower. After lengthy discussion, the proposed Bill merely included the provisions enlarging the Commission and defining the chairman's status. It was uncontroversial and was passed by Parliament in the summer of 1953 as the Monopolies and Restrictive Practices Act.[68] Although *The Economist, The Times*, and other papers expressed support for any measure which reduced the "unconscionable delay" in the Commission's reports, they regretted that the legislation was not stronger.[69] Yet according to one Conservative official the "balance of political advantage" favored the modest approach. The Conservatives "could claim credit for not letting a point of political doctrine stand in the way of changes which people of all political persuasions would be glad to see."[70]

After an inquiry lasting two and half years, Parliament received, in July, 1955, the Commission's Report on the Section 15 general reference. But for exceptional circumstances, the Report declared, all the forms of restrictive agreements examined "create[d] an undue rigidity which may affect the numbers and kind of concerns engaged in a trade, the trading methods adopted by those established in the trade and the level of prices both generally and to different classes of buyers." The economic inefficiency resulting from this "rigidity" was rooted in the ability of "combinations of traders... to exercise the powers over individuals which some price maintenance associations have acquired... through private tribunals whose procedure cannot provide the safeguards which public justice requires." The exercise of such private methods of collective self-regulation and enforcement were "particularly open to objection when they are used against concerns which are not members of the associations or have not entered into any contractual obligation to observe the rules enforced against them." Finally, the "general effect" of such exclusive dealing and preferential price agreements was "against the public interest."[71]

Agreement on these findings did not result in consensus on recommendations to Parliament. The Commission's Report explicitly favored competition over restriction. Competition facilitated consumer choice and encouraged experimentation among manufacturers and distributors in order to adapt to changing market conditions. It also permitted the entry of new firms. Business claimed it could better achieve such goals through self-regulation based wherever necessary on trade restraints. The Report declared, however, that private interests were less effective policymakers concerning these matters than an independent official body might be.[72]

Regarding what policy might best foster competition and replace private with public enforcement the Commission divided. A majority recommended legislative prohibition of the condemned practices, recognizing exemption under special circumstances. A new law would establish clearly defined criteria, including criminal liability, controlling the process of prohibition and approval of exemption. An independent official authority reporting to a Minister would decide upon the request for exemptions and lay the determination before Parliament. Three of the ten Commission members dissented, however; they opposed prohibition, favoring merely the registration of restrictive agreements. The Minority believed that the resulting publicity would reveal any abuse requiring investigation by an appropriate public body. In a Note of Dissent the Minority also singled out RPM as too complicated to be dealt with effectively under the majority's "prohibition/exemption" procedure.[73]

During the next year the Commission's Section 15 Report was central to the Conservative Government's policy discussions. Peter Thorneycroft, President of the Board of Trade, had primary responsibility for developing a legislative proposal by the fall of 1956. The issues of prohibition and registration involved difficult legal points which went beyond those raised by the 1948 and 1953 Monopolies legislation. Thus Thorneycroft's "aim [was] to get the Attorney General, deeply and personally involved in this work. Ideally, it should be our [the Board's] solution, but the Attorney General should think it is his."[74]

The Bill evolved amidst contention. First it was necessary to decide whether to adopt the majority or the minority view, or some combination of both, as the starting point of policymaking. The majority's recommendation of subjecting the restrictive practices to legislative prohibition was especially controversial. Approximating American policy, prohibition was an approach that most British public officials and private interests consistently had rejected. In one form or another, however, prohibition was proposed in the Gaitskell–Allen memorandum of 1943, urged by Wilson, the President of the Board of Trade, and recommended in Labour's White Paper of 1951. In addition, said one Board official, the minority's trust solely in registration would, in light of the evidence uncovered in the Commission's lengthy Section 15 investigation, appear to "public opinion...[to be] a ludicrously inadequate response." In fact, the Commission's experience demonstrated that "an industry whose practices are condemned...invariably seeks to argue its case all over again with the competent Minister." The industry mobilized "all the Parliamentary support" it could, presenting the "unhappy Minister" with a "string of Parliamentary questions." Thus, if at all possible, it was expedient to remove what were "essentially non-political questions" from a "partisan political atmosphere."[75]

Other considerations favored a "non-political" remedy. Always difficult in any examination of restrictive practices was determining the "criteria for identifying the public interest." The choice was between broadly or "very precisely" defined terms. A related and complicated issue was the treatment of RPM. Even Wilson had grudgingly accepted the Lloyd Jacob Commission's conclusion that not individual but collective enforcement of RPM, especially through private courts, was the primary evil. What institutional forum might best remedy such difficult policy questions? The Conservative Government's answer was to follow the recommendation of the Commission's majority report to establish some sort of tribunal, preferably a court. The Federation of British Industries eventually supported a court also. A court was not only independent of politics but also (unlike the Commission) capable of enforcing its own decisions. Such a novel approach, however, "raised some of the most difficult problems in the Government's monopoly policy." Not the least of which was establishing the jurisdictional boundary between any new tribunal and the Monopolies Commission.[76]

Labour stated forcefully its own proposals. Generally, the Party urged adaption of the Commission's Majority report, including a general prohibition subject to exemptions. Labour also favored compulsory registration of all restrictive agreements. Concerning RPM they broadly followed the proposals of the 1951 White Paper which had grown out of Wilson's efforts, especially prohibition of all forms of collective enforcement. They urged too the protection from discriminatory practices of Cooperative Society dividends and similar devices. Labour also wanted to link these measures to a general supervision of prices. Finally, they preferred establishing a new tribunal, while conceding the difficulty of defining the criteria of the public interest and the jurisdictional relationship to the Monopolies Commission.[77]

Under Thorneycroft's leadership, except on the issue of price controls, there was a substantial convergence of the two views. The policy which gradually emerged made the provision for prohibition dependent on findings arising from the process of registration. The American experience showed that outright prohibition often enmeshed decisionmaking in lengthy court proceedings, Thorneycroft said. Accordingly, he favored subjecting a wide range of restrictive agreements to compulsory registration. A tribunal would then "call up for examination" these agreements "and the onus would be on the industry to show that their practices were not against the public interest. If the tribunal found against the practice it would have to be stopped." This approach assumed that there might be exemptions. As for RPM, Thorneycroft recognized that some but not all forms might be prohibited, which at least partially coincided with Labour's view. Generally, he also did not oppose Labour's argument regarding the Cooperatives. Only concerning the supervision of prices did Thorneycroft reject altogether Labour's points. When it came to defining the public interest standard and the new tribunal's jurisdiction, moreover, the need to compromise was accepted.[78]

The Government's response to business views emphasized compromise. As their adamant opposition to the Wilson-inspired White Paper recommendations of 1951 showed, leading business groups initially resisted increased public control of trade restraints. And they counted on the Conservative Party to maintain that position. Indeed, an official of the Board charged with preparing policy papers noted in another context, that if the Government's measure became law, the Party would "certainly be accused of weakening very considerably the effectiveness of a [RPM] practice which they are thought to support."[79] A letter from an executive in a major Midlands business demonstrated the Party's problem. The writer was the "Treasurer of an important Conservative Branch" who like many other "businessmen" had "supported this Government financially and in every other respect." He stated the "widespread feelings of alarm and disgust that a Conservative Government should attempt to place such one-sided and ill-conceived legislation on the Statute Book." Passage of such a Bill, he predicted, "would sweep the Conservative Party clean out of the House...it [could] only damage business in general and the Party in particular." Such legislation would also "drive businesses into amalgamation to escape its provisions and so lead to more and more monopoly in Industry."[80]

Yet letters to Thorneycroft from small- and modest-sized firms concerning the restrictive practices Bill confirmed that other business leaders were more accommodating. The director of a Lancashire construction firm wrote that the proposed "Monopolies Bill" had "many features to which no reasonable man in industry could object." He observed, however, that the current era of full employment could not last, in which case business cooperation of the sort common during the 1920s and 1930s might again become necessary. In which case, he resisted outright prohibition of trade restraints in favor of a more flexible approach.[81] Another letter from a small ironmonger firm asserted that the "only object in writing" was to emphasize the "desirability of dealing with 'exclusive' trading whilst you are dealing with other restrictive trade practices."[82] Similarly, another businessman wrote that in order to weaken the "protected state" in which manufacturers were "now living" the legislation should make it "unlawful for retailers to prevent a manufacturer, *if he so desires*, selling direct to a consumer." This principle would defeat the "stranglehold" the retailer possessed by "trade custom."[83] In yet another case a British agricultural machinery manufacturer wanted exclusive dealing outlawed because American firms used it against him in the British home market.[84]

The position of the FBI reflected the multiplicity of business concerns. The FBI vigorously had voiced the united business opposition to Wilson's efforts during 1949–51. But their response to the Conservative's more far-reaching measures was accommodating. To be sure the FBI wanted the Government's proposals made as "innocuous" as possible. After initial resistance on the grounds that administrative bodies were better equipped to handle complex industrial issues, however, the FBI accepted the Government's contention that the "non-political" courts were a better remedy. Thus, once the Government convinced the FBI that it "meant business," the body's official position became one favoring the "judicial solution ... whereby the last word will rest with the courts and not, as would have been the case with any administrative tribunal, with a Minister and Parliament."[85]

There were further indications of the FBI's flexible stance. Despite the insistence of many of its constituents, it did not insist upon including unions or the nationalized industries in the restrictive practices Bill. As was the case during the revision of the Monopolies Act in 1953, the Government made it clear that those issues were politically too sensitive. The Government rejected, however, Labour's attempt to extend supervision of prices. Finally, the FBI did not push the claim that the proposed Bill's failure to deal with large corporations unfairly discriminated against small firms.[86]

By the fall Parliament enacted the Government's Bill as the Restrictive Trade Practices Act of 1956. The Act established a Registrar who registered Restrictive Trade Agreements; it also created a new judicial tribunal as part of the High Court of Justice, the Restrictive Practices Court. According to a two-step procedure it made compulsory, subject to criminal penalty, the registration of a wider range of trade restraints than the Commission's Section 15 Report covered, including the fixing of common prices. Mitigating the traditional *Mogul* doctrine, the law placed the "onus of proof" on the industry to show whether "on balance" the advantage of a given restrictive agreement would rebut the presumption of operating contrary to the public interest. That standard recognized very broadly an element of economic judgment, suggesting indirectly some concern not only for efficiency and employment considerations, but also the interests of consumers. It was incumbent upon industry to prove to the Court that in light of some specific purpose the employment of the practice was "reasonable."[87]

Based on a showing of evidence, the Act provided for certain exemptions or "gateways." On the whole, however, the expectation was that the Court would decide against most agreements, whereupon they would be discontinued but if continued the parties would be in contempt of the court. The rules of evidence admissibility were made more flexible than in ordinary courts; the right of appeal, however, was more circumscribed. If it chose to do so the Court might hear the opinions of economists. The Act prohibited the collective enforcement of RPM but strengthened an individual manufacturer's right of enforcement through litigation. The law also instituted a new, smaller Monopolies Commission whose jurisdiction extended only to large "single firm monopolies" and registered restrictive agreements in the export industry.[88]

The Restrictive Trade Practices Act thus established dramatic but not unprecedented new policy. The Conservative Government's announcement early in 1956 stated that the measure was partially "a compromise between the [Commission's Section 15] Majority and Minority recommendations." However, in "the main" the proposal went "considerably beyond either set of recommendations," because it applied to "all the known restrictive practices affecting the production, processing and supply of goods in the United Kingdom." In addition, it went further than the "Minority because, although the practices [were] not to be prohibited outright, without judicial investigation, the onus of showing that they [were] in the public interest rests with those who wish to continue them."[89] Shaping this mix of compromise and innovation were the changed economic conditions and alignment of interest group pressures which the Conservative Government faced during the mid-1950s. Yet the Labour Government's 1951 White Paper foreshadowed the new law, while it implemented many of the central recommendations of the Gaitskell–Allen memorandum thirteen years later.[90]

During the 1960s this policy consensus resulted in further legislative refinements. As business leaders predicted, the legislative limitation of cartel practices encouraged mergers, which peaked during the late 1960s. Following the passage of the Restrictive Trade Practices Act of 1956, however, various expert studies revealed how effective lawyers were in providing business ways around the prohibition of certain collectively enforced RPM agreements. The Conservative Government attacked the problem in the Resale Prices Act of 1964 which prohibited RPM except in cases where it was proven to be consistent with the public interest. The Conservative Government's reaction to the growing merger wave also resulted in a 1964 White Paper which recommended giving the Board the authority to refer to the Monopolies Commission those mergers in which the acquired assets had a value of more than £25 million or which might result in the firm controlling over one-third of the market. The proposal expanded the criteria of public interest, strengthening the Commission's power. The year the White Paper was published, a Labour Government returned whereupon it supported the proposals in the Monopolies and Mergers Act of 1965. Somewhat paradoxically, the following year Labour also created the Industrial Reorganization Corporation (IRC), empowered to promote appropriate mergers in the spirit of rationalization. In 1968 Labour also passed another Restrictive Practices Act requiring registration of various "information agreements."[91]

The triumph of managerial capitalism in Britain thus coincided with the strengthening of anti-cartel and merger policies. Business groups had supported the investigation–publicity approach instituted in the Monopolies Act of 1948. But when Wilson attacked RPM and Labour published the 1951 White Paper, various segments of the business community balked, fearing that the protective system of self-regulation was fundamentally threatened. Reflecting the post-war bipartisan political consensus supporting full employment and economic efficiency the Conservatives nonetheless accepted the Commission's Section 15 report as grounds for enacting the Restrictive Trade Practices Act of 1956. Divisions among business interests permitted the Conservatives to succeed where Labour had failed. As the anti-cartel policy generally succeeded, however, both leading parties wrestled with the rising merger wave which peaked in 1968. While Labour was more willing to promote "rationalization" mergers through the IRC, both parties approved expanding the

Monopolies Commission's authority to police mergers in the name of competition. Notwithstanding significant limitations, business self-regulation had given way to public control.

THE AMERICAN REVIVAL OF ANTITRUST: THEORIES OF EFFICIENCY VERSUS REPUBLICAN VALUES, 1948–1968

Unlike British postwar policymaking, American antitrust, of course, built upon a long-established tradition. Returned to office in 1948, the Truman Administration attempted to revive antitrust enforcement. Until the Korean conflict compelled a change in priorities, the Justice Department and the FTC pushed for a return to policies more consistent with the republican values associated with Brandeis, while the Democratic Congress amended the Clayton law with the Celler-Kefauver Anti-merger Act of 1950. The Republican Eisenhower Administration, moreover, succeeded in winning from the federal courts victories supporting the old policy and the new law. Sustained in sweeping terms by the Supreme Court, the Kennedy and Johnson Administrations maintained policy continuity with their successors. Generally, Democrat and Republican presidents respected the interests of small business in merger cases and defended competition in cartel suits. In addition, after Truman, all three Justice Departments opposed fair trade laws and other antitrust exemptions. The mix of policies reflected the ambiguous political status of large and small business, while the resulting tensions gave rise to economic theories emphasizing efficiency. The interplay of government policies, interests, and theory facilitated the conglomerate mergers of the 1960s.

After Truman's election victory the relation between antitrust and big business remained ambivalent. In part, popular distrust of big government limited the Administration's effectiveness. Pressure from large and small business groups, antagonistic newspaper editorials, and division within the Administration prevented passage of legislation which would have established a Small Business Agency. There was widespread resistance also to government prosecution of the A & P Company solely because of bigness. The public and Congress opposed the Small Business Agency as indicative of the slide toward collectivism and the A & P prosecution as an ill-conceived attack on consumers. On the grounds of free enterprise and states' rights, however, Congress established new antitrust exemptions, first in the fields of cooperative rate-making practices known as the basing-point system and second in the states' Fair Trade Laws.[92]

The antimerger amendment to the Clayton Act also received serious consideration. Theoretically, the legislation avoided the "big-government" stigma because it increased federal antitrust authority to protect small firms in the name of free enterprise, without enlarging the size of the federal bureaucracy. During 1949 there was a recession which continued until the Korean conflict. While the new Democratic congressional majority supported antimerger legislation, the environment of uncertainty led a Republican Senator to admit that rising "antibigness" criticism was not politically partisan, but consistent with a long American tradition. The critics directed their antagonism not toward merchandizing firms such as A & P, but at such corporate giants as General Motors and DuPont. Most of the modest-sized enterprisers represented by the Small Business Federation were within the distribution sector; since the TNEC they had pressured Congress to close the Clayton Act's asset-loophole. Also, unlike the proposal for the small business administration, the antimerger provision did not suggest the need for increased taxes to fund a new agency.[93]

Nevertheless, the law was the object of contention. The leading proponents were Congressman Emmanuel Celler and Senator Estes Kefauver who supported much the same measures which Congress had rejected in 1947. *Business Week*, *Fortune*, and principally Republican conservatives retorted that these proposals were based on resistance to bigness per se. According to the rule of reason, they rightly claimed, bigness in and of itself was not "bad." Celler and Kefauver, the FTC, the Council of Economic Advisors, and their small-business constituents repudiated this argument. Appealing to the distrust of bigness, the FTC's economist Corwin Edwards said, "From an economic standpoint, all businesses reach a point where they begin to lose their efficiency because of their size." Similarly, Celler stated, "The individual and small business man cannot flower amidst the weeds of monopoly."[94] Kefauver and Celler argued further that the antimerger amendment to the Clayton Act was indispensable for the very reason that the federal courts in such cases as *Columbia Steel* had made the prevention of merger by government prosecution virtually impossible. With Truman's support, Celler's House Committee conducted the most thorough investigation of mergers since the TNEC.[95]

After protracted debate and parliamentary maneuvering Congress passed and Truman signed in December, 1950 the Celler-Kefauver Antimerger Act. Yet, during the rest of Truman's Administration, the new Act and antitrust generally was relatively quiescent. The Korean conflict, combined with conflicts within the Justice Department, limited the implementation of a coherent enforcement strategy. The various cases the Justice Department and the Antitrust Division had initiated against the big firms remained active. After 1950, however, the Administration's main antitrust activities involved efforts to provide small firms with a fair proportion of military contracts. Thus, despite the enactment of the most stringent antitrust measure since the Sherman Act, and the Justice Department's willing return to a Brandeisian "big-is-bad" philosophy, American antitrust enforcement suffered the same fate as Thurman Arnold's activism of twenty years earlier.[96]

President Dwight Eisenhower consummated and extended what the Truman Administration had begun. Numerous studies by economists supported the view that the Antimerger Act facilitated the merger movement which began in the mid-fifties and peaked at the end of the 1960s. The polls of business opinion, as well as the business press indicated that antitrust generally and the law governing mergers in particular, influenced the increase of mergers. Even so the advice corporate lawyers gave their clients rested upon the substantive action of the Justice Department and the courts.[97] Shortly after Eisenhower took office in 1953, Attorney General Brownell set out a broad enforcement policy. Brownell noted that the press, lawyers, business leaders, and the general public expressed heightened interest in vigorous antitrust enforcement. Accordingly, the 1952 Platform Pledge of the Republican Party included an antitrust plank. The Party pledged equality of enforcement, simplication of administration, assistance to business seeking good-faith compliance, and "an *uncompromising determination* that there shall be no slackening of effort to protect free enterprise against monopoly and unfair competition; and most certainly – no winking at violations of the law and no wholesale dismissal of pending suits."[98]

Brownell explained how the Administration intended to fulfill this pledge. He supported the recommendations of expert legal and business groups for legislation streamlining, simplifying, and exediting antitrust prosecutions. As one who was "proud of... American capitalism," Brownell said he was nonetheless "old fashioned enough to believe... that this control should be in keeping with a middle-of-the-road political philosophy ... aimed primarily at the elimination of predatory practices." Quoting a law professor Brownell emphasized that big business had "made no important managerial policy or decision without conscious consideration of the prohibitions of the antitrust laws." The Attorney General expressed sympathy also for the "continual cry of little business that, being unable to pay large retainers to insure proper advice, it [was] the recipient of by far an undue proportion of criminal prosecutions, because of the average small business-man's inability to determine without advice whether his conduct [was] within or without the law."[99]

In the tradition of the TNEC Brownell also proposed the appointment of the "Attorney General's National Committee to Study the Antitrust Laws."[100] The publication of the Commission's report in 1955, coincided with the rise of merger activity.[101] Partisan criticism arose in Congress because of the delay. Nevertheless, an internal memorandum of September, 1953 expressed the Administration's view that the wait for the report was justified "by the great desirability of resolving uncertainty confronting business management as a means for stimulating investment and high employment as well as vigorous competition."[102] Newspapers and experts anticipated that the report would have significant impact on business structure and conduct. During the spring of 1955 the Eisenhower Cabinet considered the Commission's findings prior to publication. The Commission favored adherence to the rule of reason as applied in the *Columbia Steel* case. Bigness was not unlawful, yet enforcement of the Antimerger Act was especially necessary in cases involving vertical and horizontal mergers. The report did not mention conglomerate mergers.[103]

In addition, the Commission urged a "harmonization" of the goals of the Clayton, Robinson-Patman, and Sherman Acts. It recommended the repeal of the "fair trade" exemption, but few changes were proposed in patent law. Although the Commission rejected establishing an antitrust exemption for agreements involving foreign trade, it recommended careful attention to the needs of exporters within the existing legal framework. Finally, the report supported technical modifications of antitrust procedures, indicating that there should be greater reliance on advice and negotiation, especially through consent decrees. Government and private law suits, of course, were important, but because they often were drawn out it was necessary to rely more upon negotiation.[104]

Throughout the remaining years of Eisenhower's presidency the Commission's report guided the course of antitrust action. Within the Administration, private memoranda recognized the political usefulness of following the recommendations pertaining to small enterprise. Since the 1930s the Democrats had gained support among farmers and modest-sized retailers and wholesalers in small farming communities which were traditionally Republican constituencies. The middlemen were divided concerning fair trade laws, but generally favored Robinson-Patman. Farmers had no set position for or against the latter law; they opposed, however, fair trade statutes. Accordingly, the Administration concluded that fair trade "acts operated to the detriment of free competition" and so their repeal seemed "advantageous"; yet there was to be little interference with Robinson-Patman. The Justice Department also attacked price-fixing agreements in the name of "fighting inflation."[105] In quiet cooperation with the FTC the Justice Department negotiated important consent decrees, including one with RCA which placed valuable patent information in the public domain. The Administration also decided that vital elements of the international petroleum cartel did not violate the antitrust laws.[106]

The Commission's Report also pointed out the importance of antitrust to international business generally. Following the Commission's recommendation the Administration's Council on Foreign Economic Policy (CFEP) established an interdepartmental Task Force in spring, 1955 which included representatives from the Department of State, Justice Department, FTC, Treasury, and the National Security Council. Arguing that the law of European nations permitted greater trade restraints, American foreign-business interests such as the Chamber of Commerce of London contended that the antitrust laws hurt their competitiveness. Throughout the remainder of the Eisenhower Administration the Task Force studied this and related issues. The resulting report concluded that the nation's foreign trade, investment, and the exchange of technology were being adversely affected by the uncertainty of the law. Also, antitrust enforcement in some situations created foreign relations and national security problems with which neither the Attorney General nor the President has sufficient statutory authority to cope. There was disagreement, however, over whether to establish an administrative mechanism for "advance consultation" between business and the antitrust enforcement agencies. Brownell opposed establishing such a process without legislation, and he had higher legislative priorities of his own. Finally, the relevant government departments merely improved the means of disseminating antitrust information to foreign businesses.[107]

By Eisenhower's second term a high priority was antimerger litigation. In April, 1957 the Executive Assistant to Brownell wrote to the White House that the "most important immediate objective of the Antitrust Division...[was] to obtain an authoritative court ruling on the Anti-merger statute." The Division had reached agreement "with counsel for Bethlehem and Youngstown to speed up consideration of that merger case, which will be a test case for all industry...result[ing] in a speedy court decision on the main legal problems troubling corporate officials regarding mergers."[108] As this case and others proceeded, the Government won a noteworthy victory against DuPont, which required the firm to divest its share in the General Motors Corporation. Notwithstanding this decision, however, the necessity of an authoritative test of the Antimerger Act remained. "Striking and surprising" as the Court's *DuPont* decision was, a memorandum observed, "it will have little practical effect in both the short term and the long term." The decision might "become a factor in businessmens' decisions respecting new vertical acquisitions." But congressional unwillingness to fund an "antitrust crusade," combined with the closely divided Court handing down the decision made revolutionary consequences unlikely. Finally, the "1954 [Brown] decision on school segregation provides some lessons with respect to the speed of implementation of 'revolutionary' court actions."[109]

By the end of the Eisenhower Administration, Brownell's Antitrust Division began fulfilling the Celler-Kefauver Act's promise. Antitrust enforcers took as their point of departure the recommendations of the Antitrust Commission Report. The Antitrust Division and the FTC thus sought to undercut the legal basis of horizontal and vertical mergers. Generally they succeeded. The Department's famous DuPont victory was less important than its blocking of a merger between Bethlehem and Youngstown Steel. Brownell won the sort of case Clark had lost in *Columbia Steel*. Once corporate lawyers realized that vertical and horizontal mergers were unlikely to survive legal prosecution they advised their clients that conglomerate mergers were safe. Significantly, the Antitrust Commission had not mentioned conglomerate mergers, so the Eisenhower

Administration's antimerger policy encouraged a new merger wave. Meanwhile, in the prosecution of price-fixing agreements, the opposition to Fair Trade, and the reform of antitrust technicalities the Eisenhower antitrust officials sought to win over small business.[110]

Notwithstanding a contrary public image, the transition from Republican to Democratic antitrust enforcement was characterized by continuity. During the Kennedy Administration, the media dramatized several confrontations between Attorney General Robert F. Kennedy and certain business leaders. Yet, concerning the enforcement of antitrust itself, the reality was more prosaic. Lee Loevinger, former judge of the Minnesota Supreme court and Kennedy's first Assistant Attorney General of the Antitrust Division, said that between the two Administrations, "I don't think there was any dramatic change in policy." According to Loevinger his Republican predecessor, Robert T. Bicks, "did pretty well. I think that he ran away with it a little bit, and he probably went beyond what the Eisenhower Administration really wanted as an antitrust policy." In addition, many of the lawyers and staff Bicks employed remained under Loevinger.[111]

Loevinger and his successor William H. Orrick, Jr., as had Brownell, tried to balance coercion and restraint. The Kennedy Administration's official position was that "far from being natural enemies, government and business" were "necessary allies" in making the "free enterprise system" work. In practical terms this meant that over two-thirds of the Division's civil cases ended up in consent decrees. To facilitate the negotiational process with adequate safeguards, however, Loevinger initiated a procedure requiring public disclosure prior to entering a decree. More quietly, the Justice Department and the FTC maintained a liaison permitting private parties to submit a request for merger clearance from either agency. The Division also significantly influenced passage of the "most significant" antitrust measure since the Antimerger Act, the law for civil investigative demand. Growing out of Loevinger's recommendations, Celler and Kefauver supported the law which strengthened the Division's investigative authority, particularly where firms sought clearance to merge. Loevinger and Orrick also emphasized the education of business leaders and their lawyers through numerous public presentations.[112]

Loevinger also implemented the Republican recommendation of

creating a Foreign Commerce section within the Antitrust Division. Before Brownell took significant action on the Task Force Report of the CFEP, the Eisenhower presidency ended. As a United States representative to the Organization of Economic Cooperation and Development committee studying international restrictive practices, Loevinger understood legal issues involving foreign commerce. It was not surprising, therefore, that he implemented the Republican initiative. Among the units of the Antitrust Division, the Foreign Commerce Section coordinated matters relating to international business of foreign nationals, maintained liaison with the State Department and other federal agencies on similar matters, and carried out the Justice Department's responsibilities in connection with the OECD. The Section was small and rarely involved in litigation.[113] Loevinger observed that its existence indicated neither a "more nor less rigorous attitude toward antitrust enforcement in foreign trade, but rather a recognition of the growing importance of international trade and an effort to develop greater knowledge and expertise in this area."[114]

Efforts to maintain a balanced policy carried over into prosecutions. As Loevinger said, the "question, basically, came down to the relative emphasis that you give to pricefixing cases on the one hand and merger cases on the other." The former included the more easily won "conspiratorial action cases," whereas the latter were the harder merger cases. Initially, "congressional antitrust liberals" criticized the Justice Department's emphasis on price-fixing cases. By the time Orrick replaced Loevinger in 1963, however, the Division had "brought more merger cases than in any comparable period before or since."[115] The Court's acceptance of the federal government's arguments in these cases made it "clear" Orrick concluded, that both horizontal and vertical "anticompetitive mergers" were "now effectively prohibited by antitrust laws." As a result, he predicted an "increase in conglomerate mergers." The conglomerates were "subject to antitrust laws, but their effect on competition is more complex and therefore more difficult to establish."[116]

The search for balance reflected mixed political tensions. The Kennedy Administration's antitrust enforcement, like that under Eisenhower, recognized that on most issues small business was a divided constituency. Accordingly, the Kennedy Justice Department followed its predecessor by opposing fair-trade legislation, vigorously prosecuting price-fixing conspiracies, and working to streamline technical procedures in order to reduce the advantages large firms had in the market for lawyer services. Although not without qualification, the Federation of Small Business on the whole approved of these outcomes. Antimerger policy remained ambivalent. Publicly disclaiming support for the theory that "bigness is bad," the government actively encouraged or at least did not resist administrative procedures which facilitated advanced approval of mergers. Yet in defense of competition it attacked increased corporate concentration, overcoming adverse decisions in federal district courts to win in the Supreme Court. The result under Kennedy was the same as under Eisenhower: horizontal and vertical mergers steadily declined while conglomerate mergers increased. Antitrust liberals applauded the former and criticized the latter.[117]

The Court's landmark *Brown Shoe* decision of 1962 facilitated the antimerger policy. Initiated during the Eisenhower years, the *Brown Shoe* case applied the ALCOA "economic-effects" theory to prevent a merger of the fourth and twelfth largest shoe producers which would have established retail control of a market share totaling only 8 percent. Nevertheless, the Court decided that because the firm's increased horizontal and vertical concentration significantly enlarged its market share in various local markets, the merger violated the Celler-Kefauver Act. Said Loevinger, the decision, "prohibits acquisitions, either of stock or assets, where competition in *any* line of commerce in *any* section of the country may be substantially lessened. The test as stated in the Senate Report on the [Celler-Kefauver] Bill is whether there is a reasonable probability that competition *may* be lessened." *Brown Shoe* shaped the course of the Court's antimerger decision-making for nearly a decade.[118]

Even so, the Kennedy Administration's antimerger enforcement reflected a distrust of bigness. As had every Antitrust Division head since Thurman Arnold, Orrick insisted that this pro-competition policy rested on a rigorous analysis of economic effects. The Antitrust Division, Orrick affirmed, had "no authority to balance any violation of the law against the social, political, and economic benefits which we feel might be derived from a merger."[119] The string of cases from *Brown Shoe* on, however, indicated that a basic distrust of increased concentration and greater corporate size was central to the government arguments the Court adopted. It was noteworthy that most federal district courts rejected these arguments, making victory contingent upon a favorable review by the Supreme Court. The working assumption shared by both the antitrust prosecutors and the Court was that competition resulted from limiting the number of big firms and increasing or maintaining the number of small ones.[120]

The continuity of postwar antitrust enforcement continued during the Johnson Administration. Ramsey Clark, who followed Nicholas Katzenbach as Attorney General, supervised first Harvard Law School antitrust expert, Donald Turner, and later Turner's executive assistant, Edwin M. Zimmerman, as head of the Antitrust Division. Despite the personnel changes the mix of cases fit the pattern established since the late 1940s: the bulk involved price-fixing while the number of antimerger suits steadily rose. As had their Republican and Democratic predecessors, Clark and Turner opposed fair trade laws. Although unsuccessful on that point, they blocked attempts by the auto industry to establish antitrust exemptions for research in connection with automobile safety legislation. They also won Congressional approval for strengthened procedures in merger investigations. Through the Divisions' Foreign Commerce Section and other units in the Department, discussions with British and EEC officials on restrictive practices increased. Following the lead of the White House and State Department, Clark and Turner approached the international petroleum cartel with flexibility. On the whole, the Johnson Administration's antitrust policy successfully reconciled diverse political pressures, particularly those arising from small business.[121]

There was innovation in the field of mergers. Clark, like Katzenbach, continued to win victories in the Supreme Court applying the Antimerger Act to vertical and horizontal mergers. Yet beginning in 1965 the numbers of conglomerate mergers climbed significantly, peaking three years later. Accordingly, when Clark became Attorney General in early 1967, he called for increased prosecution of the conglomerates. As the business press and polls of business leaders showed, however, successful antitrust prosecution of vertical and horizontal mergers on grounds of their anti-competitiveness had facilitated conglomerate mergers for the very reason that uncompetitive effects were difficult to prove. Indeed, the Orrick Antitrust Division initiated very few such prosecutions because the connections between conglomerates and established antitrust competition doctrines were so complex. Undaunted, Clark attempted to persuade first Turner and then Zimmerman that stepped-up prosecution of conglomerates was vital.[122]

Turner's stance on the conglomerate issue was influential. At Harvard he had co-authored a seminal article which argued that contemporary antitrust competition doctrine permitted prosecution of conglomerates on very limited grounds. A court might accept proof of uncompetitive effects arising from "potential competition," "decisive competitive advantage," and "reciprocity." During the mid-1960s the FTC applied a "reciprocity" theory to block the merger of a producer of processed foods, Consolidated Foods, and Gentry, a manufacturer of dehydrated onion and garlic. The FTC used the same theory to prevent the merger of General Dynamics and Liquid Carbonic Company. As a result, Turner's ideas received close scrutiny from antitrust lawyers representing business and the government.[123]

"Reciprocity" and the other doctrines looked to economic effects. But the underlying presumption against concentration was consistent with a general distrust of bigness. Turner was concerned that this distrust might result in an antitrust policy based on social and political goals. Favoring a policy of support for the interests of consumers as defined by economic analysis, Turner resisted using his theories to launch a general attack on conglomerate "super concentration." He stated, "One cannot support an attack of much greater depth on conglomerates without trenching on significant economic and other values, and therefore without an unprecedented reliance on judgments of an essentially political nature."[124]

Turner denied that social or political value provided an adequate basis for antitrust policy. He told a meeting of the ABA's Antitrust Section, that achieving "order" in antitrust law was unlikely until "we can succeed in disentangling it from many policy considerations having little or nothing to do with the protection of competition." Antitrust enforcers "should not attack a merger simply because the companies are large in the absolute sense, and we should not attack aggressive but fair competitive conduct simply on the basis that some competitors are hurt." Turner observed, however, that lawyers could use these same arguments to defend increased corporate concentration. Since becoming head of the Division in 1965, he said, proponents defended contemplated mergers on the "grounds that it would promote the national defense, assist in solving the balance of payments problem, reduce unemployment and contribute to the

Administration's anti-poverty program. I fully expect to hear before long that a merger should be allowed because it will contribute to the President's program for making America beautiful."[125]

The tension between the policy preferences of Clark and Turner was evident in the Merger Guidelines of 1968. One of the most important innovations of postwar merger policy, the merger guidelines proposed statistical concentration levels that determined the basis for bringing an antitrust suit. Following the tests established in *Brown Shoe*, the basic criteria were related to market structure. "As the market share of firms increased, their ability to acquire a firm in the same market without fear of recrimination decreased," explained one expert. "In a market where concentration had increased 7 percent in the past ten years, an acquisition of only 2 percent was enough to prompt an antitrust suit." According to *Business Week*, Turner's Guidelines made "no sweeping changes." But the *Antitrust and Trade Regulation Review* observed that the guidelines made "a significant contribution to what has come to be known as the 'numbers game' – the use of market share figures to show a merger's anticompetitive effect."[126]

Turner's merger guidelines grew out of his experience as head of the Antitrust Division. Near the start of his term in 1965 he preached how important to the enforcement of antitrust was publicity. In their role as business advisors the antitrust bar was especially vital. Significant, too, was the research and writing of legal academics. Publication of the "Government's views" thus "speeds up the process of development of the law by laying the basis for a continuing dialogue among Government, the bar, business groups and the academic profession." Publication also generated "empirical data that will help us to decide whether tentative positions have gone too far or not far enough." In time, however, the pressure from "lawyers and/or their business clients... requesting general advice or 'guidelines'" became sufficiently great that Turner refused private appointments with these individuals or groups. The need to reconcile this pressure with the commitment to publicity facilitated the formulation of the guidelines.[127]

The Guidelines codified the tension between economic and sociopolitical values which had characterized the government's antitrust policies and the Court's merger decisions since ALCOA. The theoretical preoccupation with competition obscured the conflict between the triumph of oligopoly in American big business and the persistent distrust of concentration indicated by the continuing attack on horizontal and vertical mergers. Thus the "order" Turner sought to create in antitrust law assumed that limiting levels of corporate concentration did not interfere with the scale and organizational economies which resulted in benefits to consumers. Ultimately, however, this vision of competition was unable to escape the value judgments inherent in the determination of what exactly were appropriate concentration levels. The complexity of the problem was suggested by the attempt to distinguish between anticompetitive effects in horizontal and vertical mergers on the one hand and conglomerates on the other.

AN UNEVEN POLICY CONVERGENCE, 1969–1990

From the late sixties to 1990 British and American policy continued to converge. The British relied primarily upon an administrative process, whereas in America the courts exercised ultimate control. At the beginning of the Nixon Administration the Antitrust Division briefly prosecuted conglomerates. Similarly, the British government sporadically used the referral process to protect British firms from foreign takeovers and, in certain cases, the Commission's reports had the same result. By the 1980s, however, the Baxter Merger Guidelines and the Tebbit Guidelines incorporated competition policies focusing on concentration levels associated primarily with horizontal mergers. Admittedly, corporate concentration was greater in Britain, owing no doubt to the significant degree of ministerial discretion and other institutional uncertainties inherent in the reference procedure itself. But overall, British and American officials scrutinized horizontal mergers in the name of competition, while generally tolerating conglomerates. Thus, notwithstanding differing institutional arrangements, both nations' polices encouraged convergence on the basic structure of managerial capitalism.

Between 1966 and 1977 British merger and monopoly policy was ambivalent. The Act of 1965 creating the new Monopolies and Merger Commission established the "public interest investigation" as the method of control. The Commission's authority extended to firms possessing one-third market share or assets over £5 million, and reached horizontal, vertical and conglomerate, mergers. The exercise of this authority depended, however, upon a reference by the Board of Trade. During the same period, the Industrial Reorganization Corporation (IRC) encouraged various mergers in order to promote rationalization. Unlike the staff of the Commission which included economic, legal, and accountancy experts, the IRC's personnel were largely businessmen. The coincidence of the two policies facilitated ambiguity. "Mergers involving large firms [were] not, of course, necessarily harmful to the public interest... but the power of a giant, especially of two giants united, might be such as to stifle competition, or the empire created might be too large for the most efficient use of resources," a government spokesman conceded. "In judging all these cases, however, I would propose always to remember what mergers can in certain cases do to achieve greater strength for our economy at home and abroad."[128]

The influence of IRC coincided with a paucity of references. By 1969, of the 350 mergers which could have come within the Commission's jurisdiction, the Board had referred only 10. This was the case despite the intense merger activity of the late 1960s. In 1969, too, the Board revealed the operation of an interdepartmental unit within the Board known as the Merger Panel; it screened mergers and decided which ones to refer. A "close working relationship" existed between the Panel and the IRC. Although the Panel considered questions involving competition and efficiency, the degree to which one was weighted against the other was not publicized. While the Minister was not bound by the Panel's decision, the Panel nonetheless examined difficult cases through what often amounted to a "public interest" investigation not unlike that which would have been conducted by the Commission. These factors, a commentator wrote, "confirmed the impression established on enactment of the merger legislation, that relatively few mergers were thought to give rise to public interest concerns, and saw the parallel operation of a policy clearly antagonistic to merger control."[129]

The treatment of the cases the Commission *did* investigate was ambiguous. During the late 1960s the great majority of references involved horizontal mergers, but, by the early seventies the relative number of conglomerate mergers increased. Although the mergers the Commission and the IRC dealt with were similar in character, each body treated those mergers differently. The conglomerate cases, moreover, drew the Commission into the practicalities of take-over bids, encouraging its role as an arbitrator. Yet, generally, the goal of the Commission's investigations was "by no means clear at the outset."[130]

Still, public officials had established the basic rules governing future policymaking. Following the defeat of the Labour Government, the Conservatives dismantled the IRC in 1971, facilitating greater policy consistency. Even so the Board referred to the Commission all three types of mergers – conglomerate, vertical, and horizontal – though the total number remained relatively small. Similarly, the factors shaping the Commission's decisions were diverse, ranging from competition or efficiency considerations to the morale of a new firm's management. No less important than the Commission's role, moreover, was the Merger Panel's choice as to what cases to refer.[131]

These factors remained important after passage of the Fair Trading Act of 1973. The new law created a separate Office of Fair Trading (OFT) headed by the Director General. The Act changed the market-share criterion from a one-third to a quarter share of supplies and established new public interest criteria suggesting somewhat greater concern than earlier legislation for competition. The new law also delegated to the Director General the duties of the Registrar of Restrictive Practices, and the responsibility for making monopoly references to the Commission. There was less change in the field of mergers. Unlike the area of monopolies, the Director General did not have primary authority to refer merger cases to the Commission. As head of the Merger Panel he nonetheless kept abreast of proposed mergers and made referral recommendations to the Department of Trade and Industry's Secretary of State. Although these recommendations were not binding on the Secretary, generally they were followed.[132]

The initial development of the OFT coincided with a decline in the intensity of merger activity. At the same time the referral process and the Commission's investigations became enmeshed in takeover battles involving foreign firms. A notable instance was Sothebys' courting of a reference to thwart the attempted takeover by an American firm until a friendly British "white knight" appeared. By 1984 it was increasingly clear that preserving competition was only one of several factors considered in the application of the "public interest" standard by the Merger Panel, the Director General, the Secretary of State, and the Commission.[133]

These tensions engendered efforts to establish greater consistency and coherence in the law. Parliament consolidated restrictive-practices legislation in 1976. Similarly, Parliament attempted to improve the cumbersome procedures by which the Director General referred trade restraints to either the Restrictive Practices Court or the Monopoly and Mergers Commission. In 1980 the Director General received enlarged authority to investigate the restrictive practices of individual firms. If the firms failed to respond to the threat of publicity, the Director might then refer the matter to the Commission. Following the Commission's condemnation, the Minister was empowered to restrain the firm, though in actual practice compliance usually was achieved through more informal arrangements. During the same period, British policymakers and firms confronted the need to reconcile competition and restrictive-practices law to the requirements of membership in the Common Market and the European Economic Community (EEC). As a result, after the 1973 Treaty of Accession, British business was subject to two sets of rules and enforcement authorities.[134]

In 1978 an Inter-Departmental Committee chaired by senior government official Hans Liesner completed a review of UK merger, monopoly, and restrictive-practices policies. The Green Paper stated that "a more critical approach to mergers should be adopted." It recommended that the prevailing policy which minimized the risks associated with mergers "should be shifted to a neutral approach." The Liesner Committee's recommendations reflected concern about the growing level of concentration within industry. In the sphere of restrictive practices the Green Paper recommended stricter control of informal cartel arrangements.[135]

The Liesner Committee linked the concern about concentration to a policy emphasizing competition. Yet a policy based primarily upon competition could result in the limitation of references and Commission decisions since the proportion of horizontal mergers, the chief source of increased concentration, were declining. These considerations encouraged both the Labour and Conservative governments to broaden the applicability of the public-interest standard in one category of cases. When foreign investors threatened to buy up vital regional enterprises in a contested takeover, the government and the Commission defended the jobs and pride of such indigenous Scottish firms as Highland Distillers, the Royal Bank of Scotland, and House of Fraser. This policy, however, specifically encouraged domestic conglomerates.[136]

In 1984 these patterns of policymaking received formal sanction in the Tebbit Guidelines. Soon after the third reference of a contested takeover battle between Lonrho and the House of Fraser another review of merger policy within the Department of Trade and

Industry ensued. In response to a parliamentary question during July, 1984 Secretary of State Norman Tebbit publicized the policy statement resulting from this study. "I regard mergers policy as an important part of the Government's general policy of promoting competition within the economy in the interests of the customer and of efficiency and hence of growth and jobs," he said. "Accordingly my policy has been and will continue to be to make references primarily on competition grounds." How these grounds might influence the outcome of particular controversies, however, was suggested only by reference to international cases. "In evaluating the competitive situation in individual cases I shall have regard to the international context: to the extent of competition in the home market from non-United Kingdom sources and to the competitive position of United Kingdom companies in overseas markets."[137]

Tebbit's Guidelines indicated a shift in policy emphasis. Since the early 1970s the Merger Panel's selection and the Commission's settlement of references focused on competition issues involving primarily horizontal mergers. By the mid-1980s the policy toward horizontal mergers was clear enough to business decisionmakers. This heightened awareness coincided with the horizontal-merger references which generally concerned only localized markets, though some quite large horizontal mergers such as *GEC/Plessey* and vertical mergers such as *British Telecom/Mitel* were also referred.

The Guidelines' confirmation of this policy unavoidably focused attention on the scope of exceptions. Tebbit had said that references would be "primarily" made on competition grounds. The reference of a few cases in which Australian or other foreign companies used highly leveraged financing to take over British firms indicated, however, that this opening for government intervention was narrow. "No matter how large or bitterly contested a bid was," said one observer, "if no competition issues were involved a reference was unlikely." Reinforcing this predisposition toward limited action, moreover, were a few cases in which competition issues were present but not necessarily conspicuous. The Imperial Group/United Biscuits and Guinness/Distillers bids brought indirect pressure from the authorities until the bids were dropped. And yet the government did not oppose the companies' attempts to achieve similar results through modified financial arrangements.[138]

This was a change, commentators noted, which facilitated the merger boom beginning in 1985. By then the percentage by asset value of diversification mergers had risen to 54 percent and horizontal mergers had declined to 42 percent. "Two or three years previously, a contested bid could have been referred to the Commission and the arguments of competing parties analyzed in detail," wrote one economist. "Now, bitterly contested bids involving large public companies were not only not examined, but furthermore the policy concerns were dealt with in an abrupt manner to ensure that the bids could proceed with minimal interruption." As a result, there was a "limited... overlap between merger policy and the merger boom."[139]

As British policymakers wrestled with these concerns, the nation's relationship to the European Community acquired greater importance. Article 85 of the 1958 Treaty of Rome prohibited and made unlawful cartel agreements and other restraints affecting the trade of member states, subject only to certain exceptions. Article 86 prohibited the abuse of a firm's dominant position within the Common Market or a substantial part of it. The primary but not exclusive goal of these measures was to encourage competition. Yet, throughout most of the period, there was little policymaking involving mergers. Then, in the mid-1980s, the European Commission changed this policy, reflecting the increase in mergers between firms in different states of the Common Market. The change facilitated the enactment of the European Community's first significant merger regulation in September, 1990.[140]

The European Commission exercised primary jurisdiction over the enforcement of the new merger regulation. In a review given during the summer of 1990 the chairman of the UK Monopolies and Merger Commission, Sidney Lipworth, pointed out that the European Commission's jurisdiction reached generally "only... mergers of a reasonably significant size, and...exclude[d] those mergers which are largely a matter of national concern. Consequently, even fairly large mergers within a member state will fall within the jurisdiction of the state if two-thirds or more of their respective business is done there." Further limiting this jurisdiction were three important but vaguely defined exceptions, including mergers involving "distinct markets," or "legitimate national interests." The third exception involved a case in which a member state requested the European Commission to handle the mergers occurring solely within its own national borders.[141]

Despite notable differences in procedure, Lipworth noted, the

UK's and EC's use of an administrative approach was preferable to the American reliance on courts. On the whole, the two systems had the "merit of speed and finality – a comprehensive economic arbitration ... [which] makes for more business certainty." Certainty was essential in "an era of global businesses and transnational mergers. If all the relevant individual sovereign blocs ... apply their own competition and other requirements, business will be faced with increasing uncertainty and delay."[142]

As British officials assimilated EC policies, they reevaluated competition law and policy at home. During the late 1980s the Department of Trade and Industry published the results of a review conducted by an interdepartmental group again chaired by Liesner. As it investigated both restrictive practices and merger policies, Liesner's Committee maintained close liaison with the OFT and the Monopolies and Mergers Commission. The involvement of the latter two bodies was essential because recommendations would affect their organization and authority. The review itself reflected business's desire for clearer guidance, especially given the nation's growing economic integration within the EC. It also grew out of concerns about the high level of corporate concentration and the significant restructuring of British business associated with takeover battles involving the growth of conglomerates.[143]

The Liesner Committee's recommendations called for changes in law and policy. Concerning mergers, the Committee recommended establishing a non-mandatory notification system, which would facilitate legally binding negotiations between the Director General and business prior to a merger. The intent was to reduce the need for formal references to the Commission. In those cases where a reference was made, the Committee proposed to tighten the OFT's and the Commission's procedures to reduce delay in the investigation and subsequent reporting of findings. The changes involving cartels were more sweeping. In many cases the Restrictive Trade Practices Act of 1956 no longer satisfactorily policed the sophisticated informal cartel practices of the 1980s. Also, it was necessary to align British policy more closely with that of the EC. The Committee recommended extending the prohibition provision of the 1956 Act to include any agreement with an "anti-competitive effect." The old law's registration procedure would come to an end. The provision for exemptions would remain but be narrowed, especially in the case of professional services. Finally, the Committee proposed revising competition law so as to allow private legal action against prohibited agreements. By 1990 legislation enacting the merger proposals seemed likely; the status of the restrictive practices measures was, however, unclear.[144]

In America during the transition from the Johnson to the Nixon Administration many observers predicted a weakening of antimerger enforcement. At the start of 1968, ITT canceled several mergers because of Attorney General Ramsey Clark's determined opposition. After Nixon's election, however, the company once more began a series of acquisitions anticipating a more sympathetic attitude from the government. Similarly, the Johnson Administration's Antitrust Task Force headed by Dean Philip Neal of the University of Chicago Law School published its report in May, 1969. The Neal Report proposed new legislation to support a broad attack on conglomerate mergers through extensive divestiture. The next month Congress publicized the report of a commission chaired by Chicago economist George Stigler which Nixon had appointed as an interim measure. The Stigler Report expressed doubt that conglomerate mergers possessed "uncompetitive" consequences, opposed deconcentration, and therefore minimized the need for new legislation. Moreover, new Attorney General John Mitchell put Richard McLaren in charge of the Antitrust Division. McLaren was a prominent Chicago lawyer and former chairman of the ABA's Antitrust Section who had for years successfully defended business in antitrust suits.[145]

Initially, however, those expecting more lenient enforcement were disappointed. During his confirmation hearing and in other public statements McLaren favored using laws already on the books to attack conglomerates. He did not accept Donald F. Turner's position that vigorous prosecution of conglomerates required new legislation. McLaren also rejected arguments that bigness necessarily brought efficiency, asserting instead that it encouraged complacent management and weakened incentives facilitating innovation. Ever-increasing size also created large units of economic power which might result in political manipulation. "Basically, what we were shooting for, from the beginning of 1969," McLaren said, "was to stop this merger trend that was leading more and more toward economic concentration."[146]

McLaren built his campaign against conglomerate mergers on an extension of Turner's theory of reciprocity. A "community of interest" resulted when, to maintain favorable relations, suppliers of merging companies sold to other subsidiaries of the new conglomerate. This degree of interdependence, McLaren warned, inevitably reduced competition. According to Attorney General Mitchell, the "community of interest," was not "a formal agreement but merely the recognition of common goals by large diversified corporations." Such firms had "little interest in competing with each other in concentrated markets." It was thus in their "interest to maintain the status quo and not engage in the type of aggressive competition which we expect in a free market." Accordingly, the Justice Department was prepared to "oppose any merger by one of the top 200 manufacturing firms or firms of comparable size in other industries." Mitchell indicated that this goal might go beyond Turner's merger guidelines, but he was confident that it was "clearly authorized by present antitrust law."[147]

Nixon's role in the subsequent implementation of this anti-conglomerate policy was complex. As Mitchell and McLaren publicized their goals, Nixon initially advised Mitchell to "keep a close watch on... (the trustbusters). They tend, at times, to be anti-business professionals." Yet, amidst publicity surrounding the prosecution of ITT, he asked the Council of Economic Advisors for its views on the status of conglomerate mergers under the antitrust laws. Shortly thereafter, at a White House meeting devoted to antitrust policy, Nixon consistently supported McLaren, favoring the use of the law to defend small business from corporate giants. This was, Nixon said, "a tremendously potent political problem... Does it mean that Mom and Pop stores are on the way out – and supermarkets are all we'll have?" He perceived "a sociological problem here. We may be helping consumers, but we don't help the character of our people. This is an old-fashioned attitude, Dick [McLaren], I know – but I would rather deal with an entrepreneur than a pipsqueak manager of a big store."[148]

Within a year, however, Nixon withdrew his endorsement of McLaren's campaign. By September 1969, Nixon supported the view of Robert Bork that the conglomerate lawsuits were "one of the bleakest, most disappointing developments in antitrust history." Through John Ehrlichman, Nixon urged Mitchell and the Justice Department to "come up with a new approach." McLaren, however, refused. Meanwhile, the media revealed "political machinations" involving ITT. Fear of further bad press prevented interference with the Division's activities until McLaren became a federal judge in 1971. During the summer of that year one of Nixon's advisors noted that Mitchell had agreed to follow Nixon's new stance "that action be taken to reduce any...harassment [of business], apparent or real." Thomas Kauper, McLaren's successor, retreated from the anti-conglomerate suits, initiating over his four-year tenure only three cases. Nixon also appointed FTC Commissioners who backed away from the McLaren-type policy. Nevertheless, throughout the remainder of Nixon's troubled presidency, ITT and other conglomerates settled cases, agreeing to modest divestiture rather than risk defeat in the Supreme Court. In other instances the threat of antitrust enforcement prevented mergers. In any case the wave had run its course by 1971, with mergers at the lowest point in twelve years.[149]

Thus, notwithstanding a certain ambivalence, during the 1970s antitrust enforcement gradually shifted away from McLaren's policy. The traditional tension within the Justice Department involving whether to emphasize price-fixing or merger suits persisted from 1969 to 1980. Meanwhile, in 1975 the Ford Administration won congressional approval for a proposal Republican and Democratic Justice Departments had supported for twenty years: the repeal of the federal fair trade law. President Gerald Ford also signed the Hart-Scott-Rodino Antitrust Improvements Act of 1976 (HSR) which included the *parens patriae* provision whereby federal funds were allocated to state attorney generals to support state antitrust prosecutions. The HSR also required firms to inform the Justice Department and the FTC before going ahead with mergers that exceeded size limits established in the Turner guidelines. The HSR imposed, too, a mandatory waiting period before certain acquisitions and tender offers could proceed. After the mid-1970s, however, the Justice Department, the Supreme Court, and the FTC pursued a policy of leniency toward mergers. In 1979 the Court seemed to underline the shift in the *GTE Sylvania* case, applying the rule of reason to allow a territorial vertical restraint. On grounds of economic efficiency, the decision reversed a Warren Court precedent which had held that such restraints were illegal per se.[150]

Diverse political pressures reinforced this tension. Throughout the economically chaotic 1970s big business was on the defensive, as Congress enacted, and two Republican presidents supported or at least did not prevent, extensive new regulatory and environmental legislation.[151] Oregon Republican Senator Robert Packwood suggested the persistence of traditional concerns for small business in a debate of antitrust measures during 1975. New antitrust legislation was necessary in order to "breakup... the concentrations of power in the major industries in this country, oil and otherwise, so that we might return to the numerous, small- and medium-sized competitive industries that made this country grow, and continue to be needed to make this country great."[152] Congressional voting patterns revealed that local or regional considerations shaped the vote for or against the new antitrust measures. In some cases these local factors resulted in limiting or weakening the bills before they became law. In other instances the opposition prevented enactment of stronger antimerger legislation including the "no-fault" monopolization Bill, the Industrial Reorganization Act, and the Monopolization Reform Act.[153]

The growing influence of "efficiency" antitrust theory indicated further the direction of change. From the mid-1950s on the teaching of neoclassical economics and law identified with Aaron Director and others at the University of Chicago gained influence. Although the Neal Task Force Report of 1969 emphasized reciprocity, Bork dissented, arguing forcefully for the Chicago theories of efficiency. By 1974 those theories clearly dominated the Airlie House Conferences. The participants systematically repudiated the economic theories underlying the neo-Brandeisian doctrines of competition prevailing since the late 1940s. In the same year Neal and others published a collection of essays entitled *Industrial Concentration: The New Learning*, a comprehensive statement of the Chicago School approach. These academic factors coincided with the Court's acceptance of efficiency principles in *Sylvania* and other cases, and the corresponding defeat of various divestiture suits begun under McLaren.[154]

Ironically, the first extensive official adaptation of the "new learning" occurred during the Carter Administration. As late as 1979 the antimerger position identified with McLaren persisted in the National Commission for the Review of Antitrust Laws and Procedures (NCRALP). Carter's Assistant Attorney General of the Antitrust Division John Shenefield headed the Commission. It proposed amending the Sherman Act to adopt the "no-fault" monopolization procedure to facilitate suits involving monopolistic power unrelated to organizational or scale efficiencies. The Shenefield Commission also defined areas where divestiture was the recommended remedy. These recommendations, however, were not altogether inconsistent with the Chicago School efficiency doctrines. Shenefield's predecessor, Donald I. Baker *rejected* a 10-million dollar appropriation from Congress for use by the Antitrust Division to strengthen the state attorney generals' antitrust prosecutions. Although administrative considerations undoubtedly were involved in Baker's decision, it was consistent with an acceptance of the theory that most mergers were economically efficient and therefore should not be opposed. Shenefield endorsed the theory in principle. Thus his Commission's proposals were aimed primarily at limiting the most conspicuous monopolistic abuses which had no relation to a large firm's effective performance.[155]

Various factors helped to explain the Carter Administration's acceptance of the efficiency doctrine. Generally, the economic instability of the late 1970s made allocative efficiency a primary concern. More particularly the Justice Department and the FTC followed the trend established by the Supreme Court, whose precedents after all influenced the success or failure of the government's suits. In addition, the Carter years coincided with the most dramatic increase in private antitrust cases in the nation's history. The Court itself stated that these "private suits provided a significant supplement to the limited resources available to the Department of Justice for enforcing the antitrust laws and deterring violations." Similarly, despite Baker's reservations, Congress increased further the amount of federal funding channeled to state antitrust enforcement under HSR and other legislation. In this and other ways federal action helped the state attorney generals to circumvent limitations the Court imposed on state antitrust suits in the *Illinois Brick* decision of 1979. As a result, the state attorney-generals supplemented federal antitrust prosecution to a greater extent than anytime since 1918. The Carter Department of Justice initiated somewhat more criminal (particularly price-fixing) cases than civil (especially merger) cases. The decline in merger prosecutions was understandable given the Court's defeat of McLaren's conglomerate divestiture suits. Yet, at least in that category of litigation, the decrease represented a return to Turner's skepticism of conglomerate prosecutions.[156]

These considerations suggested the degree to which antitrust under the Reagan Administration represented a new departure. Throughout the 1980s a succession of Antitrust Division heads and their critics asserted that the government's policy represented a significant break with the past. Reagan's first Assistant Attorney General of the Antitrust Division was Stanford law professor William Baxter. He won the case breaking up AT & T's Bell System. In federal district court, moreover, Baxter and his successors initiated 94 cases annually, 80 criminal and 14 civil. The Carter Justice Department brought 67·5 cases annually, 30 civil and 37·5 criminal. Thus the Reagan Justice Department not only increased the total average of cases brought, but significantly altered the proportion in favor of criminal cases.[157]

But the apparent discontinuity was ambiguous. Baxter and his successors emphasized prosecution of relatively easy to prove per se offenses, including price fixing, horizontal market divisions, and bid rigging. Unlike their predecessors, the Reagan Antitrust Division declined to prosecute either price or non-price vertical restraints. Viewed in this light, there was greater consistency in that most of the government's cases involved types of cartel practices rather than mergers. Perhaps influencing the Reagan Administration's pronounced increase in the proportion of criminal over civil cases, moreover, was the Court's increased willingness to permit vertical restraints on grounds of economic efficiency. Thus the Court encouraged both a lenient approach to mergers, and a still more vigorous prosecution of the most conspicuously criminal forms of price fixing and other trade restraints. The record of the FTC was similar.[158]

Until Congress passed the HSR Act in 1976 the government's ability to influence mergers remained essentially reactive. The prior-notification and waiting-period provisions of the Act, however, made possible a *prospective* merger policy. With these provisions in place Baxter published in 1982 guidelines which enabled firms to know in advance whether a merger would likely result in prosecution. Baxter replaced Turner's measure of concentration with one known as the Herfindahl Index. Through mathematically determined thresholds the Index indicated that most vertical and conglomerate mergers would be free from prosecution, while the government would continue to scrutinize more carefully horizontal mergers.[159]

The Reagan merger policy ultimately did not escape criticism from even its successor Republican Administration. By the mid-1980s critics pointed to considerable evidence showing that the government's enforcement of the Herfindahl Index was more tolerant than ever of mergers. The critics nonetheless argued that the remedy was not a return to the values identified with Louis Brandeis, but a more faithful enforcement of Baxter's original standards. The Bush Antitrust Division responded favorably to an ABA Task Force Report whose contributors included former Antitrust Division chiefs from the Nixon and Carter Administrations. The Report suggested that Reagan antitrust officials had over emphasized the "'presumption' that most mergers are comparatively beneficial or an uncritical acceptance of an ease of entry argument or efficiencies defense that cannot be substantiated." Nevertheless, the debate was about whether the law facilitated efficiency defined as consumer welfare, not whether efficiency plus social and political values should be the goal of antitrust enforcement. More than ever before republican values had been eclipsed by a new consensus.[160]

Notwithstanding important differences, British and American policy had converged. British business, academic economists, the legal profession, and governmental policymakers did not generally accept the Chicago-type efficiency theories prevalent in America. The Tebbit Guidelines, the Liesner Committee studies of 1988 and even the EC's new merger regulation, however, incorporated a primary goal of efficiency defined in terms of competition. These policy standards in principle tolerated social and political values which American antitrust had rejected. In addition, uncertainties associated with ministerial discretion, and the referral process probably facilitated higher levels of corporate concentration than existed in America even during the Reagan years. Yet, despite these contrasts, in both nations imprecision inherent in defining oligopolistic competition, combined with a fairly consistent rejection of cartels, facilitated the relative decline of horizontal mergers in favor of conglomerates. Thus the Bush Administration's willingness to reassert the Baxter Guidelines, like the Conservative Government's acceptance of the Liesner Committee's recommendations, suggested that for some time after 1990 efficiency concerns would likely provide the basis for the continued convergence of each nation's response to big business.

Conclusion

During the formative era, American antitrust became a policy at war with itself. By establishing an amalgam of economic and moral imperatives as the basis for applying state law and the Sherman Act, state and federal authorities and the Supreme Court ironically nurtured giant corporate enterprise. The most successful big firms were able to shut out new competitors and thereby defeat one goal of antitrust policy. Yet the triumph of the rule of reason also reflected the recognition that bigness often made possible economies benefitting consumers, another purpose of antitrust law. Meanwhile, private suits and state and federal prosecution of cartel practices blocked price-fixing practices and promoted entry into the business order. Ultimately, the achievement of such divergent goals required the sort of flexible policy choices the American rule of reason facilitated.

The consensus favoring freedom of contract represented by the British courts' application of the rule of reason, however, gave lawmakers little direct influence over business structure in Britain. As a result, family enterprise preserved its influence and often impeded the attainment of organizational and production economies arising from centralized management. Without an antitrust policy, commentators believed, Britain lacked the means to influence the direction of its economy at a time when its competitors possessed such means, placing itself at a comparative disadvantage.

The rise of big business thus engendered a divergent response from British and American lawmakers. Prior to the 1880s, neither nations' courts generally enforced the restrictive practices businessmen established. Yet, by the early 1890s, British and American courts were called upon to decide the legality of new business structures. In Britain, the *Mogul* case condoned but did not enforce a sophisticated system of self-regulating cartel practices. A few years later in

Nordenfelt the House of Lords established "reasonableness" as the general rule governing exceptional cases arising from the changing economy. The self-restraint these and subsequent decisions represented, provided a legal framework for the perpetuation of family enterprise, the comparatively smaller turn-of-the-century merger wave, and the corresponding underdevelopment of large, managerially centralized corporations.

The comparison with American business and law was noteworthy. During the 1880s the inability to enforce cartel agreements encouraged businessmen to adopt Dodd's trust device. The response of the states to this new innovation, however, was ambivalent. Eventually three basic paradigms of individual merger structure evolved: the common law trust, the asset acquisition, and the holding company. Yet most states revised their laws to make restrictive trade agreements not only unenforceable but also subject to prosecution as illegal, resulting in the dissolution of the original trust. Meanwhile, the New Jersey law of 1889 allowed a tighter form of corporate structure, just as the steady increase of private suits increasingly weakened the usefulness of local cartel practices. The Supreme Court's construction of the Sherman Act broadly conformed to a similar pattern until 1903. Not before then was there a decision which looked beyond the surface legal form to the internal organizational and financial substance of a corporation, to hold that a holding company was illegal. Unlike their British counterparts, then, American businessmen between 1897 and 1903 considered merger issues not solely in investment terms, but also as the safest means of avoiding government prosecution. Market factors undoubtedly influenced the great merger wave in both nations. But, given the otherwise similar technological and industrial development of the two countries, a salient difference was the presence or lack of antitrust.

Similarly, the end of the merger wave only indirectly affected British lawmakers. The question of whether the courts should enforce loose restrictive agreements became entangled in the labor issue. Halsbury's unsuccessful efforts culminating in the Trade Disputes Act, and the specific labor concerns noted in the Australian antitrust case, suggested that the British courts perceived that the two issues were linked to preserving social order. Ultimately, the merger wave merely reinforced the law's general sanction of business self-regulation with the result that the emergence of large corporations was on a small enough scale that family enterprise maintained greater control.

In America the outcome of the merger wave was very different. More than ever before, the proliferation of giant corporations based on the attainment of vertical integration disrupted the economy's system of middlemen. Until the struggle reached this proportion the government challenged no tight corporate structure whose business unequivocally involved interstate trade as opposed to production within a single state. The Roosevelt and Taft Administrations reversed this policy. The new effort, however, required examination of the relation between internal corporate organization and external business behavior which reinforced the increasingly popular distinction between "good" and "bad" trusts. In 1911, the court announced the rule of reason which seemed to affirm that distinction. Significantly, Brandeis, who categorically repudiated any notion of a "good trust" condoned the Court's new rule thus supporting the consensus favoring an enlarged bureaucratic approach to antitrust. In addition, Chief Justice White's attempted reconciliation notwithstanding, the Court's new doctrine went beyond the narrower reasonableness standard British courts established in *Nordenfelt*.

These considerations suggested that the Court's decisions of 1911 involved not only the immediate conflicts arising from the great merger wave, but also the broader tension within republican values and *laissez-faire*. The British government's passivity and the court's self-restraint toward the restrictive practices of business were consistent with the Free Trade consensus and the fact that economic change did not directly threaten family enterprise. Thus, even the labor struggles merely reinforced the British support of self-regulating, restrictive practices. In America, however, despite the lip service given *laissez-faire* and Social Darwinist tenets the fundamental ideological confrontation was rooted in the clash between small and big business. The proponents of each system claimed that the other was economically inefficient, threatened the public welfare, and violated individual rights. Yet most Americans were unwilling either to forego the consumer benefits large corporations made possible or to give up the opportunities associated with small enterprise. Republican values exacerbated this dilemma because they rested the balance of individual and public interests on moralistic considerations. Nevertheless, White's formulation of the rule of reason implicitly incorporated this moralism to provide a standard flexible enough to satisfy even Brandeis, the arch foe of bigness. Accordingly, the Wilson Administration enacted new antitrust legislation, including the Clayton Act and Federal Trade Commission.

Comparing British and American business structures provides a basis for suggesting the broader impact of antitrust during the formative era. The principles of Free Trade and freedom of contract to which British courts adhered in applying their rule of reason reflected a preference for the invisible hand of the market; whereas, the ambivalent interpretations of the Sherman Act, culminating in the Supreme Court's rule of reason, demonstrated American confidence in the visible hand of the lawmaker. These divergent views of government intervention in the economic order grew out of different social relations and political conflicts in the two nations. Despite its inconsistencies and failures, American antitrust law at least prevented less efficient cartel practices and encouraged economies of scale arising from managerial centralization.

From World War I on, each nation's business structure and government policymaking underwent gradual if uneven convergence. The war required policymakers to make decisions involving first the extent of business–government cooperation during hostilities, and secondly its consequences for peacetime reconversion. In Britain modifications in company law favoring holding companies and court decisions sanctioning restrictive practices fostered corporate mergers and cartels. The period of post-war reconstruction from 1919 to 1921 experienced sufficient economic dislocation that British authorities briefly experimented with a type of antitrust policy. Based on investigation and publicity, the government enforced this policy through the short-lived Profiteering Acts and the Standing Committee on Trusts.

American antitrust was well-established by 1914. But preparedness, military action, and peacetime reconstruction provided the context for changing enforcement priorities. Prior to United States entry into the war the Wilson Administration urged the Court to apply the rule of reason to break up managerially centralized large corporations. The war disrupted this effort. By 1921 the Court declared that bigness was not necessarily "bad," began circumscribing the authority of the FTC, and started limiting the reach of the Clayton Act in both labor and holding-company cases. It continued, however, to uphold the government's prosecution of overt cartel practices.

Britain's wartime mobilization and peacetime reconversion engendered new tensions in values and interest. Both nations' neoclassical economic thought modified and even challenged classical theory, paving the way for a better understanding of oligopolistic competition. Many British publicists and economists adopted a faith in rationalization which supported a modest expansion of the state's supervisory role to foster cartelization and mergers. The Free Trade consensus persisted, but it was eroding. Although mergers threatened many middlemen, more small firms either remained subject to traditional competitive pressures or increasingly were protected within the system of business self-regulation. With the termination of its antitrust experiment in 1921 the government maintained a modest supervisory function which encouraged restrictive practices and tighter corporate structures.

In America, despite the war, neoclassical economic thought did not eclipse republican values. The wartime mobilization increased the awareness of the relation between fixed costs and economies of scale, which the Supreme Court indirectly affirmed in the *US Steel* decision of 1920. In addition, individuals who represented opposing political parties such as Brandeis and Hoover nonetheless favored trade associations. The flexibility of the rule of reason, moreover, enabled both big business and trade association advocates to support different forms of oligopolistic competition. Ultimately, however, Americans' attachment to the individual opportunity represented by small business and the desire for consumer goods identified with bigness perpetuated ambivalence. Accordingly, unless there was proof of pernicious conduct the law sanctioned increased managerial centralization while it condemned overt cartel practices in defense of competition and small enterprise. Both outcomes were consistent with the blend of moral and market assumptions republican values embodied.

World War I influenced the second great merger wave. Hannah argued convincingly that the 1920s merger movement established the basis of a British corporate economy which was "catching up" with the managerial structure pioneered by American big business. In the British corporate order, however, monopoly and restrictive practices were more prevalent. In America, by contrast, oligopoly was more characteristic of giant corporations, and outright cartelization – consistent with Hoover's and Brandeis's support for trade associations – was illegal. In the second as in the first merger movement, moreover, similarities in each nation's stock issues suggested that market factors alone did not explain the differing levels of managerial centralization.

Again, however, a conspicuous difference was the law. After 1921 British administrators increasingly condoned and the courts enforced restrictive practices, encouraging British businessmen to adopt the holding company. In the United States, by contrast, the Court's application of the rule of reason facilitated the development of a more unitary and multidivisional corporate organization. American as well as British economists, publicists, and policymakers used "rationalization" rhetoric. But the shaky alliance of American large and small business supporting the relaxation of antitrust could not overcome the deeper conflict reflected in the persistence of republican values. Similarly, British small enterprise remained comparatively more protected within the system of self-regulation and, therefore, less willing to challenge the "get along" ethos.

During the Great Depression and World War II each nation's policies tentatively converged. The Depression ended the second merger wave and both countries adopted cartelization policies, symbolized in Britain by final demise of Free Trade and the triumph of tariff protectionism. In America, however, the campaign to relax antitrust and foster cartels under the NRA triumphed only briefly. Despite the spread of multidivisional structure throughout American firms, British industry as a whole actually performed better during the Depression. The depth of the collapse ultimately stimulated a dramatic revival of antitrust under Thurman Arnold, which nevertheless abated once the United States entered the war. Because of the war, also, British policymakers and business groups broadly questioned whether their nation's comparatively less-developed corporate structure could compete effectively in a more prosperous post-war world. The resulting clash pitted defenders of governmentally supervised cartelization against proponents of competition enforced through some form of antitrust.

While domestic tensions most significantly shaped British policymaking, American diplomacy reinforced the proponents of competition. The Coalition Government's commitment to full employment as a primary goal of post-war economic planning was the most important factor facilitating greater government intervention. The debate within and without the government was over what form of official action would be sufficient to ensure full employment.

Many members of the Labour Party and some Tories supported the pro-competition policy proposed in the Gaitskell–Allen memorandum. Yet other segments of the Conservative Party, as well as large and small business pressure groups, advocated returning to the inter-war cartel policy, modified only by strengthened governmental supervision. The zealous American attack on international cartels associated with the bilateral negotiations involving the ITO influenced British policymakers. Ultimately, however, internal domestic conflicts led Labour to institutionalize the investigation–publicity policy in the Monopolies and Restrictive Practices Act of 1948. The experiment of the Standing Committee on Trusts which seemed consigned to oblivion in 1921, had become the law of the land. In America, too, indigenous tensions defeated the ITO and revived the Brandeisian attack on bigness inherent in the persistent acceptance of republican values.

After 1948 a gradual if uneven convergence characterized the business structure and official policymaking of both nations. Wilson's efforts culminating in Labour's 1951 White Paper and the Conservatives' enactment of the Restrictive Practices Act of 1956, represented a new bipartisan anti-cartel consensus. Division within the business community, especially among the small business supporters of resale price maintenance, enabled the Conservatives to succeed where Labour had failed. Nevertheless, by 1990, lawyers' ingenuity and uncertainties associated with membership in the European Community required Labour and Conservatives periodically to reaffirm this anti-cartel policy through legislative recommendations and laws. Meanwhile, each party's policy toward horizontal and vertical mergers was ambiguous. Following the course of American antitrust law and business, the combination of British cartel and merger policies influenced the 1960s' merger wave. Catching up with the United States and completing the organizational transformation begun during the 1920s, managerial capitalism generally displaced the British system of self-regulation, though corporate concentration was higher in Britain than America. The end of the IRC, the flexible reference procedure of the OFT and the enforcement of Tebbit Guidelines, the favorable official reception given most of the recommendations of both Liesner Committees, and the EC's 1990 merger regulation encouraged the relative increase of conglomerate mergers during the 1980s.

In the United States the mix of anti-cartel and merger policies also stimulated conglomerates. Democrat and Republican antitrust officials continued the traditional policy of emphasizing the prosecution of cartel practices. Until the mid-1970s, moreover, the Supreme Court's application of the Celler-Kefauver Act and the 1968 Guidelines also sanctioned the vigorous attack on horizontal and vertical mergers consistent with republican values. The business press and the private and public statements of federal antitrust enforcement authorities confirmed that the government's mix of policies encouraged corporate decision-makers to adopt the conglomerate structure.

The Court's and the government's increased acceptance of efficiency theory, the passage of the Hart-Scott-Rodino Act, and the revitalization of state antitrust enforcement paved the way for the significant change in the proportion of merger-cartel prosecutions of the Reagan years. The broad bipartisan support given the Baxter Guidelines, especially after it became apparent that the Reagan Antitrust Division was perhaps not enforcing them, indicated the demise of republican values. The impact of this policy on business structure nonetheless was to encourage the second conglomerate merger wave, which in turn tended to reverse the results of its 1960s' predecessor.

As each nation's business structure increasingly converged, so did the role of lawyers. During both of the post-war merger waves, the similar pattern of each nation's stock prices suggested the importance of market factors. Yet, as Hannah noted, the causal linkages reflected in the stock market remained sufficiently enigmatic to suggest that governmental policy was also an important factor influencing business strategy and structure. One indicator of this influence was that after 1948 the continuing succession of laws and policy statements compelled British business to rely more than ever before on lawyers for advice. At least since the rise of Wall Street firms and complementary market for legal services represented by Brandeis during the late nineteenth century, by contrast, American business had depended on lawyers. By the 1980s, moreover, American judges' adoption of efficiency theories engendered a degree of self-restraint more consistent with that of British courts. While American antitrust activism clearly was not dead, the new theories facilitated the lawyer's advisory role. Perhaps more than ever before, then, British and American lawyers performed a similar function in each nation's business order.

The increased role of lawyers suggested the use pressure groups made of economic thought. After World War II economic experts and publicists in both nations linked the attainment of improved employment and business efficiency to some sort of antitrust policy. Large and small business were influential in both nations, but British organized labor was more concerned about antitrust than their American counterparts. In neither country were consumers effectively organized enough to exercise continuous political clout. In Britain the advocates of governmentally promoted and supervised rationalization clashed with the defenders of competition. Notwithstanding Labour's support of IRC, the Conservatives and Labour generally agreed on a mix of anti-cartel and merger policies which reflected the divisions within large and small business and perhaps a weakening of traditional social-class values. Also, as A. D. Neale suggested, British economists accepted a more pragmatic view of efficiency than the Chicago School. The interplay between pressure groups and theory was most evident in reference decisions and Commission reports. As a result, British governmental policy encouraged the adoption of multidivisional management structures, especially conglomerates. Despite the high level of corporate concentration, this structure facilitated the adaptation of British big business to changing economic conditions.

In America the revival and subsequent demise of republican values reflected the triumph of efficiency theories. Throughout the post-war period the political fortunes of large and small business fluctuated, and generally the antitrust policies of both political parties emphasized compromise. Since Hoover and Arnold, at least, antitrust authorities had contended that economic results rather than pernicious conduct or social-political values was the goal of enforcement. Nevertheless, after World War II Democrats and Republicans and the Supreme Court linked economically oriented efficiency concerns to the threat corporate concentration posed for small business and free government. Even Donald Turner's Merger Guidelines of 1968 did not escape the value judgments implicit in the concerns involving concentration levels versus the tolerance of conglomerates. The courts' growing receptivity to Chicago-type theories and the broad bipartisan acceptance of the Baxter Guidelines seemed finally, however, to have displaced republican values. Yet the result was similar to that in Britain: shifting policy encouraged business to adopt more flexible organizational structures identified with conglomerates.

Thus antitrust constraints often encouraged each nation's business to adopt more effective management structures. The failure rate of post-war mergers, like that of earlier periods, suggested that improved managerial organization was not alone enough to avoid problems associated with adapting the corporate order to changing times. A comparison of the British and American response to big business indicated nonetheless that effective management was essential to the process of adjustment. The contribution antitrust made to this process was first to limit cartels as a viable business form. Secondly, the ambiguity of merger policy did not permit making either an easy or neat distinction between efficient and inefficient large-scale corporations. Yet in America and Britain the overall outcome of antitrust policy was to foster enough organizational flexibility that many big firms did well. Near the end of the twentieth century the British and American corporate economy experienced difficulties competing effectively with other nations. Yet, if the competitive edge was to be regained, antitrust, despite its inadequacies, clearly was part of the remedy.

Notes

INTRODUCTION

1 Alfred D. Chandler, Jr., *Scale and Scope: The Dynamics of Industrial Capitalism* (Cambridge, Massachusetts 1990), 8.
2 *Ibid.*, 286.
3 "Scale and Scope: Towards a European Visible Hand? A Review Article," *Business History* (1991 forthcoming).
4 Throughout the following pages my debt to the work of Professors Chandler and Hannah is evident. In the notes I attempt to put the reader in the way of arguments contrary to my own.

1 THE RESPONSE TO BIG BUSINESS: THE FORMATIVE ERA 1880–1914

1 Compare Samuel H. Beer, *Modern British Politics, A Study of Parties and Pressure Groups* (London, 1965); R. M. Punnett, *British Government & Politics* (Aldershot, Hampshire, 1987), 17–29, 145–172; and Tony Freyer, "Federalism," J. P. Greene, editor, *Encyclopedia of American Politic History* (New York 1984), 546–564; Tony Freyer, "Federalism," Robert J. Janosik, editor, *Encyclopedia of the American Judicial System* (3 volumes, New York 1986), III, 1089–1104; Harry N. Scheiber, "Federalism and the American Economic Order," *Law & Society Review*, X (Fall 1975), 57–118; Richard Franklin Bensel, *Sectionalism and American Political Development, 1880–1980* (Madison, Wisconsin, 1984); Elizabeth Sanders, "Industrial Concentration, Sectional Competition, and Antitrust Politics in America, 1880–1980," *Studies in American Political Development An Annual* I (New Haven, Connecticut, 1986), 142–214; Tony Allan Freyer, *Forums of Order: The Federal Courts and Business in American History* (Greenwich, Connecticut, 1979).
2 P. S. Atiyah, *The Rise and Fall of Freedom of Contract* (Oxford, 1979), 571–601; Peter Mathias, *The First Industrial Nation, An Economic History of Britain, 1700–1914* (London, 1983), 351–397; Alfred D. Chandler, Jr., *Scale and Scope* (Cambridge, Massachusetts, 1990); Leslie Hannah, *The Rise of the Corporate Economy* (London, 1983), 1–26; Jeannie Anne Godfrey Dennison, "The Reaction to the Growth of Trusts and Industrial Combinations in Britain, 1888–1921," (unpublished Ph.D.

334

Thesis, University of London, 1980) (used with permission); Tony
Freyer, "The Sherman Antitrust Act, Comparative Business Struc-
ture, and the Rule of Reason: America and Great Britain, 1880–1920,"
74 *Iowa Law Review*, (July 1989), 991–1018; Leslie Hannah, "Mergers,
Cartels, and Concentration: Legal Factors in the U.S. and European
Experience," in N. Horn and J. Kocka, editors, *Law and the Formation
of the Big Enterprises in the 19th and Early 20th Centuries* (Gottingen:
Vandenhoeck & Ruprecht, 1979), 306–315; William R. Cornish,
"Legal Control over Cartels and Monopolization, 1880–1914: A
Comparison," Horn and Kocka, editors, *Law and the Formation of the Big
Enterprises* (Gottingen, 1979), 281–303; P. L. Payne, *British Entre-
preneurship in the Nineteenth Century* (London 1988); Tony Orhnial, editor,
Limited Liability and the Corporation (London, 1982); Herbert Hoven-
kamp, "The Antitrust Movement and the Rise of Industrial
Organization," *Texas Law Review*, 68 (November 1989), 105–168;
Leslie Hannah, "Visible and Invisible Hands in Great Britain,"
in Alfred D. Chandler, Jr. and Herman Daems, editors, *Managerial
Hierarchies, Comparative Perspectives on the Rise of the Modern Industrial
Enterprise* (Cambridge, Massachusetts, 1980), 41–76; William Letwin,
*Law and Economic Policy in America, The Evolution of the Sherman
Antitrust Act* (Chicago, 1981), Hans N. Thorelli, *The Federal Antitrust
Policy, Organization of an American Tradition* (Baltimore, 1955);
Alexander M. Bickel and Benno C. Schmidt, Jr., *The Judiciary and
Responsible Government 1910–21* (New York, 1984), 86–199; Martin M.
Sklar, *The Corporate Reconstruction of American Capitalism, 1890–1916, The
Market, the Law and Politics* (Cambridge, UK, 1988); Thomas K.
McCraw, *Prophets of Regulation, Charles Francis Adams, Louis D. Brandeis,
James M. Landis, Alfred E. Kahn* (Cambridge, Massachusetts, 1984)
80–142; Edward C. Kirkland, *Industry Comes of Age, Business, Labor and
Public Policy, 1860–1897* (Chicago, 1961), 197–215, 306–24; Freyer,
Forums of Order, 99–141; Tony Freyer, "Economic Liberty, Antitrust,
and the Constitution, 1880–1925," in Ellen Frankel Paul and Howard
Dickman, editors, *Liberty, Property, and Government: Constitutional
Interpretation Before the New Deal* (Albany, 1989), 187–216; Alfred D.
Chandler, Jr., *The Visible Hand, The Managerial Revolution in American
Business* (Cambridge, Massachusetts, 1977), 315–376; Morton Keller,
Affairs of State, Public Life in Late Nineteenth Century America (Cambridge,
Massachusetts, 1977), 409–438; James May, "Antitrust Practice and
Procedure in the Formative Era: The Constitutional and Conceptual
Reach of State Antitrust Law, 1880–1918," *University of Pennsylvania
Law Review*, 135 (March 1987), 495–593; James May, "Antitrust in
the Formative Era: Political and Economic Theory in Constitutional
and Antitrust Analysis, 1880–1918," *Ohio State Law Journal* 50 No. 2
(1989), 257–395; Herbert Hovenkamp, "State Antitrust in the Federal
Scheme," *Indiana Law Journal* 58 No. 3 (1983), 375–432; Herbert
Hovenkamp, "Labor Conspiracies in American Law, 1880–1930,"
Texas Law Review, 66 (April 1988), 919–965; Herbert Hovenkamp,

"The Classical Corporation in American Legal Thought," *The Georgetown Law Journal*, 76 (June 1988), 1593–1689; Suzanne Weaver, *Decision to Prosecute: Organization and Public Polity in the Antitrust Division* (Cambridge, Massachusetts, 1977), 11–35; Louis Galambos and Joseph Pratt, *The Rise of the Corporate Commonwealth, U.S. Business and Public Policy in the Twentieth Century* (New York 1988), 56–64; Naomi R. Lamoreaux, *The Great Merger Movement in American Business, 1895–1904* (Cambridge, UK, 1985); Herbert Hovenkamp, "Antitrust's Protected Classes," *Michigan Law Review*, 88 (October 1989) 1–48.

3 Hannah, *Rise of the Corporate Economy*, 8–26; Payne, *British Entrepreneurship*, 14–20; Jonathan Barron Baskin, "The Development of Corporate Financial Markets in Britain and the United States, 1600–1914: Overcoming Asymmetric Information," *Business History Review* 62 (Summer 1988), 199–237; Paul J. Miranti, Jr., "Associationalism, Statism and Professional Regulation: Public Accountants and the Reform of Financial Markets, 1896–1940," *Business History Review* 60 (Autumn 1986), 438–468; Chandler, *Scale and Scope*; Freyer, "Sherman Antitrust Act," *Iowa Law Review*, 74 (July 1989), 991; Freyer, "Economic Liberty, Antitrust, and the Constitution," in Paul and Dickman, editors, *Liberty, Property, and Government*, 187–216; Sklar, *Corporate Reconstruction of American Capitalism*; McCraw, *Prophets of Regulation*, 80–142; Hovenkamp, "Antitrust's Protected Classes," *Michigan Law Review*, 88 (October, 1989), 1–48; Dennison, "Reaction to the Growth of Trusts"; Hannah, "Mergers," in Glenn Porter, editor, *Encyclopedia of American Economic History Studies of the Principal Movement and Ideas* (3 volumes; 1981), II, 639–651.

4 Hannah, *Rise of the Corporate Economy*, 8–26; Chandler, *Scale and Scope* 235–392; Freyer, "Sherman Antitrust Act," *Iowa Law Review*, 74 (July 1989), 991; Hannah, "Mergers," in Porter, editor, *Encyclopedia*, II, 641–632; Hannah, "Mergers, Cartels, and Concentration," Horn & Kocka, editors, *Law and the Formation of the Big Enterprises*, 306–315.

5 Hannah, "Mergers," in Porter, editor, *Encyclopedia*, II, 642.

6 K. Feiling, *History of England* (London 1948), 848.

7 As quoted, Dennison, "Reaction to the Growth of Trusts," 168. See also Beer, *Modern British Politics*; Punnett, *British Government*, 17–29.

8 See Note 4.

9 Ashworth, *Economic History*, 216–238; Atiyah, *Freedom of Contract*, 571–601; Mathias, *First Industrial Nation*, 351–397; Dennison "Reaction to the Growth of Trusts," 80–99, 164–195, 220–249; Beer, *Modern British Politics*, 54–125; Freyer, "Sherman Antitrust Act," *Iowa Law Review*, 74 (July 1989), 991; and see fuller discussion and citation, Chapters 3 and 4.

10 Freyer, "Federalism," Greene editor, *Encyclopedia of American Political History* 546–564; "Federalism," Janosik, editor, *Encyclopedia of the American Judicial System*, III, 1089–1104; Scheiber, "Federalism and the American Economic Order, *Law & Society Review*, X (Fall 1975), 57–118; Bensel, *Sectionalism and American Political Development*,

1880–1980; Sanders, "Industrial Concentration, Sectional Competition, and Antitrust Politics in America, 1880–1980," *Studies in American Political Development An Annual* I (New Haven, Connecticut, 1986), 142–214.

11 Harold C. Livesay, *Samuel Gompers and Organized Labor in America* (Boston, 1978), 144–146 148–152; William E. Forbath, "The Shaping of the American Labor Movement," *Harvard Law Review*, 102 (1989), 1109–1256.

12 *Ibid.*; Allon Gal, *Brandeis of Boston* (Cambridge, Massachusetts, 1980), 11–16, 46–65; Philippa Strum, *Louis D. Brandeis, Justice for the People* (New York, 1984), 55–113; McCraw, *Prophets of Regulation* 95–109; Bickel and Schmidt, *Judiciary and Responsible Government*, 133.

13 Mathias, *First Industrial Nation*, 356, 364–366; Payne, *British Entrepreneurship*, 17–18; Beer, *Modern British Politics*, 66–113; R. P. T. Davenport-Hines, *Dudley Docker, The Life and Times of a Trade Warrior* (Cambridge, England, 1984), 55–83; Dennison, "Reaction to the Growth of Trusts," 36–250.

14 Thorelli, *Federal Antitrust Policy*, 54–156, 235–430; Letwin, *Law and Economic Policy in America*, 53–99, 155–160, 182–279; Kirkland, *Industry Comes of Age*, 195–215, 306–324; McCraw, *Prophets of Regulation*, 95–109; Sklar, *Corporate Reconstruction of American Capitalism*, 333–431; Freyer, "Economic Liberty, Antitrust, and the Constitution," Paul and Dickman, editors, *Liberty, Property, and Government*, 187–216.

15 Dennison, "Reaction to the Growth of Trusts"; Hovenkamp, "Political Economy of Substantive Due Process," *Stanford Law Review*, 40 (January, 1988), 402–410, 437–438.

16 Hovenkamp, "Political Economy of Substantive Due Process," *Standard Law Review*, 40 (January, 1988), 411–439; and see note 14.

17 *Ibid.*; see also note 15.

18 James Bryce, *The American Commonwealth* (2 volumes, London, 1901), II, 540–541, 542.

19 See chapters 2, 3.

20 Freyer, *Forums of Order*, 99–101; see also, note 14.

21 Mathias, *First Industrial Nation*, 26, 56–58, 226.

22 Hannah, "Visible and Invisible Hands in Great Britain," in Chandler and Daems, editors, *Managerial Hierarchies*, 63–64; and see below.

23 Tony Freyer, "The Associational Economy: Debtor–Credit or Relations and Law in Antebellum America" (unpublished manuscript); Chandler, *Visible Hand*, 15–49, 315–344; Freyer, *Forums of Order*, 99–141; Charles W. McCurdy, "American Law and the Marketing Structure of the Large Corporation, 1875–1890," *Journal of Economic History*, 38 (September 1978), 631–649.

24 Henry W. Macrosty, *The Trust Movement in British Industry: A Study of Business Organization* (New York 1968, reprint of 1907 edition); P. Lesley Cook, *Effects of Mergers: Six Studies* (London 1958), 28–63 135–178; B. W. E. Alford, "Penny Cigarettes, Oligopoly, and Entrepreneurship in the UK Tobacco Industry in the Late Nineteenth

Century," in Barry Supple, editor, *Essays in British History* (Oxford, England, 1977), 69–87; Charles Wilson, *History of Unilever* (2 volumes, London, 1954) I, 30–48; Sheila Marriner and Francis Hyde, *The Senior John Samuel Swire, 1825–1898, Management in Far Eastern Shipping Trades* (Liverpool, 1967), 135–185; Robert Roberts, *The Classic Slum Salford Life in the First Quarter of the Century* (London, 1971), 26–27, 82–83.

25 See notes 9 and 11; and, Davenport-Hines, *Docker*, 25–83.

26 As quoted, Davenport-Hines, *Docker*, 39; and discussion in text. See also, Charles Dellheim, "The Creation of a Company Culture: *Cadbury's, 1861–1931,*" *American Historical Review*, 92 (February 1987), 13–44.

27 See note 11.

28 As quoted, Dellheim, "Company Culture: *Cadbury's,*" *American Historical Review*, 92 (February 1987), 27, 34.

29 See note 11.

30 *Ibid.*; Dennison, "Reaction to the Growth of Trusts," 58–59; and note 28.

31 G. C. Allen, *Monopoly and Restrictive Practices* (London, 1968), 58–59; Robert Stevens, *Law and Politics, The House of Lords as a Judicial Body, 1800–1976* (Chapel Hill, North Carolina, 1978), 95–96.

32 See chapter 4, Part 4, notes and discussion.

33 The scope and nature of "self-regulation" is developed in the following pages. I have found suggestive the use of the idea in Jonathan Lurie, *The Chicago Board of Trade, 1859–1905, The Dynamics of Self-Regulation* (Urbana, Illinois, 1979).

34 For the relation of legal rules to business structure see note 2; as this pertains to the rule of reason see chapters 3 and 4. But see also Sklar, *Corporate Reconstruction of American Capitalism*, 117–154.

35 Freyer, *Forums of Order*, 100.

36 Mathias, *First Industrial Nation*, 395–404.

37 Chandler, "Development of Modern Management Structure," McCraw, editor, *Essential Chandler*, 356; Hannah, *Rise of the Corporate Economy*, 8, 53; Chandler, "Seedbed of Managerial Capitalism," Chandler and Daems, editors, *Managerial Hierarchies*, 9–40; Hannah, "Visible and Invisible Hands," Chandler and Daems, *Managerial Hierarchies*, 41–76.

38 Hannah, *Rise of the Corporate Economy*, 23–24.

39 *Ibid.*

40 Jeremiah Jenks, as quoted, Livingston, "Social Analysis," *American Historical Review*, 92 (February 1987), 84.

41 McCraw, *Prophets of Regulation*, 70–71; Hovenkamp, "Antitrust Movement," *Texas Law Review*, 68 (November 1989), 153–166.

42 Hannah, "Visible and Invisible Hands," Chandler and Daems, editors, *Managerial Hierarchies*, 63.

43 Dennison, "Reaction to the Growth of Trusts," 196–199; and note 24.

44 As quoted, Kirkland, *Industry Comes of Age*, 196–199; and note 24.

45 As quoted, Cook, *Effects of Mergers*, 37.

46 "Report of the Committee on Trusts," *Parliamentary Papers*, XIII (1918), 17; See also note 43.
47 Note 44; and Louis Galambos, *Competition & Cooperation The Emergence of a National Trade Association* (Baltimore, 1966).
48 As quoted, "Report of the Committee on Trusts," *Parliamentary Papers*, XIII (1918), 3.
49 William Reader, as quoted, Chandler, *Scale and Scope*, 292.
50 Notes 43, 44, 46, 47.
51 Chandler, *Visible Hand*, 317.
52 As quoted, Kirkland, *Industry Comes of Age*, 203.
53 As quoted, Cook, *Effects of Mergers*, 46.
54 Hovenkamp, "Labor Conspiracies in American Law," *Texas Law Review*, 66 (April 1988), 932–933.
55 *US* v. *Addyston Pipe & Steel Co.*, 85 F. 271, 279 (6th Cir., 1898), *aff'd*, 175 U.S. 211 (1899).
56 See chapter 4; and Freyer, "Sherman Antitrust Act," *Iowa Law Review*, 74 (July 1989), 991.
57 As quoted, McCraw, *Prophets of Regulation*, 97.
58 Hovenkamp, "Antitrust Movement," *Texas Law Review*, 68 (November 1989), 153–166.
59 See chapter 4.
60 Freyer, *Forums of Order*, 109–110; McCurdy, "American Law and the Marketing Structure of the Large Corporation," *Journal of Economic History*, 38 (September 1978), 631–649; Thorelli, *Federal Antitrust Policy*, 96–107.
61 See discussion and citations in chapters 3 and 4.
62 The argument and evidence presented in chapters 3 and 4 supports Chandler and Hannah, cited notes 37. For an opposing view see Sklar, *Corporate Reconstruction of American Capitalism*, 163–166. In chapters 3 and 4, I attempt to show interplay between changing market relations and state and federal law and a comparison of the results with Britain. Such an analysis suggests the shortcomings of an interpretation which departs from Chandler and Hannah.
63 See chapters 3 and 4.
64 *Ibid.*
65 Chapter 4 attempts to make the case for this thesis. But see Sklar, *Corporate Reconstruction of American Capitalism*, 146–166.
66 Chandler, *Visible Hand*, 229; McCraw, *Prophets of Regulation*, 101–108.
67 Chandler, *Scale and Scope*, 250, 251–252.
68 See note 62. For the argument that American antitrust favored oligopoly over monopoly and competition over cartels see: Alfred D. Chandler, Jr., "The Coming of Oligopoly and Its Meaning for Antitrust," *National Competition Policy, Historians' Perspectives on Antitrust and Government-Business Relationships in the United States* (Washington, D.C., 1981), 62–96; McCraw, *Prophets of Regulation*, 144–146.
69 Marriner and Hyde, *The Senior*, 160.
70 *Ibid.*, 135–184; see also the manuscript records of the Peninsular &

Orient Co., located in National Maritime Museum (Greenwich, England): P&O/52/1, "Answers by the Sub-Committee held on 5 April 1907," 1–9; P&O/52/3, Sir Thomas Sutherland, "Minute on Shipping Conferences," 1–7, P&O/52/2. "Royal Commission on Shipping Conferences…19 May 1890," 1–35. See also Dennison, "Reaction to the Growth of Trusts," 226–242.

71 P&O/12/1, 3, 4 Letterbook: Freshfields to Taylor, 3 June 1914; Waltons & Co. to Freshfields, 10 June 1914; Chairman to Board (Secret) 22 May 1914.

72 Dear Sir or Madam, 16 June 1914, 1, 2, 5, 6.

73 Chandler, *Visible Hand*, 438–444.

74 *Ibid.*, as quoted, 442.

75 Louis Galambos, "Loose Combinations and Their Public Control Over Time," *National Competition Policy*, 144–206.

76 Note 62.

77 Chandler, *Scale and Scope*, 255–261.

78 *Ibid.*

79 Chandler, *Visible Hand*, 209–239.

80 *Ibid.*, 285–376.

81 *Ibid*, 321–326.

82 *Ibid.*, 323–326.

83 *Ibid.*, 321; Freyer, *Forums of Order*, 103–104.

84 Bruce Bringhurst, *Antitrust and the Oil Monopoly, The Standard Oil Cases, 1890–1911* (Greenwich, Connecticut, 1979). For fuller discussion see chapter 3.

85 Joseph A. Pratt, "The Petroleum Industry in Transition: Antitrust and the Decline of Monopoly Control in Oil," *Journal of Economic History*, 40 (December 1980), 815–837.

86 Chandler, *Visible Hand*, 326–336; and see chapter 3.

87 *Ibid.*

88 Mary Yeager, *Competition and Regulation: The Development of Oligopoly in the Meat Packing Industry* (Greenwich, Connecticut, 1981).

89 Chandler, *Visible Hand*, 382–391.

90 Chandler, *Scale and Scope* 242–246; Dellheim, "Company Culture: Cadbury's," *American Historical Review*, 92 (February 1987), 13–44.

91 Chandler, *Scale and Scope* 246–249; Alford, "Penny Cigarettes," Supple, editor, *Essays in British Business History*, 49–69; Macrosty, *Trust Movement*, 229–238.

92 *Ibid.*

93 Chandler, *Scale and Scope*, 378–388; Macrosty, *Trust Movement*, 203–209; Wilson, *Unilever*, I, 130–148.

94 The Solicitor General's brief in *U.S.* v. *Joint Traffic Ass'n*, 171 U.S. 505 (1898), as quoted, Hovenkamp, "Antitrust Movement," *Texas Law Review*, 68 (November 1989), 133–134. Chapters 3 and 4 sets forth the evidence for the argument stated here. See also, Freyer, "Sherman Act," *Iowa Law Review*, 74 (July 1989), 991. But see Sklar, *Corporate Reconstruction of American Capitalism*, 163–166.

95 Freyer, *Forums of Order*, 99–120; Hovenkamp, "Classical Corporation in American Legal Thought," *Georgetown Law Journal*, 76 (June 1988), 1593–1689, Chandler, *Visible Hand*, 315–344, 373–374; James C. Bonbright and Gardiner C. Means, *The Holding Company, Its Public Significance and Its Regulation* (New York 1969); William J. Reader, "Versatility Unlimited – Reflections on the History and Nature of The Limited Liability Company," in Tony Orhnial, editor, *Limited Liability and the Corporation* (London 1982), 191–204; Hannah, *Rise of the Corporate Economy*, 8–26; Payne, *British Entrepreneurship*, 14–28; Macrosty, *Trust Movement*, 1–23.

96 Freyer, *Forums of Order*, 101, 107; Macrosty, *Trust Movement*, 15–16; Chandler, *Visible Hand*, 315–320; Bonbright and Means, *Holding Company*, 1–76; A Report of the Committee on Trusts," *Parliamentary Papers*, XIII (1918), 31–34.

97 Chandler, *Visible Hand*, 319–332; see also chapter 3.

98 Hannah, *Rise of Corporate Economy*, 8–26; Payne, *British Entrepreneurship*, 14–28; Macrosty, *Trust Movement*, 15–16; Reader, "Versatility Unlimited," Orhnial, editor, *Limited Liability*; 191–204; "Report of the Committee on Trusts," *Parliamentary Papers*, XIII (1918) 18–19, 31–34.

99 S. B. Saul, as quoted, in Davenport-Hines, *Docker*, 52–53.

100 Chandler, "Development of Modern Management Structures," McCraw, editor, *Essential Chandler*, 364; Chandler, *Visible Hand*, 332–334; chapter 3. But see Sklar, *Corporate Reconstruction of American Capitalism*, 162–164.

101 McCraw, *Prophets of Regulation*, 69–70; Hovenkamp, "Antitrust Movement," *Texas Law Review*, 68 (November 1969), 105–168; Bonbright and Means, *Holding Company*, 1–76; Chandler, *Visible Hand*, 1–14, 315–376.

102 "Report of Committee on Trusts," *Parliamentary Papers*, XIII (1918), 40.

103 *Ibid.*, 40–41; and note 98.

104 As quoted, Kirkland, *Industry Comes of Age*, 213.

105 As quoted, Davenport-Hines, *Docker*, 30.

106 As quoted, Chandler, *Scale and Scope*, 291.

107 Hannah, "Visible and Invisible Hands," Chandler and Daems, *Managerial Hierarchies*, 71; Hannah, "Mergers," Porter, editor, *American Economic History*, 643; Chandler, *Visible Hand*, 337–339; Lamoreaux, *Great Merger Movement*.

108 McCraw, *Prophets of Regulation*, 76.

109 Dellheim, "Company Culture: *Cadburys*," *American Historical Review* , 92 (February 1987), 43–44; Chandler, *Scale and Scope*; Mathias, *First Industrial Nation*, 350–393; Bernard Elbaum and William Lazonik, editors, *The Decline of the British Economy* (Oxford, England, 1986); Hannah, *Rise of Corporate Economy*, 24–26.

110 Chandler, *Scale and Scope*; Elbaum, "The Steel Industry Before World War I," Elbaum and Lazonik, editors, *Decline of British Economy* 51–81.

111 Hannah, "Mergers," Porter, editor, *American Economic History*, 642–

643; Hannah, *Rise of Corporate Economy*, 2–23; Chandler, *Visible Hand*, 331–339. For a different, though not necessarily a contrary, view see, Lamoreaux, *Great Merger Movement*; Hannah, "Visible and Invisible Hands," Chandler and Daems, editors, *Managerial Hierarchies*, 70–71.

112 Edward Q. Keasbey, "New Jersey and the Great Corporations," *Harvard Law Review*, 13 (November 1899), 275–276.

113 Chapters 3 and 4.

114 *Ibid.*

115 Chandler, *Visible Hand*, 332–334.

116 Hannah, *Rise of the Corporate Economy*, 23–24.

117 Notes 105 and 106.

2 THE DIVERGENCE OF ECONOMIC THOUGHT

1 Although there are numerous studies of Anglo-American social and economic thought, there are few which relate these ideas to the formative development of antitrust in Britain and America. A pioneering effort to compare elements of legal culture having some relevance to antitrust is Richard A. Cosgrove, *Our Lady the Common Law: An Anglo-American Legal Community 1870–1930* (New York, 1987). More directly on point are excellent articles by Herbert Hovenkamp: "The Political Economy of Substantive Due Process," *Stanford Law Review*, 40 (January 1988), 379–447, which expressly compares British and American economic thought; and "Labor Conspiracies in American Law, 1880–1930," *Texas Law Review*, 66 (April 1988), 919–965. See also William Letwin, *Law and Economic Policy in America, The Evolution of the Sherman Antitrust Act* (Chicago, 1981), 18–52; and James May, "Antitrust in the Formative Era: Political and Economic Theory in Constitutional and Antitrust Analysis, 1880–1918," *Ohio State Law Journal*, 50 No. 2 (1989), 257–395. For an initial attempt at suggesting the place of economic thought in a comparison of British and American approaches to antitrust see Tony Freyer, "The Sherman Antitrust Act, Comparative Business Structure, and the Rule of Reason: America and Great Britain, 1880–1920," *Iowa Law Review*, 74 (July, 1989), 991. For a more complex picture it is necessary to drawn upon relevant studies of economic thought in each nation. For the British side nothing compares to the superb work of Jeannie Ann Godfrey Dennison entitled, "The reaction to the Growth of Trusts and Industrial Combinations in Britain, 1888–1921" (unpublished Ph.D. thesis, University of London, 1980) (available at Senate House Library). This study is used with her kind permission. See also Leslie Hannah, *The Rise of the Corporate Economy* (London, 1983); P. S. Atiyah, *The Rise and Fall of Freedom of Contract* (Oxford, England, 1985); Robert Skidelsky, *John Maynard Keynes; Hopes Betrayed, 1883–1920* (London, 1983), 32–50, 206–232. Although the American materials are voluminous, for the purposes of this study the following are most useful: Hans B. Thorelli, *The Federal Antitrust Policy,*

Organization of an American Tradition (Baltimore, 1954), 54–163, 235–368; Edward C. Kirkland, *Industry Comes of Age, Business, Labor, and Public Policy, 1860–1897* (Chicago, 1967), 195–222, 262–77, 306–24; Martin J. Sklar, *The Corporate Reconstruction of American Capitalism, 1890–1916, The Market, the Law and Politics* (Cambridge, England, 1988), 57–78; Tony Freyer, "Economic Liberty, Antitrust, and the Constitution, 1880–1925," in Ellen Frankel Paul and Howard Dickman, eds., *Liberty, Property, and Government: Constitutional Interpretation Before the New Deal* (Albany, 1989), 187–215; Tony Allan Freyer, *Forums of Order: The Federal Courts and Business in American History* (Greenwich, Connecticut, 1979), 99–141, and Joseph Dorfman, *The Economic Mind in American Civilization, 1865–1918* (3 volumes, New York, 1949–1959).

2 The following discussion will explore this perceptible shift in public discourse and the opinion of professional economists as it coincided with changing market conditions, especially the great merger wave. Although the works cited in note 1 discuss changes in economic thought, except for Dennison, "Reaction to the Growth of Trusts," they make little effort to relate the change to the business cycle.

3 Dennison, "Reaction to the Growth of Trusts," 44, 148–152; James Bryce, *The American Commonwealth* (2 volumes, London, 1901), I 449, 535–48,. 715, II, 154–65, 238–855.

4 Henry Carter Adams, "Relation of the State to Industrial Action," Joseph Dorfman, editor (New York, 1954, reprint of original article, 1887), 89–90.

5 Hovenkamp, "Political Economy of Substantive Due Process," *Stanford Law Review*, 40 (Jan, 1988), 402–30.

6 *Ibid.*, 407–21; Skidelsky, *Keynes*, 32–48; Sklar, *Corporate Reconstruction of American Capitalism*, 57–78.

7 Francis Wayland, *The Elements of Political Economy* (New York 1837), vi, as quoted, Hovenkamp, "Political Economy of Substantive Due Process," *Stanford Law Review*, 40 (January 1988), 413.

8 Hovenkamp, "Political Economy of Substantive Due Process," *Stanford Law Review* 40 (January 1988), 415–420.

9 Sklar, *Corporate Reconstruction of American Capitalism*, 57–78, 334–364.

10 As quoted, John Milton Cooper, Jr., *The Warrior and the Priest, Woodrow Wilson and Theodore Roosevelt* (Cambridge, Massachusetts, 1983), 161.

11 Freyer, "Economic Liberty, Antitrust, and the Constitution."

12 Hovenkamp "Labor Conspiracies," *Texas Law Review*, 66 (April 1988), 935–45; Hovenkamp "Political Economy of Substantive Due Process," *Stanford Law Review*, 40 (January 1988), 407–410; Sklar *Corporate Reconstruction of American Capitalism*, 57–78; Skidelsky, *Keynes*, **32**-48, 206–32.

13 *Political Economy* (Boston, 1888), 263, as quoted, Hovenkamp, "Labor Conspiracies ," *Texas Law Review*, 66 (April 1988), 936.

14 Bryce, *American Commonwealth*, II, 535–548. For my attempt to develop this point see the following discussion.

15 Compare Thorelli, *Federal Antitrust Policy*, 109–116, Hovenkamp, "Political Economy of Substantive Due Process," *Stanford Law Review*, 40 (January 1988), 417 (from which I draw the quoted phrases), and Atiyah, *Rise and Fall of Freedom of Contract*, 285–286.

16 There is no study of American popular opinion showing the reaction to big business as a new phenomenon which matches the detail and quality of Dennison, "Reaction to the Growth of Trusts," though Thorelli, *Federal Antitrust Policy*, 108–163 is an excellent start. Also useful in a general way is Edward C. Kirkland, *Dream and Thought in the Business Community 1860–1900* (Ithaca, 1956).

17 Unless otherwise noted, all directly quoted references of original sources are taken from Dennison, "Reaction to the Growth of Trusts," 37–55.

18 *Ibid.*, as quoted, 41.

19 *Ibid.*, as quoted, 42, 43.

20 *Ibid.*, as quoted, 49.

21 *Ibid.*, as quoted.

22 *Ibid.*, as quoted, 50.

23 *Ibid.*, as quoted, 55.

24 *Ibid.*, as quoted, 46.

25 *Ibid.*, as quoted, 42.

26 *Ibid.*, as quoted, 50.

27 *Ibid.*, as quoted, 52.

28 *Ibid.*, as quoted, 54.

29 Unless otherwise noted, the following directly quoted references are from Thorelli, *Federal Antitrust Policy*, 134–151.

30 *Ibid.*, as quoted, 134.

31 *Ibid.*, as quoted, 135.

32 *Ibid.*, as quoted, 135, note 101.

33 As quoted, Kirkland, *Industry Comes of Age*, 311, 313.

34 As quoted, Thorelli, *Federal Antitrust Policy*, 147.

35 *Ibid.*, 148–149 for discussion of Gomper's vacillation on the antitrust issue.

36 *Ibid.*, as quoted, 148.

37 *Ibid.*, as quoted, 147.

38 *Ibid.*, as quoted, 150.

39 *Ibid.*, 150–151 for the discussion of the incorporation of the antitrust plank into the platforms of the two major national party organizations beginning in 1888. For the growing conflict between the NAM and the unions see Harold C. Livesay, *Samuel Gompers and Organized Labor in America* (Boston, 1978), 145–148, 162.

40 Kirkland, *Industry Comes of Age*, 126; Thorelli, *Federal Antitrust Policy*, 350–351.

41 Thorelli, *Federal Antitrust Policy*, 149.

42 Proceedings in Relation to Trusts, H. Rep. No. 3112, 50th Cong., 1st Sess. (1888), 433.

43 As quoted, Thorelli, *Federal Antitrust Policy*, 129.

44 *Ibid.*, 116.
45 As quoted, Kirkland, *Industry Comes of Age*, 309.
46 "The Standard Oil Company," *North American Review*, 136 (February 1883), 188.
47 See discussion, chapters 1, and 3 and 4.
48 As quoted, Kirkland, *Industry Comes of Age*, 309–310.
49 See discussion in chapters 1 and 3 for further consideration of the pervasiveness of conflict among interest groups and its consequences.
50 *Ibid.*
51 James May, "Antitrust Practice and Procedure in the Formative Era: The Constitutional and Conceptual Reach of State Antitrust Law, 1880–1918," *University of Pennsylvania Law Review*, 135 (Mar. 1987), 521–535.
52 Unless otherwise noted all directly quoted references to original sources are taken from Dennison, "Reaction to the Growth of Trusts," 60–68, 80–96. The Marshall reference is as quoted, 60.
53 Except where otherwise noted, the directly quoted references to American professional economists are from either Thorelli, *Federal Antitrust Policy*, or May, "Antitrust in the Formative Era," *Ohio State Law Journal* 50, No. 2 (1989), 257–395.
54 As quoted, Dennison, "Reaction to the Growth of Trusts," 62.
55 *Ibid.*, as quoted, 61.
56 *Ibid.*, as quoted, 64.
57 *Ibid.*, as quoted, 63.
58 *Ibid.*, as quoted, 64.
59 *Ibid.*, as quoted, 83.
60 *Ibid.*, as quoted, 65.
61 *Ibid.*, as quoted, 66.
62 *Ibid.*, 83, and generally, pp. 80–96.
63 As quoted, May, "Antitrust in the Formative Era," *Ohio State Law Journal* 50 (1989), 271.
64 *Ibid.*, as quoted, 274, 275 (italics in original).
65 *Ibid.*, as quoted, 277 (italics in original).
66 Thorelli, *Federal Antitrust Policy*, 117–27.
67 *Ibid.*, as quoted, 123.
68 *Ibid.*, as quoted, 132.
69 *Ibid.*, as quoted, 124 (italics in original).
70 *Ibid.*, as quoted, 127, 128.
71 As quoted, Hovenkamp, "Labour Conspiracies," *Texas Law Review*, 66 (April 1988), 938.
72 See note 68.
73 In the following I attempt to show not that American and British public officials consciously used marginalist theory to justify increased bureaucratic regulation. Rather, the argument is that the policy-maker's resort to enlarged administrative authority was merely *consistent with* the gradual emergence of marginalist theory in the work of Marshall and others. Moreover, the suggestion is that changes in

policy and theory followed the transformation brought about by the merger wave.

74 Except where otherwise noted the following directly quoted references are taken from Dennison, "Reaction to the Growth of Trusts," 101–195.

75 *Ibid.*, as quoted, 148.

76 *Ibid.*, as quoted, 127.

77 *Ibid.*, as quoted, 110.

78 *Ibid.*, as quoted, 130.

79 *Ibid.*, as quoted, 126.

80 *Ibid.*, as quoted, 136.

81 *Ibid.*, as quoted, 138.

82 *Ibid.*, as quoted, 136.

83 *Ibid.*, as quoted, 126.

84 *Ibid.*; Henry W. Macrosty, *The Trust Movement in British Industry, A Study of Business Organization* (London, 1907), 284–307. See also chapter 3.

85 Dennison, "Reaction to the Growth of Trusts," 147.

86 *Ibid.*, 139; Macrosty, *Trust Movement*, 203–209, 261, 265; C. Wilson, *The History of Unilever, A Study in Economic Growth and Social Change* (2 volumes, London, 1954) I, 30–48. See also chapter 3.

87 Thorelli, *Federal Antitrust Policy*, 329–43. Unless otherwise noted the following directly quoted references are from these pages.

88 *Ibid.*, as quoted, 339.

89 *Ibid.*, 340–342.

90 As quoted, Freyer, "Economic Liberty, Antitrust, and the Constitution," 206.

91 Compare *Ibid.*; Thorelli, *Federal Antitrust Policy*, 331–332; Hovenkamp, Political Economy of Substantive Due Process," *Stanford Law Review*, 40 (January, 1988), 417–420; Atiyah, *Freedom of Contract*, 285–286.

92 Thorelli, *Federal Antitrust Policy*, 331.

93 *Ibid.*, 341, as quoted.

94 See chapter 3.

95 Thorelli, *Federal Antitrust Policy*, 332, as quoted.

96 May, "Antitrust Practice and Procedure in the Formative Era," *University of Pennsylvania Law Review*, 135 (March 1987), 561–571.

97 As quoted, Bickel and Schmidt, *Judiciary and Responsible Government*, 130.

98 *Ibid.*, as quoted, and the accompanying text.

99 Compare May, "Antitrust in the Formative Era," *Ohio State Law Journal* 50 (1989), 203; and Bickel and Schmidt, *Judiciary and Responsible Government*, 135.

100 As quoted, Bickel and Schmidt, *Judiciary and Responsible Government*, 133.

101 *Ibid.*, 135–39. Brandeis did not disclose that he had drafted one of the major Progressive legislative proposals that was then being debated in the Congress.

102 *Ibid.*, as quoted, 135.
103 *Ibid.*, as quoted. See also McCraw, *Prophets of Regulation*, 109–113 discussing Brandeis's evolving view of the appropriateness of an antitrust commission.
104 See chapter 4.
105 For the reference to the control of assets see McCraw, *Prophets of Regulation*, 98.
106 As quoted, James Livingston, "The Social Analysis of Economic History and Theory: Conjectures on Late Nineteenth-Century American Development," *American Historical Review*, 92 (February 1987), 86.
107 *Ibid.*, as quoted, 84.
108 See chapters 1, 3, and 4.
109 McCraw, *Prophets of Regulation*, 112–142.
110 As quoted, Dennison, "Reaction to the Growth of Trusts," 142.
111 *Ibid.*, 226–242.
112 *Ibid.*, as quoted, 166.
113 *Ibid.*, as quoted, 186.
114 Compare Macrosty's views with those of American economists discussed below.
115 Dennison, "Reaction to the Growth of Trusts," 196–199. For the triumph of the "getting along" ethos see chapter 1.
116 *Ibid.*, as quoted, 189.
117 *Ibid.*, as quoted, 203, 204, 208.
118 *Ibid.*, as quoted, 209.
119 *Ibid.*, as quoted, 210. See also, R. P. T. Davenport-Hines, *Dudley Docker The Life and Times of a Trade Warrior* (Cambridge, UK, 1984), 66. Compare to Brandeis discussed above.
120 Dennison, "Reaction to the Growth of Trusts," 226–242.
121 See chapter 3.
122 See chapter 4. For the failure to enact the "rationalization measures" see Leslie Hannah, *The Rise of the Corporate Economy* (London, 1983), 27–40.
123 Thorelli, *Federal Antitrust Policy*, 311–328, 369–431; Letwin, *Law and Economic Policy*, 71–77, 197–98; Sklar, *Corporate Reconstruction of American Capitalism*, 57–78.
124 Letwin, *Law and Economic Policy*, 198.
125 As quoted, Livingston, "Social Analysis of Economic History," *American Historical Review*, 92 (February, 1987), 84.
126 As quoted Thorelli, *Federal Antitrust Policy*, 324–325.
127 Kirkland, *Industry Comes of Age*, 312.
128 Sklar, *Corporate Reconstruction of American Capitalism*, 57–62.
129 *Ibid.*
130 As quoted, Livingston, "Social Analysis of Economic History," *American Historical Review*, 92 (February 1987), 92. Compare discussion of Brandeis above.
131 Thorelli, *Federal Antitrust Policy*, 314–315.

132 *Ibid.*, as quoted, 312–313.
133 McCraw, *Prophets of Regulation*, 109–128; Letwin, *Law and Economic Policy*, 270–278.

3 THE POLITICAL RESPONSE

1 Samuel H. Beer, *Modern British Politics, A Study of Parties and Pressure Groups* (London, 1965); William Ashworth, *An Economic History of England, 1870–1939* (London, 1982), 216–238; P. S. Atiyah, *The Rise and Fall of Freedom of Contract* (Oxford, 1979), 571–601; Peter Mathias, *The First Industrial Nation, An Economic History of Britain, 1700–1914* (London, 1983), 351–397; Alfred D. Chandler, Jr., *Scale and Scope* (Cambridge, Massachusetts, 1990); Leslie Hannah, *The Rise of the Corporate Economy* (London, 1983), 1–26; Jeannie Anne Godfrey Dennison, "The Reaction to the Growth of Trusts and Industrial Combinations in Britain, 1888–1921," (unpublished Ph.D. Thesis, University of London, 1980) (used with permission); Tony Freyer, "The Sherman Antitrust Act, Comparative Business Structure, and The Rule of Reason: America and Great Britain, 1880–1920, 74 *Iowa Law Review* (July 1989), 991; Leslie Hannah, "Mergers, Cartels, and Concentration: Legal Factors in the U.S. and European Experience," in N. Horn and J. Kocka, editors, *Law and the Formation of the Big Enterprises in the 19th and Early 20th Centuries* (Gottingen: Vandenhoeck & Ruprecht, 1979), 306–315; William R. Cornish, "Legal Control over Cartels and Monopolization, 1880–1914: A Comparison, " Horn and Kocka, editors, *Law and the Formation of the Big Enterprises* (Gottingen, 1979), 281–303; P. L. Payne, *British Entrepreneurship in the Nineteenth Century* (London, 1988); Tony Orhnial, editor *Limited Liability and the Corporation* (London, 1982); Herbert Hovenkamp, "The Antitrust Movement and the Rise of Industrial Organization," *Texas Law Review*, 68 (November 1989), 105–168.

2 William Letwin, *Law and Economic Policy in America, The Evolution of the Sherman Antitrust Act* (Chicago, 1981); Hans B. Thorelli, *The Federal Antitrust Policy, Organization of an American Tradition* (Baltimore, 1955); Alexander M. Bickel and Benno C. Schmidt, Jr., *The Judiciary and Responsible Government 1910–21* (New York, 1984), 86–199; Martin M. Sklar, *The Corporate Reconstruction of American Capitalism, 1890–1916, The Market, the Law and Politics* (Cambridge, England 1988); Thomas K. McCraw, *Prophets of Regulation, Charles Francis Adams, Louis D. Brandeis, James M. Landis, Alfred E. Kahn* (Cambridge, Massachusetts, 1984) 80–142; Edward C. Kirkland, *Industry Comes of Age, Business, Labor and Public Policy, 1860–1897* (Chicago, 1961), 197–215, 306–324; Tony Allan Freyer, *Forums of Order, The Federal Courts and Business in American History* (Greenwich, Connecticut, 1979), 99–141; Tony Freyer, "Economic Liberty, Antitrust, and the Constitution, 1880–1925," in Ellen Frankel Paul and Howard Dickman, editors, *Liberty, Property, and Government: Constitutional Interpretation Before the New Deal* (Albany,

1989), 187–216; Alfred D. Chandler, Jr., *The Visible Hand, The Managerial Revolution in American Business* (Cambridge, Massachusetts, 1977), 315–376; Morton Keller, *Affairs of State, Public Life in Late Nineteenth Century America* (Cambridge, Massachusetts, 1977), 409–438; James May, "Antitrust Practice and Procedure in the Formative Era: The Constitutional and Conceptual Reach of State Antitrust Law, 1880–1918," *University of Pennsylvania Law Review*, 135 (March 1987), 495–593; James May, "Antitrust in the Formative Era: Political and Economic Theory in Constitutional and Antitrust Analysis, 1880–1918," *Ohio State Law Journal* 50 No. 2 (1989), 257–395; Herbert Hovenkamp, "State Antitrust in the Federal Scheme," *Indiana Law Journal* 58 No. 3 (1983), 375–432; Herbert Hovenkamp, "Labor Conspiracies in American Law, 1880–1930," *Texas Law Review*, 66 (April 1988), 919–965; Herbert Hovenkamp, "The Classical Corporation in American Legal Thought," *The Georgetown Law Journal* 76 (June 1988), 1593–1689; Suzanne Weaver, *Decision to Prosecute: Organization and Public Policy in the Antitrust Division* (Cambridge, Massachusetts, 1977), 11–35; Louis Galambos and Joseph Pratt, *The Rise of the Corporate Commonwealth, U.S. Business and Public Policy in the Twentieth Century* (New York, 1988), 56–64; Naomi R. Lamoreaux, *The Great Merger Movement in American Business, 1895–1904* (Cambridge, UK, 1985). Herbert Hovenkamp, "Antitrust's Protected Classes," *Michigan Law Review*, 88 (October 1989) 1–48.

3 Chapter 4 focuses primarily on the courts, whereas this chapter, though including discussion of the judiciary wherever appropriate, emphasizes the wider political context. For a general discussion of the role of the federal courts in overcoming the costs of federalism, see Freyer, *Forums of Order* 99–141.

4 Compare Cornish, "Legal Control over Cartels and Monopolization," 283; Letwin, *Law and Economic Policy*, 42–46; Elisha Greenhood, "General Restrictions on Business Freedom," *Central Law Journal* 19 (July, 1884), 62–68; May, "Antitrust in the Formative Era," *Ohio State Law Journal* 50 No. 2 (1989), 309–331 to Sklar, *Corporate Reconstruction of American Capitalism*, 93–100. See also chapter 4.

5 As quoted, Dennison, "Reaction to the Growth of Trusts," 40 and accompanying text.

6 *Mogul Steamship Co.* v. *McGregor, Gow & Co.*, 66 *Law Times* 1 (1982); G. C. Allen, *Monopoly and Restrictive Practices* (London, 1968), 58.

7 *Thorsten Nordenfelt* v. *Maxim Nordenfelt Guns and Ammunition Co.*, 1894 AC 564; quoted passage is from Allen, *Monopoly and Restrictive Practices*, 59; see also Letwin, *Law and Economic Policy*, 42; May, "Antitrust in the Formative Era," *Ohio State Law Journal* 50 No. 2 (1989), 309–331. To support the contention that reasonableness had a nontechnical meaning prior to *Nordenfelt* compare *Mitchel* v. *Reynolds*, 1 Peere Wms 181 (1711) to Judge Nathaniel Lindley's opinion in *Mogul* 62 *Law Times*, 820, 838 (1889) the implications of which are explored in chapter 4.

8 *Ibid.*; and Sklar, *Corporate Reconstruction of American Capitalism*, 98, 184–203.

9 Allen, *Monopoly and Restrictive Practices*, 59; and see chapter 1, which explores this proposition.

10 As quoted, Dennison, "Reaction to the Growth of Trusts," 54, 56 and discussion in the text.

11 Chandler, *Visible Hand*, 320–325; Hovenkamp, "Labor Conspiracies," *Texas Law Review*, 66 (April 1988), 932–933; Freyer, *Forums of Order*, 99–141; Thomas S. Berry, "The Effect of Business Conditions on Early Judicial Decisions Concerning Restraint of Trade," *Economic History Review*, 10 (1950), 30–44; May, "Antitrust in the Formative Era," *Ohio State Law Journal* 50 No. 2 (1989), 309–331.

12 As quoted, Berry, "Effect of Business Decisions," *Economic History Review*, 10 (1950), 31.

13 Greenhood, "General Restrictions on Business Freedom," *Central Law Journal* 19 (July, 1884), 62.

14 *Ibid.*

15 Berry, "Effect of Business Decisions," *Economic History Review*, 10 (1950), 30–44.

16 George Candee Gale, "The Doctrine of Ultra Vires," *Central Law Journal* 48 (1899), 236. Compare, Keller, *Affairs of State*, 432–433; Charles W. McCurdy, "The Knight Sugar Decision of 1895 and the Modernization of American Corporation Law, 1869–1903," *Business History Review*, 53 (Autumn 1979), 304–343; and Hovenkamp, "Classical Corporation," *Georgetown Law Journal* 76 (June 1988), 1662–1667.

17 Judy Slinn, *A History of Freshfields* (London 1984), 109.

18 *Ibid.*, as quoted, 109.

19 *Ibid.*, as quoted, 109–110. However, this general concern for a liberal company law did not mean that solicitors or barristers challenged accountants as those primarily responsible for managing self-regulating, anticompetitive practices. See discussion chapter 4.

20 Macrosty, *The Trust Movement in British Industry* (London, 1907), 15–16; Chandler, *Scale and Scope*.

21 As quoted, Dennison, "Reaction to the Growth of Trusts," 207.

22 Payne, *British Entrepreneurship*, 16.

23 *Ibid.*, as quoted, 16, 17.

24 *Ibid.*, as quoted, 19.

25 Macrosty, *Trust Movement*, 16.

26 As quoted, William J. Reader, "Versatility Unlimited: Reflections on the History and Nature of the Limited Liability Company," in Orhnial, editor, *Limited Liability*, 200.

27 As quoted, Dennison, "Reaction to the Growth of Trusts," 70, 121, 124.

28 Freyer, *Forums of Order*, 101.

29 *Ibid.*, 104.

30 Chandler, *Invisible Hand*, 321–326.
31 Freyer, *Forums of Order*, 101.
32 Morris D. Forkosch, *Antitrust and the Consumer* (Buffalo, 1956), 223–224, 416–417; May, "Antitrust Practice and Procedure in the Formative Era," *University of Pennsylvania Law Review*, 134 (March 1987), 497–517. But see Sklar, *Corporate Reconstruction*, 154–173.
33 *Ibid.*
34 As quoted, Freyer, "Economic Liberty," in Paul and Dickman, editors, *Liberty, Property and Government*, 195–196.
35 *Ibid.*, as quoted, 196.
36 *Ibid.*, as quoted, 197.
37 As quoted, Thorelli, *Federal Antitrust Policy*, 155, note 193.
38 As quoted, Forkosch, *Antitrust and the Consumer*, 416–417, and see generally Section 2 or Appendix "A" for excerpts of state statutes involving antitrust enacted before or contemporaneously with the passage of the Sherman Act of 1890.
39 For general pattern of local protectionism see Freyer, *Forums of Order*, 99–141. More particularly, see May, "Antitrust Practice and Procedure in the Formative Era," *University of Pennsylvania Law Review*, 135 (March 1987), 507–540; May, "Antitrust in the Formative Era," *Ohio State Law Journal* 50 No. 2 (1989), 313–391.
40 As quoted, May, "Antitrust in the Formative Era," *Ohio State Law Journal* 50 no. 2 (1989), 333.
41 *The American Commonwealth* (2 volumes, 1901), II, 162.
42 As quoted, Jonathan Lurie, *Law and the Nation, 1865–1912* (New York 1983), 32.
43 See note 39; and McCurdy, "Knight Sugar Decision," *Business History Review*, 53 (Autumn 1979), 322; Bruce Bringhurst, *Antitrust and the Oil Monopoly, The Standard Oil Cases, 1890–1911* (Westport, Connecticut, 1979); Chandler, *Visible Hand*, 319–320, 323–333.
44 *Ibid.*; and James Willard Hurst, *Law and Social Order in the United States* (Ithaca, 1977), 252–253; and chapter 4. But see, Sklar *Corporate Reconstruction of American Capitalism*, 154–166.
45 Freyer, *Forums of Order*.
46 See note 39.
47 139 US 24 (1890); McCurdy, "Knight Sugar Decision," *Business History Review*, 53 (Autumn 1979), 320–321; Thorelli, *Federal Antitrust Policy*, 432–499.
48 For public opinion on this point see chapter 2.
49 See chapters 1 and 2.
50 Beer, *Modern British Politics*, 54–124.
51 P. J. Cain, "Railways 1870–1914: The Maturity of the Private System," *Transportation in Victorian Britain*, W. J. Freeman and D. H. Aldcroft, editors, (Manchester, 1986) 92–133; T. R. Gourvish, "The Railways and the Development of Managerial Enterprise in Britain, 1850–1939" in K. Kobayashi and H. Morikawa, editors, *Development*

of Managerial Enterprise (Tokyo, 1986), 185–210; P. J. Cain "Railway Combination and Government, 1900–1914," *The Economic History Review,* 25 (November 1972), 623–641.

52 As quoted, Cain, "Railways 1870–1914," Freeman and Aldroft, editors, *Transport in Victorian Britain,* 115.

53 *Ibid.,* as quoted, 113–114.

54 See note 51.

55 Beer, *Modern British Politics,* 109–125, 245–276. See also Ashworth, *Economic History,* 216–238; Atiyah, *Freedom of Contract,* 571–601.

56 *Ibid.;* Dennison, "Reaction to the Growth of Trusts." For the *Taff Vale* and Trade Disputes Act controversy see Robert Stevens, *Law and Politics, The House of Lords as a Judicial Body, 1800–1976* (Chapel Hill, 1978), 94–95, 114n, 124, 196n.

57 Stevens, *Law and Politics,* 94–95, 114n, 124, 196n.

58 As quoted, Dennison, "Reaction to the Growth of Trusts," 58, 59.

59 *Ibid.,* 54–56.

60 *Ibid.,* as quoted, 160–196.

61 *Ibid.,* as quoted, 166–167.

62 *Ibid.,* 169–172.

63 For example see below, discussion of Royal Commission on Shipping Rings.

64 Dennison, "Reaction to the Growth of Trusts," 44–72, 101–154; Hannah, *Rise of Corporate Economy,* 8–26.

65 *The Trust Movement in British Industry A Study of Business Organization* (London, 1907), 58.

66 There is little agreement on what the original intent of the Sherman Act was in so far as "protected groups" is concerned. Thorelli, *Federal Antitrust Policy* said the framers intended primarily to maintain competition, whereas Robert Bork, "Legislative Intent and the Policy of the Sherman Act," *Journal of Law & Economics* 9 (1966), 7 contended protection of consumers defined solely in terms of neoclassical efficiency. Except for those who accept Bork's ideological agenda, most writers see a multiplicity of goals, to some extent contradictory, influencing the legislative process. A sophisticated discussion following this argument is Hovenkamp, "Antitrust Protected Classes," *Michigan Law Review,* 88 (October 1989), 1–48 which confirms Letwin, *Law and Economic Policy,* 53–99. For another view see Sklar, *Corporate Reconstruction of American Capitalism,* 93–117.

67 As quoted, McCurdy, "Knight Sugar Decision," *Business History Review,* 53 (Autumn 1979), 324.

68 As quoted, Hovenkamp, "State Antitrust," *Indiana Law Journal* 58 (1983), 379.

69 As quoted, Weaver, *Decision to Prosecute,* 20–21.

70 *Ibid.,* as quoted.

71 As quoted, Letwin, *Law and Economic Policy,* 97.

72 As quoted, Sklar, *Corporate Reconstruction of American Capitalism,* 115–116. For the comparison of British and American judges see

Freyer, "Sherman Act," *Iowa Law Review*, 74 (July 1989); and see chapter 4.

73 Sherman Antitrust Act, ch. 647, 26 Stat. 209 (1890).

74 As quoted, Weaver, *Decision to Prosecute*, 25.

75 See chapter 4, and above.

76 As quoted, McCurdy, "Knight Sugar Decision," *Business History Review*, 43 (Autumn 1979), 323, 327.

77 Chandler, *Visible Hand*, 438–450.

78 Thorelli, *Federal Antitrust Policy*, 266.

79 May, "Antitrust Practice and Procedure," *University of Pennsylvania* 135 (March 1987), 500–503.

80 May, "Antitrust in the Formative Era," *Ohio State Law Journal* 50 No. 2 (1989), 331–340; Freyer, *Forums of Order*, 100–104; Morris D. Forkosch, *Antitrust and the Consumer* (Buffalo, 1956), 223–224, 416–417; Hovenkamp, "Antitrust Movement," *Texas Law Review*, 68 (November 1989), 130–134. See also chapter 2 and chapter 4.

81 As quoted, May, "Antitrust in the Formative Era," *Ohio State Law Journal* 50 no. 2 (1989), 336.

82 *Ibid.*, as quoted, 333, 336.

83 James C. Bonbright and Gardiner C. Means, *The Holding Company, Its Public Significance and Its Regulation* (New York, 1969), 66, 68–69.

84 Thorelli, *Federal Antitrust Policy*, 436–444, but see private suits where the reverse was true, 477–499. Perhaps the greatest divergence was in the antitrust decisions of the 5th and 2nd US Circuit Courts: Dwight M. Jett, Jr. "A Comparison of the 5th and 2nd Circuit Antitrust Decisions in the 1890s" (unpublished law student paper 1989); and Letwin, *Law and Economic Policy*, 144–152.

85 *US* v. *E. C. Knight Co.*, 156 U.S. 1 (1895). Compare: McCurdy, "Knight Sugar Decision," *Business History Review*, 53 (Autumn 1979), 304–343; Thorelli, *Federal Antitrust Policy*, 445–448; Letwin, *Law and Economic Policy*, 121–127. See also chapter 4.

86 *US* v *Trans-Missouri Freight Ass'n*, 166 U.S. 290 (1897); and commentary (including relation to Debs and the Pullman strike): Letwin, *Law and Economic Policy*, 123–142, 153–181; Sklar, *Corporate Reconstruction of American Capitalism*, 124–145; Thorelli, *Federal Antitrust Policy*, 452–470. These reverences also include discussion of the cases where there was, arguably at least, some modification of Peckham's literal interpretation, the most important of which was *US* v.*Addyston Pipe and Steel Co.*, 175 US 211 (1899). See also Chandler, *Visible Hand*, 331–334; and chapters 1 and 4 for further analysis, including the affect of uncertainty on corporate lawyers.

87 *Ibid.*, and notes 83–85.

88 13 (November 1899), 199. But see Sklar, *Corporate Reconstruction of American Capitalism*, 162–163.

89 Bonbright and Means, *Holding Company*, 67–69; Edward Q. Keasbey, *Harvard Law Review*, 13 (November 1899), 201; and chapters 1 and 4.

90 For the relative security or insecurity of middle men as a source of

interest-group pressure or its lack compare Chandler, *Scale and Scope* 255–260, and *Visible Hand*, 209–239, 315–375. See generally, Macrosty, *Trust Movement.*

91 Macrosty, *Trust Movement*, 81. See also Dennison, "Reaction to the Growth of Trusts," 101–120; and P. Lesley Cook, *Effects of Mergers, Six Studies* (London 1958), 28–63, 133–177, 215–225, 279–296.

92 Macrosty, *Trust Movement*, 82, 128–129.

93 *Ibid.*, 163; and Cook, *Effects of Mergers*, 28–63, 133–177, 215 225, 279–296; Dennison, "Reaction to the Growth of Trusts," 101–120.

94 G. C. Allen, *Monopoly and Restrictive Practices* (London 1968), 58–59. See also chapters 1 and 4.

95 Chandler, *Scale and Scope* 242–248; Macrosty, *Trust Movement*, 230–239; B. W. E. Alford, "Penny Cigarettes, Oligopoly, and Entrepreneurship in the UK Tobacco Industry in the Late Nineteenth Century," in Barry Supple, editor, *Essays in British Business History* (Oxford 1977), 49–68.

96 *Ibid.*

97 Macrosty, *Trust Movement*, 238, 239.

98 *Ibid.*, 204, 205.

99 *Ibid.*, 261, 263; Charles Wilson, *History of Unilever* (2 volumes, London 1954), I, 30–48; Ruth Cohen, "The Soap Industry," in Cook, *Effects of Mergers*, 215–228.

100 *Ibid.*; for quote, Wilson, *History of Unilever*, I, 88.

101 *Ibid.*

102 See notes 50–53 and discussion in text.

103 As quoted, Cain, "Railways 1870–1914," in Freeman and Aldcroft, editors, *Transportation in Victorian Britain*, 120.

104 Macrosty, *Trust Movement*, 290–307, quote at 307. See also, Dennison "Reaction to the Growth of Trusts." 226–242; and chapter 1.

105 *Ibid.*

106 As quoted, Dennison, "Reaction to the Growth of Trusts," 230, 235, 236.

107 *Ibid.*, as quoted 235–236, 237.

108 *Ibid.*, 237.

109 *Royal Commission on Shipping Rings*, 1909 (Col. 4668), 117, 118.

110 As quoted, Dennison, "Reaction to the Growth of Trusts," 241.

111 *Ibid.*, 241–242.

112 *Ibid.*, 238.

113 See chapter 1 and above.

114 Compare note 109, and notes chapter 1.

115 The literature on the Progressive-era Presidents' response to the trust issue, particularly the growing reliance on bureaucracy, is large. An influential view remains Richard Hofstadter, *The Age of Reform* (New York 1955). Except for the treatment of the rule of reason, probably the best recent work is Sklar, *Corporate Reconstruction of American Capitalism*, 285–430. See also McCraw, *Prophets of Regulation*, 108–142. An excellent overview, including an incisive discussion of the rule of

reason, is Bickel and Schmidt, *Judiciary and Responsible Government*, 86–199.

116 As quoted, Livingston, "Social Analysis of Economic History," *American Historical Review*, 92 (February 1897), 84.

117 Thorelli, *Federal Antitrust Policy*, 254–368; Kirkland, *Industry Comes of Age*, 201–215, 262–277, 306–324; McCraw, *Prophets of Regulation*, 108–142; Sklar, *Corporate Reconstruction of American Capitalism*, 285–430; Freyer, "Economic Liberty," in Paul and Dickman, editors, *Liberty, Property and Government* (Albany 1989), 187–216.

118 As quoted, Lewis L. Gould, *The Presidency of William McKinley* (Lawrence, Kansas, 1983), 163.

119 As quoted, Freyer, "Economic Liberty," in Paul and Dickman, editors, *Liberty, Property and Government* (Albany 1989), 204–205.

120 *Ibid.*, as quoted, 197.

121 *Ibid.*, as quoted, 205.

122 *Ibid.*, as quoted.

123 May, "Antitrust in the Formative Era," *Ohio State Law Journal* 50 No. 2 (1989), 313–340; May, "Antitrust Practice and Procedure in the Formative Era," *University of Pennsylvania Law Review*, 135 (March 1987), 507–540; Bringhurst, *Antitrust and the Oil Monopoly*, 10–108; Joseph Pratt, "The Petroleum Industry in Transition: Antitrust and the Decline of Monopoly Control in Oil, *Journal of Economic History* 40 (1980), 40–59.

124 As quoted, Richard A. Hofstadter, *The Progressive Movement 1900–1915* (New York, 1963), 141–142; and as quoted William Lee Baldwin, *Antitrust and the Changing Corporation* (Durham, North Carolina, 1961), 37.

125 As quoted, Hofstadter, *Progressive Movement*, 143.

126 Thorelli, *Federal Antitrust Policy*, 534–549; Weaver, *Decision to Prosecute*, 27–28.

127 *US* v. *Northern Securities Co.*, 193 US 197 (1904); Thorelli, *Federal Antitrust Policy*, 420–431, 470–475; Letwin, *Law and Economic Policy*, 207–237. See also chapter 4.

128 See discussion and materials cited, chapter 4.

129 As quoted, Letwin, *Law and Economic Policy*, 237.

130 Compare, Sklar, *Corporate Reconstruction of American Capitalism*, 179–203; Thorelli, *Federal Antitrust Policy*, 551–55.

131 As quoted, Carl Resek, editor, *The Progressives* (Indianapolis, Indiana, 1967), 192.

132 Sklar, *Corporate Reconstruction of American Capitalism*, 182, 189, 203–286.

133 *Ibid.*, 183–203.

134 See discussion above, notes 4–14, 66–72; and the fuller analysis developed in chapter 4.

135 Sklar, *Corporate Reconstruction of American Capitalism*, 184–203, 334–364.

136 Bickel and Schmidt, *Judiciary and Responsible Government*, 95–100, 126–141.

137 *Ibid.*, 136–137; McCraw, *Prophets of Regulation*, 109–126.

138 Bickel and Schmidt, *Judiciary and Responsible Government,* 110–111.
139 *Ibid.,* as quoted, 95.
140 *Ibid.,* as quoted, 97.
141 *Standard Oil Co.* v. *US,* 221 US 1 (1911); *US* v. *American Tobacco Co.,* 221 US 105 (1911). For discussion and analysis see chapter 4.
142 *Ibid.*
143 As quoted, Bickel and Schmidt, *Judiciary and Responsible Government,* 123.
144 *Ibid.,* 107–129; and chapter 4.
145 As quoted, Freyer, "Economic Liberty," in Paul and Dickman, editors, *Liberty, Property, and Government* (Albany 1989), 204.
146 Bickel and Schmidt, *Judiciary and Responsible Government,* 127–129; Sklar, *Corporate Reconstruction of American Capitalism,* 364–382.
147 As quoted, McCraw, *Prophets of Regulation,* 111. For rest of discussion in this paragraph, compare McCraw and Sklar, *Corporate Reconstruction of American Capitalism,* 383–430.
148 Freyer, "Economic Liberty," in Paul and Dickman, editors, *Liberty, Property and Government* (Albany 1989), 204–210.
149 Sklar, *Corporate Reconstruction of American Capitalism,* 335–430.
150 Note 148; and chapter 4.
151 *Ibid.;* for McReynolds, as quoted, Bickel and Schmidt, *Judiciary and Responsible Government,* 117.
152 Note 123.
153 Bonbright and Means, *Holding Company,* 57.
154 McCraw, *Prophets of Regulation,* 144–145.
155 *Ibid.;* Sklar, *Corporate Reconstruction of American Capitalism,* 151–152, 420; Freyer, "Economic Liberty," in Paul and Dickman, editors, *Liberty, Property, and Government* (Albany 1989), 204–210.
156 Sklar, *Corporate Reconstruction of American Capitalism,* 90, 171n, 187, 172, 285, 328–332, 381, 420–424; McCraw, *Prophets of Regulation,* 112–142.

4 THE COURTS RESPOND TO BIG BUSINESS

1 *The Anti-Trust Act and the Supreme Court* (New York, 1914), 4, 47.
2 *Mogul Steamship Co.* v. *McGregor, Gow & Co.,* 59, *Law Times* 514, 520 (1888).
3 *Mogul Steamship Co.* v. *McGregor, Gow & Co.,* 62, *Law Times* 820 (1889); *Mogul Steamship Co.* v. *McGregor, Gow & Co.,* 66, *Law Times* 1 (1892).
4 See chapter 3, and discussion in text and notes below for evidence supporting this view. But see Martin J. Sklar, *The Corporate Reconstruction of American Capitalism, 1890–1916, The Market, the Law, and Politics* (Cambridge, England 1988), and Donald Dewey, "The Common-Law Background of Antitrust Policy," *Virginia Law Review,* 41 (October 1955), 759–786. Herbert Hovenkamp, "Labor Conspiracies in American Law, 1880–1930," *Texas Law Review,* 66 (April 1988) especially pages 932–933 notes the fallacy which flawed Dewey's

argument. See also James May, "Antitrust in the Formative Era: Political and Economic Theory in Constitutional and Antitrust Analysis, 1880–1918," *Ohio State Law Journal*, 50, no. 2 (1989), 311–331.

5 See discussion below; May, "Antitrust in the Formative Era," *Ohio State Law Journal*, 50 (1989), 311–331; and chapter 3.

6 See discussion below.

7 62, *Law Times* 820, 838 (1889).

8 *US* v. *Addyston Pipe & Steel Co.*, 85 F. 271 (6th Cir. 1898), at 283. See Robert Bork, *The Antitrust Paradox: A Policy at War with Itself* (New York, 1978), 27 noting that Taft's opinion was not so much a restatement as a new departure, a view confirmed by May, "Antitrust in the Formative Era," *Ohio State Law Journal*, 50 (1989), 311–331.

9 As noted above, Sklar, *Corporate Reconstruction of American Capitalism*, adopts Taft's view that the rule of reason was always inherent in the British and American common law governing restrictive business practices. This chapter, continues, the argument of the preceding chapters in the attempt to suggest the need for an alternative thesis.

10 William R. Cornish, "Legal Control over Cartels and Monopolization, 1880–1914: A Comparison," in Norbert Horn and Jurgen Kocka, eds., *Law and the Formation of Big Enterprises in the 19th and Early 20th Centuries* (Gottingen; Vandenhoeck & Ruprecht, 1979); Hans B. Thorelli, *The Federal Antitrust Policy* (Baltimore, 1955), 9–53, 280–303; William Letwin, *Law and Economic Policy in America, The Evolution of the Sherman Antitrust Act* (Chicago, 1981), 19–52; P. S. Atiyah, *The Rise and Fall of Freedom of Contract* (Oxford, U.K., 1979), 697–700. For a view which assumes that the English law *was* static see Sklar, *The Corporate Reconstruction of American Capitalism*, 154–166. See also, Tony Freyer, "The Sherman Act, Comparative Business Structure, and the Rule of Reason: America and Great Britain, 1880–1920," 74, *Iowa Law Review*, July 1989) 991–1018.

11 *Thorsten Nordenfelt* v. *Maxim Nordenfelt Guns and Ammunition Co.* 1894 AC 535, 564.

12 Cornish, "Legal Control over Cartels," 281–282; Letwin, *Law and Economic Policy*, 32–52; see also chapter 3.

13 1894 AC, 564.

14 *Ibid.*, 565; Letwin, *Law and Economic Policy*, 42–45; Cornish, "Legal Control over Cartels," 284–285. For the implications of the law for family enterprise see chapter 1 and below.

15 *Mogul Steamship Co.* v. *McGregor, Gow & Co.*, 59, *Law Times* 514 (1888); *Mogul Steamship Co.* v. *McGregor, Gow & Co.*, 62, *Law Times* 820 (1889); *Mogul Steamship Co.* v. *McGregor, Gow & Co.*, 66, *Law Times* 1 (1892). For the business dimensions of the conference system see chapter 1.

16 For the votes see the decisions cited in notes 2 and 3. Fry's quote is at 61 *Law Times* 828.

17 61 *Law Times*, 826, 827, 829.

18 66 *Law Times* 4.
19 See chapter 1.
20 *Maxim Nordenfelt Guns and Ammunition Co.* v. *Nordenfelt*, 67 *Law Times* 469 (1892); *Maxim Nordenfelt Guns and Ammunition Co.* v. *Nordenfelt*, 68 *Law Times* 833 (1892); *Maxim Nordenfelt Guns and Ammunition Co.* v. *Nordenfelt*, 69 *Law Times* 471 (1893); *Nordenfelt* v. *Maxim Nordenfelt Guns*, 1894 A.C. 535.
21 1894 A.C. 533, 555.
22 *Ibid.*, 558, 561.
23 *Ibid.*, 575.
24 *Ibid.*, 565.
25 *Ibid.*, 551.
26 *Elliman, Sons & Co.* v. *Carrington & Son, Ltd.*, 1901 2 Ch. 275.
27 *Ibid.*, 279, 280. Note that the Court declined to enforce the agreement by issuing an injunction. Compare, Atiyah, *Freedom of Contract*, 699.
28 *British United Shoe Machinery Co. Ltd.* v. *Somervell Bros.*, 95 *Law Times* [Ch.] 711, 713, 714 (1907). BUSM was a subsidiary of the American company. See *US* v. *United Shoe Manufacturing Co.*, 258 U.S. 451 (1915).
29 *USMC of Canada* v. *Brunet*, 1909 A.C. 330, 343, 344.
30 *Attorney-General of the Commonwealth of Australia* v. *The Adelaide Steamship Co. Ltd.*, 1913 A.C. 781, 782.
31 *Ibid.*, 800, 801, 802, 810, 813.
32 *North Western Salt Co. Ltd.* v. *Electrolytic Alkali Co., Ltd.*, 1913, 3 K.B. 422; *North Western Salt Co. Ltd.* v. *Electrolytic Alkali Co., Ltd.*, 1914, A.C. 46.
33 1914 A.C. 469, 471.
34 Letwin, *Law and Economic Policy*, 265, though noting the similarity between the British and American rule, nevertheless, describes the degree to which Chief Justice White's formulation (see below) was "idiosyncratic." For a somewhat different perspective which follows closely the material presented in this and the previous section, see Freyer, "Sherman Act, Comparative Business Structure, and the Rule of Reason."
35 Alfred D. Chandler, Jr., *The Visible Hand, The Managerial Revolution in American Business* (Cambridge, Massachusetts, 1977), 315–344, 375–376; and Leslie Hannah, "Mergers, Cartels and Concentration: Legal Factors in the US and European Experience," in Horn and Kocka, eds. *Law and the Formulation of Big Enterprise*, 306–315, argue for the linkage between antitrust and business, a thesis developed in Freyer, "Sherman Act, Comparative Business Structure, and the Rule of Reason." But see Sklar, *Corporate Reconstruction*, 154–175; and Thorelli, *Federal Antitrust Policy*. For citation to cases, see below.
36 Freyer, "Sherman Act, Comparative Business Structure, and the Rule of Reason;" *Iowa Law Review*, 74 (1989); Alfred Chandler, "The Development of Modern Management Structure in the US and UK," in Thomas K. McCraw, ed., *The Essential Alfred Chandler: Essays Toward A Historical Theory of Big Business*, 364. Interestingly, Sklar,

Corporate Reconstruction, 317–318 provides some evidence for this view. See also James C. Bonbright and Gardiner C. Means, *The Holding Company* (New York, 1969), 51–65.

37 Chandler, *Visible Hand*, 377–454.

38 *State* v. *American Cotton Oil Trust*, 1 *Ry. & Corp. L.J.* 509 (La. 1888); *People* v. *Chicago Gas Trust Co.*, 130 Ill. 268 (1889); *State* v. *North River Sugar Refining Co.*, 121 N.Y. 582 (1889); *People* v. *American Sugar Refining Co.*, 7 *Ry. & Corp. L.J.* 83 (Cal. 1895); *State* v. *Nebraska Distilling Co.*, 29 Neb. 700 (1890); *Distilling & Cattle Feeding Co.* v. *People*, 156 Ill. 448 (1895); *State* v. *Standard Oil Co.*, 49 Ohio St. 137 (1892); and Charles W. McCurdy, "The *Knight* Sugar Decision of 1895 and The Modernization of American Corporation Law, 1869–1903," *Business History Review*, LIII (Autumn 1979), 304–342. For the revisions of state common law and statutes in order to strengthen the means of prosecution see: Morris D. Forkosch, *Antitrust and the Consumer* (Buffalo, 1956), 223–224, 416–417; and especially James May, "Antitrust Practice and Procedure in the Formative Era: The Constitutional and Conceptual Reach of State Antitrust Law, 1880–1918," *University of Pennsylvania Law Review*, 135 (March 1987), 497–517. See also Thorelli, *Federal Antitrust Policy*, 259–265; Bruce Bringhurst, *Antitrust and the Oil Monopoly, the Standard Oil Cases, 1890–1911* (Westport, Connecticut, 1979). But see Sklar, *Corporate Reconstruction*, 154–173.

39 Bringhurst, *Oil Monopoly*, 10–68; Joseph A. Pratt, "The Petroleum Industry in Transition: Antitrust and the Decline of Monopoly Control in Oil," *Journal of Economic History*, 40 (December 1980), 815–837.

40 Herbert Hovenkamp, "State Antitrust in the Federal Scheme," *Indiana Law Journal*, 58 (Spring 1983), 378–379.

41 Bonbright and Means, *Holding Company*, 70–71.

42 28 So. Rep. 669, 670 (Alabama, 1900).

43 *Ibid.*, 672–673. Compare, discussion of *Nordenfelt*, above.

44 May, "Antitrust Practice and Procedure," 503.

45 *Federal Antitrust Policy*, 266.

46 McCurdy, "*Knight* Sugar Decision," 304–342; Letwin, *Law and Economic Policy*, 85–181; Thorelli, *Federal Antitrust Policy*, 96–107; May, "Antitrust Practice and Procedure," 507–521.

47 Letwin, *Law and Economic Policy*, 108–115; Thorelli, *Federal Antitrust Policy*, 369–388. Compare, the *Adelaide Steamship* case discussed above.

48 *US* v. *EC Knight Co.*, 156 US 1 (1895); Letwin, *Law and Economic Policy*, 121–122, 161–167; McCurdy, "*Knight* Sugar Decision," 328–340. Further discussion below. But see Sklar, *Corporate Reconstruction*, 160–161.

49 Robert L. Raymond, "The Federal Antitrust Act," *Harvard Law Review*, 23 (February 1910), 376–377; Bonbright and Means, *Holding Company*, 49; and discussion below. But see Sklar, *Corporate Reconstruction*, 162–163.

50 See notes 35, 38, 44, and 45.

51 *In re Debs*, 158 US 564 (1895); Letwin, *Law and Economic Policy*, 123–130, 155–161; William E. Forbath, "The Shaping of the American Labor Movement," *Harvard Law Review*, 102 (February 1989), 1160–1165.

52 *US* v. *Trans-Missouri Freight Association*, 166 US 290 (1896); Letwin, *Law and Economic Policy*, 167–172. But see Sklar, *Corporate Reconstruction*, 161.

53 166 US 290, 322–323.

54 *Ibid.*, 323, 324. But see Robert Bork, *The Antitrust Paradox: A Policy at War with Itself* (New York, 1978), 25.

55 Hannah, *Rise of Corporate Economy*, 23. For further discussion of the interconnection between legal and financial factors see chapters 1 and 3.

56 *Addyston Pipe and Steel Co.* v. *US*, 175 US 211 (1899); *US* v. *Joint Traffic Association*, 171 US 505 (1898); *Hopkins* v. *US*, 171 US 578 (1898). For discussion see Letwin, *Law and Economic Policy*, 172–181.

57 *US* v. *Northern Securities Co.*, 193 US 197 (1903). Letwin, *Law and Economic Policy*, 201–237. Although the *E. C. Knight* case involved a holding company, the issue of interstate commerce was raised by neither the Justice Department nor the majority opinion. Until *Northern Securities* every other case involved a "loose" business structure, such as a price-fixing agreement. These decisions and those of the states, as well as the government's failure to challenge "tight" corporate structures provided lawyers with the only basis for advising their clients. For general discussion see below.

58 *Loewe* v. *Lawlor*, 208 US 274, 307 (1908). See Sklar, *Corporate Reconstruction*, 223–226; and Letwin, *Law and Economic Policy*, 275.

59 *US* v. *Standard Oil*, 221 US 1, 56, 62, 75 (1911).

60 *US* v. *American Tobacco*, 221 US 106, 179 (1911).

61 *Ibid.*

62 Alexander M. Bickel and Benno C. Schmidt, Jr., *The Judiciary and Responsible Government, 1910–1921* (New York, 1984), 108–109.

63 See discussion of the *Mogul* and *Nordenfelt* case above.

64 220 US 373 (1911); see also Bickel and Schmidt, *Judiciary and Responsible Government*, 703–706.

65 Bickel and Schmidt, *Judiciary and Responsible Government*, 136, 704, 707–708; McCraw, *Prophets of Regulation*, 101–108.

66 A. D. Neale and D. G. Goyder, *The Antitrust Laws of The United States of America, A Study of Competition Enforced by Law* (Cambridge, UK, 1982), 249–253.

67 Thomas K. McCraw, *Prophets of Regulation, Charles Francis Adams, Louis D. Brandeis, James M. Landis, Alfred E. Kahn* (Cambridge, Massachusetts, 1984), 144–147. For private suits see above.

68 *US* v. *Aluminum Co. of America* (1912), in Antitrust Consent Decrees, 1906–1966 (American Enterprise Institute, Washington, DC, 1968), 217; *U.S. American Telephone and Telegraph Co.* (1914), *ibid.*, 275;

George David Smith, *From Monopoly to Competition The Transformation of Alcoa, 1888–1986* (Cambridge, England, 1988), 111–113; Bickel and Schmidt, *Judiciary and Responsible Government*, 170; *US* v. *E. I. DuPont*, 188 Fed. Rep. 127 (Circuit Court D. Delaware, 1911).

69 Later, this outcome resulted because the law's framers were unable to agree upon language which simply denied that the statute applied to labor. Instead, they resorted to ambiguous phraseology which said that the antitrust laws were not to be construed to prohibit labor unions or the lawful conduct thereof. For cases which construed the Act's ambiguous language so as to defeat union activity see: *Duplex Printing Press Co.* v. *Deering*, 254 US 443 (1921); *American Steel Foundries* v. *Tri-City Central Trades Council*, 257 US 184 (1921). For a view of the Clayton Act which differs sharply from Letwin's and that presented here see: A. T. Mason, *Organized Labor and the Law* (Princeton, 1925) 119–131.

70 Morton Keller, "The Pluralist State: American Economic Regulation in Comparative Perspective, 1900–1930," Thomas McCraw, ed., Regulation in Perspective: Historical Essays, 76–78 (Boston, 1981). Bickel and Schmidt, *Judiciary and Responsible Government*, 662–663. The Federal Trade Commission Act of 1914 established a federal agency with power to forbid unfair competitive or deceptive practices; it left to the agency, however, the power to determine what "unfair" meant. Although Brandeis, who had influenced the law's passage, had hoped the Commission would use its ambiguous authority to support the practices of small business and defeat those of big business, the Supreme Court, as it had with the Clayton Act, construed the grant of authority quite narrowly. As a result, the Commission was able primarily only to research and publish information pertaining to "unfair practices," but lacked the power to actually prevent most such practices. See *F.T.C.* v. *Gratz*, 253 US 421 (1920).

71 See note 36.

72 As quoted, John Braeman, *Before the Civil Rights Revolution The Old Court and Individual Rights* (Westport, Connecticut, 1988), 27.

73 As quoted, Robert Stevens, *Law and Politics, The House of Lords as a Judicial Body, 1800–1976* (Chapel Hill, 1978), 103.

74 *Ibid.*, as quoted, 104.

75 *Ibid.*, 149–181; Brian Abel-Smith and Robert Stevens, *Lawyers and the Courts, A Sociological Study of the English Legal System, 1750–1965* (Cambridge, Massachusetts, 1967), 112–115.

76 As quoted, Stevens, *Law and Politics*, 160.

77 As quoted, Abel-Smith and Stevens, *Lawyers and the Courts*, 112.

78 *Mogul Steamship Co.* v. *McGregor, Gow & Co.*, 23 (1889) Q.B. 598, 626.

79 On the limited, though important scope of Macnaghten's activism, see Stevens, *Law and Politics*, 99, 117. On the prevalence of freedom of contract and free trade see Atiyah, *Rise and Fall of Freedom of Contract*, 697–699.

80 *Allen* v. *Flood* (1898), A.C. 1. Abel-Smith and Stevens, *Lawyers and the Courts*, 112.

81 *Quinn* v. *Leatham* (1901), A.C. 495, 506; *Taff Vale Railway Co.* v. *Amalgamated Society of Railway Servants* (1901), A.C. 426. Stevens, *Law and Politics*, 91–92.

82 As quoted, Stevens, *Law and Politics*, 94; and see generally, 92–96.

83 *Ibid.*, as quoted, 96.

84 For the relation of self-restraint to the comparative unimportance of courts to British business, see Abel-Smith and Stevens, *Lawyers and the Courts*, 79–100. See also, discussion below.

85 On the use of republican values and the ambivalence of American popular attitudes toward big and small business, see, Tony Freyer, "Economic Liberty, Antitrust, and the Constitution, 1880–1925," in E. F. Paul and H. Dickman, editors., *Liberty, Property, and Government* (SUNY, Binghampton, 1989) 187–215; P. S. Atiyah and Robert S. Summers, *Form and Substance in Anglo-American Law, A Comparative Study of Legal Reasoning, Legal Theory, and Legal Institutions* (Oxford, UK, 1987), 245–257.

86 As quoted, May, "Antitrust Practice and Procedure," 532.

87 For the interplay of national party politics, the Court's labor injunction decisions, organized labor, and the irony that similar ideology supported labor and the NAM's attack upon it see: Sklar, *Corporate Reconstruction*, 223–228, 356–357, 405–406; Forbath, "American Labor Movement," 1148–1179.

88 *People of California* v. *American Sugar Refining Co.*, *Ry. & Corp. L.J.*, VII (1890), 83, 86.

89 See above, and chapter 3.

90 See note 56.

91 See note 56 and 57.

92 As quoted, Bickel and Schmidt, *Judiciary and Responsible Government*, 180.

93 Bickel and Schmidt, *Judiciary and Responsible Government*, 144–199; McCraw, *Prophets of Regulation*, 144–147.

94 Sklar, *Corporate Reconstruction*, 151–154; Chandler, "Modern Management Structure in the US and UK," 364.

95 The characterization of White's formulation of rule of reason as "idiosyncratic" comes from Letwin, *Law and Economic Policy*, 265. Here generally I follow Letwin, though for broader discussion of the decision and republican values, see Freyer, "Economic Liberty." See also the comparison of White's rule of reason to Macnaghton's rule of reasonableness discussed above.

96 Atiyah and Summers, *Form and Substance*, 240–255.

97 See above.

98 As quoted, May, "Antitrust Practice and Procedure," 586, 587. For Holmes and positivism generally see Atiyah and Summers, *Form and Substance*, 246–248, 251–252.

99   As quoted Bickel and Schmidt, *Judiciary and Responsible Government*, 704.
100 As quoted, May, "Antitrust Practice and Procedure," 587.
101 As quoted, Richard A. Cosgrove, *Our Lady The Common Law : An Anglo-American Legal Community, 1870–1930* (New York, 1987), 107.
102 White to Henry P. Dart, 13 February 1917; White to Henry P. Dart, 21 April 1917. Archives and Manuscripts Department of the Earl K. Long Library of the University of New Orleans.
103 Abel-Smith and Stevens, *Lawyers and the Courts*, 79.
104 *Ibid.*, as quoted, 81.
105 As quoted, Tony Allan Freyer, *Forums of Order : The Federal Courts and Business in American History* (Greenwich, Connecticut, 1979).
106 As quoted, Bickel and Schmidt, *Judiciary and Responsible Government*, 140.
107 As quoted, Stevens, *Law and Politics*, 284.
108 See above.
109 *Ibid.*
110 As quoted, May, "Antitrust Practice and Procedure," 505.
111 As quoted, Stevens, *Law and Politics*, 85.
112 *Ibid.*, 84–104; and the cases discussed above.
113 Freyer, *Forums and Order*, 99–142.
114 See above.
115 Bickel and Schmidt, *Judiciary and Responsible Government*, 71.
116 As quoted, Abel-Smith and Stevens, *Lawyers and the Courts*, 209–210, 227.
117 *Ibid.*, 209.
118 *Ibid.*, as quoted, 179, 167, 229.
119 As quoted, Bickel and Schmidt, *Judiciary and Responsible Government*, 705.
120 John C. Gray, *The Nature and Sources of the Law* (New York, 1909), 369.
121 Robert L. Raymond, "The Federal Anti-Trust Act," *Harvard Law Review*, 23 (February 1910), 354.
122 As quoted, Bickel and Schmidt, *Judiciary and Responsible Government*, 166.
123 "The Present Legal Status of Trusts," *Harvard Law Review*, 7 (October 1893), 162.
124 "Federal Anti-Trust Act," 375.
125 As quoted, Bickel and Schmidt, *Judiciary and Responsible Government*, 141.
126 Lawrence M. Friedman, *A History of American Law* (New York, 1985), 636–641. Nancy Lisagor and Frank Lipsius, *A Law Unto Itself, The Untold Story of the Law Firm Sullivan & Cromwell* (New York, 1988).
127 Lisagor and Lipsius, *A Law Unto Itself*, 26, 27.
128 *Ibid.*, as quoted, 34; for the *Northern Securities Case*, and after, see *ibid*, 38.
129 The study of this second market for legal services is just beginning. Brandeis, of course, is the most famous representative (see below for

discussion and references). Friedman, *History of American Law*, 305–306, 482, 648 and Tony Freyer, "The Supreme Court and Progressivism: Bickel and Schmidt's *History of the Supreme Court,*" *American Bar Foundation Research Journal*, 1987 (Fall 1987), 824–826 are suggestive. See also references to Frederick Newton Judson, in Sklar, *Corporate Reconstruction*, 210, 211, 285, 288; and McCraw, *Prophets of Regulation*, 101–108.

130 As quoted, Tony Freyer, *Harmony & Dissonance: The Swift & Erie Cases in American Federalism* (New York, 1981), 95.

131 *Ibid.*, as quoted.

132 *Ibid.*, as quoted, 96.

133 Allon Gal, *Brandeis of Boston* (Cambridge, Massachusetts, 1980), 11–16. See also Philippa Strum, *Louis D. Brandeis Justice for the People* (New York, 1984), 30–41.

134 As quoted, Gal, *Brandeis of Boston*, 25–26.

135 McCraw, *Prophets of Regulation*, 101–108; Bickel and Schmidt, *Judiciary and Responsible Government*, 136, 706–709.

136 For the private suits and successful federal prosecutions, see: May, "Antitrust Practice and Procedure," 503; Bickel and Schmidt, *Judiciary and Responsible Government*, 180–199.

137 Bickel and Schmidt, *Judiciary and Responsible Government*, 106, 170–171, 180–199; McCraw, *Prophets of Regulation*, 144–145.

5 THE IMPACT OF WORLD WAR I, 1914–1921

1 Useful overviews of the organizational impact of the war on both the public and private sectors of the British and American economies are: Sidney Pollard, *The Development of the British Economy, 1914–1980* (London, 1983), 1–50; Leslie Hannah, *The Rise of the Corporate Economy* (London, 1983), 27–53; Robert F. Himmelberg, *The Origins of the National Recovery Administration, Business, Government, and the Trade Association Issue, 1921–1933* (New York, 1976), 5–25; Robert D. Cuff, "Business, the State, and World War I: The American Experience," Jordan A. Schwartz, editor, *The Ordeal of Twentieth-Century America: Interpretive Readings* (Boston, 1974), 48–63; Robert F. Himmelberg, "Business, Antitrust Policy, and the Industrial Board of the Department of Commerce, 1919," *Business History Review*, 42 (Spring 1968), 1–19. Alfred D. Chandler, Jr. *Scale and Scope* (Cambridge, Massachusetts, 1990).

2 *Economist*, December 1 (1917), 868; Hannah, *Corporate Economy*, 41–53. For a more detailed discussion see text and references below notes 7–9, 75–94.

3 Himmelberg, *Origins of the National Recovery Administration*, 5–25; Cuff, "Business, the State, and World War I," in Schwartz, editor, *Ordeal*, 48–63; Himmelberg, "Business, Antitrust Policy, and the Industrial Board," *Business History Review*, 42 (Spring 1968), 1–19; Robert D. Cuff, "Antitrust Adjourned: Mobilizations and the Rise of the

National Security State," *National Competition Policy Historians' Perspectives on Antitrust and Government-Business Relationships in the United States* (Washington, DC, 1981), 208–259.

4 *Report of the Committee on Trusts Parliamentary Papers*, XIII (Cmd 5835, 1918), 17, 32–34, directly quoted at 34. For the American side, see text and references below, notes 97–117. The direct quote is from *American Column Co.* v. *US*, 257 US 377 (1921) at 384.

5 Pollard, *Development of the British Economy*, 1–12, 19–38; J. D. Gribbin, *The Post-War Revival of Competition As Industrial Policy, Government Economic Service Working Paper No. 19* (December 1978), 1, 5; *Report of the Committee on Trusts*, 13 (1918), 1–43; Hannah, *Corporate Economy*, 27–28.

6 Chandler, *Scale and Scope*; *Report of the Committee on Trusts* (1918), 1–43; Gribbin, *Revival of Competition*, 1, 5.

7 Pollard, *Development of the British Economy*, 29–38; William F. Notz and Richard S. Harvey, *America Foreign Trade As Promoted by the Webb-Pomerene and Edge Acts* (Indianapolis, 1921), 134–139; Hannah, *Corporate Economy*, 27–43.

8 "The Pre-War Position [of the public policy toward monopoly]" 3–4, BT64/318.

9 *Ibid.*

10 R. P. T. Davenport-Hines, *Dudley Docker The Life of a Trade Warrior* (Cambridge, UK, 1984), 78–83.

11 *Ibid.*, as quoted, 81.

12 *Ibid.*, 105–132. See also the history of the Standing Committee on Trusts, below, texts and references, notes 75–94.

13 *Ibid.*, as quoted, 85.

14 *Ibid.*, as quoted. For the rationalization movement, generally see Hannah, *Corporate Economy*, 27–40. Though the ideas which became identified with the movement can be traced to the 1880s, the organizational experiences of World War I helped to popularize them. Even so the movement did not really attain its greatest influence until the late 1920s and the 1930s. See Jeannie Anne Godfrey Dennison, "The Reaction to the Growth of Trusts and Industrial Combinations in Britain 1888–1921" (unpublished thesis University of London, 1981), 250–299. The thesis is used with the author's kind permission.

15 *Report of the Committee on Trusts*, 13 (1918), 24, 25. For the "get-along" ethos see chapter 1.

16 Pollard, *Development of the British Economy*, 38–50.

17 See chapters 1 and 2.

18 See text and references below, notes 60, 75–94.

19 *Ibid.*

20 Cuff, "Business, the State, and World War I," in Schwartz, editor, *Ordeal*, 50–51.

21 *Ibid.*, as quoted, 51–52.

22 *Ibid.*, 55–61. See also other references, note 4.

23 *Ibid.*; Himmelberg, *Origins of the National Recovery Administration*, 5–25;

Louis Galambos, "Loose Combinations and Their Public Control Over Time," *National Competition Policy Historians' Perspectives* (Washington, DC, 1981), 144–206.

24 Paul J. Miranti, Jr., "Associationalism, Statism, and Professional Regulation: Public Accountants and the Reform of the Financial Markets, 1896–1940," *Business History Review*, 60 (Autumn 1986), 449–451.

25 As quoted, Thomas K. McCraw, *Prophets of Regulation* (Cambridge, Massachusetts, 1984), 133, 134.

26 Notz and Harvey, *American Foreign Trade as Promoted by the Webb-Pomerene and Edge Acts*, 308–312; Davenport-Hines, *Docker*, 85.

27 As quoted, Notz and Harvey, *American Foreign Trade As Promoted by the Webb-Pomerene and Edge Acts*, 309, 310.

28 *Ibid.*, 157–352, for complete legislation.

29 Himmelberg, *Origins of the National Recovery Administration*, 29.

30 Tony Freyer, "Economic Liberty, Antitrust, and the Constitution, 1880–1925," in Ellen Frankel Paul and Howard Dickman, editors, *Liberty, Property, and Government: Constitutional Interpretation Before the New Deal* (Albany, 1989), 209. See also text and references below, notes 116 and 117.

31 See chapters 1, 3, and 4.

32 Alfred D. Chandler, Jr., *The Visible Hand, the Managerial Revolution in American Business* (Cambridge, Massachusetts, 1977), 89, 189, 202, 204, 469; George David Smith, *From Monopoly to Competition, the Transformation of Alcoa, 1888–1986*, 60–38.

33 Chandler, *Visible Hand*, 375–376, 495. See also, Chandler, "The Coming of Oligopoly and Its Meaning for Antitrust," *National Competition Policy Historians' Perspectives* (Washington, DC), 62–96.

34 Himmelberg, *Origins of the National Recovery Administration*, 5–25; McCraw, *Prophets of Regulation*, 126–142.

35 Miranti, "Associationalism," *Business History Review*, 60 (Autumn 1986), 450–451.

36 As quoted, Walter Lippmann, *Drift and Mastery* (New York, 1914), 141.

37 *Ibid.*, 142.

38 As quoted, Harold C. Livesay, *Samuel Gompers and Organized Labor in America* (Boston, 1978), 156. See also Himmelberg, *Origins of the National Recovery Administration*, 81–85.

39 See text and references below, notes 97–115.

40 See note 3.

41 As quoted, Cuff, "Business, The State, and World War I," in Schwartz, editor, *Ordeal*, 56, 57.

42 *Ibid.*, 62.

43 As quoted, Himmelberg, "Business, Antitrust Policy, and the Industrial Board," *Business History Review*, 42 (Spring, 1968), 6, 7.

44 *Ibid.*, 9–21; Himmelberg, *Origins of the National Recovery Administration*, 5–25.

45 Ellis W. Hawley, "Herbert Hoover and the Sherman Act, 1921–1933: An Early Phase of a Continuing Issue," *Iowa Law Review*, 74 (July 1989), 1067–1103; Robert F. Himmelberg, "President Hoover, Organized Business, and the Antitrust Laws: A Study in Hooverian Ideology and Policy," *Herbert Hoover Reassessed, Senate Documents*, Vol. 9, 96 Cong. 2D Session, January 3, December 16, 1980 (Washington, DC, 1981), 123–144.

46 As quoted, Himmelberg, *Origins of the National Recovery Administration*, 11. For the agreement with Brandeis see text and references below, notes 109–111.

47 See especially chapters 2 and 3 for the pre-war ideologies and economic thought.

48 As quoted, Dennison, "Reaction to the Growth of Trusts," 251.

49 As quoted, Notz and Harvey, *American Foreign Trade As Promoted by the Webb-Pomerene and Edge Acts*, 132.

50 Dennison, "Reaction to the Growth of Trusts," 261, 274, 276.

51 *Ibid.*, as quoted, 260, 268.

52 *Ibid.*, 267–269.

53 *Ibid.*, as quoted, 272.

54 *Ibid.*, as quoted, 263.

55 *Ibid.*

56 *Ibid.*, 250–273; *Report of the Committee on Trusts*, 13 (1918), 1–43; Hannah, *Corporate Economy*, 41–53.

57 *Report of the Committee on Trusts*, 13 (1918), 7, 11, 20.

58 *Ibid.*, 30.

59 *Ibid.*, 28.

60 *Ibid.*, 13–14.

61 See especially chapters 2 and 3, and notes 36 and 37 above.

62 See notes 24, 25, and 45. Hawley, "Hoover and the Sherman Act," *Iowa Law Review*, 74 (July 1989), 1095 noted in passing the Hoover–Brandeis connection. An earlier discussion is Joseph Dorfman, *Economic Mind*, vol. 4, 48–49, 147–159, though Dorfman does not attempt to reconcile his seemingly contradictory descriptions of Hoover as a conservative and Brandeis as a liberal. Hawley's discussion of Hoover, taken together with McCraw, *Prophets of Regulation*, 133–134, 146 on Brandeis, shows there is little or no contradiction, given the organizational and social values the two shared.

63 Himmelberg, *Origins of the National Recovery Administration*, 17; Dorfman, *Economic Mind*, 4, 48–49; Hawley, "Hoover and the Sherman Act," *Iowa Law Review* 74 (July 1989), 1068–1074. For Brandeis and the *Hardwood* decision see below text and references notes 109–111.

64 *Drift and Mastery*, 24–25, 44–45.

65 *Ibid.*, 45–46.

66 As quoted, Dorfman, *Economic Mind*, vol. 3, 490, 494, and surrounding text. For pre-war economic thought see chapter 2.

67 Compare Dorfman, *Economic Mind*, vol. 3, 385, vol. 4, 353, vol. 5, 555;

William E. Kovacic, "Failed Expectations: The Troubled Past and Uncertain Future of the Sherman Act as a Tool for Deconcentration," *Iowa Law Review*, 74 (July 1989), 1130; Herbert Hovenkamp, "The Antitrust Movement and the Rise of Industrial Organization," *Texas Law Review*, 68 (November 1989), 160–163.

68 Dorfman, *Economic Mind* vol. 4, 353–395, especially, 383, 387–388.

69 Chapter 4 explored the implications of the judiciary's self-restraint. The *Report of the Committee on Trusts*, 13 (1918), 1–43 detailed the growth of monopoly and restraints during the war.

70 *The Report of the Committee on Trusts*, 13 (1918), 18.

71 *Herbert Morris, Ltd.* v. *Saxelby* 1915 2 Ch. 57.

72 *Morris* v. *Saxelby* 1916 A.C. 688, 716.

73 *Joseph Evans & Co. Ltd.* v. *Heathcote* 1918 1 K.B. 418; *McEllistrim* v. *Ballymacelligott Co-operative Agricultural Society Ltd.* 1919 A.C. 53. *Rawlings* v. *General Trading Co.* 1919 1 K.B. 635.

74 *The Report of the Committee on Trusts* (1918), 31, 32, 33, 34.

75 Dennison, "Reaction to the Growth of Trusts," 250–289; and Hannah, *Corporate Economy*, 43–46, note the Standing Committee on Trusts but the treatment is far from exhaustive.

76 *Ibid.* The reference to *The Times* is as quoted, Dennison, "Reaction to the Growth of Trusts," 276.

77 "Board of Trade Standing Committee on Trusts, Parts I and II, meetings 1–71, October 1919 to May 1921" (BT 55/55 PRO, Kew Gardens). This material includes, primarily, typescript minutes of day-to-day meetings. The minutes of each meeting are numbered, but, of course, the entire manuscript series is not numbered consecutively. The following discussion is a composite of the entire manuscript. Generally, wherever a significant passage is quoted directly, the reference is to the number of the meeting or meetings (i.e. no. 1). In other cases the directly quoted reference is from published material, or separate, typescript memoranda included among the manuscripts.

78 Meeting nos. 8, 20, 39.

79 No. 1.

80 Nos. 1, 3, 7.

81 No. 8.

82 No. 8, 10.

83 Nos. 19, 20, 33.

84 No. 21.

85 Nos. 33, 42; J. E. Edgecomb, Director [The Electric Lamp Manufacturers' Association of Great Britain] to the President of the Board of Trade [Sir Robert Horne], 31 March 1920. The letter ended with the PS: "A similar letter has been addressed to the Prime Minister." Edgecomb's letter is a lengthy critique of the SCT's subcommittee report, *Electric Lamp Industry Profiteering Act, 1919 Findings and Decisions* (Cmd. 622, 1920), 1–15. Taken together the letter and the report showed the extent of horizontal cartel practices among the members of the Association and vertical ones between producers and middlemen.

Also the competitive pressure from foreign, particularly Dutch competitors was documented.

86 No. 33.
87 No. 37.
88 No. 49.
89 No. 52. See also note 76.
90 Nos. 52, 54, 57, 61, 62.
91 Nos. 55, 56, 65.
92 "To the President of the Board of Trade Deputation Regarding Trust Legislation," 1–3.
93 *Ibid.*
94 No. 71.
95 James May, "Antitrust in the Formative Era: Political and Economic Theory in Constitutional and Antitrust Analysis, 1880–1918," *Ohio State Law Journal*, 50 (1989), 258–395; James May, "Antitrust Practice and Procedure in the Formative Era: The Constitutional and Conceptual Reach of State Antitrust Law, 1880–1918," *University of Pennsylvania Law Review*, 135 (March 1987), 495–593.
96 See chapters 3 and 4.
97 See notes 32 and 33, and text and references below notes 98, 99, 100, 101.
98 Alexander M. Bickel and Benno C. Schmidt, *The Judiciary and Responsible Government* (New York, 1984), 144–171; Chandler, *Visible Hand*, 375–376; Hovenkamp, "Antitrust Movement," *Texas Law Review*, 68 (November 1989), 151–153; Peter C. Carstensen, "How to Assess the Impact of Antitrust on the American Economy: Examining History or Theorizing?" *Iowa Law Review*, 74 (July 1989), 1198–1214. *US v. American Can Co.*, 230 F. 859 (D.Md. 1916), *appeal dismissed*, 256 US 706 (1921); *US v. Corn Products Ref. Co.*, 234 F. 964 (SDNY 1916), *appeal dismissed*, 249 US 621 (1918). For US Steel and International Harvester especially see text and references, notes 32, 33, 99, 100.
99 Bickel and Schmidt, *Judicial and Responsible Government*, 157–160; Chandler, *Visible Hand*, 375–376.
100 As quoted, Naomi R. Lamoreaux, *The Great Merger Movement in American Business, 1895–1904* (Cambridge, England, 1985), 176.
101 *US v. US Steel Corp.*, 251 US 417, 447–448 (1920). See also Lamoreaux, *Great Merger Movement*, 175–177, 180–181; Bickel and Schmidt, *Judiciary and Responsible Government*, 144–171; Carstensen, "How to Assess the Impact of Antitrust," *Iowa Law Review*, 74 (July 1989), 1212; Leslie Hannah, "Mergers," Glenn Porter, editor, *Encyclopedia of American Economic History Studies of the Principal Movements and Ideas* (3 volumes, New York, 1981), II, 642–644; Chandler, *Visible Hand*, 375–376.
102 Carstensen, "How to Assess the Impact of Antitrust," *Iowa Law Review*, 74 (July 1989), 1198–1210. See also Mary Yeager, *Competition and Regulation: The Development of Oligopoly in the Meat Packing Industry* (Greenwich, Connecticut, 1981) 219–244.

103 Bickel and Schmidt, *Judiciary and Responsible Government*, 171–177.
104 *Ibid.*, 180–199.
105 McCraw, *Prophets of Regulation*, 144–147.
106 See chapter 4.
107 246 US 231, 237 (1918).
108 *Ibid.*, 238, 239, 241. For the Brandeisian rhetoric of the 1912 campaign and the coincident attack on *Dr. Miles*, see chapters 3 and 4. See also Bickel and Schmidt, *Judiciary and Responsible Government*, 177–180.
109 Bickel and Schmidt, *Judiciary and Responsible Government*, 179–180, 707–713. For Brandeis and Hoover on trade associations see note 62.
110 *Ibid.*, 257 US 377, 412, 413–419 (1921).
111 257 US at 419.
112 See notes 24, 44–46.
113 253 US 421, 427–428 (1920). Bickel and Schmidt, *Judiciary and Responsible Government*, 661–665.
114 253 US at 433, 434, 435, 440.
115 *FTC* v. *Beech-Nut Packing Co.*, 257 US 441, 456 (1921). For *Dr. Miles* see note 108 and chapter 4.
116 *Duplex Printing Press Co.* v. *Deering* 254 US 443, 479 (1920); *American Steel Foundries* v. *Tri-City Central Trades Council* 257 US 184 (1921). For the status of labor during World War I see note 38.
117 *Truax* v. *Corrigan* 257 US 312, 342, 354 (1921).

6 TENTATIVE CONVERGENCE, 1921–1948

1 For Britain see: Leslie Hannah, *The Rise of the Corporate Economy* (London, 1983), 54–143; Sidney Pollard, *The Development of the British Economy, 1914–1980* (Baltimore, Maryland, 1983), 51–234; Paul H. Guénault and J. M. Jackson, *The Control of Monopoly in the United Kingdom* (London, 1967), 6–35; G. C. Allen, *Monopoly and Restrictive Practices* (London, 1968), 50–69; G. C. Allen, "Monopoly in the United Kingdom," in Edward H. Chamberlin, editor, *Monopoly and Competition and their Regulation* (London, 1954), 88–109; J. D. Gribbin *The Post-War Revival of Competition as Industrial Policy, Government Economic Service Working Paper No. 19* (London, 1978), 1–15. For the United States see: Alfred D. Chandler, Jr., *Scale and Scope, The Dynamics of Industrial Capitalism* (Cambridge, Massachusetts, 1990); Neil Fligstein, *The Transformation of Corporate Control* (Cambridge, Massachusetts, 1990), 75–173; Ellis W. Hawley, "Herbert Hoover and the Sherman Act, 1921–1933: An Early Phase of a Continuing Issue," *Iowa Law Review*, 74 (July 1989), 1067–1104; Ellis W. Hawley, *The New Deal and the Problem of Monopoly, A Study in Economic Ambivalence* (Princeton, 1974); Robert F. Himmelberg, *The Origins of the National Recovery Administration, Business, Government, and the Trade Association Issue, 1921–1933* (New York, 1976); Robert F. Himmelberg, "President Hoover, Organized Business, and the Antitrust Laws: A Study in Hooverian Ideology and Policy," in *Herbert Hoover Reassessed*, Volume

9, Senate Documents, Serial 13313, nos. 96–63, 96 Congress, 2nd Session (Washington, DC, 1981), 123–144; Corwin D. Edwards, "Thurman Arnold and the Antitrust Laws," *Political Science Quarterly*, 58 (September 1943), 338–355; Leslie Hannah, "Mergers," in Glenn Porter, editor, *Encyclopedia of American Economic History Studies of the Principal Movements and Ideas* (3 volumes, New York, 1981), II, 639–651; William E. Kovacic, "Failed Expectations: The Troubled Past and Uncertain Future of the Sherman Act as a Tool for Deconcentration," *Iowa Law Review*, 74 (July 1989), 1105–1150.

2 See chapter 5. For a full analysis of the concept of "unitary" operational structure see Fligstein, *Corporate Control*, 75–115.

3 Hannah, *Rise of the Corporate Economy*, 97.

4 Gribbin, *Post-War Revival of Competition*, 1–15; Pollard, *Development of the British Economy*, 98–114; Hannah, *Rise of Corporate Economy*, 135–142. Carl Eis, *The 1919–1930 merger movement in American Industry* (New York, 1978).

5 Kovacic, "Failed Expectations," *Iowa Law Review*, 74 (July 1989), 1122.

6 Hannah, "Mergers," 644. See also Fligstein, *Corporate Control*, 98; Chandler, *Scale and Scope*, 72–73, 230–231.

7 Note 4; Chandler, *Scale and Scope*, 287–88, 296, 303, 311, 312, 320, 370, 379; and chapter 5.

8 Chandler, *Scale and Scope*, 287–88, 296, 303, 311, 312, 320, 370, 379.

9 T. B. Robson, *Holding Companies and Their Published Accounts* (London, 1936), 1–27.

10 William L. Baldwin, *Antitrust and the Changing Corporation* (Durham, North Carolina, 1961), 51; *FTC* vs. *Western Manufacturing Co., et al.* 272 US 554 (1926); A. D. Neale and D. C. Goyder, *The Antitrust Laws of the United States of America* (Cambridge, England, 1982), 181–186.

11 Chandler, *Scale and Scope*, 361; Fligstein, *Corporate Control*, 123.

12 As quoted, Fligstein, *Corporate Control*, 133.

13 *Ibid.*, as quoted, 127, 128.

14 Compare, Chandler, *Scale and Scope*, 295–392; and Hannah, *Rise of the Corporate Economy*, 90–143. See also, W. J. Reader, *Imperial Chemical Industries: A History* (2 volumes, London, 1975).

15 For this point I am indebted to Professor Leslie Hannah.

16 Chandler, *Scale and Scope*, 390.

17 As quoted, Sidney Hyman, *The Lives of William Benton* (Chicago, 1969), 280.

18 Judy Slinn, *A History of Freshfields* (London, 1984), 152–155; Interview L. C. B. Gower, 6 November 1989; Robson, *Holding Companies*, 11–20, 25–26, quote at 20.

19 James C. Bonbright and G. C. Means, *The Holding Company* (New York, 1969), 28, 31–32, 39–49, quote at 28. The continuing significance of private suits is suggested by the activism of such lawyers as Samuel Untermeyer who, following the Brandeisian tradition of the People's Lawyer worked against trade associations during the 1920s.

See Himmelberg, *Origins of the NRA*, 14. Other indirect evidence is suggested by several lawyers contributing to the National Economic Committee, who had a similar practice. See below.

20 See notes 4 and 14.

21 *Ibid.* For America see Himmelberg, *Origins of the NRA*, 88–223; Hawley, *Problem of Monopoly*; Hawley, "Hoover and the Sherman Act," *Iowa Law Review*, 74 (July 1989), 1085–1103; Fligstein, *Corporate Control*, 116–179.

22 As quoted, Pollard, *Development of the British Economy*, 104.

23 See note 21.

24 Chandler, *Scale and Scope*, 230–233; Fligstein, *Corporate Control*, 116–160.

25 Fligstein, *Corporate Control*, 118–119.

26 See note 14.

27 See notes 6, 24.

28 Pollard, *Development of the British Economy*, 192–234; Gribbin, *Post-war Revival of Competition*, 6–15; Edwards, "Arnold and the Antitrust Laws," *Political Science Quarterly*, 58 (September 1943), 338–355; Fligstein, *Corporate Control*, 167–173. For full discussion and citation see below, fourth section on the international cartel issue during World War II, and chapter 7.

29 See chapters 2 and 5 for the gradual breakdown of classical theory of perfect competition, which paved the way for the triumph of the theory of imperfect competition discussed below.

30 Joan Robinson, *The Economics of Imperfect Competition* (London, 1933); E. H. Chamberlin, *The Theory of Monopolistic Competition* (Cambridge, Massachusetts, 1933). For general discussion see Baldwin, *Antitrust and the Changing Corporation*, 67–117.

31 Baldwin, *Antitrust and the Changing Corporation*, 67–76. See also Himmelberg, *Origins of NRA*, 183–184, 192; Hawley, *New Deal and the Problem of Monopoly*.

32 As quoted, Baldwin, *Antitrust and the Changing Corporation*, 93.

33 R. H. Coase, "The Nature of the Firm," in *The Firm the Market and the Law* (Chicago, 1988), 33–56, quoted at 37. But see also Herbert Hovenkamp, "The Antitrust Movement and the Rise of Industrial Organization," *Texas Law Review*, 68 (November 1989), 165–166.

34 Hannah, *Rise of the Corporate Economy*, 27–90.

35 J. M. Rees, as quoted, Jeannie Anne Godfrey Dennison "The Reaction to the Growth of Trusts and Industrial Combinations in Britain, 1881–1921" (unpublished Ph.D. Thesis, University of London, 1980), at 251. This fine work is used with permission.

36 Hannah, *Rise of the Corporate Economy*, 46–47 notes how few were the small business opponents of rationalization.

37 As quoted, Himmelberg, *Origins of the NRA*, 58.

38 *Ibid.*, 221. Himmelberg is the best indepth study of the entire period, 1919–1933. See also, Hawley, *New Deal and the Problem of Monopoly*, 447–449, and Hawley, "Hoover and the Sherman Act," *Iowa Law Review*, 74 (July 1989), 1067–1104.

39 Hawley, *New Deal and the Problem of Monopoly*, 420–455; Fligstein, *Corporate Control*, 116–123, 161–173; Baldwin, *Antitrust and the Changing Corporation*, 101–114.
40 "Minutes," 5 April 1943, Alex Kilroy, BT64/318.
41 See chapters 3 and 5.
42 Himmelberg, *Origins of the NRA*, 81–85, 91–93, 110–116, 117–125; Hawley, *New Deal and the Problem of Monopoly*, 452; Edwards, "Arnold and the Antitrust Laws," *Political Science Quarterly*, 58 (September 1943), 346–348.
43 Hannah, *Rise of the Corporate Economy*, 24, 47, 49–50; Guénault and Jackson, *Control of Monopoly*, 19–27; Hyman, *William Benton*, 278–283.
44 As quoted, Hyman, *William Benton*, 281.
45 Dennison, "Reaction to the Growth of Trusts," 289–299.
46 "Monopoly and the Law An Economist's Reflections on the *Crofter* Case," *The Modern Law Review*, 6 (April 1943), 97–111.
47 *Ibid.*, 102, 103, 104.
48 *Ibid.*, 107, 108.
49 *Ibid.*, 109, 110–111.
50 As quoted, Baldwin, *Antitrust and the Changing Corporation*, 61, 62.
51 *Ibid.*, as quoted, 60.
52 Hawley, "Hoover and the Sherman Act," *Iowa Law Review*, 74 (July 1989), 1067–1104; Himmelberg, "Hoover, Organized Business, and the Antitrust Laws," *Hoover Reassessed*, volume 9, Senate Documents, 96 Congress, 2nd Session, December 1980 (Washington, 1981), 123–144.
53 Kovacic, "Failed Expectations," *Iowa Law Review*, 74 (July 1989), 1134.
54 Thurman Arnold, "Antitrust Law Enforcement, Past and Future," *Law and Contemporary Problems*, 7 (Winter 1940), 10–11.
55 *Ibid.*, and note 52. For Lewis, see note 47.
56 Arnold, "Antitrust Law Enforcement," *Law and Contemporary Problems*, 7 (Winter 1940), 11, 12, 14.
57 As quoted, Baldwin, *Antitrust and the Changing Corporation*, 112, 113.
58 See pp. 223–232 and chapter 7.
59 As quoted, Hyman, *William Benton*, 278.
60 Note 40.
61 Robert E. Cushman, *The Independent Regulatory Commissions* (New York, 1941), 502, 503, 504.
62 "Control of Monopolies in the Public Interest," May 1943, 7–9, BT64/318.
63 For the earlier developments see chapters 1 and 3. For the interwar period see note 4.
64 As quoted, "Control of Monopolies in the Public Interest," May 1943, 7, BT64/318.
65 *Ibid.*, as quoted, 8.
66 As quoted, Pollard, *Development of the British Economy*, 105.
67 Notes 4, 43, 62.

68 "Control of Monopolies in the Public Interest," May 1943, 7–8, BT64/318; Pollard, *Development of the British Economy*, 106. See also, Hyman, *William Benton*, 281–283.

69 W. Friedmann, "The Harris Tweed Case and Freedom of Trade," *The Modern Law Review*, 6 (December 1942), 1–21 is a good overview. For earlier period see chapter 4. See also Robert Stevens, *Law and Politics, the House of Lords as a Judicial Body, 1800–1976* (Chapel Hill, North Carolina, 1978), 185–321.

70 Friedmann, "Harris Tweed Case," *Modern Law Review*, 6 (December 1942), 14.

71 *Sorrel* v. *Smith*, (1925), AC 700.

72 Friedmann, "Harris Tweed Case," *Modern Law Review*, 6 (December 1942), 8.

73 *Ibid.*, 18.

74 *Ibid.*, 19; (1937), AC 797 is the case citation.

75 Note 69.

76 Friedmann, "Harris Tweed Case," *Modern Law Review*, 6 (December 1942), 14.

77 *Ibid.*, 17. W. Arthur Lewis's article, discussed in notes 46–49 above, suggested the consequences for economic efficiency arising from *Harris Tweed* and other decisions. Especially concerning the labor dimensions of the case, see also Stevens, *Law and Politics*, 279n, 301, 331n, 396.

78 Chapter 7 explores how this consensus evolved during and immediately after World War II.

79 See notes 38, 39.

80 Phrases, as quoted, Hawley, "Hoover and the Sherman Act," *Iowa Law Review*, 74 (July 1989), 1075, 1076, 1077, 1082. For the continuity between Hoover and Brandeis, see chapter 5.

81 *Ibid.*, 1078–1091. Case citations are: *Maple Flooring Mfrs. Ass'n.* v. *United States*, 268 US 563 (1925); *United States* v. *Trenton Potteries Co.*, 273 US 392 (1926) (case decided, 21 February 1927); *United States* v. *International Harvester Co.*, 274, US 693 (1927).

82 Hawley, "Hoover and the Sherman Act," *Iowa Law Review*, 74 (July 1989), 1085–1101. Quotation and case cited: *United States* v. *Swift* & *Co.*, 286 US 106, 118 (1932).

83 Hawley, "Hoover and the Sherman Act," *Iowa Law Review*, 74 (July 1989), 1085–1101; Hawley, *New Deal and the Problem of Monopoly*.

84 As quoted, "Hoover and the Sherman Act," *Iowa Law Review*, 74 (July 1989), 1091, 1092.

85 Note 83.

86 288 US 344 (1933); *Schechter Poultry Corp.* v. *United States*, 295 US 495 (1935).

87 Neale and Goyder, *Antitrust Laws*, 134–137, 212–214, 241–245, 262–265. See also, for parallel with British law and business, chapter 4.

88 Baldwin, *Antitrust and the Changing Corporation*, 101–114.

89 Compare discussion and notations note 84; Hawley, *New Deal and the Problem of Monopoly*, 439–455.

90 As quoted, Fligstein, *Corporate Control*, 169.

91 Hawley, *New Deal and Problem of Monopoly*, 447–449; Baldwin, *Antitrust and the Changing Corporation*, 113–114.

92 George David Smith, *From Monopoly to Competition, The Transformation of Alcoa, 1888–1986*, 193–214.

93 148 F.2d 416 at 427, 431 (1945).

94 Smith, *From Monopoly to Competition*, 213, notes, that despite the modest decree, the "practical results" of the case "proved beneficial over time. The oligopoly that emerged in the aluminum industry ... enlivened the industry and spurred the development of new markets well beyond what Alcoa alone might have been able to accomplish."

95 For detailed discussion of the British side of the story see chapter 7. For Johnson-Benson visit see Hyman, *William Benton*, 278–283.

96 Edwards, "Arnold and the Antitrust Laws," *Political Science Quarterly*, 58 (September 1943), 339, 344–345, 350–353.

97 *Ibid.*, 344–345. See also Edwards, editor, *A Cartel Policy for the United Nations* (New York, 1945).

98 Fritz Machlup, "The Nature of the International Cartel," Edwards, editor, *Cartel Policy*, 1.

99 78th Congress 2nd Session, Senate, Subcommittee Report 4, November 13 (Washington, 1944). See also "Economic and Political Aspects of International Cartels," 78th Congress 2nd Session Senate Committee Report (Washington, 1944).

100 Cartel Memo 98, 18 November 1944, 1–5, in Rand Records, Committee for Economic Policy, 1954–1961, 524, Folder 3, Roger C. Dixon to Joseph Rand, 23 December 1955, Eisenhower Library.

101 See chapter 7.

102 As quoted, Machlup, "International Cartel," Edwards, editor, *Cartel Policy*, 2.

103 Hyman, *William Benton*, 278–283.

104 Note 100.

105 As quoted, note 102.

106 Chapter 7.

107 Machlup, "International Cartel," 14; and see affiliations of Corwin D. Edwards, Theodore J. Kreps, Ben W. Lewis, Fritz Machlup, Robert P. Terrill, contributors to Edwards, editor, *Cartel Policy*.

108 Edwards, "The Possibilities of An International Policy Toward Cartels," Edwards, editor, *Cartel Policy*, 48.

109 *Ibid.*, as quoted, 97.

110 *Ibid.*, 97–98.

111 Notes 100, 101. For British and American bilateral foreign-policy dimensions see chapter 7.

112 "Cartels and National Security," 78th Congress 2nd Session Senate

Subcommittee Report No. 4, November 13, (Washington, 1944), 1–13.
113 *Ibid.*, quote at 3.
114 See note 100.
115 *Ibid.*
116 As quoted, Edwards, "Possibilities," in Edwards, editor, *Cartel Policy*, 101.
117 *Ibid.*, 100–102.
118 Chapter 7.
119 As quoted, Edwards, "Possibilities," in Edwards, editor, *Cartel Policy*, 102–103.
120 Chapter 7.
121 As quoted, Edwards, "Possibilities," in Edwards, editor, *Cartel Policy*, 102.
122 Alan S. Milward, *The Reconstruction of Western Europe, 1945–51* (Berkeley, California, 1984), 88, 195, 219, 241–246, 279; Paul H. Guénault and J. M. Jackson, *The Control of Monopoly in the United Kingdom* (London, 1960), 36–51. For a fuller discussion see chapter 7.
123 Robert L. Branyon, "Antimonopoly Activities during the Truman Administration," (unpublished Ph.D. dissertation, 1961), 68–78.
124 *Ibid.*, 111–114.
125 Fligstein, *Corporate Control*, as quoted, 170; see also 181–184.
126 *Ibid.*, 172–173. See also note 124.
127 Branyon, "Antimonopoly Activities," 81–83. *US* v. *Columbia Steel Co.*, 334 US 495 (1948).
128 Fligstein, *Corporate Control*, 173–174. See also note 124.
129 *Ibid.*; and note 127.
130 *Ibid.*

7 A BRITISH ANTIMONOPOLY POLICY EMERGES, 1940–1948

1 Although the issue of the nationalization of private industry influenced policymaking, it will be considered here only in passing because there was no significant parallel with American developments. The emergence of Britain's antimonopoly policy during World War II is outlined generally in: Sidney Pollard, *The Development of the British Economy, 1914–1980* (Baltimore, 1983), 200–210, 229–234; J. M. Jackson and Paul H. Guénault, *The Control of Monopoly in the United Kingdom* (London, 1967), 25–26; G. C. Allen, *Monopoly and Restrictive Practices* (London, 1968), 61–62; G. C. Allen, "United Kingdom," in E. H. Chamberlain, ed., *Monopoly and Competition and their Regulation* (London, 1954), 88–109. These works, however, were impressionistic because the manuscript materials necessary to explore the inner history of the issue were not open to the public until the 1970s. A pioneering study based upon an initial reading of these sources was

J. D. Gribbin, *The Post-War Revival of Competition As Industrial Policy, Government Economic Service Working Paper no. 19* (London, December 1978), who revealed that the tension between the proponents of competition and defenders of cartels shaped initial policymaking. Mr. Gribbin kindly gave me an interview on 6 July, 1989 in which he enlarged upon the material presented in his *Post-War Revival of Competition* (cited hereafter, Gribbin Interview). He also shared a soon to be published paper entitled "The Contribution of Economists to the Origins of UK Competition Policy" (July 1990 London), 1–27. Gribbin and Allen also suggested that American diplomatic pressure influenced the policymaking process. This chapter analyzes the Gribbin–Allen insights in light of the framework developed in chapter 6; it draws upon an extensive reading of manuscript material to provide an inside story of how Britain's antimonopoly policy emerged from 1941 to 1948. Unless otherwise noted all sources are located in BT64, Public Record Office, Kew Gardens.

2 Gribbin, *Post-War Revival of Competition Policy*, 6–15; Gribbin, "Contribution of Economists," 1–27. See also Pollard, *Development of the British Economy*, 200–210, 224–234.

3 "Industrial Organization-Position of Trade Association," 1 August 1942, BT64/318.

4 H. C. [Henry Clay], 30th December 1941, BT64/394.

5 Ruth L. Cohen, "Trade Associations", 22 December 1941, BT64/318 summarized the Innes Memorandum. See also Gribbin Interview 6 July 1989; Gribbin, "Contribution of Economists," 1–27.

6 See chapters 5 and 6; and Gribbin Interview 6 July 1989; Gribbin, "Contribution of Economists," 1–27.

7 See note 5.

8 *Ibid.*

9 H. C. [Henry Clay], 27 January 1942, BT64/394; see also Gribbin "Contribution of Economists," 1–27.

10 Cohen [handwritten note], 16 March 1942, BT64/394.

11 C. K. Hobson [handwritten note], 25 June 1943, BT64/318.

12 "Note on the Attitude of the Law towards Price Fixing and Analogous Agreements For Trade Protection" [no date], BT64/318.

13 P. T. O. [initialed, no date], BT64/318.

14 Quote at C. I. [probably Sir Charles Innes], 29 July 1942, BT64/318.

15 "City Notes, Big Business and Little," *Finance & Commerce*, Tuesday – 26 May 1942; "Government and Industry, An Industrialist's View – Mr. Courtauld's Reflections," *The Times*, 13 April 1942; "Control of Combination: Between Public Interest and Private Rights," *The Times*, 4 April, 1942. "Plea for the Little Man," British Dislike of Over Planning [source and date illegible]. All collected BT64/318.

16 C. H. [initials perhaps H], 28 July 1942, BT64/318.

17 Note 14.

18 Note 3.
19 *Ibid.*
20 Gribbin Interview, 6 July 1989; Pollard, *Development of the British Economy*, 229–230; quoted in "Restrictive Practices in Industry Memorandum by the Board Trade" [Spring 1943], BT64/318.
21 Gribbin, "Contribution of Economists," 11–19, and as quoted at 12.
22 *Ibid.*, 6–11.
23 "Review of the United Kingdom Press on Post-War Commercial Policy, 1st–31st July 1943," BT64.318. See also Sydney Hyman, *The Lives of William Benton* (Chicago, 1969), 278–283.
24 "Restrictive Practices in Industry Memorandum by the Board of Trade" [Spring 1943], BT64/318.
25 Kilroy to Allen, 29 March 1943, BT64/318.
26 *Ibid.*
27 Allen to Kilroy, 31 March 1943, BT64/318.
28 *Ibid.*
29 "Note on the Desirability of an Enquiry into Monopolistic Practices;" and "United States Experience," BT64/318.
30 Note 24.
31 Alex Kilroy "Monopoly-Comments on Professor Allen's Paper," 7 August 1943, BT64/318.
32 The full Memorandum, dated 17 July 1943, is located in BT64/318; it is the culmination of the research effort, notes 24 and 29. I am indebted to Helen Mercer for my copy, and to Denys Gribbin for suggesting its significance.
33 G. C. Allen, "Synopsis on Report on Monopoly Now Being Prepared," 7 July 1943, BT64/318.
34 "Control of Monopoly," 12.
35 *Ibid.*, 18–30.
36 Allen, "Synopsis," 1.
37 *Ibid.*, 1–2.
38 "Control of Monopoly," 24.
39 Allen, "Synopsis," 2.
40 G. L. Watkinson, "Monopolies," 21 July 1943, BT64/318.
41 Ibid.
42 J. E. M., 22 July 1943, BT64/318.
43 Gribbin, "Contribution of Economists," 19–22.
44 R. L. Cohen to R. F. Kahn, 23 November 1943, BT64/318.
45 G. H. Andrew, 26 February 1944, BT64/260.
46 *Ibid.*
47 Minute Sheet, exchanges between Andrew, Kilroy, and others dated 18 January 1944 – 7 December 1944, BT64/316.
48 *The Organization of British Industry, Report of the FBI Organization of Industry Committee*, October 1944.
49 Minute Sheet, Andrew, 18 January 1944, BT64/316.
50 Note 45.

51 Minute Sheet, Kilroy, 16 October 1944, BT64/316.
52 "Restrictive Practices Draft paragraph on Main Job of Staff of Commission," October 1944, BT64/316.
53 *Ibid.*
54 *Ibid.*
55 John Jewkes to Alex Kilroy, 10 October 1944, BT64/316.
56 Minute Sheet, Andrew, 7 December 1944, BT64/316.
57 *Ibid.*
58 D. N. Fyfe to Alex Kilroy, 18 January 1945; "Note Accompanying Revised Draft Heads of Bill on Restrictive Practices and Monopolies," BT64/316.
59 Minute Sheets, 25 January 1945–6 March 1945, BT64/316.
60 *Ibid.*, 2 February 1945.
61 "Restrictive Practices," 6 February 1945, BT64/316.
62 Minute Sheet, Andrew, 17 February 1945.
63 *Ibid.*, 21–22 February 1945.
64 Minute Sheet, G.L.W., 6 March 1945.
65 "Restrictive Practices and Monopolies, Instructions to Parliamentary Counsel to Prepare A Bill," BT64/316.
66 Watkinson to Doc. [G. C. Allen], 12 March 1945, BT64/394.
67 "The Legislative Program, 1944–45 Session" [initialed] G. E. P., 2 May 1945, BT64/316.
68 "Supplies & Services (Transitional Powers) Bill," G. S. W. [initialed], 3 August 1945, BT64/316.
69 The degree of consensus was suggested by newspaper reports and editorials involving the issue during the summer of 1945. See, "Labour shows the way, Industry Tories allowed to rot," by Lincoln Evans, *Daily Herald*, 29 June 1945; "Monopolies and Industrial Efficiency," *Sunday Observer*, 17 June 1945; "Cartels and Monopolies" *Financial News*, 21 June 1945; "The Four Parties Discuss Monopolies," *Daily Express*, 2 June 1945; "Bill to Deal with Abuse of Monopolies," *Daily Telegraph*, 26 June, 1945; "Combines and Control," *Financial Times*, 27 June 1945; "Private v. Public Monopolies," by Arthur Greenwood, *Daily Express*, 29 May 1945; "Public Ownership Must Begin Now," *Daily Herald*, 20 October 1944. All collected BT64/394.
70 Gribbin, "Contribution of Economists," 1–27. For fuller discussion see chapter 6.
71 Minute Sheet, R. L. C [ohen], 1 May 1944, BT64/317; G. C. Allen [handwritten] 1 May 1944.
72 H. J. H., 4 April 1944, BT64/317.
73 Minute Sheet, R. L. C., 1 May 1944, BT64/317.
74 To Anthony Eden, 17 May 1944, BT64/317.
75 "U.S.A. and the Cartel Question," 1944, BT64/317.
76 See unsigned Memorandum, dated 9th November, 1944, and the "Report of the Sub-Committee on War Mobilization of the Committee on Military affairs, US Senate, on Cartels and National Security,"

BT64/394. The file included a copy of the Kilgore Report. Corwin Edwards and his research findings were well known to members of the Board of Trade, because of numerous exchanges involving the international cartel issue. Gribbin Interview, 6 July 1989.

77 See notes 67 and 68, and chapter 6.

78 "Article VII. Resumption of Informal Talks with American Officials. Summary of 13th Meeting, held at the Board of Trade on Tuesday, 30 January 1945." 1–10, dated 31 January 1945, BT64/317.

79 *Ibid.*

80 *Ibid.*

81 *Ibid.*

82 *Ibid.*

83 "Article VII. Continuation of Informal talks with American Officials. Summary of 8th meeting of second series, held at the Board of Trade on 27 June 1945." Dated June [no date] 1945, BT64/414.

84 Minutes, Andrew, 24 August 1945, BT64/414.

85 "Cartels," R. Shakle, 28 August 1945, BT64/414.

86 Alan S. Milward, *The Reconstruction of Western Europe 1945–51* (Berkeley, California, 1984), 88, 195, 219, 241–46, 279; Randall Bennett Woods *A Changing of the Guard Anglo-American Relations, 1941–1946* (Chapel Hill, North Carolina, 1990), 188, 218; Guénault and Jackson, *Control of Monopoly*, 37; Gribbin, "Contribution of Economists," 6–13.

87 P. W. S. Andrew [untitled], 8 January 1946, BT64/260.

88 *President's Morning Meeting Restrictive Practices: I Note – by the Department,* 27 January [?] 1946, BT64/260.

89 See note 87.

90 See note 88.

91 "Extract from Fortnightly Economic Summary," *Cartels,* BT64/394.

92 G. H. Andrew, *Cartels and Article VII,* 29 August 1946, BT64/414.

93 See note 88.

94 *Weekly Newsletter Restrictive Practices,* 8 October 1946, BT64/260.

95 P. W. S. Andrew, *Restrictive Practices: I – Registration,* 1–15 October 1946 [?], BT64/260.

96 See note 86.

97 A. Kilroy [untitled], 28 April 1947, BT64/260.

98 *A Committee on the Distribution of Building Materials His Majesty's Government's Policy on Restrictive Practices Memorandum by the Board of Trade* [no date], BT64/260.

99 See note 97.

100 G. H. Andrew to C. H. Blagburn, 18 February 1947, BT64/260.

101 P. W. S. Andrew to A. Kilroy, "Possible Chairman of a Restrictive Practices Panel and Commission," 10 February 1947, BT64/260.

102 *Draft Paper on Restrictive Practices Policy,* 10 November 1947, BT64/460; G. H. Andrew, *Marshall Plan, Paragraph on Cartels for paper on Economic Integration of Europe,* 17 July 1947, BT64/494.

103 Extract from Speech by Sir Stafford Cripps at Central Hall, 12 September 1947; Board of Trade, postponed from Friday, 7th to

Thursday, 13th November 1947, BT64/498. *Parliamentary Debates, House of Commons, Standing Committee B Official Report, Monopoly (Inquiry and Control) Bill*, Tuesday, 11th May 1948 (London, 1948), BT64/492.

104 *Parliamentary Debates... Monopoly... Bill*, Tuesday, 11th May 1948 (London, 1948), 14; Guénault and Jackson, *Control of Monopoly*, 36–40.

105 *Ibid.*

106 *Ibid.*, as quoted, Guénault and Jackson, *Control of Monopoly*, 40.

8 UNEVEN CONVERGENCE SINCE WORLD WAR II

1 Works which provide a basis for a comparison of the interaction between business structure and government policy in both nations during the post-war era are: Leslie Hannah, *The Rise of the Corporate Economy* (London, 1983), 123–163; Leslie Hannah, "Scale and Scope: Towards a European Visible Hand? A Review Article," *Business History* (forthcoming, January 1991); Leslie Hannah, "Mergers," Glenn Porter, editor, *Encyclopedia of American Economic History* (3 volumes, New York, 1979), II, 645–651; Alfred D. Chandler, Jr. *Scale and Scope: The Dynamics of Industrial Capitalism* (Cambridge, Massachusetts, 1990), 605–628; Alfred D. Chandler, "The Enduring Logic of Industrial Success," *Harvard Business Review* (March/April 1990), 434–444; Neil Fligstein, *The Transformation of Corporate Control* (Cambridge, Massachusetts, 1990), 161–314; James Fairburn and John Kay, editors, *Mergers and Merger Policy* (Oxford, England, 1989); J. D. Gribbin, *the Post-War Revival of Competition As Industrial Policy, Government Economic Service Working Paper No. 19* (December 1978), 15–58; A. D. Neale and D. G. Goyder, *The Antitrust Laws of the U.S.A.* (Cambridge, England, 1982); Sidney Pollard, *The Development of the British Economy, 1914–1980* (London, 1985), 250–261, 301–315; G. C. Allen, *Monopolies and Restrictive Practices* (London, 1968), 61–164; Paul H. Guénault and J. M. Jackson, *The Control of Monopoly in the United Kingdom* (London, 1967), 150–194; E. Victor Morgan, *Monopolies, Mergers and Restrictive Practices: UK Competition Policy, 1948–1987* (Edinburgh, 1987); D. C. Elliot and J. D. Gribbin, "The Abolition of Cartels and Structural Change in the United Kingdom," in A. P. Jacquemin and H. W. de Jong, editors, *Welfare Aspects of Industrial Markets* (2 volumes, Leiden, 1977), II, 344–365. Also useful is Richard Critchfield, *An American Looks at Britain* (New York, 1990).

2 The works noted above provide evidence directly or indirectly relating to economic thought and to pressure groups. On efficiency theory particularly see: William Lee Baldwin, *Antitrust and the Changing Corporation* (Durham, North Carolina, 1961), 118–284; R. H. Coase, *The Firm, the Market and the Law* (Chicago, 1988); Tim Frazer, *Monopoly, Competition and the Law: The Regulation of Business Activity in Britain, Europe and America* (New York, 1988); Frank H. Stephen, *The Economics of Law* (Ames, Iowa, 1988); Valentine Korah, *Competition Law of Britain and the Common Market* (The Hague, 1982); R. B. Stevens

and B. S. Yamey, *The Restrictive Practices Court: a Study of the Judicial Process and Economic Policy* (London, 1965); Herbert Hovenkamp, "The Antitrust Movement and the Rise of Industrial Organization," *Texas Law Review*, 68 (November 1989), 163–168; Herbert Hovenkamp, "Marginal Utility and the Coase Theorem," *Cornell Law Review*, 75 (May 1990), 783–810; Herbert Hovenkamp, "Antitrust's Protected Classes," *Michigan Law Review*, 88 (October 1989), 1–48; William H,. Page, "The Chicago School and the Evolution of Antitrust: Characterization, Antitrust Injury, and Evidentiary Sufficiency," *Virginia Law Review*, 75 (October 1989), 1221–1310; Terry Calvani and Michael L. Sibarium, "Antitrust Today: Maturity of Decline," *The Antitrust Bulletin*, 35 (Spring 1990), 123–218; Herbert Hovenkamp, "The Sherman Act and the Classical Theory of Competition;" William E. Kovacic, "Failed Expectations: The Troubled Past and Uncertain Future of the Sherman Act as a Tool for Deconcentration;" Peter C. Carstensen, "How to Assess the Impact of Antitrust on the American Economy: Examining History or Theorizing," *Iowa Law Review*, 74 (July 1989), 1019–1066, 1105–1150, 1175–1217. For references to the legal profession see below, notes 36–39.

3 Hannah *Corporate Economy*, 144–145; Hannah, "Mergers," Porter ed., *Encyclopedia*, II, 646–647, 650; James A. Fairburn and John A. Kay, "Introduction;" Fairburn, "The Evolution of Merger Policy in Britain;" Stephen Littlechild, "Myths and Merger Policy," in Fairburn and Kay, eds., *Mergers*, 1–29, 193–230, 301–321.

4 Hannah, "Mergers," Porter, editor, *Encyclopedia*, 646; "1980s Mergers Reverse the 1960s," *Christian Science Monitor*, Friday, 6 July 1990, at 6.

5 Littlechild, "Myths and Mergers," in Fairburn and Kay, editors, *Mergers*, 304; Derek Sach, "Nothing Ventured, Nothing Gained," *London Times*, Thursday, 2 November 1989, at 37.

6 Hannah, *Corporate Economy*, 145, 149.

7 Hannah, "Mergers," Porter, editor, *Encyclopedia*, 647. See also Fligstein, *Transformation of Corporate Control*, 238–258.

8 *Mergers Policy A Department of Trade and Industry Paper on the Policy and Procedures of Merger Control* (HMSO, London, 1988), 38; Hannah, *Corporate Economy*, 161.

9 For overview see Guénault and Jackson, *Control of Monopoly*, 150–194; Gribbin, *Post-War Revival of Competition*, 18–58; Elliott and Gribbin, "Abolition of Cartels," Jacquemin and de Jong, eds., *Welfare Aspects*, 345–365, quote at 356.

10 Fairburn, "Evolution of Merger Policy," in Fairburn and Kay, eds., *Mergers*, 191–207; Pollard, *Development of the British Economy*, 307.

11 Fairburn, "Evolution of Merger Policy;" Littlechild, "Myths," in Fairburn and Kay, eds., *Mergers*, 191–230, 303–305.

12 Hannah, "Mergers," Porter, editor, *Encyclopedia*, 645–650; Fligstein, *Transformation of Corporate Control*, 161–295.

13 Calvani and Sibarium, "Antitrust Today," *Antitrust Bulletin*, 35 (Spring 1990), 183–188; "Interview with Ira Millstein: Task Force

Chair Reviews ABA Report on Antitrust Division," *Antitrust* (Fall/Winter 1989), 4–7; Linda Himelstein, "Ronald Reagan's Legacy, Antitrust Enforcement Stumbles in Court," *Legal Times*, 13 No. 9, Week of 23 July 1990, 9–11. As quoted, "States Hit US Antitrust Stance, United to Stem 'Mega-Mergers,'" *Los Angeles Times*, Wednesday, 11 March 1987. See also "Bush Favors Review of Takeover Rules," *Tuscaloosa News*, 16 January 1989, at 16.

14 Compare Hannah, *Corporate Economy*, 149–150; and Fligstein, *Transformation of Corporate Control*, 197–225; and Hannah, "Mergers," Porter, editor, *Encyclopedia*, 647–649. See also author's interview with L. C. B. Gower, 6 November 1989.

15 As quoted, Fligstein, *Transformation of Corporate Control*, 250.

16 "Takeovers: More Winners than Losers," *London Times*, Wednesday, 3 December 1986, at 32.

17 Steve Lohr, "Financial Scandal Roils Britain," *New York Times*, Friday, 30 January 1987, at 25. For the pervasiveness of this clash of social-class values see Critchfield, *America Looks at Britain*, 89–158, 436–465.

18 *Merger Policy Blue Paper* (HMSO, London, 1988); *Review of Restrictive Trade Practices Policy A Consultative Document* (HMSO, London, 1988); Sydney Lipworth, "Development of Merger Control in the UK and the European Community," Denning Lecture 1990 (unpublished manuscript), 1–35.

19 Ernest Connine, "Naked Greed Can't Be Bottom Line," *Los Angeles Times*, Monday, 23 February 1987, at 5. See also Lawrence R. Klein, "Market Needs Infusion of Morality," *Los Angeles Times*, Tuesday, 24 February 1987, at 3.

20 For the impact of the earlier merger waves see Chapters 1, 6. The vacillating political clout of each of these pressure groups is discussed in David Vogel, *Fluctuating Fortunes: The Political Power of Business in America* (New York, 1989); Samuel Lubell, *The Future of American Politics* (New York, 1965); John Brooks, *The Great Leap: the Past Twenty-five Years in America* (New York, 1966).

21 Hannah, *Corporate Economy*, 145, 149; Neale, *Antitrust Laws*, 476; Guénault and Jackson, *Control of Monopoly*, 1501–194. For more on the pressure groups see below.

22 A. D. Neale, *The Antitrust Laws of the United States of America* (First Edition, Cambridge, England, 1960), 487. For a useful overview see Baldwin, *Antitrust and the Changing Corporation*, 118–284; Stephen, *Economics of Law*; Frazer, *Monopoly, Competition and Law*.

23 On the influence of Coase see Hovenkamp, "Antitrust Movement," *Texas Law Review*, 68 (November 1989), 163–168; Hovenkamp, "Marginal Utility and the Coase Theorem," *Cornell Law Review*, 75 (May 1990), 783–810, quotes at 808, 809.

24 Neale, *Antitrust Laws*, (First Edition, 1960), 498, 502.

25 As quoted, Kovacic, "Failed Expectations," *Iowa Law Review*, 74 (July 1989), 1133, 1135–1136.

26 Author's interview with Aaron Director, 1 April 1988; Edmund W. Kitch, editor, "The Fire of Truth: A Remembrance of Law and Economics at Chicago, 1932–1970," 163–234; Aaron Director and Edward Levi, "Law and the Future of Regulation," *Northwestern University Law Review*, 51 (1956), 281–296.

27 As quoted, Fligstein, *Transformation of Corporate Control*, 220, 221.

28 Fligstein, *Transformation of Corporate Control*, 203–206, 213, 214, 218, 219.

29 "A Look at the Merger Problem," February 12, 1966, Milwaukee, Wisconsin, Clark Papers Box 40 File, "Antitrust, 1966–1967," JPL.

30 See note 2.

31 Alan Neale to Author, 10 September 1990; Interview, 15 December 1986. Interview V. Korah, 7 December 1986; Korah, *Competition Law*.

32 Note 11.

33 Neale, *Antitrust Laws*, (First Edition, 1960), 501.

34 See below notes 40–43.

35 Calvani and Sibarium, "Antitrust Today," *Antitrust Bulletin*, 35 (Spring 1990), 135–179; Bernard G. Segal, "A Lawyer Looks at the Antitrust Client," in *Economic Facts and Antitrust Goals; Inputs for Corporate Planning: Tenth Conference on Antitrust Issues in Today's Economy* (New York, 1971), 39–47.

36 Interview, L. C. B. Gower, 5 November 1989; interview, Christopher Bellamy, 5 July 1989; interview V. Korah, 7 December 1986.

37 *Ibid.*; and Stevens and Yamey, *Restrictive Practices Court*, 26–27, 175–192.

38 *Review of Restrictive Trade Practices Policy*, 23.

39 Note 36; interview Mr Jonathan Green, Senior Economist, MMC, 19 December 1986. See also Neale and Goyder, *Antitrust Laws* (Third Edition, 1982), 475–497.

40 Note 35; Fligstein, *Transformation of Corporate Control*, 212–222.

41 "A Lawyer Looks at the Antitrust Client," in *Economic Facts*, 41, 45.

42 As quoted, Fligstein, *Transformation of Corporate Control*, 217–218.

43 Calvani and Sibarium, "Antitrust Today," *Antitrust Bulletin*, 35 (Spring 1990), 175–179; "A Lawyer Looks at the Antitrust Client," in *Economic Facts*, quote at 42.

44 *Ibid.*; and notes 2, 40.

45 Notes 31, 36, 39.

46 *Ibid.*; and notes 37, 38.

47 As quoted, J. M. Evans, *De Smith's Judicial Review of Administrative Action*, (Fourth Edition, London, 1980), 32–33, 34. See also Kenneth Culp Davis, "The Future of Judge-Made Public Law in England: A Problem of Practical Jurisprudence," *Columbia Law Review*, 61 (January 1961), 201–220.

48 Notes 2, 42, 43.

49 Willis P. Whichard, "A Common Law Judge's View of the Appropriate Use of Economics in Common Law Adjudication," *Law and Contemporary Problems*, 50 (Autumn 1987), 257.

50 Page, "Chicago School," *Virginia Law Review*, 75 (October 1989), 1307, 1308.

51 A good overview of these issues is Guénault and Jackson, *Control of Monopoly*, 36–162. See also, Allen, *Monopoly and Restrictive Practices*, 61–164; and Pollard, *Development of the British Economy*, 250–261, 301–315.

52 As quoted, *Resale Price Maintenance (Report)*, *Oral Answers*, 2 June 1949, BT64/556. See also *Justification of Governments [RPM] Proposals*, BT64/4882.

53 [A. D. Neale], *Draft Action on Resale Price Maintenance*, BT64/556; see also Alan Neale to author, 10 September 1990.

54 *Monopolies and Restrictive Practices Commission Inquiries arising from the publication of the Resale Price Maintenance Report* BT64/556.

55 Note 52.

56 *Ibid.*

57 Minute Sheet, "Daily Press Summary," 25 July 1949, BT64/556.

58 *Ibid.*; Bernard Floud, 26 July 1949.

59 Minute Sheet, Bernard Floud, 11 February 1950, BT64/556.

60 *Note of Meeting on Thursday, 28th July – Resale Price Maintenance*, BT64/556.

61 Note 53.

62 Minute Sheet, 6 March 1950 [italics in original], BT64/556.

63 Alan Neale to Author, 10 September 1990. See also Note 53.

64 Minute Sheet, A. C. Hill, 29 January 1952, BT64/4908.

65 Minute Sheet, James Helmore, 1 February 1952, BT64/4908.

66 Guénault and Jackson, *Control of Monopoly*, 150–162.

67 *Ibid.*

68 *Ibid.*, 40–51; Minute Sheet, *Monopolies Legislation*, A. C. Hill, 25 March 1953, 28 March 1953, BT64/4988.

69 "More Lances Against Monopoly," *The Economist*, 18 July 1953, 155, 15; "Inquiries Into Monopolies Bill to Strengthen Commission," *The Times*, 3 July 1953; "Changes in Monopolies Commission, State Industries Still Not Included," *Manchester Guardian*, 3 July 1953, all collected BT64/4988.

70 [No title, author] addressed to Rt. Hon. R. Assheton, MP, March 1953, BT64/4988.

71 As quoted Guénault and Jackson, *Control of Monopoly*, 154, 158.

72 *Ibid.*, 160–161.

73 *Ibid.*

74 Minute Sheet, *Future Legislation Monopolies*, F. W. Glaves-Smith, 25 July 1955, BT64/4827.

75 *Monopolies Commission Report on Collective Discrimination*, 4 July 1955, BT64/4827. For earlier recommendations see note 63 and chapter 7.

76 *The Ministerial Committee on Monopolies*, M. H. M. Reid, 18 July 1955, BT64/4827.

77 *Proposed New Legislation on Restrictive Practices: President's Meeting with*

Representatives of the Trades Union Congress, 29 October 1955; *Note of Meeting: TUC Views on the Government's Proposals on New Legislation on Restrictive Practices, C. B. Nixon,* 7 *November* 1955, BT64/4765.

78 *Note of a Meeting T.U.C. Views...,* C. B. Nixon, 7 November 1955, BT64/4765.

79 *Restrictive Practices Legislation,* 1 September 1955, BT64/4827.

80 President, Midland & South Staffordshire Brick Association, to D. Derek Walker Smith, MP, 2 March 1956, BT64/4774.

81 Director, Tobb Bros. Ltd. to Rt. Hon. Sir Anthony Eden, 24 February 1956, BT64/4774.

82 Director, Freck H. Burgess Ltd. to Rt. Hon. Peter Thorneycroft, M.P., 23 April 1956, BT64/4774.

83 "Captain Guinness" to Mr. President [Thorneycroft], 16 April 1956, BT64/4774.

84 See note 82.

85 *Restrictive Business Practices, Federation of British Industries on Government's Proposals for Future Legislation,* T. K. Rees, 19 September 1955, BT64/4827; *Restrictive Practices Act of 1956 A Guide for the Industrialist* (London, 1956), 2; *Monopolies Legislation,* G. H. Andrew, 1 October 1955, BT64/4827.

86 *Ibid.*

87 Guénault and Jackson, *Control of Monopoly,* 163–169; Stevens and Yamey, *Restrictive Practices Court,* 23–157; *Note of the President's Meeting with Members of the Monopolies and Restrictive Practices Commission on Tuesday, February 14, 1956,* 15 February 1956, BT64/4832.

88 *Ibid.*

89 *Publication of Restrictive Trade Practices Bill,* 15 February 1956, BT64/4832.

90 See Gribbin, *Post-War Revival of Competition,* 23; Note 63; and chapter 7.

91 Fairburn, "Evolution of Merger Policy in Britain," in Fairburn and Kay, editors, *Mergers,* 193–200; Korah, *Competition Law;* Stevens and Yamey, *Restrictive Practices Court,* 26–27, 175–192.

92 Branyon, "Antimonopoly Activities," 65–98, 133–208.

93 *Ibid.,* 78–83, 123–133.

94 Fligstein, *Transformation of Corporate Control,* as quoted, 188, 189.

95 *Ibid.,* 190.

96 *Ibid.,* 197; and notes 92, 93.

97 Fligstein, *Transformation of Corporate Control,* 195–225, 230–238. For an overview of the Eisenhower antitrust policy see: Theodore Philip Kovaleff, *Business and Government During the Eisenhower Administrative: A Study of the Antitrust Policy of the Antitrust Division of the Justice Department* (Athens, Ohio, 1980).

98 "Our Antitrust Policy," Friday, 26 June 1953, 2, 3. Neil Jacoby, Box 3, EPL.

99 *Ibid.,* 6.

100 Kovaleff, *Business and Government*, 17–48.
101 See note 92.
102 Neil H. Jacoby to Arthur F. Burns, 21 September 1953, Neil Jacoby Box 3, File "Antitrust," EPL.
103 Note 100. See also Robert Gray to Brownell [no date]; and "Preview of the Report of the Attorney General's Committee to Study the Antitrust Laws," 16 March 1955, White House, Cabinet, 1953–1960, Box 1. File "Antitrust," EPL.
104 *Ibid.*
105 *Ibid.*; and see Lubel, *Future of American Politics*, 167, 170–171; Estes Kefauver, "Anti-Trust Laws: Progress in Reverse," *The New Leader*, 28 February 1955, 12–14.
106 Brownell to Eisenhower, 15 September 1954, Areeda Papers, Box 5, File, "Antitrust (Oil) Cartels," EPL; Harold H. Healy to A. J. Goodpaster and Albert P. Toner, 19 February 1958, White House Staff Research Group, Box 13, File "Justice," EPL.
107 The CFEP files are extensive in the Eisenhower Library. For summary see "Report of the Antitrust Task Force of the Council on Foreign Economic Policy," CFEP Records, 1954–1961, Box 4, File 524, EPL.
108 Harold, H. Healy to A. J. Goodpaster and Albert P. Toner, 9 April 1957; Healy to Goodpaster and Toner, 17 December 1956, White House Office Staff, Box 12, File "Justice 1–100," EPL.
109 Irving H. Siegal to Paul W. McCracken, "A Note on the Supreme Court Decision in DuPont Case," 17 June 1957, Areeda Papers, Box 5, File "Antitrust," EPL.
110 Note 97.
111 "Oral History Interview with Lee Loevinger," 13 May 1966, 7, 8, 9, quote at 10, KPL.
112 *Ibid.*, quote at 4, 12, 22–23.
113 *Ibid.*, 40–44.
114 "Summary of Discussion with Assistant Attorney General Lee Loevinger... Concerning the Policies, Operation and Organization of the Antitrust Division," 28 January 1963; quote at 5, Personal Papers of Ramsey Clark, Box 40, JPL.
115 "Oral History Interview with Loevinger," 12,
116 "The Antitrust Division – Should its Powers be Expanded or Restricted?" 5, 6, Orrick Papers, Box 15, drafts of talk for Meeting of the Commonwealth Club, 9 March 1965, KPL.
117 *Ibid.*, Fligstein, *Transformation of Corporate Control*, 201–203.
118 Fligstein, *Transformation of Corporate Control*, as quoted 201, and text, 201–203.
119 "The Antitrust Division – Should its Powers be Expanded or Restricted?" 7, 8, Orrick Papers, Box 15, drafts of talk for Meeting of the Commonwealth Club, 9 March 1965, KPL.
120 Note 118; and Neale and Goyder, *Antitrust Laws*, 186.
121 "Justice Department History Antitrust Division," "Administrative

History of the Justice Department," Volume 8, Part 12; James M. Frey to James Gaither, 25 November 1966, Office Files of James Gaither, Antitrust General, JPL; *Attitudes of Independent Business Proprietors Toward Antitrust Law, 1943 to 1963* (National Federation of Independent Business, San Mateo, California, 1963).

122 Fligstein, *Transformation of Corporate Control*, 203–206; notes 116–119; "Conglomerates Beware," *Forbes*, 1 November 1967, 27–30.

123 Fligstein, *Transformation of Corporate Control*, 204–206.

124 *Ibid.*, 205–206.

125 "Address," Delivered before Antitrust Section of the ABA, Miami, Florida, 10 August 1965, at 8–9, Personal Papers of Ramsey Clark, Box 40, "Antitrust Division 1965," JPL.

126 As quoted, Fligstein, *Transformation of Corporate Control*, 219, 220.

127 "Address," Miami, 10 August 1965, 6–7; Turner to Clark, 7 December 1965, Clark Papers, "Antitrust Division," Box 40, JPL.

128 Fairburn, "Evolution of Merger Policy in Britain," in Fairburn and Kay, editors, *Mergers*, 195, 196.

129 *Ibid.*, 196, 198.

130 *Ibid.*, 199, 200; Littlechild, "Myths," in Fairburn and Kay, editors, *Mergers*, 304.

131 Fairburn, "Evolution of Merger Policy in Britain;" Sir Gordon Borrie, "Merger Policy: Current Policy Concerns;" Swift, "Merger Policy: Certainty or Lottery?," in Fairburn and Kay, editors, *Mergers*, 199–200, 246–263, 264–280. Mrs Korah brought home to me how deep was the controversy over the references process, Interview, 7 December 1986.

132 Fairburn, "Evolution of Merger Policy in Britain," Fairburn and Kay editors, *Mergers*, 200–204; Pollard, *Development of the British Economy*, 307; Korah, *Competition Law*.

133 *Ibid.*

134 Korah, *Competition Law*.

135 As quoted, Littlechild, "Myths," in Fairburn and Kay, eds., *Mergers*, 302, and text, 301–321. See also my interview with Mr. Hans Liesner, 2 November 1989.

136 Notes 132.

137 Fairburn, "Evolution of Merger Policy in Britain," 204, and as quoted, Swift, "Merger Policy: Certainty or Lottery?," Fairburn and Kay, editors, *Mergers*, 267.

138 Fairburn, "Evolution of Merger Policy in Britain," Fairburn and Kay, editors, *Mergers*, 204, 205.

139 *Ibid.*, 206; *Competition Policy in OECD Countries, 1985–1986* (Paris, 1987), 215.

140 Note 36; Korah, *Competition Law*, 13–14; Lipworth, "Development of Merger Control," 1–35, Denning lecture 1990.

141 Lipworth, "Development of Merger Control," 18.

142 *Ibid.*, 31, 34.

143 Note 18. See also Liesner Interview, 3 November 1989.
144 *Ibid.*; for resistance to the restrictive practices proposals see Leslie Ainsworth, "The UK Government's Proposal on Restrictive Trade Practices," *Financial Times*, 11 January 1990.
145 Fligstein, *Transformation of Corporate Control*, 207–212. Kovacic, "Failed Expectation," *Iowa Law Review*, 74 (July 1989), 1126.
146 *Ibid.*, as quoted, 207.
147 *Ibid.*, as quoted, 208.
148 *Ibid.*, as quoted, 209.
149 *Ibid.*, 210, and as quoted, 211.
150 Kovacic, "Failed Expectations," *Iowa Law Review*, 74 (July 1989), 1126; Calvani and Sibarium, "Antitrust Today," *Antitrust Bulletin*, 35 (Spring 1990), 123–217. *Continental T. V., Inc.* v. *GTE Sylvania, Inc.*, 433 US 36 (59–147).
151 Vogel, *Fluctuating Fortunes*, 59–147.
152 As quoted, Kovacic, "Failed Expectations," *Iowa Law Review*, 74 (July 1989), 1126.
153 *Ibid.*, 1126–1128; Elizabeth Sanders, "Industrial Concentration, Sectional Competition, and Antitrust Politics in America, 1880–1980," *Studies in American Political Development*, 1, 195–212.
154 Notes, 26, 28, 35; and Kovacic, "Failed Expectations," *Iowa Law Review*, 74 (July 1989), 1138–1139.
155 Kovacic, "Failed Expectations," *Iowa Law Review*, 74 (July 1989), 1138; Calvani and Sibarium, "Antitrust Today," *Antitrust Bulletin*, 35 (Spring 1990), 185; Fligstein, *Transformation of Corporate Control*, 194.
156 Calvani and Sibarium, "Antitrust Today," *Antitrust Bulletin*, 35 (Spring 1990), 175–188. Quote, *Reiter* v. *Sonotone Corp.*, 442 U.S. 330 (1979) at 34; *Illinois* v. *Illinois Brick Co.*, 431–US 270 (1977). See also notes 127, 145.
157 Calvani and Sibarium, "Antitrust Today," *Antitrust Bulletin*, 35 (Spring 1990), 179–183. See also Baxter Interview with Author, 1 April 1988; and my interview, Former FTC Commissioner Terry Calvani, 31 July 1990. For *AT & T* case see Peter Temin, *The Fall of the Bell System, A study in Prices and Politics* (Cambridge, England, 1987).
158 *Ibid.*
159 Donald F. Turner, "Observations on the New Merger Guidelines and the 1968 Merger Guidelines," *Antitrust Law Journal*, 51 (August 1982), 307–315; Interview, FTC Commissioner Calvani, 31 July 1990.
160 As quoted, "ABA Task Force Calls for Stepped Up Antitrust Enforcement," *Antitrust* (Fall.Winter 1989), 7.

Index